THE FADDAN MORE PSALTER

The Discovery and Conservation of a Medieval Treasure

First published in 2021 by the National Museum of Ireland
In association with the Wordwell Group

First Edition

National Museum of Ireland
Ard-Mhúsaem na hÉireann
Kildare Street
Dublin 2
Ireland
www.museum.ie

Wordwell Group
Unit 9, 78 Furze Road
Sandyford
Dublin 18
www.wordwellbooks.com

ISBN: 978-1-914470-00-4

A CIP catalogue record of this book is available from the National Library of Ireland, the British Library and the Library of Congress.

Designed by Fiachra McCarthy
Copyedited by Emer Condit
Printed by Gráficas Castuera, Spain

Cover image: The Faddan More Psalter before conservation (NMI)

THE FADDAN MORE PSALTER

The Discovery and Conservation of a Medieval Treasure

JOHN GILLIS

museum
National Museum of Ireland
Ard-Mhúsaem na hÉireann

CONTENTS

FADDAN MORE PSALTER

List of illustrations

Acknowledgements

I am indebted to a number of individuals for getting me over the line with this body of work. There is no doubt that without their contributions there would be no volume. The acknowledgements that follow necessarily start with the Leonard brothers, Patrick and Kevin, owners of the Faddan More Bog, and their eagle-eyed digger operator, Edward Fogarty, who spotted one button from the cover of the psalter peeking out from a bucketload of peat. The immediate and responsible action taken by Kevin and Patrick ensured that no further deterioration occurred before Museum staff arrived on site.

In its former guise, this volume formed the basis of my Ph.D thesis and this phase included the involvement of some of the finest scholars on our island. Dr Laura Cleaver, as my supervisor, guided, directed and redirected my efforts with a calmness that on many occasions converted my blind panic into productive writing. My other 'hand-holder' throughout was my good friend Tim O'Neill; his advice, guidance and expertise are to be seen on every page. I had the *crème de la crème* of proofreaders: Dr Bernard Meehan, who also worked directly on the project while in the National Museum; he was a tough but wise taskmaster and kept me on track. Dr Paul Mullarkey shared his extensive knowledge in this field, and his advice provided much in the way of supporting material. Jessica Baldwin scrutinised my every word and reorganised my writing, providing that final polish.

In the early stages, when I doubted whether I could realistically do justice to this work, the encouragement, support and occasional cajoling from Professor Dáibhí Ó Cróinín, Felicity O'Mahony, Dr Jane Maxwell and Professor Roger Stalley ensured that I didn't fall at the first fence. Dr Rachel Moss scrutinised my early chapters and throughout offered support and helpful advice.

Maeve Sikora of the National Museum of Ireland, who was lead archaeologist for the Faddan More Psalter (now Keeper of Irish Antiquities), was a constant source of assistance and advice as I attempted to put the manuscript in context. Maeve continued to support me in my efforts to publish this work and in tandem with Dr Audrey Whitty made it a reality. Carol Smith, who was conservator for the related material from Faddan More, generously shared her discoveries, which greatly assisted in making sense of the material nature of the project. Patrick Boyle magnanimously gave up space in his area of the Museum's Conservation Department, where I installed a large vacuum machine that would be in constant use during my time there. Rolly Read, Head of Conservation in the Museum, welcomed me and facilitated my many requests and whims. The National Museum of Ireland, my home for four and a half years during the conservation process, advanced my knowledge of the find in many ways, including inviting leading experts from a range of disciplines to visit and report; among these were the late

Christopher Clarkson, Michael Gullick, Fr Martin McNamara and Dr Roy Thompson, all of whom made valuable contributions to this work.

The remarkable facilities made available to me during my two 'visiting scholar' trips to the Getty Research Institute in Los Angeles greatly progressed my research. The Getty also supported my introduction of the Faddan More Psalter to America, through a series of lectures on both coasts. While there, I was greatly supported and assisted by Nancy Turner, Dr Alexa Sekyra and the rest of the team 'on the hill', with a particular mention to Angie Donougher. The genuine interest and support of my colleagues in the Conservation Department in Trinity kept me focused, believing and grounded over the seven years of writing and research. I am thankful to the then Librarian, Robin Adams, and Susie Bioletti for releasing me from Trinity in the first instance.

When Professor Matthew James Driscoll and Professor Pádraig Ó Macháin gave their collective stamp of approval to my efforts, I was encouraged, by them, to take the work from the scope of an academic audience into the wider domain and what follows is the end result.

FADDAN MORE PSALTER

Preface

It has been fifteen years since the Irish Antiquities Division Duty Officer, Fiona Reilly, received a call from the Leonard brothers reporting the discovery of a book in their bog at Faddan More, Co. Tipperary. The manuscript, identified by Raghnall Ó Floinn as an early medieval psalter, had been discovered by digger driver Eddie Fogarty, who noticed it fall open as he scooped a bucketful of peat from the section of the bog. The relationship between the National Museum and the Leonard brothers—Patrick and Kevin—dates back to 1999, when an early medieval leather bag was discovered in Faddan More Bog.

The following day, National Museum staff visited Faddan More to collect the psalter and to investigate the site. In the weeks that followed, staff of the Irish Antiquities Division and Conservation Department excavated the find-spot, while parallel investigations into the conservation of the manuscript commenced. Although many other antiquities have been found in Irish bogs, this was the first time that a manuscript had been discovered. Its conservation thus required specialist expertise not held within the NMI. What emerged was a four-year collaborative project between the National Museum and Trinity College to research and conserve the manuscript.

This publication charts the conservation of and research on the psalter by John Gillis. The project involved collaboration between Gillis and archaeological conservators at the National Museum, in particular Carol Smith, experienced in treating waterlogged organic artefacts and human remains from bogs in Ireland. Invaluable input was also generously given by Dr Bernard Meehan, then Keeper of Manuscripts and Early Printed Books at Trinity College Library.

As the manuscript was revealed and researched, new insights were gained into the manufacture and use of early medieval manuscripts in Ireland. The psalter was effectively excavated under laboratory conditions, each fragmented bifolio separated and recorded before conservation. The cover, at the bottom of the block, was the last element to be investigated, and it revealed evidence of a papyrus lining on the inside and numerous incised motif pieces on the outside. Many early medieval manuscripts survive through having been rebound and kept in libraries over hundreds of years. The Faddan More Psalter is different; it was probably deposited within a century of being written. The survival of a contemporary cover with the manuscript is almost unique in an early medieval Irish context.

Other objects discovered at the find-spot, including a leather bag and an animal pelt, are undergoing research and conservation and will be published separately along with the excavation report. Although some associated finds were present, the reasons why the psalter should have been deposited in such a place and in such a manner are still unclear. What is certain is that it represents one of the most remarkable chance discoveries in Ireland in many decades. The fact that such a fragile organic object survived for a millennium in wet conditions, the fact that it was noticed by Eddie Fogarty, and the fact that a full bifolio survived and allowed Gillis to ascertain the codicological details of the psalter are all very much against the odds.

The cover and a selection of the manuscript bifolios, conserved by John Gillis, are now on permanent display at the National Museum of Ireland, Kildare Street.

Many people have been involved in this project and special thanks are due to Bernard Meehan and John Gillis of Trinity College Dublin, and to Patrick Wallace, Raghnall Ó Floinn, Eamonn Kelly, Anthony Read, Fiona Reilly, Margaret Lannin and Carol Smith of the National Museum of Ireland. Of all those involved, however, the Leonard family—Patrick, Kevin and Denise—stand out as model finders and citizens who by their actions have enriched our national collections. We are indebted to them. This foreword is dedicated to the memory of the late Patrick 'Podge' Leonard, a remarkable man who sadly did not live to see the psalter on display or this publication coming to fruition.

MAEVE SIKORA
Keeper of Irish Antiquities

FADDAN MORE PSALTER

Introduction

When in 2006 an early medieval Insular manuscript surfaced from the Faddan More Bog in north County Tipperary, the event afforded a unique opportunity to study in detail all aspects of what is now 'one of the National Museum of Ireland's top ten treasures' (Fig. A).[1] Entombed in its own inhospitable time capsule, many features of the original book have survived. One particularly unexpected feature was the vegetable-tanned leather cover, which seemed to draw stylistically on Near Eastern models for its form.

The manuscript now popularly referred to as the Faddan More Psalter (hereafter FMP) was discovered on 20 July when the operator of a peat-digger, Edward Fogarty, unearthed what he recognised as a book. The commercial bog owned by the Leonard brothers, Patrick and Kevin, is located in the townland of Faddan More (derived from the Irish name *Feadán Mór*) in the parish of Loughkeen, Co. Tipperary. Identification of the manuscript as a psalter or book of psalms was quickly established on site by Raghnall Ó Floinn, then Head of Collections of the National Museum of Ireland, based on a small area of writing, containing the key words *in valle lacrimarum* 'in the valley of tears', that was visible among the mass of peat surrounding the manuscript. It was the image of these few words from Psalm 83:4–9 that was flashed around the world's media as news of the discovery spread.

My involvement with the project began when I was invited by Rolly Read, then Head of Conservation at the National Museum, to examine and comment on the find. The FMP, like the majority of early medieval manuscripts, was produced on parchment, but as an untanned animal skin it presented a new conservation challenge. Archaeological survival of parchment is extremely rare and no major survival of this material and antiquity had previously been retrieved and conserved from a bog environment. This, combined with the complexity of unravelling the structure of an early medieval book in such a poor state of preservation, prompted a broad consultation and gathering of expertise. I was seconded to the National Museum as the lead conservator for the project with responsibility to carry out initial investigation and all practical treatments, including recording the find. A team of experts from several fields was assembled to form a steering committee to guide this complex project to a conclusion. The team consisted of Dr Patrick Wallace (Director of the National Museum of Ireland, NMI), Mr Eamonn Kelly (Keeper of Irish Antiquities, NMI), Mr Raghnall Ó Floinn (Head of

1 Dr Patrick Wallace, then Director of the National Museum of Ireland, in a national radio interview some years after the discovery of the Faddan More Psalter.

Fig. A—Faddan More Bog, Co. Tipperary.

Collections, NMI), Mr Anthony Read (Head of Conservation, NMI), Dr Bernard Meehan (Keeper of Manuscripts, Trinity College Dublin), Mr John Gillis (Senior Conservator, Trinity College Dublin), Fr Martin McNamara (Professor Emeritus, Milltown Institute of Theology and Philosophy) and Professor Dáibhí Ó Cróinín (School of History, National University of Ireland, Galway). Such was the significance of the FMP in relation to the history of Irish book-making that the National Museum commissioned a filmed documentary of the conservation as it progressed. This was broadcast on RTÉ in 2010 and subsequently on the History Channel for a period after that. It also provided an additional format for the conservation record of the project.

The first task was to record the psalter in its as-found state. The main aim here was to establish the make-up of the quires and to produce a collation map, a feature used in the codicological examination of a book. This work, however, was greatly complicated by the lack of surviving backfolds and the highly disturbed and fragmented nature of the folios. Once this had been achieved, over several months and after a number of failed attempts, it was possible to produce a definitive make-up of the manuscript quires. The next stage of the programme was to employ a drying system to allow the extant fragments of the vellum folios to be taken from their saturated state to a dry and stable condition by removing the excess free water. Because of the unique conditions in which the manuscript had remained for over a millennium, I could find no published comparative conservation treatments that might guide the de-watering of the saturated vellum. It is known that, unlike tanned leather, vellum was and is a material produced under high tension, resulting in a fibre network aligned at a low angle of weave, and this, combined with poor hydrothermal stability, meant that shrinkage through the drying process was a major concern. After much experimentation and consultation, an in-house method was developed and executed with only marginal loss of dimension, and although the dry vellum now has little if any fold endurance it is stable and robust.[2]

With the completion of the drying stage, my focus turned to the identification and relocation of floating fragments, the development of a housing system and further recording of codicological features such as ruling, pricking, line count, edge trimming, margins, stitching, the use of colour etc. The second major component of this manuscript, the tanned leather cover, was also in a saturated state and was maintained as such until the vellum folio fragments were conserved. This in many ways formed a separate project, as the requirements and materials were very different from that of the vellum text block. Because the cover was an object produced from vegetable-tanned leather, I was able to draw from the world of archaeological conservation and employ a tried and tested method for de-watering the binding to reach a successful outcome (see Chapter 1). The discovery of both a number of trial motifs and small fragments of papyrus adhering to the leather (Fig. B) prompted much speculation regarding the origin of the cover and these became fundamental aspects of research.

After completion of the conservation and the design and construction of a storage and display system for the manuscript, I focused my attention on the relocation of folio fragments with identifiable text. It was evident from the early stages of the conservation that the project would generate questions in relation to the materials used and methods employed to make this manuscript. Questions concerning the origins of the structure, the chronology of the cover and its features required answers. In addition, this was an unknown manuscript and presented a unique opportunity to contextualise it in relation to other manuscripts from the same epoch. These questions prompted me to continue working with the FMP in the form of a doctoral thesis. A dedicated and permanent exhibition of the FMP in the National Museum of Ireland opened in 2010.

The research has an interdisciplinary outcome, as during the four-and-a-half-year conservation process I collaborated with Dr Bernard Meehan, Fr Martin McNamara and Timothy O'Neill in relation to the palaeography and orthography of the FMP. This included noting abbreviations, spelling changes, scribal errors such as haplography and variations from the standard Vulgate psalter. Although this is not my area of expertise, such has been my exposure to the manuscript that I have become quite adept at deciphering the hand, often difficult to read owing to physical deterioration. I have employed current technology in digital imaging techniques to aid this aspect of the work in providing palaeographical assistance to Fr McNamara. I worked with staff from Digital Humanities in NUI Maynooth on hyperspectral imaging of the psalter folio fragments in an attempt to enhance and record difficult-to-decipher writing. A supplement produced as a result of the deciphering of the FMP is my identified text of the complete 150 psalms as they survive in this manuscript (see Appendix 4). My research in this area will feed into the proposed production of a full transcription of the FMP by the relevant scholars. I also worked closely with Timothy O'Neill, a leading calligrapher and authority on the Irish manuscript tradition. His suggestion for threads of relevant research feature throughout.

From a codicological viewpoint, the body of work will add to our meagre understanding of early medieval book-making through the detailed examination of all aspects of the FMP. It is worth emphasising that the cover of the manuscript is the only one of its kind extant in a Western context and, as such, is a particularly valuable contribution to our understanding of early medieval book-making. Additional research into relevant material, manuscripts and artefacts will provide a more informed and accurate picture of book-making practice in the Insular world. By studying the individual components employed to produce the FMP we can learn more about its makers and their access to the raw materials

2 Gillis 2012.

Fig. B—SEM image of papyrus fragment from the inside cover of the FMP.

required, some of which were locally sourced and in common use while others were imported through trade links, either specifically for use in book production or adapted from other tasks. This study aims to add to existing information on the transfer of goods and technologies between the eastern Mediterranean and the western extremities of Europe. Examination of the trial motifs on the FMP cover will elucidate the process of decoration of liturgical material in an Irish monastic setting.

The psalter played an important role in Christian liturgical devotion, and in Ireland it had an additional function as a teaching aid for Latin. Martin McNamara has written extensively on the psalter, its editions and influence. He was directly involved in the early stages of this project and with the clarification of the surviving text, and it is hoped that the FMP will contribute its unique features to the corpus of extant psalters. The quality and palaeographical comparisons of the writing, which is in an Irish majuscule hand, can be analysed. In this regard I have drawn on the work of Timothy O'Neill, Bernhard Bischoff and William O'Sullivan, among others. The extant decorated lettering also allows for comparative study, and work by Gifford Charles-Edwards, John Higgitt and Nicolete Gray assists in placing and, importantly, dating the manuscript. Finally, although scant, surviving decoration can be analysed and assessed against other Insular manuscripts of the early medieval period. Fortunately, unlike codicological studies, this area of manuscript studies is well researched, and I have referenced important scholarly material from Françoise Henry, J.J.G. Alexander and Rachel Moss to assist in placing the decorative aspects of the FMP in context. The overall analysis will also contribute to a greater understanding of the family of Insular manuscripts and the FMP's place within that group.

It is clear that there was a hierarchy of book production within the Insular monastic world and, comparatively speaking, a relatively abundant number of highly decorated and probably once-bejewelled gospel-books survive: the Book of Kells (Dublin, TCD MS 58), the Lindisfarne Gospels (London, BL Cotton MS Nero D.IV) and the Echternach Gospels (Paris, Bib. MS lat. 9389), to name but a few, all destined for display on the altar and/or commissioned to celebrate a particular saint's life or a significant occasion. Conversely, there are the everyday copies required for canonical hours and didactic purposes, few of which have come down to us. One example is the eighth-century Northumbrian Gospel (London, Royal MS 1.B.VII). The FMP sits more comfortably in the latter category but serves as a reminder that the distinction was not always clear-cut.

I have studied the FMP primarily as an archaeological object. I base my research on completed scientific analyses, including investigation of the black dye on the leather cover by Brian W. Singer at Northumbria University, radiocarbon dating of components from the manuscript and surrounding find-spot by the ^{14}CHRONO Centre of Queen's University Belfast, palaeoenvironmental research of the find-spot by the School of Geography, Archaeology and Palaeoecology, Queen's University Belfast, analyses of samples of the vellum text block by Rene Larsen at the Royal Danish Academy of Fine Arts and investigation of the leather of the cover by Roy Thomson, formerly of the Leather Conservation Centre, Northampton. In addition, I have identified other areas for attention, including a palaeographical study of the hand or hands in the FMP and comparison with other manuscripts of similar date and possibly from the same general location. Investigation of this material, combined with my own observations documented over the four years of the conservation process, will result in a detailed description of the FMP as a material object from early medieval Ireland. Research will include codicological comparisons with other Insular manuscripts, particularly those in contemporary bindings such as the Cadmug gospel-book (Fulda, Landesbibliothek Codex Bonifatianus 3), which, like the FMP, is enclosed by a cover with definite eastern Mediterranean features. Researching literary sources from related areas of study, such as monastic life, Insular art, saints' Lives and the social history of the period, will clarify the setting in which the FMP was produced. The combination of this scientific and humanities research will inform us better as to what influenced the choices of both book-maker and scribe, culminating in the style and format of the FMP.

THE FADDAN MORE PSALTER

The surviving manuscript contains five quires of varying folio counts and layout, with two quires containing ten leaves and a count of twelve, thirteen and fifteen for the remaining three quires, giving a total of 60 folios. There are no flyleaves, although the last folio of the fifth quire is blank. The layout does not follow the Insular practice whereby the hair side of one folio faces the flesh side of another, nor is it consistent with having the hair side on the outside of the quire, a convention also associated with Insular practice.[3] Likewise, the Continental rule of 'like facing like', also known as 'Gregory's rule', is not evident.[4] It is more accurately described as an indiscriminate quire arrangement, in a tradition observed among the majority of other early medieval Irish manuscripts. There are, however, exceptions, such as the ninth-century St Gall Priscian (St Gallen Cod. Sang. 904), a product of a northern Irish monastery, which I observed to be more consistent in its make-up.

The FMP manuscript is written in long lines in an Irish majuscule hand. There are approximately 32

3 T.J. Brown 1974; J. Brown 1993, 126.

4 Named after the American-born (1846) German Casper Rene Gregory, professor of theology, who is credited with discovering this feature in medieval manuscripts.

lines to a page and the text block measures approximately 305mm x 226mm. There are clear indications that, at the very least, the individual quires had tackets of vegetable fibres through the backfolds in order to keep the bifolios together, and this may have extended to connecting one quire to the next in a form of unsupported sewing. The material is calfskin vellum and, allowing for trimming, it is likely that one skin provided two bifolios. This takes into account that cattle then were generally smaller than they are today,[5] so somewhere in the region of fifteen animals would have been required to produce the FMP. The writing and substrate of the psalter's text block will be discussed in detail in this book.

THE COVER

However dishevelled the cover of the FMP may appear, it is predominantly intact and complete. This situation is exceptional and affords the opportunity to examine in detail the materiality surrounding its manufacture. The codicological study of medieval bindings more typically requires searching for clues or 'shadows' of the now-lost original structure. This is the unfortunate consequence of a revered manuscript remaining in use over a substantial period of time, with the likelihood of its being re-bound in the style of the day by its custodians at various times. This in turn results in the loss of the original binding structure and sewing, and, in the majority of cases, in the trimming of the leaves to suit the new binding or to 'tidy up' the appearance, which is even more injurious. In the case of the more elaborate manuscripts, the often bejewelled and highly decorative bindings were sometimes plundered by the latest invaders or opportunist thieves, with obvious disastrous results (see Chapter 6). Evidence of this is clear when one considers how few contemporary manuscript bindings survive today from the early Middle Ages and how many of our important manuscripts—famously including the Book of Kells—now display cropped text and decoration owing to careless trimming. All this activity robs us of key codicological information. Rare surviving bindings from the early Middle Ages include the late seventh-century St Cuthbert's Gospel (London, British Library Add. MS 89000) and the eighth-century Cadmug Gospels. Given the rarity of bindings from this period, it is even more unlikely that the plain and simple limp cover of the FMP would have survived in its present form had it not been buried below ground for such an extended period.

The simple construction of the cover of the FMP, made from a single piece of leather folded and creased to form a wallet-like enclosure for its contents, reaches back to technology employed at the earlier stages of the development of the codex. Thus far the physical description of the cover of the FMP allows for an obvious comparison with the Coptic Nag Hammadi bindings, discussed in more detail in Chapter 4. The similarities were mooted at an early stage of the discovery, despite there being a 400-year time-gap and origins in two different continents.[6] Conversely, it would be easy to argue, given the straightforward nature of the technology involved in producing this type of book cover, that one did not influence the other; rather it was a more 'organic' development influenced by the everyday surrounding domestic objects, such as containers, satchels or even clothing. A study of the materials employed in making the cover of the FMP suggests, however, a more direct link between the two bookbinding forms. Initial comparative research was focused on the Nag Hammadi codices, which I examined at close quarters in the Coptic Museum in Cairo in 2010, and the research was extended to locate and study similar covers from the same region or of the same type but closer in date to the FMP.

Close study of the cover reveals wear and tear from use over an extended period, evidenced by splits

5 Wilde 1857–61.

6 Respected experts in the fields of medieval book structures and codicology, including Dr Christopher Clarkson, Michael Gullick and Anthony Cains, examined the manuscript shortly after its discovery and, by request, submitted initial reports on their findings.

along crease lines and the rounding-off of corners. Allied to this are the cut edges and lack of turn-ins, which could be the result of trimming. This may have been carried out to tidy up earlier damage or to improve the fit for the psalter, having been originally made for a larger volume. A detailed description of the visible evidence on the cover will be presented in Chapter 4. Discovered at an advanced stage of the conservation process was a collection of trial motifs displaying strong Insular characteristics on the surface of the cover. This utilitarian treatment of the binding of the FMP is somewhat at odds with the spiritual significance of devotional books. In the Christian tradition the book had its own meaning as witness to the promise of salvation and was almost as potent a symbol as the cross.[7] This is reinforced when one takes account of how often the image of a book appears in the Christian codex among miniatures, historiated initials and in the stonework of Irish high crosses of the Middle Ages. For example, on the west face of the Monasterboice Tall Cross (Co. Louth) Christ is shown giving the key of the new Church to St Peter and the book of the new law to St Paul. The Insular habit of housing books in highly decorated and bejewelled book-shrines, often centuries after they were written, usually because they were believed or desired to be associated with a particular saint, also demonstrates the important symbolic nature of the Christian book.[8] Clearly the FMP received no such reverential treatment, and it is for that reason that a higher percentage of the de luxe volumes have come down to us while their more utilitarian counterparts have not survived in the same numbers. During the period of their production, however, the contrary was surely the more likely scenario: the number of everyday working manuscripts coming from the scriptorium would have been considerably higher than the illuminated manuscripts intended for display on the altar or raising the status of the church that possessed it. These 'de luxe' manuscripts required much in the way of resources, skills and materials, if not time to produce.

When the evidence is considered, both stylistically and in terms of the materials employed to produce the cover of the FMP, a strong association with eastern Mediterranean or, more specifically, Coptic book-making is apparent. Initial thoughts may seem to suggest that the cover is an anomaly, a stray that somehow found its way to the western edge of Europe and as such should be categorised as a one-off. The binding of the Cadmug gospel-book, however, which is considered to be contemporary with its contents, is typically described as an Eastern type with unsupported sewing. The other early medieval Insular manuscript that retains its original binding is St Cuthbert's Gospel, recently purchased by the British Library. This again has a clear indication of Eastern influence in the form of unsupported sewing. This theme continues with the binding of red goatskin moulded over raised decoration contained within a panel, also raised. The surface displays tooling with interlace patterns, which were inpainted. This combination bears strong stylistic links to both Coptic and later Islamic leatherwork. Finally, I refer to the comments of Sir William Betham on his opening of the *Cathach* (Dublin, RIA MS 12 R 33)[9] book-shrine in 1813, describing the additional material found inside: a thin piece of board covered with red leather, very like that with which Eastern manuscripts are bound.[10] Unfortunately, Sir William had no regard for what may well have been the original binding of the *Cathach* and it was discarded.

The following chapters will commence with a detailed description of the conservation process and how the many features identified during this work prompted the necessity for further research into

7 Pächt 1986, 10.

8 Stokes 1932, 72.

9 Royal Irish Academy. The *Cathach* is the oldest extant Irish manuscript of the psalter. Although there is no definite date for its production, it has historically been linked to St Columba, but current thinking cast doubts on his authorship. It is dated to the late sixth or early seventh century.

10 Ó Cróinín 2009, 6.

the manuscript in a wider context. The second chapter presents an examination of the remains of the vellum text block; despite the fragmented condition and extensive lacunae, many manufacturing features are visible, supplying clues to production. In addition, codicological evidence is to be found throughout in the form of pricking and ruling, and these conventions are examined and compared. The third chapter focuses attention on the different forms of writing employed in the FMP, its quality, chronology and how it compares with other manuscripts of the period. The scant surviving decoration is also scrutinised and categorised. It is in this chapter that the date of the manuscript is discussed, given the palaeographical evidence combined with art-historical and scientific findings. Chapter 4 describes in detail the unusual yet simple binding structure and how its form and materials suggest a Coptic influence or even manufacture. Similar extant examples and contemporary illustrated versions are discussed, including two Insular manuscripts: the Cadmug Gospels from the mid-eighth century and the Mac Durnan Gospels (London, Lambeth Palace Library MS 1370)[11] from the late ninth or early tenth century. Both contain miniatures depicting the evangelists John and Luke respectively, each holding a book clearly similar in construction to the cover of the FMP. The multiple trial motifs inscribed randomly on the binding of the FMP are catalogued and described in Chapter 5. Among the designs there is interlace work inside a border, curvilinear and key patterns. Other, more typical trial motifs produced on bone are compared, with an example excavated from Fishamble Street in Viking Dublin displaying a very similar cross to one of the motifs on the FMP. Comparable examples of the individual motifs are listed from various sources, mostly as components on the decorated folios of manuscripts. The question of where the FMP might have been produced is addressed in Chapter 6 by examining the landscape in the immediate region around where the manuscript was found. This part of Ireland is associated with many ecclesiastical sites, and their documented history from around the time when the FMP was circulating is examined. The 'how and why' the manuscript was found in a bog is investigated in Chapter 7, considering particular physical features of the manuscript as it survives today combined with archaeological reports on the find-spot. Although it is impossible to be definitive, certain scenarios describing the circumstances leading to the deposition of the manuscript are proposed. Finally, the conclusion places the FMP among the corpus of Insular manuscripts and demonstrates its role as an archetypal Insular manuscript of the early medieval period. The particular features of what appears to be an object of two discrete parts are discussed.

DEVELOPMENT OF THE CODEX AS A SUBSTRATE FOR THE WRITTEN WORD

Before beginning analysis of the FMP as an early medieval book structure, a summary of the current understanding of the genesis of the codex up to the early Middle Ages may be helpful.

It was clear to the authors of our first written records that it would be necessary to devise a system for protecting the information of their transcripts. It should be recognised, however, that very little concerning the methods and means of early book production has come down to us through either pagan or Christian written sources. Most of our evidence comes from the archaeological study of finds, either directly from the discovery of fragmented books or indirectly through iconographic illustrations of the book in contemporary art. In addition, clues can be extracted from casual references to the codex in early texts. One of the earliest substrates for the written word to be produced in any great numbers was the papyrus scroll. The date of invention of this historically significant material is uncertain but it can be traced as far back as the fourth millennium BC in Egypt.[12] The source of the raw material is a species

11 Scribe named as Maelbrigte Mac Durnan; written in Ireland or Iona.

12 Skeat 1969, 58.

of reed, *Cyperus papyrus*, which grew in great quantities in Egypt, particularly along the Nile Delta, but also in other areas of the Near East and Sicily. The transformation of plant stem, typically 3m in length, to flat sheet involves the removal of the triangular outer rind to expose the white pith within. The pith is cut into strips, which are laid side by side with a slight overlap; the operation is repeated to create a second layer, this time with the strips lying at right angles to the layer beneath. The two layers are hammered and pressed before being allowed to dry out. Pliny the Elder (AD 23–79) gives us an eyewitness description of its production during Roman occupation: 'being first inclined, the leaves of papyrus are laid upon it lengthwise, as long indeed as the papyrus will admit of, the jagged edges being cut off at either end; after which a crossed layer is placed over it ... When this is done, the leaves are pressed together, and then dried in the sun.'[13] This cross-layer provided the writing surface, as it ran parallel to the direction of the script.

Throughout its long history of production, two layers of fibres appear to have been the standard thickness for papyrus, with only the occasional sheet of three layers being identified. The surface of the dry sheet is finished by dressing with pumice and finally by burnishing with a polishing tool of ivory or stone. Intentionally or not, as writing was executed on the inside horizontal surface of the roll, the contents were protected when the roll was not in use; the roll thus acted as a form of cover, performing the same function as later intentionally produced book structures in a variety of formats. Papyrology studies have shown us that scribes employed, in the main, only the inside/horizontal fibre face of the roll; where writing is found on the vertical fibre face, it is more often the recycling of a discarded roll, where more ephemeral texts, such as notes, registers etc., are recorded on the blank surface of the outside of the roll.[14] The development of the papyrus roll was widespread not only in Egypt, the main source of the raw materials, but also in the world of her conquerors: Greece by the time of Alexander in 332 BC, and later the Roman Empire, which adopted the Greek language in addition to the vernacular, along with the roll for use in administrative documents. As the main surface for writing, papyrus was produced in abundant quantities and appears to have been treated very much like our modern machine-made paper, being discarded when no longer required. An example of this abundance can be read in the documented travels of the Egyptian Wen-Amon (*c.* 1090 BC), who is recorded as carrying 500 blank rolls of papyrus 'of the finest quality' to Phoenicia to barter for wood.[15]

As a product of the Roman Empire, papyrus found its way into many regions, but the climatic conditions became less and less favourable as one travelled west, resulting in today's minimal survival of papyrus documents or even fragments from western Europe. There are some intriguing exceptions to this, albeit in almost fossilised form. A quantity of British coins, *potin* or *speculum*, thought to date from between 54 BC and AD 43, display the impression of fine parallel lines running perpendicular to each other on the surface in low relief. These surface markings are not woven but rather lie one on top of the other, in the same manner as a finished papyrus sheet. The markings appear only on the 'flan' or the flat surface onto which any decoration or figure is worked. One expert concluded that papyrus was used as part of the manufacturing process of the coins, perhaps as a release from the clay mould.[16] There are also extant a small quantity of actual documents, written in Ravenna in the fifth century AD, that survived in the slightly more 'papyrus-friendly' climate of Italy.[17] The conservative papal chancery continued with the use of papyrus into the eleventh century with occasional survivors.[18]

---

13 Bostock and Riley 1855, 189–91.

14 Skeat 1969, 56.

15 Elliott 2004, 38.

16 Wild 1966.

17 Wood 2013, 48.

18 McCormick 2001, 704-8; Bischoff 2008, 8.

It is thought that the individual sheets of a roll were initially attached to each other by sewing, attaching the trailing edge of one sheet to the leading edge of the next with some form of thread.[19] The brittle nature of papyrus is likely to have resulted in premature failure at the point of stitching and so the use of glue or paste to carry out the task was introduced to great success, with seamless joins between sheets allowing scribes to write easily across the overlap. There is also an indication that no adhesive was required to join the two sheets, particularly if the roll was formed during the manufacture of the papyrus sheets. Simply hammering the overlap between the two sheets before they had fully dried created a strong bond between the cell tissues of both layers.[20] All of this indicates that a deliberate effort was made during early development of the book structure to extend its life and retain its contents—an aspect of the book that in future centuries would carry particular significance with the arrival of Christianity and the dissemination of the word of God. Typically, the blank papyrus was supplied in rolls by the manufacturer to the scribe, who could extend the length of the roll by simply attaching additional sheets. Papyrus was rolled, as mentioned above, with the horizontal fibres on the inside, thus reducing the stress on the written surface, while the vertical fibres on the outside ran in the same direction as the roll. It was also possible for a scribe to purchase individual leaves, which would suffice for shorter documents. Extant examples include British Museum Pap. 128 (the *Iliad*), in which the sheets measure 250mm x 121mm. Writing was in columns and the Graeco-Roman scribe worked without the pricking and ruling guides associated with later parchment manuscripts. The ink was for the most part carbon-based, employing the by-products from burned timber or oil mixed with a gum to bind it together. Pliny (*Natural History*) comments on the production of ink, listing soot and gum in the ingredients. It is worth noting that papyrus was not the only substrate employed to create a roll for writing purposes; bark, leather, textiles and even metal have been found in the book-roll format.[21] Copper scrolls (dating from the third to the first century BC) were among the rolls found in the caves of the Wadi Qumran region near the Dead Sea.[22]

Alternative formats for the roll were to be found in antiquity, and wooden tablets (the word 'tablet' comes from the Latin *tabula*, meaning 'board') were in everyday use in ancient Rome.[23] Writing was inscribed directly onto the thin plates of local wood, prepared specifically and finished to a polished surface. A collection of handwritten documents found during excavations of the Roman fort of Vindolanda, located on Hadrian's Wall in northern Britain, has proved a valuable window into the everyday life of a Romano-British garrison and testifies to the educated status of the occupants of the fort. The tablets are made of local timbers—birch, oak and alder—and are fashioned into thin plates measuring approximately 200mm x 80mm and up to 3mm in thickness. The Old Roman Cursive script is written in iron gall ink. Nearly 500 tablets have been recovered, dating from the first and second centuries AD.[24]

Of particular interest is the folding of the tablets by scoring down the centre to form a diptych, but also technically a step towards the codex format and away from the roll or tablet. This form of tablet was likely the antecedent of the 'wax tablet', a development that improved both the finished product and the speed with which it could be written on. Production involved coating the surface of the wooden plates with a thin layer of wax (often black), which could be easily inscribed with a pen-like tool known as a stylus. A further refinement saw a recessed trough cut into the face of the timber to

---

19 Diringer 1982, 138.

20 Parkinson and Quirke 1995, 15.

21 Diringer 1982, 44–6.

22 Davies *et al.* 2002, 108–13.

23 Joyce 1997, 482.

24 Vindolanda Tablets Online: see http://vindolanda.csad.ox.ac.uk/about.shtml.

allow a deeper layer of wax to be applied. The writing could be easily erased by smoothing out the surface of the wax; indeed, some styli had a spatula-like end for just such a function.[25] These tablets were useful for ephemeral writings, teaching purposes and legal documents. They were used singly or as two tablets joined together (known as a diptych), or three (making a triptych); tablets joined in any greater numbers are referred to as polyptychs. Typical species of wood used in ancient Rome included beech, cedar and boxwood.[26] Extant examples of the polyptych from the Roman world in the early Christian period display deliberate notches and holes along one long edge (being rectangular in shape), components of a sewing system used to join the leaves together. A similar system was employed to join the multi-quire codices of the same period. Georgios Boudalis has convincingly argued that the type of stitching that might have been employed to join the individual plates was likely adopted from craft methods such as basketry.[27]

We retain an early medieval example of a polyptych in Ireland, namely the Springmount Bog Wax Tablets,[28] discovered in the north of Ireland in the early twentieth century by a man cutting turf in Springmount Bog, Co. Antrim. Now in the National Museum of Ireland, they consist of six wooden (yew) tablets in a 'landscape format', measuring 75mm x 210mm and 6mm thick.[29] These tablets have a trough hollowed out on both sides to accommodate the wax and to allow for recto and verso use. The first and last tablets, however, are hollowed out only on the verso and recto respectively and as such form proper book covers. The outer surfaces are smooth and shaped through manufacture and extensive handling in use. This contributes to the book-like impression of the object, which comes to hand in a very satisfying manner. The tablets contain the text of Psalms 30, 31 and 32 of the Vulgate psalter, written with a drypoint stylus. The writing appears to be the hand of a competent scribe, familiar with Irish majuscule script. The tablets have been dated to the late sixth or early seventh century.[30] Two holes have been bored through the assembled tablets along one long edge, through which wedge-shaped leather thongs were passed, anchoring all six along this edge and forming a spine and, as such, a proper codex. Although not as refined as the stitched type produced in the Roman world, this stab-sewing method survived through the evolution of binding structures and into the modern era. There were two secondary leather loops, only one of which is extant. These fitted the circumference of the book at each end and had the effect of keeping the book closed. They are a forerunner to the fastenings found on many Carolingian bindings from the eighth and ninth centuries. Attached to the loops was a longer strap, allowing the tablets to be carried over the shoulder or around the neck, like a book-satchel. It can reasonably be argued that the Springmount Bog Tablets represent Ireland's earliest book.

Along with the text of the psalter, the wooden wax tablets would have been essential tools for the elementary studies which were practised in Irish monasteries by the *oblati* or young novices. After a period under the guidance of a cleric or hermit, permission was sought to enter the monastic order. The young student would learn through Latin, which was propagated through books, as opposed to native learning, which was oral—hence the monastic term for study was the Latin word *lectio*, 'reading'.[31] Instruction also involved the art of writing and committing to memory the 150 psalms which formed the principal part of the canonical hours. The wax tablets allowed the novice to practise perfecting the Irish majuscule and minuscule hand without the consumption of expensive

25 Brown 1994, 119; Bologna 1978, 3.

26 Diringer 1982, 29.

27 Boudalis 2018, 29.

28 National Museum of Ireland S.A. 1914:2.

29 Webster and Backhouse 1991, 80–1; Wallace and Ó Floinn 2002, 181, 191.

30 Charles-Edwards 2002, 27.

31 Pedersen 1909–13, I, 222.

and precious vellum. We see the benefit of this when we read of a student whose scribal attempts were so poor that 'none could tell whether it was caused by a human hand or by a bird's claw!'.[32] As a student progressed, it is reasonable to assume that he may well have produced his own personal copy of the psalter, even though personal possessions were frowned on in monastic tradition. This would prove a most useful tool, given the prominent role of the psalms. We also find reference to the tablet in contemporary written sources; St Ciaran (*c.* 512–*c.* 549) is recorded as writing on staves.[33] In addition, we are very fortunate to have a somewhat romanticised description of the production of a wax tablet in the *Hisperica Famina*, a seventh-century collection of rhetorical descriptive poems written in Hiberno-Latin, possibly as grammatical exercises: 'The wooden tablet was made from choice pieces; it contains rubbing wax from another region; a wooden median joins the little divided columns, on which lovely carving has played ...'.[34]

The Romans are credited with influencing the development of the next significant format for transmitting the written word—the codex (from the Latin *caudex*, meaning the trunk or stem of a tree), which, it has been suggested, developed directly from wooden tablet diptychs in Roman Egypt,[35] replacing the timber with a more flexible substrate. Our modern definition of the codex, firmly linked to the first centuries of Christianity, can be loosely described as a stack of papyrus or parchment leaves folded in half, written on both sides, with some form of tacket employed to keep the stack together, either passed through the backfold or stab-sewn through the side, close to the back edge. A clear descendant of the wooden polyptych, the papyrus or parchment leaves were far lighter and more portable and, although now requiring the use of some form of ink, they remained reusable, as the surface could be scraped with a knife to erase unwanted text, particularly in the case of parchment. In the first century AD the Romans employed a new format for taking notes and recording day-to-day business; typically a rough parchment was used and these notebooks were called *membrane*, reflecting the origin of the folios.[36] More permanent works were also being scribed into codex form; in the first century AD, the Roman poet Martial mentions a parchment codex containing Homer's *Iliad*, clearly not an ephemeral work.[37] Another reference appears in the New Testament in Paul's request to Timothy in II Timothy 4:13: 'When you come, bring the cloak that I left with Carpus at Troas, and my scrolls, especially the parchments'.

These first codices were composed of a single quire, which sometimes contained a staggeringly large number of pages. One extant example is the Milan BA MS P. Vogliano V, a single-quire codex of papyrus with over 140 leaves containing a Coptic edition of St Paul's letters. Later, multi-quire codices eased the strain and improved the function of the text block, which was mechanically fixed to some form of cover or binding. It is likely that these early codices were bound first and then written, with the reverse becoming the norm in later centuries when monastic centres became the producers of Christian literature. There is a suggestion that the new Christian religion chose the codex format over the more popular and abundant roll in an attempt to differentiate itself from pagan religions and the Jewish faith.[38] As a general rule, the majority of earlier codices tended to use papyrus leaves (all extant single-quire codices are on papyrus) rather than parchment, with a gradual reversal of the situation, so that by the fifth century parchment had become the material of choice. Historical records document the

32 Plummer 1910, II, 13.

33 Joyce 1997, 483.

34 Herren 1974, 107.

35 Meyer 2007.

36 Skeat 1969, 66.

37 Roberts and Skeat 2004, 24–9.

38 Skeat 1969, 72.

dramatic arrival of parchment as the usurper of papyrus in the second century BC. In Book XIII of his *Natural History* Pliny relates a story of tension between two dynasties: 'owing to the rivalry between King Ptolemy and King Eumenes about their libraries, Ptolemy suppressed the export of papyrus, parchment was invented at Pergamum as an alternative and afterwards the employment of the material on which the immortality of human beings depends, spread indiscriminately'.[39] The events in Pergamum give us our root word for 'parchment' today, although forms of parchment were in common use long before the second century BC, possibly as early as the Middle Kingdom of ancient Egypt (about 2000 BC), not only as a writing surface but also used in many applications that exploited its particular qualities, including drum heads and other percussion instruments.[40] In an Irish context the *bodhrán*, traditionally covered in goatskin, is a good example of the use of parchment for other purposes. These skins, however, were less refined than those developed in Pergamum and were typically more akin to leather, as the process involved some form of tanning agent.[41]

The clearest evidence of how the early Christian books were bound comes from a collection of surviving single-quire codices found in 1945 buried in an urn near Nag Hammadi, a city in Upper Egypt on the West Bank of the Nile.[42] These limp and semi-limp structures are discussed in detail in Chapter 4. As the multi-quire codex became more commonplace, there was a notable change to the binding format as the limp and semi-limp style of covers of the Nag Hammadi manuscripts were replaced by stiff-boarded bindings of laminated papyrus sheets, or of timber, covered in leather. This afforded a higher degree of protection for the contents but the convenient and more easily produced nature of the limp structures ensured their continued production into the eighteenth century and beyond, with the tanned leather covers being superseded by covers of parchment. The attachment system of the quires initially continued to employ direct tacketing between cover and text block. In later centuries this changed, developing into supported sewing systems in the Western tradition and unsupported sewing in the Mediterranean world, both systems no longer mechanically connecting the individual quires directly to the cover.

To date, the study of bookbinding structures has leaned heavily on a few scholarly works published over the past hundred years. These include G.D. Hobson's *English binding before 1500* (published in 1929), *Binding structures in the Middle Ages* by Berthe van Regemorter (1992) and the most complete overview to date in J.A. Szirmai's *The archaeology of medieval bookbinding* (1999). These volumes offer, in varying degrees of thoroughness and accuracy, the technical descriptions of a range of bookbinding structures, and chart, sometimes in fine detail, changes in the various elements and techniques, influenced by geographical and chronological boundaries. Such publications proved helpful when trying to make sense of the FMP, yet many questions remained unanswered, primarily because the binding structure of the FMP is not represented among the historically recorded types fitting the criteria of time, place and form.

The study of early medieval bookmaking, unlike other disciplines within the area of manuscript studies, poses specific difficulties in any meaningful research leading to firm conclusions, primarily because codicology requires study of the original source material; digital copies are no substitute. There are other contributing factors leading to the dearth of research in this area. First, medieval manuscript study has historically focused on content and context and scholars often ignored the carrier of that information, the binding, a fact regularly bemoaned by today's codicologists. Second, the quantity of

39 Reed 1975, 7; Diringer 1982, 170.

40 Ryder 1960.

41 Reed 1975, 43.

42 Krause 1975.

early medieval manuscripts, western or otherwise, still in their contemporary or even first replacement binding is a very small percentage of the very small percentage of extant manuscripts from this period. Finally, the availability of the source material for codicological study is limited, as such material is usually subject to severely restricted access, particularly when that study requires physical examination and manipulation of the book. The current situation is summed up by Julia Miller in her recent publication, *Books will speak plain*: 'The book as an artefact occupies the most tenuous and complex position, perhaps of all the items made by the human hand: it is at once treasured *and* cavalierly interfered with on a whim'.[43] It is the intention of this volume to tell the story of the FMP and, in doing so, to add to our knowledge of the early medieval book as an artefact and how this particular manuscript might have been perceived and utilised by its custodians.

43 Miller 2010, 37.

CHAPTER 1

Conservation of the Faddan More Psalter

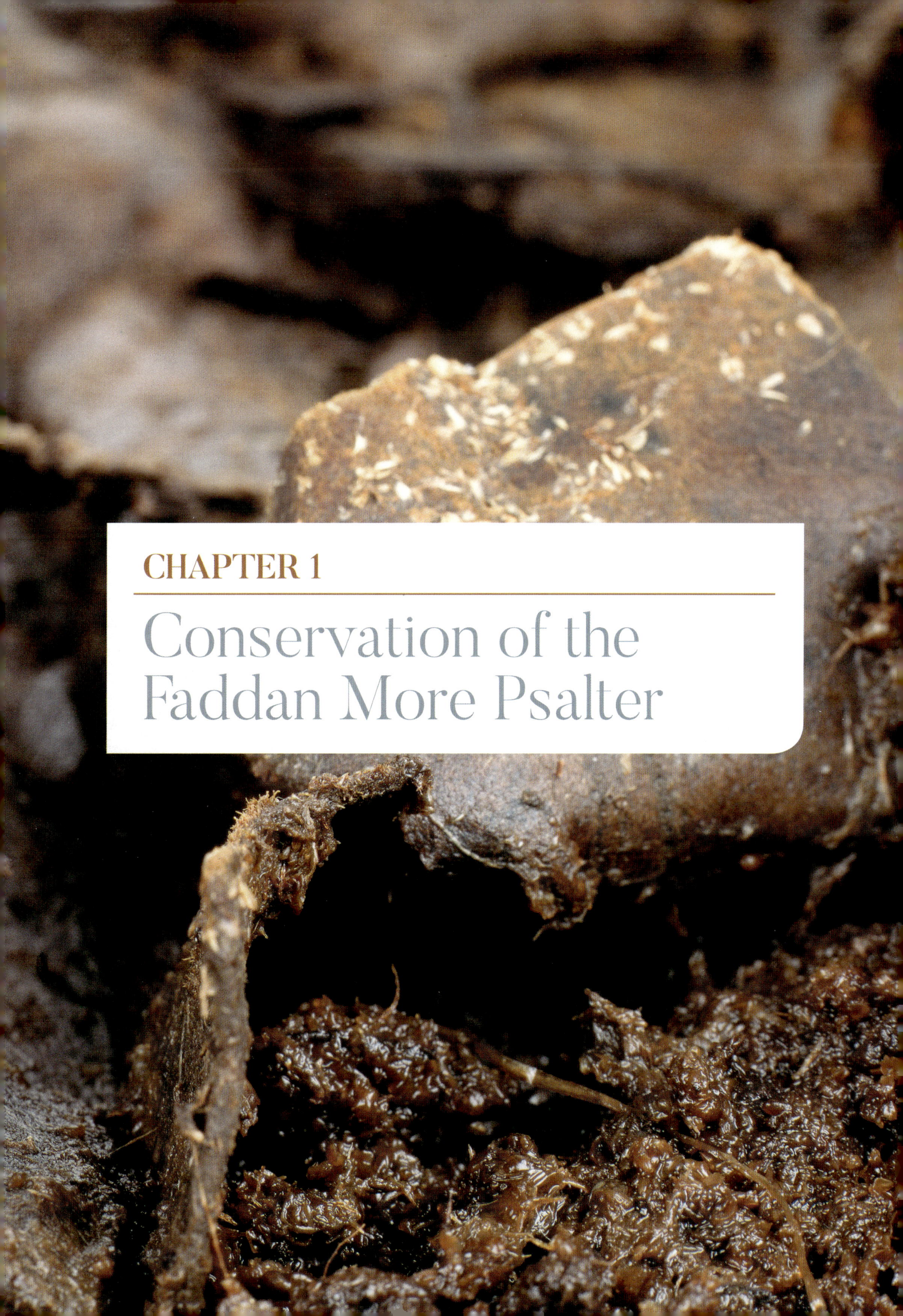

CHAPTER 1

Conservation of the Faddan More Psalter

The hands-on conservation of any object brings its conservator into a level of contact far above that of any other person engaging with the artefact, either prior to the conservator's involvement or afterwards, with the exception of its original creator. This highly focused evaluation of the materiality of the object allows much valuable information to be extracted. This information, once studied, analysed and deciphered, can reveal details relating to the object's original manufacture and to events that affected it over the passage of time. These clues can be many and varied—for example, the discovery of some minuscule fragments of extraneous material hidden in the body of the object, or particular markings on its surface not directly related to its manufacture or everyday use. The archaeology of the FMP posed several questions in relation to its origins, use and, ultimately, its disposal. Many codicological features of particular interest also came to light; indeed, much of the content of this book is based on questions raised and answers presented. This chapter will chart the lengthy and unique conservation process, which continued uninterrupted to its completion. Although aspects of the conservation work have been published, this is the first full documented report of the four-and-a-half-year process.

ASSESSMENT

On arrival at the Conservation Department of the National Museum of Ireland in July 2006, the excavated remains of the manuscript and associated material were placed in a walk-in cold store at 4°C. The saturated moisture values were maintained throughout the investigative stages by monitoring and occasional spraying with deionised water (Fig. 1.1). The conglomeration sat on a plywood base and a grain sack, items which had been employed during the difficult on-site excavation. Exposure to the atmosphere was restricted by covering the collected mass with layers of Cellocast®, a resin-impregnated bandage which is activated by water. Once dry, this material forms a rigid shell, profiled to the approximate shape of the form underneath. The extremities of the

Fig. 1.1 — The psalter as found.

hardened shell were screwed down to the plywood base, further improving the enclosed environment. Examination of the manuscript was restricted during the initial stages of conservation in order to maintain the high level of moisture. Failure in this regard would result in uncontrolled drying-out of the fibrous collagen material of which both the vellum and the leather of the manuscript were constructed, this in turn leading to irreversible shrinkage of the fibres.[1] The purpose at this initial stage was to preserve as much of the artefact as feasible in the state in which it was found.

On first examination of the manuscript, it was evident that, owing to the combination of trauma as a result of its unearthing and the hostile environment in which the organic materials had been entombed for a considerable time, many additional recording procedures would need to be carried out before any conservation could commence. Such was the condition of the manuscript that in the early stages, prior to any conservation, the number of folios and even the number of quires were incorrectly estimated and reported.[2] Given the significance of the codicological study of a manuscript and the clues this offers as to where and when the book was made, a primary aim was to establish a collation map for the extant folios.[3] This would tell us how many leaves in how many gatherings had been employed in the making of the manuscript. In addition, as well as identifying the animal type, it was hoped that the hair/flesh orientation of the skins and perhaps even the spine direction could be established. In order to achieve these aims, the first stage involved examining the manuscript without any disturbance of the mass of material in an attempt to identify backfold areas of bifolios where they lay (Fig. 1.2). This task was greatly complicated because of severe trauma, both historical and recent, which had in effect torn the quires horizontally in two across the middle of the folios. Besides the damage suffered during its unearthing, research would show that the manuscript also appears to have suffered considerable damage in its past (see Chapter 7). Careful study of the manuscript followed under the restrictive conditions previously outlined, and several detailed photographs were taken both by the author as working images and by the Photographic Department of the National Museum. These were studied at length and a preliminary folio layout was recorded, which at this early stage allowed me to confirm the presence of five quires of an inconsistent folio count. Another codicological feature identified was the lack of any flyleaves at the start and finish of the folios. Later examination after dismantling of the text block would reveal the exclusive use of calfskin vellum, which was established through the study of extant follicle patterns under magnification. The identification of the spine direction on the bifolios was much more challenging, given the condition and percentage of survival. Nevertheless, I believe that I have identified a spine pattern on the one almost intact bifolio, ff 29–32, with the spine running across the skin from fore-edge to fore-edge. This is important, as it feeds into codicological conventions on the make-up of quires and can help in narrowing down the place of manufacture.

The steering committee listed in the Introduction, composed of both National Museum staff from relevant departments and a number of external specialist scholars, met at regular intervals throughout the project. Policy decisions were made in many areas, including the proposed major conservation operations. Once a decision had been reached to dismantle the find and to conserve the individual components rather than simply to stabilise the mass as an archaeological object, further analytical investigation was suggested before the separation process began.

The additional procedures included an MRI (magnetic resonance imaging) scan, which was carried out at Trinity College Institute of Neuroscience with the intention of identifying the layers between folios and possibly even areas of decoration within the manuscript. While this proved to be

1 Cameron *et al.* 2006, 245.

2 Kelly 2006, 4.

3 Brown 1994, 42.

Fig. 1.2—Backfolds visible prior to removal.

an interesting exercise, particularly as the software for processing the images gave results in 3D and certain features, such as the edges of folios, were visible inside the mass, the scan did not provide the level of detail necessary to guide the subsequent conservation process. Computed tomography (CT scans) and X-radiography were excluded from the outset owing to concerns over accelerated degradation of the fragile vellum matrix. The final recording procedure in the manuscript's 'as found' state was the use of high-resolution digital video. This involved passing mobile cameras over the material on motorised gantries. The resulting images proved useful as reference material at later stages in the conservation process.

Although not strictly a conservation process, the recording by Crossing the Line Films, an independent film company commissioned to record the project, should be mentioned. Over a four-year period, many aspects of the work were recorded with the intention of producing a factual documentary for national television. Ultimately, this provided a visual record of the processes involved in this unique and highly complex project. As the conservator appointed to record, conserve and display the FMP, I was involved in all decision-making aspects of the work. This centred on assessing the conservation merit against risks to the manuscript, costs incurred and the potential value of any results arising from investigative procedures.

In addition to establishing the condition of the vellum from an overall macro perspective, it was essential to establish the level of degradation at a cellular level. Vellum which looks and handles as expected may in fact have suffered damage to its collagen network, which is much exposed as a result of the manufacturing process—a procedure that strips away proteins, elastin and fats, leaving the fibre network vulnerable.[4] Gelatinisation can take place without being perceptible to the naked eye. It was decided that two small samples of vellum from the psalter would be sent under licence to the Royal Danish Academy of Fine Arts School of Conservation. Under the supervision of Dr Rene Larsen, the samples were put through the range of tests developed for the IDAP (Improved Damage Assessment of Parchment) programme, with an additional amino-acid test. The evaluation included assessment of the fibre condition and measurement of hydrothermal stability. The chosen samples were representative of different visual conditions of the psalter vellum:

> **Sample A: vellum in reasonable condition that had been exposed to the bog material. Responds well to the drying process and has a tanned appearance once dry.**
>
> **Sample B: very degraded and gelatinised vellum appears 'pulped up' and unstable. When cleaned before drying, often only the text (written in iron gall ink) remains, with the vellum disintegrated.**

The Academy team commenced their analysis by examining the samples under 40x magnification to study the fibre structure, consisting of collagen, a major protein from which skin is formed. The triple helix defines the structure of the collagen molecule[5] (Fig. 1.3). Results from this examination found both samples classed as category 4, heavy damage, on a scale of 1–4. It was even suggested that if a category 5 had been available the Faddan More vellum would have qualified, such was the level of deterioration of the fibre structure. Establishing the shrinkage temperature under magnification acts as a further indicator of the level of deterioration of the fibre structure. Surprisingly, both of the Faddan More samples displayed values comparable to that of good-quality new parchment, probably because of the partial tanning of the vellum by organic tannins in the bog. The amino-acid analysis was employed to measure the degree of oxidation of the vellum. Both samples displayed moderate levels, scoring a 2 on a scale of 1–4. The anaerobic environment of the bog played a major role in this result. The report concluded that:

> *'Taken together, the analyses of the fibre samples show parchment structures that are heavily fragmented and partly gelatinised, although the remaining fibre structure has a high hydrothermal stability. This combination of characteristics may make the parchment very unstable in dry conditions, making it inflexible, brittle and very sensitive to handling and changing environmental conditions.'*[6]

Having established the condition of the psalter vellum at a microscopic/cellular level, I considered it essential for any proposed conservation process to understand the general reactive condition of the material, given its long-term exposure to the extreme environment of Faddan More Bog. The fibre structure of vellum retains tension throughout its manufacture, making it sensitive to adjustments in relative humidity and temperature owing to low hydrothermal stability.[7] A small vellum fragment with no writing on its surface which could not be located in the text block was selected for testing. It was flattened out and the outline was traced onto a piece of Mylar®. The fragment was then allowed to air-dry in normal ambient conditions. The change in its physical condition was so marked that the results were difficult to assess accurately. The air-dried fragment

---

4 Woods 2006, 204.

5 Haines 2006, 6.

6 Larsen *et al.* 2007.

7 Larsen *et al.* 2002.

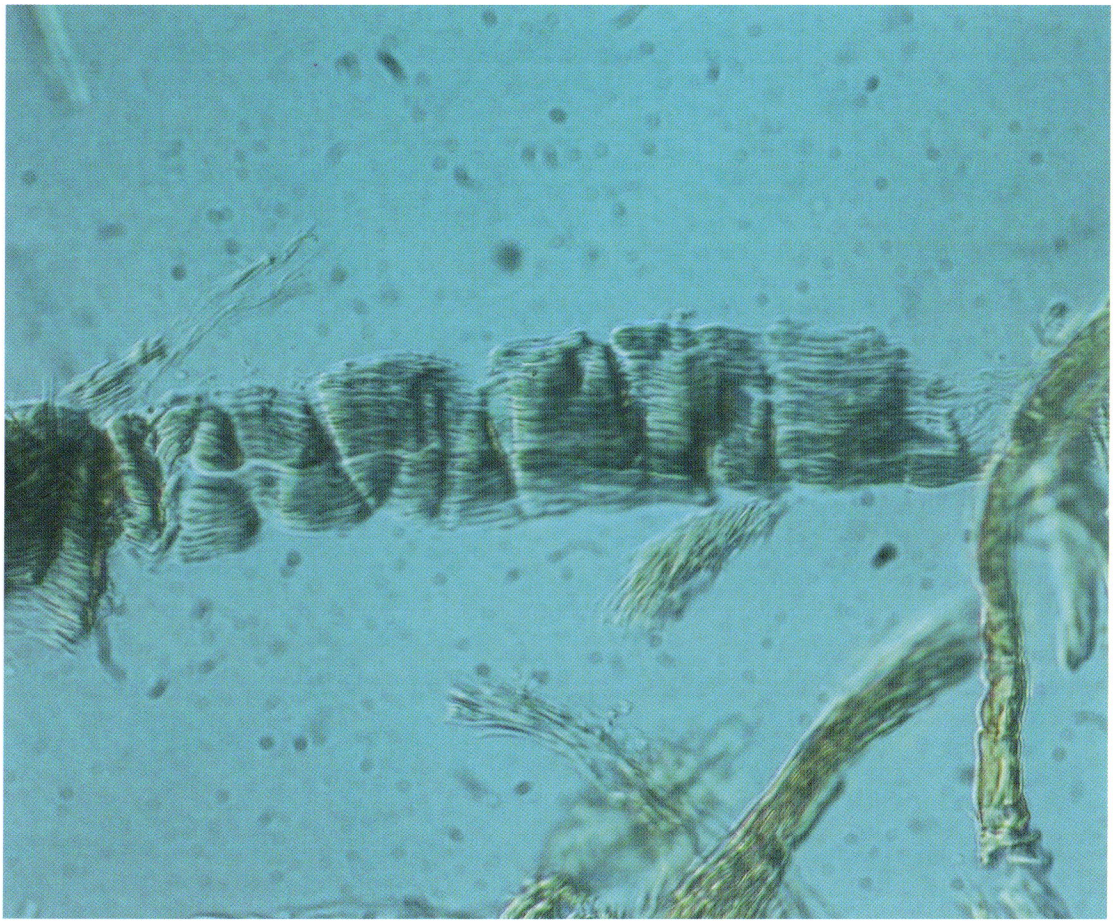

Fig. 1.3—Vellum fibres under x40 magnification.

Fig. 1.4—Air-dried vellum sample; outline shows size before drying.

was now very brittle and had shrunk to less than half its original dimensions. It was also very dark and almost unrecognisable as vellum (Fig. 1.4). Although a similar reaction would be expected in modern vellum, it appeared exaggerated in the case of the Faddan More sample. This reinforced the findings of the Royal Danish Academy's test results and emphasised the need to find an effective method of de-watering the extant fragments of the psalter's folios while controlling dimensional stability.

DE-WATERING

The next phase of the conservation process was to establish a procedure for the removal of the excess or unbound water from all components of the manuscript. It became evident during the investigative stage of the project that no vellum had ever previously been retrieved and dried from a wetland environment; as a result, there was little or no published material available for comparison. Consequently, in my role as conservator, I began to experiment in order to develop a method of completing this stage of the project successfully. Trials were carried out with vellum test samples which were conditioned in an attempt to mimic the current state of the vellum in the FMP. The source material for the trials consisted of discarded vellum flyleaves from an eighteenth-century binding. In order to reproduce some level of degradation akin to that of the FMP, the test vellum was hydrated and placed between saturated (with tap water) sheets of blotting-paper. The 'sandwich' was then placed inside a zip-lock bag under a light weight and left at ambient values for about a month. These conditions resulted in thoroughly saturated vellum with clear microbiological growth and evidence of degradation of the collagen protein. The production of vellum in the early Middle Ages varied somewhat from that of the eighteenth century, as did the end-product, but the conditioned samples were considered similar enough to render meaningful results during the subsequent de-watering trials.

To prepare the test vellum for the several trials that were to follow over the next six months, samples were cut into triangles measuring 43mm x 43mm x 60mm. The shape was chosen to provide the maximum number of test pieces from a limited supply (Fig. 1.5). Three tangible comparators were employed to assess results before and after the de-watering trials. First, thickness was measured with a dial micrometer at a number of sites on the sample and an average figure calculated. Second, the flexibility of the sample was compared to one of four plastic discs of varying thickness, by which a value could be assigned. Lastly, colour value was measured by assessing each sample under a fixed light value of 1,000 lux through a small viewing hole and comparing and allocating a value based on the Colour Atlas 96, Natural (Fig. 1.6). The remainder of the limited test vellum was cut into larger pieces in order to have samples of a more representative size as we homed in on a workable methodology. These larger samples were treated 'roughly', i.e. they were scrunched up, cuts were added, and they were wetted and re-wetted after partial drying. From the outset it was decided that no chemical additives would be used to aid the drying of the FMP's folio fragments for fear of traces remaining in the vellum; moreover, I had concerns about the possible long-term effects of chemicals such as polyethylene glycol and glycerol on the inks and pigments present in the manuscript and their potential to obstruct future non-destructive analysis. This decision ruled out some established archaeological conservation drying techniques often employed for organic material such as leather and timber.

It was clear from the outset that the physical restraint of the vellum fragments would be a major issue as unbound water was removed during the change from a saturated state to a dry one. This would potentially be a problem no matter which method was chosen for drying. The drying of collagen-based materials from a saturated state presents particular challenges owing to the nature

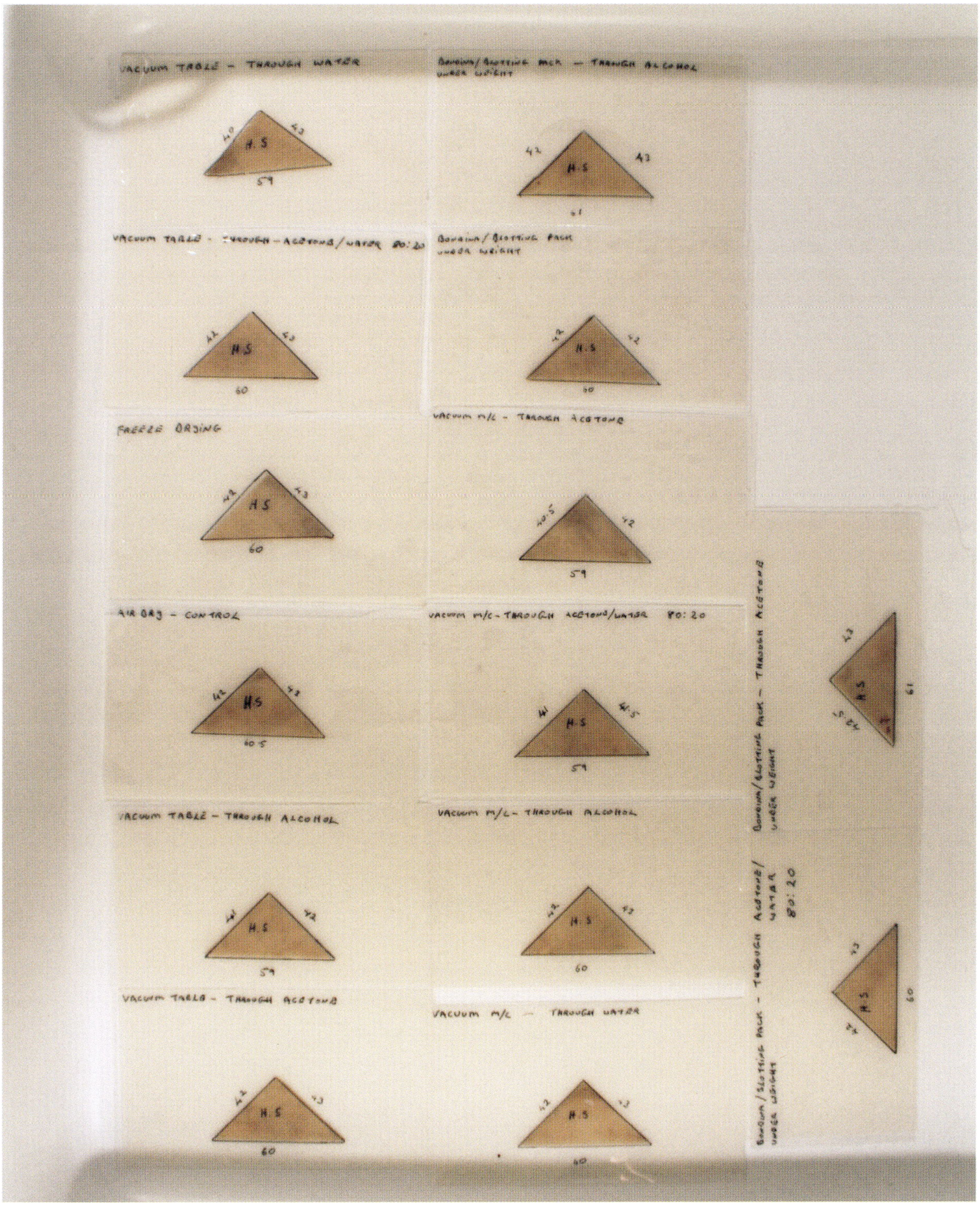

Fig. 1.5—Test samples of saturated vellum with dimensions recorded.

of their make-up.[8] During the manufacture of vellum, the cell structure is drawn into a low angle of weave and any uncontrolled removal of unbound water will result in a loss of this tension, as well as in unacceptable levels of shrinkage and irreversible gelatinisation as the fibres stick to each other. Normally this is avoided by physically restraining the vellum around its circumference as the drying process proceeds.[9] This procedure has been illustrated in numerous engravings among the pages of early

8 Ganiaris *et al.* 1982, 18.

9 Baldwin and Gillis 2006, 65.

Fig. 1.6—Colour Atlas 96 under 1,000 lux.

printed books, displaying scenes of a stretched skin suspended inside a wooden frame known as a 'herse' with the *Parchmenter* at work. The folio fragments of the FMP, however, were markedly too degraded for this approach. Four alternative methods of restraint were assessed using the test vellum samples.

For the first test method, a saturated sample was placed on a low-pressure suction table and the surface of the table masked off as required. Pressure was set at 28in. of H_2O (about 6.9kPa) with ambient values of 20°C and 57% RH. In order to reduce cupping as the sample dried, layers of Bondina® masking were placed around its circumference. As drying of the sample neared completion, pressure was reduced to 13in. of H_2O (about 3.2kPa). The use of this equipment was quickly eliminated because of the difficulty in holding the sample vellum in place once evaporation had begun. Varying the suction settings and masking of the base proved ineffective for the most part.

The second piece of equipment to be tried was an Audionvac 401H vacuum machine[10] (Fig. 1.7). The principle here is to reduce air pressure inside a container, in this case a proprietary vacuum bag, which is 'gas-tight' to below that of atmospheric pressure, measured at 1bar. Although absolute vacuum is not achieved, the removal of gas from the bag allows atmospheric pressure to be applied to the sealed contents. This has the effect of holding those contents in place with an even pressure being applied on all surfaces, including the edges. The type of vacuum chamber used in our trials was developed

10 The use of a vacuum machine was suggested by Christopher Clarkson, private book conservator, who had already discussed the possibilities of drying parchment with Stuart Welch, formerly of Conservation by Design. The latter had established the vacuum machine as a conservation tool in the area of disaster recovery, and he organised the loan of a vacuum machine for our trials.

Fig. 1.7—Audionvac 401H vacuum machine.

principally for the packing of perishable foodstuffs, and an option of 'soft ventilation' was available which extended the ventilation period and was designed for packing pressure-sensitive products. This would later prove useful for the ultimate stage of the project, to house the fragments of the FMP. For present purposes, a piece of the saturated triangular test vellum was placed between sheets of 100% cotton blotting-paper and then into an Archipress® vacuum bag. A vacuum was pulled for 35 seconds, and the bag was seam-welded for five seconds. The bag remained sealed for 24 hours before it was opened and the results observed. The recorded results from this test gave a shrinkage value of approximately 1.5%, with no distortion or change in thickness. A significant shift in colour value and a degree of translucency not present prior to testing did, however, occur. The flexibility remained at the same value.

The next test method employed a vacuum freeze-drying unit. This involves sublimation, the transition of a solid to a gas without passing through the liquid phase. For the purpose of our trial, the saturated test vellum sample was frozen and then, while under vacuum, dried by passing from its frozen state to a dry state without first reverting to the water stage, a process which took three days. The end results did not fulfil our criteria, with considerable change in colour, particularly on the hair side, becoming almost white, and a 'pulping up' of the vellum with a noticeable increase in thickness.

The third test method took a less interventionist approach: drying under light pressure. The sample was placed between sheets of 100% cotton blotting-paper and pressed under glass weights, and after two or three hours the blotting-paper was replaced by dry sheets. This process continued until the vellum reached ambient values. Although the trial vellum showed little distortion and maintained both flexibility and shrinkage values that were deemed acceptable, there was a marked increase in translucency, which suggested a gelatinisation of the collagen fibres owing to insufficient tension to keep them apart while the drying proceeded.[11]

In addition to establishing a method of de-watering the folio fragments of the FMP, we needed to demonstrate that a solvent exchange system could be used in tandem with the chosen drying method. The reasoning here is based on the premise that water as a solvent has a high surface tension, and as it retreats during the drying process it can collapse the cell structure of the polar collagen, causing excessive shrinkage and possible visual changes to the vellum. It is well documented in conservation practice that the tendency of certain organic material to shrink is reduced by replacing water with a non-polar or low polar solvent with a lower surface tension, then drying through the chosen solvent.[12] Vellum, made almost entirely of collagen, will react in such a manner.[13] The transfer is achieved by immersion of the water-saturated folio fragment in the solvent of choice, the fragment remaining in the bath until the solvent replaces the unbound water. A range of non-polar solvents and less polar solvents are available. Their working characteristics, polarity and toxic values were examined, given that I would be working in close proximity with high volumes of the chosen solvent over a lengthy period of time, and a short list was drawn up. Based on the criteria listed, the final choice was solvent exchange through denatured ethanol, although a 98:2 solution of denatured ethanol and H_2O ran a very close second and may even be preferable where the saturated vellum is less degraded.

During the trials, the vacuum machine showed great promise from the outset, as it delivered the required criteria in a controllable fashion. The main advantage proved to be the ability of the blotting-paper sandwich inside the vacuum bag to begin the drying process through capillary action by the transfer of solvent (after the exchange bath) from vellum to blotting-paper while maintaining the integrity of the vellum. After further successful trials using some of the larger pieces of test vellum, a small fragment of the FMP, with no writing and no clear evidence of its correct location, was chosen. It was processed through denatured ethanol solvent exchange, followed by drying through vacuum. I observed that the solvent exchange system also dealt with the issue of colour change experienced when drying through water in the vacuum machine, with only a slight lightening in value. Shrinkage did increase to an average of 3.5% but this was deemed well within acceptable levels, particularly considering that the saturated vellum of the psalter was likely to have been expanded beyond its original format, reinforcing the success of such small dimensional changes. Based on the successful treatment of this fragment, I repeated the process, this time with a larger fragment of a folio that also displayed some writing. Again, this satisfied the criteria laid down.

Fine-tuning the operation, with some adjustments to the interval times and materials, resulted in the following: the alcohol-saturated fragment was placed between two sheets of Bondina® after correcting any distortion or misalignment. The layers were placed between double sheets of 100% cotton blotting-paper and into the Archipress® vacuum bag. The 'sandwich' pack was placed into the vacuum machine and a vacuum pulled for 40 seconds with a five-second seal. The pack was left for three to four hours, after which it was opened and the blotting-paper replaced with dry sheets and the polythene bag discarded. The pack was then placed under pressing boards and a weight. After a further three to four hours, the blotting-paper was again replaced with dry sheets and the weight on the pressing boards was reduced. This process could be repeated if required, and further blotting-paper changes made, until the fragment came into equilibrium with ambient values. The moisture content of the processed vellum was monitored using an Aqua Boy® metre with surface probe. For some of the larger folio fragments, owing to the volume of alcohol to be displaced, a

11 Woods 2006, 205.

12 Peacock 1992.

13 Woods 2006, 204.

Fig. 1.8—Grid bridge with the psalter below.

vacuum was pulled twice before continuing with the remainder of the drying stages.

The procedure was put before the Faddan More Steering Committee and approval was given to proceed with the complete remains of the vellum text block—a process that continued over the next two years before all folio fragments were in a dry and stable state.

Taking a retrospective view of this procedure at a distance of some years, and considering that it was and is in essence a unique conservation treatment developed for a unique project, the approach has much to recommend it. The folio fragments remain stable in their inert environment, with no visible change in condition some ten years on. The decision not to employ traditional repair methods maintains the original 'as found' integrity of the calfskin vellum. In addition, should the location of any of the remaining smaller text fragments be identified in the future, uniting them with their folio fragment is relatively straightforward owing to the built-in reversibility of the housing system, detailed later in this chapter. The physical properties of the vellum, while much changed, are now accessible and it will be possible for scholars and researchers to study the content of what is Ireland's earliest psalter text after the *Cathach*.[14] If our bogs decide to give up another early book in the future, I would confidently apply the same methods, with perhaps a more exhaustive system of recording prior to de-watering.

DISMANTLING

Having established the required methodology to de-water the folio fragments of the FMP, the next conservation stage involved the dismantling of the text block. Although the manuscript was stored in the Conservation Department cold store at 4°C, there remained the risk of biological attack, now that the conditions were far more aerobic than prior to the excavation. Micro-organisms that require oxygen

14 RIA MS 12.R.33.

are mostly fungi, moulds and bacteria; the latter, however, do not like the acid conditions of leather (the cover).[15] Close inspection and monitoring were carried out continually during dismantling until the entire manuscript was in a dry and stable state. The anatomy of the manuscript as found dictated the order of work. Prior to the removal of any folio fragment, a Perspex® (PMMA) grid bridge with x- and y-axes of my own design was employed. The manuscript mass was placed beneath this prior to the commencement of a given day's work, and a grid reference was allocated to the part or fragment about to be removed; a digital image of the same area was taken through the grid (Fig. 1.8). Often a working day would be spent studying the small area of backfolds remaining on a given quire fragment prior to removal and recording as much codicological information as possible to aid future identification. All statistics gathered were fed into a database (FileMaker Pro) which I developed in-house to cope with the large volume of information generated. Typically, the type of information gathered prior to intervention included recording matching 'cut patterns' to the edges of two or more folio fragments. Owing to the haphazard nature of the edge trimming of the FMP, it was sometimes possible to match the jagged edges, thus aiding identification of which folios were adjacent to each other, even those disturbed during excavation. An example of this is seen on the trimmed edges of folios 59 and 60: both present a 'step' in the trimming of their top edges at the same point about 60mm in from the fore-edge.

The work began by locating a natural separation layer from the top down, usually found between two quires. A thin slip of aluminium printer's plate was cut to the width of a folio fragment and then covered with a fold of silicone-coated Mylar® (polyester film). The plate was slowly eased between the vellum layers to separate and support the top layer. Spraying with deionised water at the separation point reduced surface friction and assisted the transmission. This process continued until the delineation between the layers was no longer in evidence. The remaining material was a single mass of gelatinised vellum, surviving ink letters and bog material, containing plant roots, seed pods and degraded plant matter; the manuscript vellum here was at a more advanced stage of deterioration. The intact folio fragments were lifted away and in a separate operation the associated mass material was removed for separate treatment.

The next stage was to open out the vellum quire fragment, as all quire fragments of the manuscript remained closed, with their folios facing each other (Fig. 1.9). Once opened, they could be separated into individual bifolio fragments. Pre-facing with smooth Bondina®, a non-woven polyester material held in place through the surface tension of the saturated vellum, helped with this stage of the work (Fig. 1.10). Again, tracking and identifying as work progressed was essential, particularly as often a fragment of a bifolio might display no extant text to help identify its location and I was dependent on the physical position within the quire fragment to indicate to which folio it was likely to belong. At this stage other codicological features could be examined, such as the identification of singletons by examining the few millimetres of surviving backfold under magnification, or the location of pricking marks used to guide ruling of the folios. When compared to more typical codicological examination of medieval manuscripts, the discovery of these features and others was hard-earned because of the extremely poor state of preservation of the FMP and the difficulty of deciphering it. Nevertheless, this work resulted in making the FMP comprehensible as a book and laid the foundations for its future study.

CLEANING

Once they had been separated out, the next task involved the cleaning of the individual folio fragments. Work commenced by laying a saturated folio fragment (on its Bondina® support) onto a sheet of glass;

15 Reed 1972, 18.

another sheet of Bondina® was laid on top and the fragment was sprayed with deionised water. This allowed the piece to 'float' somewhat and to be manipulated to lie as flat as possible, removing folds and creases in the vellum. Excess water was sponged off and the top sheet of Bondina® was lifted away; this unintentionally started the cleaning operation, as it had the effect of lifting away some of the looser debris. The one single advantage of working with a saturated material is the ability to use water as a cleaning agent.

The method employed utilised a number of tools and techniques, depending on the condition of the vellum in any given area of the fragment. In short, the main approach was to use a soft-bristle Japanese brush and, while keeping the area flooded and working under magnification, to brush the debris off the surface. This worked for the looser material, composed mostly of bog material and plant matter, and was followed by patting the surface with a small block of conservation sponge (a hydrophilic closed-cell structure) to pick up smaller pieces, which were attracted to the sponge as it absorbed the water around it. Ultimately, however, it was necessary to resort to fine No. 3 tweezers in order to pick thousands of seed pods one by one from the surface of the vellum. All the above stages were carried out under a three-dioptre illuminated magnifier lamp. Once cleaned and still saturated, the folio fragment was faced with a sheet of Silicone Mylar® and turned over to allow the operation to be repeated on the other side.

The final cleaning stage involved the addition of denatured ethanol to introduce the solvent to the vellum in a weak solution before total immersion as part of the de-watering technique. The clean and saturated folio fragment could be further manipulated at this stage into its correct shape, as all the larger fragments had become 'set' in a distorted form over the long period of their entombment (Fig. 1.11). At this stage a final alignment of surviving edges, consisting of narrow strips of vellum no more

Fig. 1.9—Saturated folios being separated.

Fig. 1.10—A separated quire supported between Bondina® sheets.

Fig. 1.11—Folio 13r after removal and cleaning.

than a few millimetres wide, was carried out prior to the solvent exchange process.[16] After cleaning, a sheet of Mylar® was placed over the fragment and the piece mapped using a permanent pen. Selected datum points were chosen, measured and marked on the Mylar® sheet, as was the centrefold line, given that this feature was not always easy to locate once the bifolio fragment was dry.

The procedures above document the approach used when dealing with folio fragments of the FMP in which the collagen structure retained some integrity, but this level of survival applies to only 12–15% of the text block. Most of the folios have reacted in a more predictable manner for vellum that has been sitting in a saturated environment for over a millennium, dissolving into a gelatinous mass that leaves little evidence of its existence. There is, however, a unique and unexpected by-product of this destructive process: it would appear that particular components in the iron gall ink employed to write the manuscript had a partial or mild tanning effect on the vellum, but only where it made direct contact with the surface. This had the effect that where the spaces between the letters dissolved into the bog, the surface of the vellum occupied by the ink survived. In this fragile state, however, the matrix of letters did not maintain their position on the page and, as a result of free water and shifting within the bog, these letters were picked up and moved out of position. This conclusion was reached after repeatedly finding clumps of this material with letters no longer in a regimented line of text but instead upside down, sideways and anywhere except where they should have been, all in a kind of alphabet soup. In addition, over an extended period these displaced manuscript fragments were engulfed by the organic material of the bog, which had found its way between the covers of the manuscript and the folios. After identification and recording of the general location of this material within the manuscript mass, segments were lifted away. Because of their saturated state, it was acceptable to immerse them in a Pyrex® dish filled with deionised water. From here the task was to separate out the remaining word fragments, individual letters and letter fragments from the detritus around them. Once removed, these smaller fragments were laid on Bondina® on glass and kept wet until they could be de-watered by the same method used for the larger folio fragments (Fig. 1.12). The result is several thousand individual letters, partial letters, words and partial words. In some cases where the words or partial words were identified these could be reunited with their associated larger extant fragment of the psalm.

The process of separating out the smaller fragments was often hindered by the combination of very fragile degraded vellum and high surface tension of the water in which the fragments were suspended, causing them to clump and stick together. The situation was much improved by spraying between the two layers that were being separated with a 40% alcohol solution; this had the effect of reducing the surface tension enough to improve the chances of lifting away an individual fragment intact. It was also observed during the de-watering trials that immersion or spraying the folio fragments with denatured alcohol had the effect of stiffening the vellum. It was possible to use this to good effect when dealing with the smaller fragmented letters and words, as it allowed a degree of manipulation of the often very delicate matrix of the surviving material and in addition, as with the larger folio fragments, introduced the solvent to the saturated vellum. Several hundred partial word fragments and several thousand individual letter fragments are now stable and preserved. The NMI has no immediate plans for them, but they will be available for future researchers.

IDENTIFICATION AND RELOCATION OF FOLIO FRAGMENTS

The main aid to establishing the collation map of the FMP and the identification of the individual folios was the content of the manuscript. The text of the 150 psalms is readily available either printed

16 Gillis 2012.

Fig. 1.12—Removal of a letter from bog material.

or online and both were used extensively during this stage of the conservation project. The initial identification of folios and quires was made *in situ*, with all findings entered into the aforementioned database. Once removed, separated and cleaned and prior to de-watering, the process of confirming folio identification involved reading the extant text, often with the aid of enlarged and enhanced digital images (Fig. 1.13), and comparing this to an online searchable version of the Vulgate Bible.[17] During the initial on-site examination of the manuscript shortly after discovery, in addition to identifying the text as a psalter it was suggested that the version was the Gallican.[18] This version is St Jerome's second and more complete revision of the old Latin version against the Hexapala of Origen, which he produced near the end of the fourth century AD. The Gallican was the most popular version of psalms used in Ireland during the early medieval period and is the same version as the *Cathach* (*c*. 600), Ireland's oldest—albeit incomplete—copy of the Book of Psalms.[19] At a later stage of the project it was noted that the psalms of the FMP lacked the non-biblical headings (*tituli*) found in many early medieval psalters, including the *Cathach*.[20]

The larger and more intact folio fragments were photographed digitally at high resolution in their wet state, and these images, along with the actual fragment (now dry), were studied simultaneously to identify the psalm and verse. Because the order of work was dictated by the position of the quires as

17 *Biblia Sacra, Iuxta Vulgatam Versionem* (Deutsche Bibelgesellschaft, Stuttgart, 1994).

18 Raghnall Ó Floinn, 'Identification', *Archaeology Ireland* **20** (3) (supplement), s. 8.

19 RIA MS 12.R.33.

20 Martin McNamara, pers. comm., 2009.

they lay, the allocation of folio numbers was provisional, and a definitive version was not produced until all the larger folio fragments had been examined and identified. The identification of folio fragments where no text was extant and only ribbon-like strips of the folio edges remained was wholly dependent on position in relation to an adjacent folio fragment where identifiable text had survived. All of the above information, including the location and re-location of fragments, was recorded on the database. As a result, all major folio fragments of the manuscript can be tracked from their removal from the saturated mass through to their eventual folio allocation and display housing.

It was decided, once the de-watering process was under way, to record photographically all folio fragments with discernible writing. This process was carried out at a fixed focal length with the digital camera set perpendicular to the fragment. Both sides were recorded and all photographic values, such as exposure and light levels, were kept constant throughout. This operation continued over a two-year time-span of the de-watering process and, besides the larger areas of psalm fragments, groups of the rescued smaller text fragments were also recorded. This database is archived in the Museum's Conservation Department.

During the process it became evident that it would be possible to identify some of these smaller fragments of psalms and relocate them within the larger extant folio fragments. In order to achieve this with some accuracy, a 'character count' was calculated. This involved working out an average character count per line of text and employing this to locate the physical position of fragments on a folio that did not continue directly from the preceding text. The method of working out the 'character count' involved counting the characters on eight full lines of text starting at Ps. 72:14. The sample area was chosen as typically representative of the layout of the manuscript, although there wasn't much in the way of choice, given the survival rate of folios. The results gave values of between 41 and 48 characters

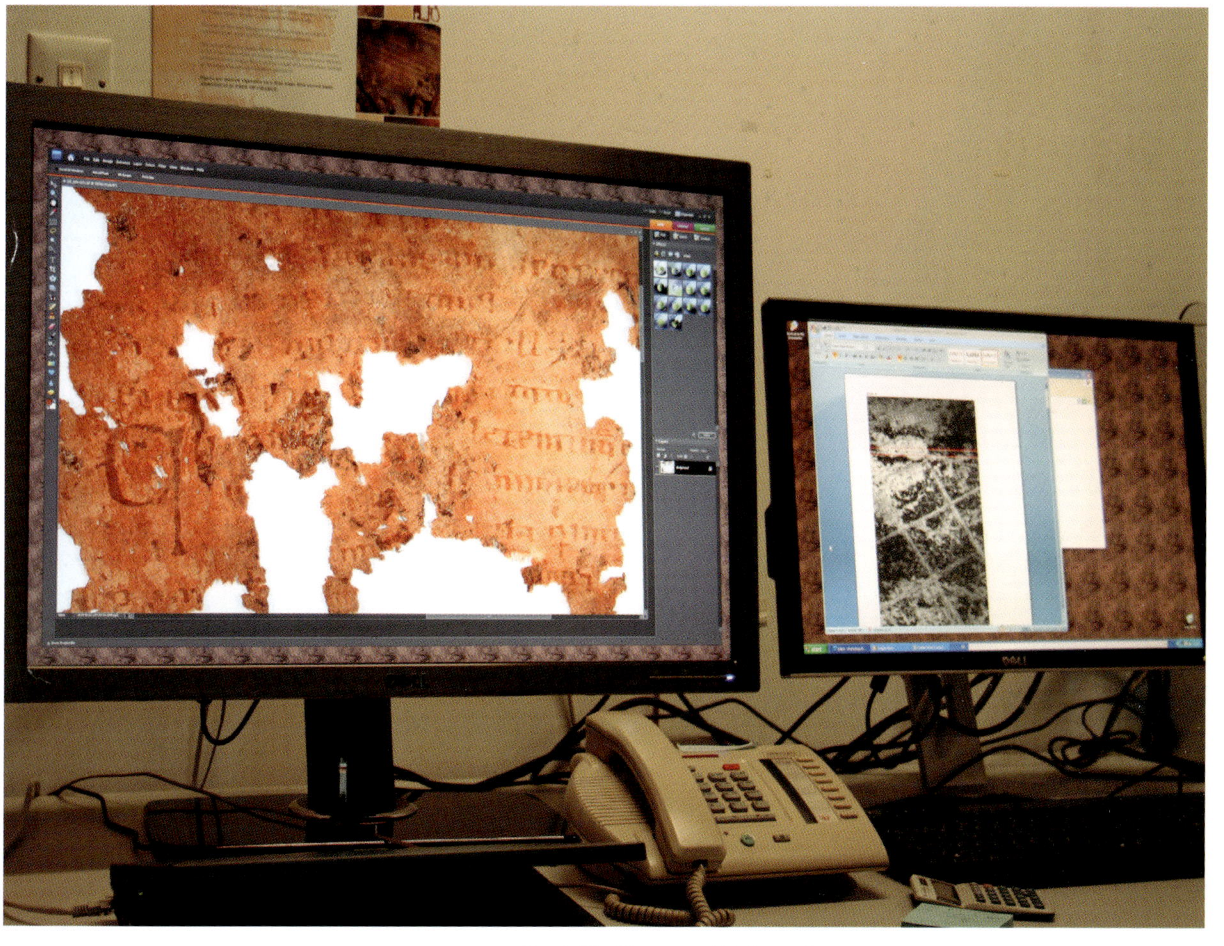

Fig. 1.13—The use of high-resolution screens to assist psalm identification.

Fig. 1.14—Virtually assembled bifolio (7v–6r) from identified fragments.

per line. The total was divided by eight and multiplied by 31, denoting the number of lines per folio (although a folio with 32 lines was identified). This gave an average of 1,364 characters per page (as this accounts for one side of the folio only). This exercise was repeated three times in different areas of the manuscript, resulting in a final mean average figure of 1,336 characters per folio. The calculation was tested by locating the beginning of a psalm in the manuscript and identifying another point two or three folios further on. Then, by using the Vulgate, it was possible to calculate the number of characters from the starting position to the finish, and then compare this to the calculated finish point using the estimated values. Allowance was made for the typical use of abbreviations and contractions in Irish writing. Results were positive and confirmed when the same exercise was replicated from a different area of the psalter.

The FMP displays little in the way of decoration to take up space on its folios. This is evidenced by the fact that very few additional decorated fragments were found, apart from those allocated to the tripartite division of the psalms. It therefore seemed logical that the decoration of the FMP was restricted to these areas of the manuscript, an arrangement adopted in other early medieval Insular psalters.[21] Further confirmation was possible where no clearly identifiable decoration remained but was expected (Psalm 101), and the shifted position of the calculated characters after this point strongly suggests that decoration did exist.

When a smaller fragment of a folio was identified as a result of reading the text on one side of the vellum or, on occasion, both sides (in general the iron gall ink survived better on the flesh side of

21 The Southampton Psalter (Cambridge, St John's College MS C.9); the Basel Greco-Latin Psalter (Basel, Universitätsbibliothek MS A.vii.3).

the skin and thus was easier to decipher), the task of correctly positioning the piece in relation to the larger surviving folio fragment was achieved by using the character calculation. Very often the correct position resulted in a gap where no text was extant, and the identified small fragment was located 'floating' in the middle of the bifolio mount. Another factor that assisted in positioning a fragment was the hair/flesh orientation, which could be matched with the main folio fragment. Additionally, sometimes the run or angle of the hair follicles gave clues as to its position. Once a fragment had been positively located, the operation had to be repeated 'virtually'. This involved cutting and pasting the digital image of the fragment from the newly created digital library of the manuscript and repositioning it with its now-identified folio fragment. In this instance it had to be carried out twice, because there were separate images for the recto and for the verso. Because all images were taken at the same focal length with the same values, a seamless image matching the actual fragment was recorded (Fig. 1.14). In addition to assisting with the location of small fragments, the character count also assisted in the recognition of anomalies in the collation map of the manuscript, where the folio count fails to tally with the position of a psalm. This in turn prompts further investigation and the possibility of further virtual reconstruction at some point in the future.

HOUSING/DISPLAY

When the conservation process had reached the stage that allowed a definitive collation map to be produced, and the identification and location of the vast majority of the text fragments had been established, the focus turned to the long-term storage of the manuscript. Given the fragmentary nature of the folios and the loss of almost all fold endurance of the vellum, it was evident that the FMP could not be returned to any form of codex. Investigation into the housing of double-sided vellum or parchment material began, resulting in the examination of a range of methods employed by conservators to deal with historical documents on collagen-based substrates, typically single items or small collections of documents. None of the systems investigated proved viable, based as they were on reasonably sound material with an intact structure. The Dead Sea Scrolls had been mentioned during the media coverage of the FMP shortly after its discovery. This comparison prompted some research into their conservation treatment over the decades and their current status. It should be noted that even these fragmented ancient documents, dating from the third century BC to the first century AD, were in a more stable state than the FMP. One interesting aspect of the current conservation of the scrolls was the reversal of previous conservation treatments carried out in the 1950s;[22] this, and the fact that no physical repair or materials had been employed in the treatment of the FMP to date, prompted trials for a system that required no new material to be introduced to the substrate in the form of support or adhesive. A number of suspension systems were tried out, involving strips of polyester material suspended inside a rigid frame. The strips were slit to allow the folio fragment to be inserted between the cuts, leaving it suspended in position inside the rigid frame. The number of smaller now-identified fragments, combined with the highly reactive nature of the FMP vellum (vellum by its nature is very hygroscopic, reacting to small changes in humidity and temperature, and the vellum of the FMP seemed to be even more reactive than would be expected[23]), rendered this approach unworkable.

Further research included a retrospective look back as far as the nineteenth century and the traditional methods used to display and house fragile papyrus fragments and other badly degraded

22 See https://www.deadseascrolls.org.il/learn-about-the-scrolls/conservation?locale=en_US, accessed 13 January 2019.

23 Woods 2006, 204.

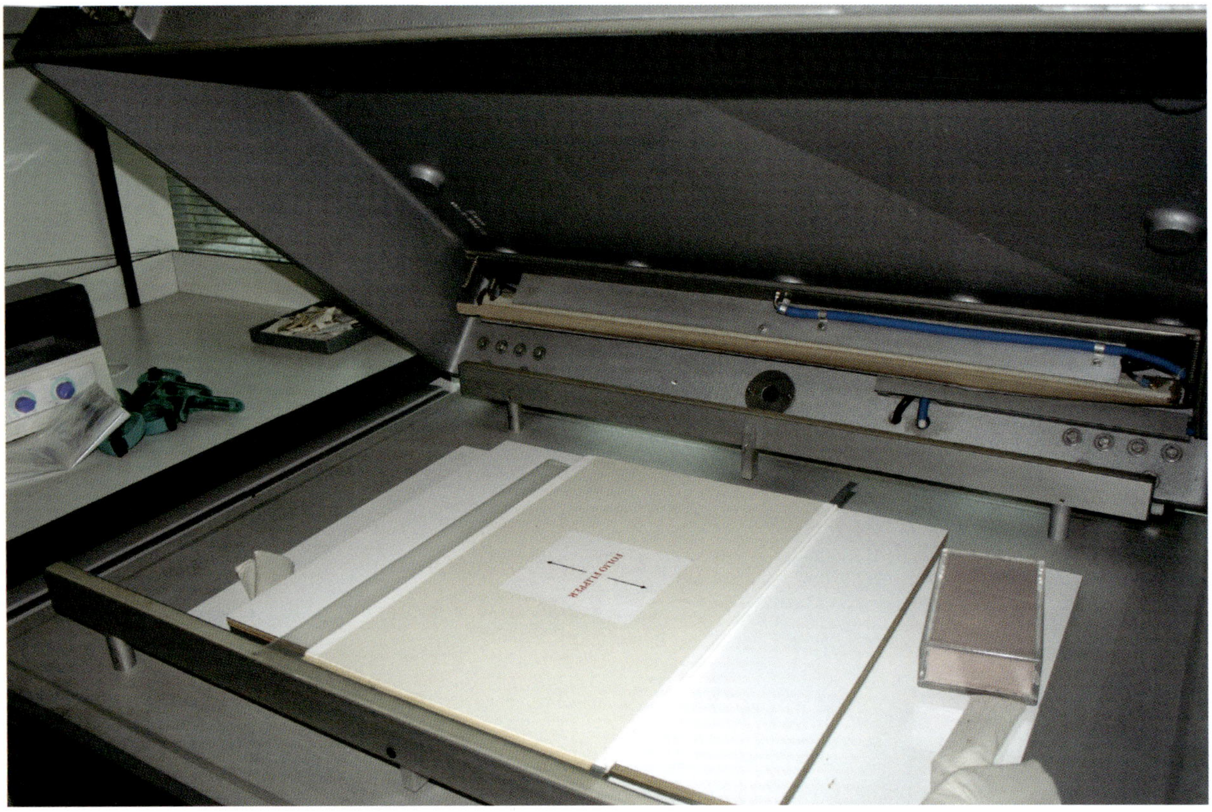

Fig. 1.15—Folio fragment in 'Folio Flipper', awaiting vacuum.

material. The use of thin sheets of glass on either side of the folio, fragment or textile, which were sealed around the edge with some form of tape, was and continues to be practised in museums, libraries and galleries around the world.[24] The system does have its drawbacks: the weight of even twenty items in a box can be substantial, while the danger of breaking the glass and the chances of failure of the edge seal allowing ingress of airborne dirt are weaknesses. Despite these issues, it came to my attention that, in the absence of any much-improved alternative, it remains a valid system because of its simplicity and lack of interference with the object. It was further observed that the fragments of the FMP were in their most secure and stable state when under vacuum as part of the de-watering process. To investigate further, some dry test vellum was placed under vacuum inside the Archipress® polyethylene bag but without the blotting-paper sandwich employed for drying. Tests were carried out, varying the vacuum time and employing the 'soft seal' system of the Audionvac 401H. This method proved very promising, meeting all our required criteria and with an outcome similar to that achieved with the long-employed glass sheets. Replacing the glass with polyethylene, however, had the distinct advantage of reducing the weight and improving the air-tightness, thus obviating the particular risks mentioned above. In addition, there is no risk of breakage if dropped.

Although polyethylene is considered reasonably inert, we wanted to ensure the optimum standard of material, given that it would be in long-term direct contact with the folio fragments of the FMP. The search quickly led to Escal® film, a material specifically designed for permanent storage of museum artefacts where an anaerobic environment is preferred and with a specific resistance to oxygen permeation. The inner layer of Escal® is polypropylene, while the outer barrier layer is a vacuum-deposited ceramic on a PVA substrate. Oxygen permeability is 0.05cc/m^2/24hrs; water vapour transmission is 0.01g/m^2/24hrs. Polyethylene is a standard material for sealing films.[25] Additional trials

24 Leach 2005, 194–5.

25 Jerry Shiner, 'Barrier films', Keepsafe Microclimate Systems, 2009 (http://keepsafe.ca/ESCAL.htm, accessed September 2012).

commenced with the Escal® film. The material is supplied on a roll or as pre-formed enclosures with a single opening; the former was chosen owing to the difficulty of positioning all the components to be sealed through the one open edge of an enclosure. The roll, on the other hand, gives complete control over the format of the housing and a much less tortuous assembly of the contents. It was decided for aesthetic purposes, and in order to convey the form of a bifolio, that the void—that is, the area where the vellum was lost—should be infilled. The material chosen was Ligfree® card, which, as well as being lignin-free and of a conservation standard, is also similar in thickness and colour to the FMP vellum. A profile of the missing area was cut out and placed adjacent to the folio fragment without actually making contact. Because of the difficulties in handling the fragile folio fragments and maintaining their position inside the fold of Escal® film prior to the vacuum process, a hinged folder of rigid boards was made. All components were placed inside this during assembly, which aided the handling during the positioning of fragments, a procedure that required viewing both verso and recto. The assembled material remained inside this 'Folio Flipper' during transport to the vacuum machine and while in the machine during the vacuum operation.

The housing of each folio fragment of the FMP proceeded as follows. A sheet of Escal® film was cut to a size of 760mm x 500mm and then folded in half along the long edge to give a finished folder measuring 380mm x 500mm. The film was placed open in the Folio Flipper and the folio fragments, along with the profiled card infill, were placed on the film with the aid of additional support material. The Folio Flipper was closed and turned over, and then opened for the removal of the support material, leaving the components to be vacuumed in position on the Escal® film. The film was folded over and a final alignment check made of the folio fragments before the Folio Flipper was closed over. One of the three unsealed edges of the Escal® film was left protruding from the Folio Flipper and this rested on the sealing bar inside the vacuum machine (Fig. 1.15). A board weight was placed on top of the assemblage and the cast-iron lid of the vacuum machine was closed. The first 'pass' had no vacuum time and served only to seal the open edge of the Escal® film. This was repeated on the second open short edge by rotating the Folio Flipper and contents and exposing the edge to the sealing bar. For the third and final open edge a 'soft' vacuum was also pulled for eight seconds before sealing. A sealing time of five seconds proved best for the film-to-film contact to create a strong bond. A narrow border was created through the sealing process and this was replicated along the top folded edge by inserting a strip of card as a distancing piece while positioning the fragments and infill. A small identification tab was attached to the lower edge of the mounted folio fragment once complete.

The finished product greatly alters the handling parameters of the manuscript. Without any direct intervention of additional adhering materials or added chemicals, the folio fragments are stable enough for both study and display. In addition, the methodology employed is easily reversed, should this be required (Fig. 1.16). Between singletons and bifolios, this process generated a total of 33 encapsulated folio fragments, representing approximately 12–15% of the manuscript. I took the opportunity at this stage to make a facsimile copy of the five quires of the text block, tracing all fragments onto double or single sheets of paper cut to the 'guesstimated' size of the original manuscript. The identified psalm number and verse are written on the traced fragment, along with the hair/flesh identification. This has proved a useful reference tool for what goes where and, because of the accurate tracing, even for comparing cut edges to check possible matching folios. It is kept inside an accurate replica of the leather cover.

Once complete, the collection of mounted folio fragments was sorted into their five quires and assembled in order. A series of tabbed four-flap folders were made, with tabs identifying the folio numbers. The final phase of the housing process involved the construction of a purpose-made 'document'-style box (Fig. 1.17). This substantial assembly, constructed from high-standard conservation materials, houses the more than 30 folders containing the folio fragments of the five

Fig. 1.16—Vacuum-housed bifolio fragment (ff 12v–1r) in its storage folder.

quires. The vertical storage of the folios ensures that there are none of the pressure or friction issues that would occur with a horizontal housing. In addition, the system allows the best use of the tabulated folders and easy location of specific sections of the psalter. This storage method will allow safe access and handling for future scholars and researchers.

One of the additional responsibilities of the Steering Committee was the display of the FMP as part of the revamped permanent Treasury Exhibition in the National Museum in Kildare Street. A dedicated and separated space was allocated to the psalter's display, accompanied by associated material and a video recounting the story of its discovery and conservation. It was decided that two folio fragments would be displayed in vertical two-sided display cases with internal fibre-optic lighting. The standard requirement for controlling the specific environment needed for the safe display of vellum or parchment was for the most part negated by the vacuum housing system, which enclosed each folio fragment in its own stable micro-climate. I submitted a proposal for a pair of two-sided window mounts made from powder-coated mild steel, on the inner face of which were placed registers for the mounted folio fragments made from a flexible magnetic material. This system allows rotation of the folio fragments on display at predetermined intervals (typically every twelve weeks). The folio fragment is positioned in one side of the window mount, with the extended borders registering with the guides. The two halves of the mount are brought together and held secure by the magnetic registers. The front-opening wall display case contains a platform for the window mounts, which are further secured by framing strips once in position. The system is designed to allow for easy rotation of the folio fragments. The lighting proved somewhat more challenging, given the slightly reflective nature of the Escal® film combined with often difficult-to-interpret content. The employment of a professional company[26] for this and the remainder of

26 Sutton Vane Associates, Dimes Place, 106–108 King Street, London, W6 0QP, United Kingdom.

Fig. 1.17a—Tabbed folders for each folio fragment.

Fig. 1.17b—Vertical storage box for folders.

Fig. 1.17c—Completed box.

Fig. 1.18—Dedicated display space for the psalter.

the Treasury Exhibition was essential to the successful outcome achieved. Lighting levels are controlled, with lux values in the space maintained around 50 and ultraviolet screening on all glass (Fig. 1.18).

THE LEATHER COVER

The simple leather binding of the FMP lay beneath the mass of material composed of the vellum folio fragments, bog matter and evidential fragments of other deposited organic material. The 'as found' structure dictated the order of the subsequent conservation procedures, as work commenced from the top down. The consequence of this approach resulted in the cover being the final major component of the manuscript to be conserved. When it was finally released, initial observations confirmed much of what information I had been able to gather while it was *in situ*; it was a single piece of tanned leather folded to form a front and back cover, a spine and a fore-edge flap. Three buttons had been attached to the flap using leather thongs (Fig. 1.19) (for a detailed description of the FMP cover see Chapter 4).

Although both the leather of the cover and the surviving vellum folio fragments originated from the same source (the hide of a calf), once flayed and dehaired they were treated very differently. Man's awareness of the need to stabilise the rawhide of an animal in order to make best use of its many attributes dates back to the Stone Age, at least 20,000 years ago. This is based on the discovery of fine leather-working tools, such as needles and awls, whose delicate nature suggests a well-refined and supple end-product.[27] The flayed hide consists of three distinct layers. The *epidermis*, which contains dead and

27 Waterer 1950, 3.

Fig. 1.19—The tanned leather cover in its wet state after cleaning.

Fig. 1.20—The cover submerged in a 15%vv glycerol bath.

Fig. 1.21 – The leather cover, dry and stable; note the black dye surviving on the surface.

dying cells, is the area of the skin exposed; this layer also contains hair or wool follicles and sweat glands. The *dermis* or *corium* lies beneath the epidermis and consists of the fibre network of collagen that gives leather its unique characteristics. It also often contains some follicle, which is essential in visual species identification once converted to leather or parchment. The final layer is the *hypodermis* or flesh layer, which is a membrane of mostly fat cells connecting the hide to the animal; neither this nor the epidermis is required by the leather or parchment maker and both are removed in manufacture. Vellum remains in effect a rawhide product, an attribute of which is its tendency to dissolve in water, hence the miraculous partial survival of the folios in the FMP. Vegetable-tanned leather, on the other hand, remains more or less unaffected, even after prolonged immersion in saturated conditions, as witnessed by numerous leather artefacts retrieved from wetland environments, including the cover of the FMP.

Taking the same conservation approach as in the treatment of the vellum folios, the cover was maintained fully saturated during all stages prior to de-watering and while the folio fragments were undergoing treatment. This was achieved in the same manner as with the vellum, by spraying with deionised water and maintaining a low storage temperature of 4°C. It was initially hoped that a similar approach to the drying process used for the vellum could also be applied to the vegetable-tanned leather of the cover. A database was set up and trials were carried out to establish whether a solvent exchange system similar to that employed for the vellum folio fragments would yield the same successful outcome. The leather drying trials were greatly assisted by having access to suitable material, very similar in type and close in date to the leather of the cover. The source was a limited number of small vegetable-tanned leather offcuts from the 1980s excavations at Wood Quay in Dublin.[28] These were discarded fragments from leather found in a spoil heap, the result of craft-making activities in the Viking settlement during the manufacture of shoes, bags, belts and other day-to-day items of the settlers. The collection amounted to several thousand fragments of leather, all of which had been maintained in a saturated state and at low temperature to reduce the risk of microbiological activity.

The trials involved the use of the same solvents and solvent exchange methods that were employed for the vellum de-watering tests. Similar parameters were also recorded before and after each treatment: thickness, colour and flexibility. Unlike vellum, during the production of leather the spaces between the fibre bundles remain, being filled with the jelly-like 'ground substance';[29] in addition, and again unlike vellum, the angle of weave is little changed. It is these features that give leather its soft feel and flexible nature. It became apparent at an early stage of these tests that, regardless of the solvent or drying method employed, the end result rendered a material that lost a high percentage of its natural flexibility. It is possible that this characteristic might be restored through physical 'working' of the leather during the final stages of evaporation, but clearly this would not be an option for the ancient leather of the FMP cover. While the lack of fold endurance and flexibility was not an issue for the vellum fragments, it was a cause of concern for the leather cover.

Discussions with the Steering Committee commenced as to the shape or form (i.e. open or closed) in which the cover should be placed before de-watering, given that it would be 'set' in whichever was chosen. The committee found this stark choice unsatisfactory, so the trials were extended. The additional tests involved drying straight from the unbound water, drying through PEG 400 (polyethylene glycol) and drying through 15%vv glycerol, the latter two being more traditional archaeological approaches. Sublimation is required for both the PEG and glycerol, and so the second part of the treatment requires vacuum freeze-drying. The test results from the glycerol were, unsurprisingly, very promising. The method involves the water-bound tanned leather being immersed in the glycerol solution until saturated; this is

28 Cameron 2007.

29 Thomson 2006a, 1.

judged by experience and, depending on the dimensions of the material, may occur over a 24-hour period. Once the solution has been fully taken up, the leather is placed in the vacuum freeze-drying unit, which, as previously described, removes excess moisture through sublimation.[30] The test leather emerged from the unit after three days, retaining its colour and thickness and with the flexibility properties associated with good-quality vegetable-tanned leather. There was concern about the effects of this treatment on the remnants of surface colour discovered on the cover at an earlier stage. A minute sample of the black pigment was sent for analysis[31] and proved to be of a charcoal type (see Chapter 4). In order to establish whether this might be an issue, a piece of the saturated Viking leather offcut that also displayed the remains of a surface colour was chosen. This was put through the glycerol method and the pigment displayed no change or loss once dry. This test fragment and the previous glycerol-treated leather were monitored over the following number of weeks to see whether any changes occurred, such as alteration of the surface texture or excess solution moving from the dermal layer outwards to the surface. Thankfully, the samples remained stable. The results were reported to the Steering Committee and agreement was reached that the cover of the FMP should be de-watered through the glycerol/vacuum freeze-drying method.

The saturated leather cover was laid flat on a support sheet of Bondina® and, working under a three-dioptre illuminated magnifier, debris was removed from the outer surface, employing the same methods as those used to clean the folio fragments. It was at this stage that several trial motifs inscribed into the leather were noticed (see Chapter 5). The inner surface was also cleaned and finally, while still in a saturated state, the cover was recorded photographically in detail by the Museum's Photographic Department. The 15%vv glycerol solution was prepared in a large developing tray. The leather cover, supported on the underside by a sheet of Bondina®, was lowered in until submerged. The top of the tray was covered and it was monitored over an eighteen-hour period, until the leather was deemed to have reached full saturation of the solution (Fig. 1.20). Once removed, a Polyzote® form wrapped in Bondina®, which had been constructed to represent the size and shape of the text block, was inserted inside the cover. The covers were closed over and the leather flap rested on the top surface of the front/left-hand cover. The 15%vv glycerol-saturated binding was wrapped in insulation layers and brought to the vacuum freeze-drying unit of the National Museum in Lanesborough, Co. Longford. The cover was placed inside the capacious chamber and, once filled, mostly with large ships' timbers, the unit was sealed and the freezing process started. The cover remained in the unit for almost three weeks. On removal, the leather of the cover displayed handling conditions that would allow some degree of flexibility. Although somewhat desiccated, the cover can, with expert handling, be opened out and returned to its closed state without injury. The leather now has the typical hue of a vegetable-tanned skin and the pigment remnants remain intact. The attached horn buttons were unaffected by the process. The incised trial motifs remained visible, perhaps even more clearly visible. A new former, this time more aesthetically pleasing, was constructed to support the closed covers, and this remains in position while the cover is on display in its climate-controlled case in the Museum's Treasury Exhibit (Fig. 1.21).

CONCLUSION

During the process of conservation, every component part of the FMP was quite literally under the microscope. While the overarching aim of the project during the conservation period was to stabilise the manuscript, many features were noted that potentially, with further study, will better inform us

30 See xviii above.

31 Singer 2008.

about the making of the manuscript and its associated cover. There was little doubt and complete consensus among all those who engaged with the manuscript, in whatever capacity, that the FMP had many unique features, and this conclusion was reached before any investigation or conservation had started. This had the immediate effect of influencing the conservation approach, with emphasis placed on recording the manuscript in its pre-treatment state, given that any conservation process, regardless of how carefully planned and executed, is a disruptive process that results in loss of evidence. A typical example would be the displacement of fragments from their as-found position within the body of the object; this matters because the as-found position can inform us about how the object was deposited and what condition it was in at the time of deposition. A more specific example relating directly to the FMP was the minute areas of backfolds that survived within the folio fragments and were identifiable, as the curve of the vellum could be observed to locate the exact fold point. Once the de-watering process had taken place, however, this fold in the vellum was lost and was no longer detectable. Conservation proceeded with these factors very much in mind, and there was a concerted effort to observe and record all evidential detail. Many of the observations made relate to physical features of the manuscript and will be discussed in later chapters.

Reflecting on the interventive aspect of the conservation, it can be said that the learning curve was a steep one. Even though all involved from the National Museum were fully supportive of the need for a well-researched approach to the conservation of the FMP, other factors did impose limitations on the process. Time was one such factor. For a conservator on secondment, there was a 'ticking clock' that influenced what was achievable within the time-frame. Interestingly, even though extensions were requested and granted, it was financial restrictions that finally brought matters to a close. Budgetary constraints also influenced what was available to purchase in terms of very specialist equipment which might well be redundant after its use in the project. When you find yourself totally absorbed in a project, you incline to the opinion that there should be no limits when it comes to doing all that is possible to preserve and conserve such an object; the reality, however, is somewhat different and ultimately compromise is required to see the project through.

It was clear from the moment the first folio fragment was removed from the de-watering pack that the legibility of the text would present difficulties for scholarly study or research. The reading of certain psalms is more akin to trying to decipher a faint palimpsest. Although the conservation process was not capable of correcting this feature, by using the latest digital technologies we were able to have the complete manuscript captured by Hyper Spectral Scanning.[32] These very large files, stored on a dedicated server, are available for the application of other imaging processes or further manipulation on the spectral range, with the goal of improving clarity of writing and possible analysis of inks.

I suggest that two important goals were successfully achieved. First, the conserved material is now accessible for research and display purposes; this is the result of the purpose-devised housing system that allows the delicate and fragmented material to be handled safely. Second, the project meets a prime conservation goal of reversibility. In the case of the FMP this is particularly straightforward, since the lack of repairs or supports added to the material means that removal from its housing is simply a matter of cutting open the Escal® enclosure. In order to glean meaningful information from the folios of the FMP it was essential to unravel and stabilise the saturated mass of vellum. The conservation process delivered this successfully. The following chapter examines the manuscript folio by folio, extracting further clues that would not have been possible without the major conservation intervention.

32 An Foras Feasa: Maynooth University, Institute for the Humanities.

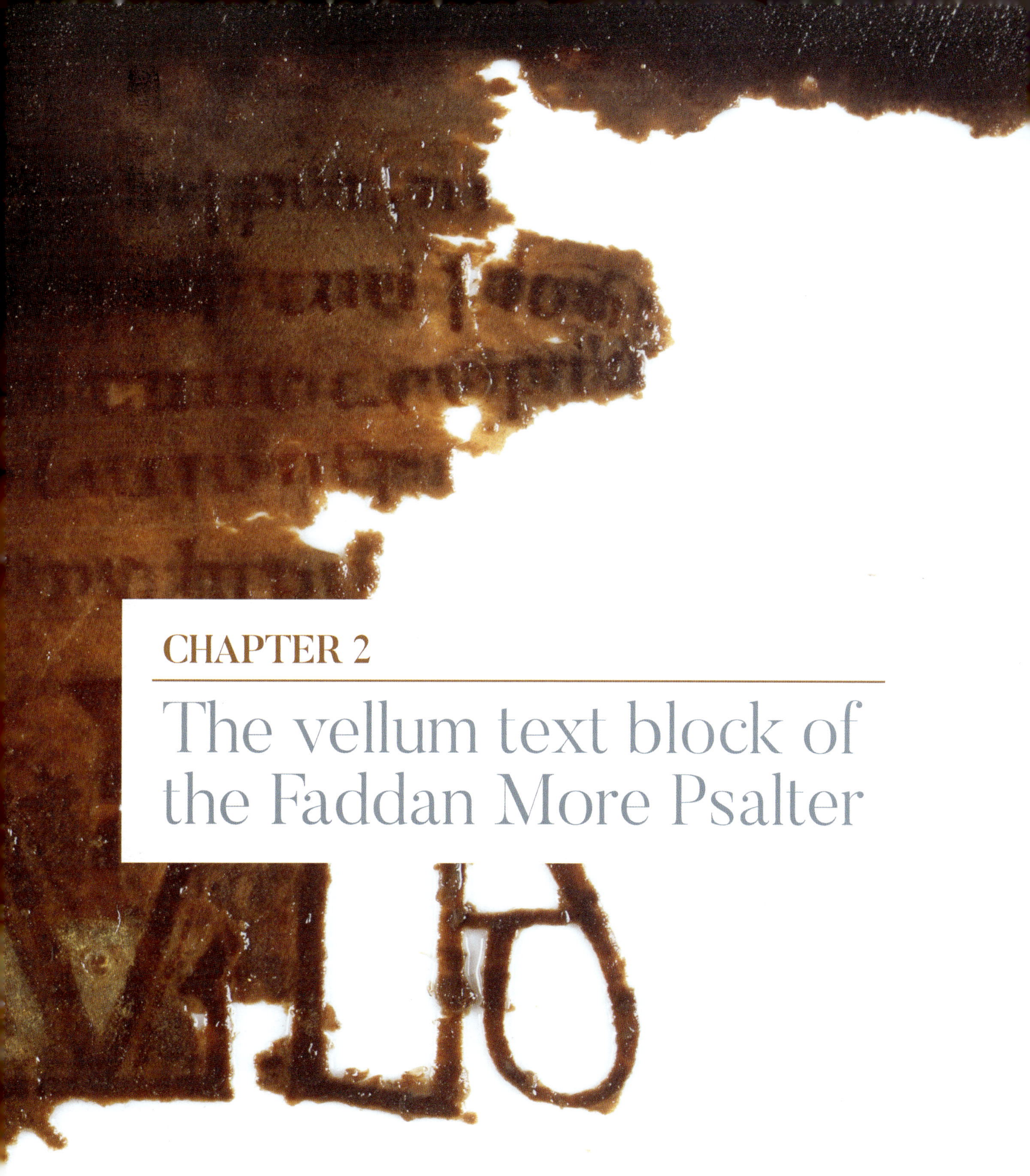

CHAPTER 2

The vellum text block of the Faddan More Psalter

CHAPTER 2

The vellum text block of the Faddan More Psalter

A range of different components are brought together to make up a medieval manuscript book, typically including leather, timber, thread, ink, pigments and the material that constitutes the bulk of the end-product, parchment. All but the timber were found as components of the FMP during its conservation. Close examination of the parchment can inform us about aspects of its life, from original construction and place of production to changes made and events experienced over time; this physical evidence can corroborate or contradict palaeographical arguments. In addition, features of the construction of the text block, which is produced before the binding, can help to narrow the window of manufacture. In this chapter the parchment and text block of the FMP are scrutinised with the intent of extracting such information, despite the dearth of surviving material and the effects of the extreme conditions in which the manuscript survived. The conservation process, as expected, did not provide all the answers in relation to the text block, and separate examination of the now-stable material was necessary. It did, however, confirm that the manuscript was an early medieval book—that is to say, in this context, belonging to the corpus of extant manuscripts such as the Book of Kells, the Book of Durrow, the Book of Dimma and the Book of Armagh, among others. Approaching any additional study through what is already known about other early book-making practices could therefore shed light on the genesis of the FMP.

In what follows, the development of parchment as the essential material of the medieval manuscript is examined, from its origin to its arrival and use in Ireland. The term 'Insular parchment' is a commonly used idiom in the study of the manuscripts of western Europe and this description is scrutinised and compared with the vellum of the FMP. The conversion of the prepared skins into a text block ready for the ink of the scribe follows a range of conventions and, once the text has been written, the gathering and sewing also follow known practice. These features are observed and compared on the vellum folio fragments of the FMP.

The conversion of the raw pelt, flayed from the animal, into a robust and long-lasting material has been familiar to man since prehistoric times. Animal skin is a multi-layered tissue, the most substantial element of which is the *corium*, a network of long fibres of collagen protein molecules interweaving together to form a cohesive and flexible structure. Between these fibres is a matrix of ground substance, which acts as a lubricant with high water-binding capacity. It is predominantly this section of the skin that is converted into leather, parchment and other ancient material such as rawhide. Additional processes of tawing and chamoising also produced leather-like products. It is thought that the Irish word for the traditional hide-covered boat, *curach*, originated from the Latin *corium*, used by Julius Caesar to describe the small seagoing vessels he encountered during his expeditions in 55 and 54 BC.[1]

Simplified descriptions of the difference between leather and parchment usually state that leather undergoes a tanning process while parchment does not. This is not an accurate representation, and many medieval parchment-makers and scribes used various tanning solutions, either during manufacture, while still on the 'herse' or frame, or afterwards in the scriptorium, in order to enhance its handling properties and the writing surface. Other substances, including fats, oils and salts, were also known to have been added to the prepared skins. This indicates a sound understanding of the material, as a significant effect of these post-process applications was to restrict the entry of water vapour and bind the fats already present, both of which improve the product. I believe that the Irish parchment-makers readily embraced these additional processes. The true constant that identifies leather from parchment is that the production of the latter requires it to be dried under tension, drawing the fibre bundles into a low angle of weave. A secondary distinction is the ability of tanned leather to resist prolonged immersion in water, often with little change to its working and handling characteristics. Parchment, however, will at best gelatinise or completely dissolve under the same conditions, as it succumbs to putrefaction. The discovery of the FMP perfectly demonstrated these differing properties, with the leather cover surviving almost unscathed over a millennium whereas only 15% of the 60 vellum folios endured through to excavation.

The story of the invention of true parchment as a writing substrate can be traced back to the second century BC at Pergamum in Asia Minor, now in modern-day Turkey, and the friction between two kings, Ptolemy V Epiphanes of Egypt and Eumenes II of Pergamum. The source of the account is found in Pliny's *Natural History* 13:21 (first century AD). Ptolemy had halted all export of papyrus to Pergamum owing to his jealousy of Eumenes's library, which rivalled his own library at Alexandria, thus forcing Eumenes to invent a new material. Because hides were imported from the Black Sea area into the city and the use of tanned leather as a substrate for writing was already known, the unprocessed hides would have suggested themselves as a suitable material for experiment. The finished product was *pergamena*, parchment, named after its place of origin, although the term was not typically in use before the fourth century AD.[2] The material proved more suitable and longer-lasting than the papyrus it replaced. The validity of this tale is uncertain, as forms of parchment are known to have already existed by this period,[3] but it is possible that techniques or recipes were improved in Pergamum, resulting in a material closer to the folios that would shortly be employed in the first Christian codices. It should be noted that at this period 'books' were for the most part in scroll form.

If it was no surprise that an early medieval book retrieved from a bog in central Ireland should be a psalter, then equally no eyebrows were raised when it was found to have been written on calfskin vellum. The use of the term 'vellum' as an alternative for 'parchment' is based on the popular description of vellum as being manufactured from the skins of young calves, the root coming from the Old French word *velin* for calfskin. This is by no means conclusive, however, the words 'vellum' and

---

1 Reed 1975, 15.

2 Ryder 1960, 392.

3 Reed (1975) is of the opinion that parchment, or parchment-like material, was available in the ancient world, possibly as far back as 2500 BC, although not necessarily for the use of scribes. Reed (1972, 118) also references a discovery in Hebron, Jordan, in 1969 of documents, dated to around the eighth century BC on palaeographical grounds, which were produced from camel skin and are of a type of parchment.

'parchment' being used interchangeably, both historically and currently. A useful exercise is to look at some dictionary definitions of vellum, where it is defined as 'a fine-grained unsplit lambskin, kidskin, or calfskin' (Merriam–Webster) or as 'made from the skins of young animals, especially cows or sheep' (Cambridge). The use of young cattle to produce a writing substrate by Irish scribes in the early medieval period is so consistent that it can be considered a codicological aid to identifying the makers of Insular manuscripts from the early centuries of Irish Christianity.

Those early scribes were for the most part monks, a result of the monastic church's dominance in Ireland by the sixth century.[4] The production of books copied from exemplars was required for both the liturgy (including gospels, psalters and martyrologies) and books for teaching. Once firmly established on home soil, the Irish monks carried their mission as *peregrini* beyond this island and brought their books, written in a distinctive Irish hand on vellum folios, with them. Surviving material fitting this pattern attests to the practice; Codex Ambrosianus C.301 inf., a manuscript from the monastery at Bobbio, the Irish foundation of St Columbanus (d. 615) established with the help of the Lombard King Agiluf in the Apennines of modern-day northern Italy, is a good example. Like many manuscripts that originated in Bobbio, it was transferred to the Ambrosiana Library in Milan in the seventeenth century as the Bobbio library was dispersed. The main content of MS C.301 inf. is a Latin commentary on the psalms with extensive Irish glosses.[5] According to E.A. Lowe (1966, III, 326), it is written in an 'Irish minuscule hand, saec. VIII–IX'. It is now generally accepted that the commentary was produced in Ireland at some point in the early ninth century.[6] Atypically for Mediterranean book production, which favoured sheep or goatskin parchment, the manuscript is written on calfskin vellum.[7]

Another manuscript firmly associated with an Irish foundation in Europe is the St Gall Gospels (Cod. Sang. 51), located in the monastery of the same name in north-eastern Switzerland. This illuminated manuscript is thought to be an import from Ireland and, according to O'Sullivan, a product of one of the cluster of monasteries located in the centre of the country. This is based stylistically on the majuscule hand, 'which substitutes compressed rectangularity for roundness'.[8] It was produced around the middle of the eighth century, again on calfskin vellum. Of additional interest is the attention that has been drawn by more than one scholar to the palaeographical similarities between the St Gall Gospels and the FMP, which was discovered in the same geographic area as O'Sullivan's Midlands group.[9] The use of vellum folios can be traced back to the earliest extant codex produced in Ireland or by Irish scribes abroad and the fragmented pre-Vulgate Gospel of Usserianus Primus (TCD MS 55). The 182 fine and expertly produced folios are all on calfskin vellum, as suggested by Tony Cains and previous examiners of the manuscript[10] and positively identified by my detailed examination of the work in 2017. Such was the degree of preparation of the skins that determining features were difficult to locate and led to erroneous identification as sheepskin, an opinion likely influenced by its reported

4 Hughes 2008, 311; McGrath 1979, 72.

5 Richter 2008.

6 Richter points to an Irish origin in the early ninth century and includes the use of vellum as opposed to parchment as an indicator. Lowe suggests Bangor as a location. Martin McNamara identifies the single scribe of the manuscript as Diarmait (d. 825), grandson of Áed Rón, from Castledermot, Co. Kildare. Pádraig Ó Riain (2011, 262) identifies the same Diarmit (Diarmuid) in *A dictionary of Irish saints* but suggests that there is little evidence that it is the same Diarmait in the colophon of the manuscript.

7 Reed 1975, 75.

8 O'Sullivan 2005, 533.

9 Farr 2017, 184; Timothy O'Neill, pers. comm., January 2018.

10 Cains 1992, 53.

connections with Bobbio.[11] The manuscript, dating from around AD 600 and possibly earlier,[12] can be cited as the starting-point for the use of calfskin as the substrate of choice for Irish writing and lends weight to the argument for Irish manufacture (Fig. 2.1). This enthusiasm for the use of vellum is also attested in the corpus of Irish manuscripts and those produced under Irish influence in England during the pre-Carolingian period. In summary, it is one of the few constants relating to book-making when many other conventions of the craft tended for the most part to be ignored by the Irish scribe.

Long before the first extant codex was copied and bound in Ireland, the mainstay of domestic stock farming was predominantly the rearing of cattle. Although archaeological evidence for Iron Age animal husbandry is scant, cattle are presumed to have been the dominant species.[13] In the early Middle Ages the status quo was maintained and their importance both as a source of product and income and as an indicator of status continued. The archaeological evidence from the period affirms that cattle accounted for 40–50% of the main domesticates on most sites.[14] Collating the Irish place-names associated with cattle—such as Inisbofin (*Inis Bó Finne*, 'island of the white cow'), Aghaboe (*Agha Bó*, 'ox field') and Doonamo (*Dún na mBó*, 'cattle fort')—demonstrates their prominence across the country. Further evidence for the importance of cattle within the societal structure of pre-Christian Ireland can be found on the vellum folios of a manuscript produced at Clonmacnoise in the last quarter of the eleventh century, *Lebor na hUidre* (the Book of the Dun Cow) (RIA MS 23.E.25). The much-damaged and reworked manuscript contains among its historical sagas, tracts and legends of Irish kings an incomplete version of the *Táin Bó Cuailgne* ('The cattle-raid of Cooley'), the epic tale of Queen Medbh of Connacht and her husband, King Ailill, who each desired to own the best bull in Ireland. This rivalry impelled Medbh into war with Ulster, ultimately leading to the celebrated hand-to-hand combat between her champion, Ferdia, and Ulster's Cúchulainn. The very name of the manuscript refers to cattle and to a narrative concerning the founder of the monastery at Clonmacnoise, St Ciaran (AD 516–48). Legend has it that a cow followed Ciaran and his companions on a journey from Clonard, Co. Meath, to Clonmacnoise and provided them with the necessary sustenance. Ciaran later used the skin of this cow, named *Odhar Chiaráin*, to write down the tale of *Táin Bó Cuailgne*.

A further reference to the importance of cattle is found in the Martyrology of Oengus the Culdee, an early ninth-century text surviving in at least ten manuscripts dating from the fifteenth century. Among the contents are the four laws of Erin: Patrick's Law, forbidding the killing of clerics; Adamnán's Law, forbidding the killing of women; Dáire's Law, forbidding the killing of kine; and the Law of Sunday, forbidding any transgression on that day.[15] In addition to the provision of an abundance of calves as a source of writing material, the prominence of cattle in the social structure of Ireland and their presence in Irish legend would make them an obvious choice as the 'carrier' of sacred writings for the Christian religion. The dominance of cattle-rearing in Ireland continued up to the beginning of the ninth century; thereafter an increase in arable agriculture, combined with greater diversity in livestock, saw a shift in balance, although some parts of the country, including Brega, the Southern Uí Néill stronghold on the east coast, were slower to change.[16] Archaeological evidence confirms this shift in agricultural practice with the emergence of platform ringforts, not suitable for the rearing of cattle; early medieval ringforts were for the most part farmsteads, and this would have included their function as cattle enclosures.

---

11 O'Sullivan 1985, 353.

12 Bischoff 1990, 83.

13 Raftery 2005, 153.

14 McCormick 2014.

15 Stokes 1905, 211.

16 Stout 2017, 134.

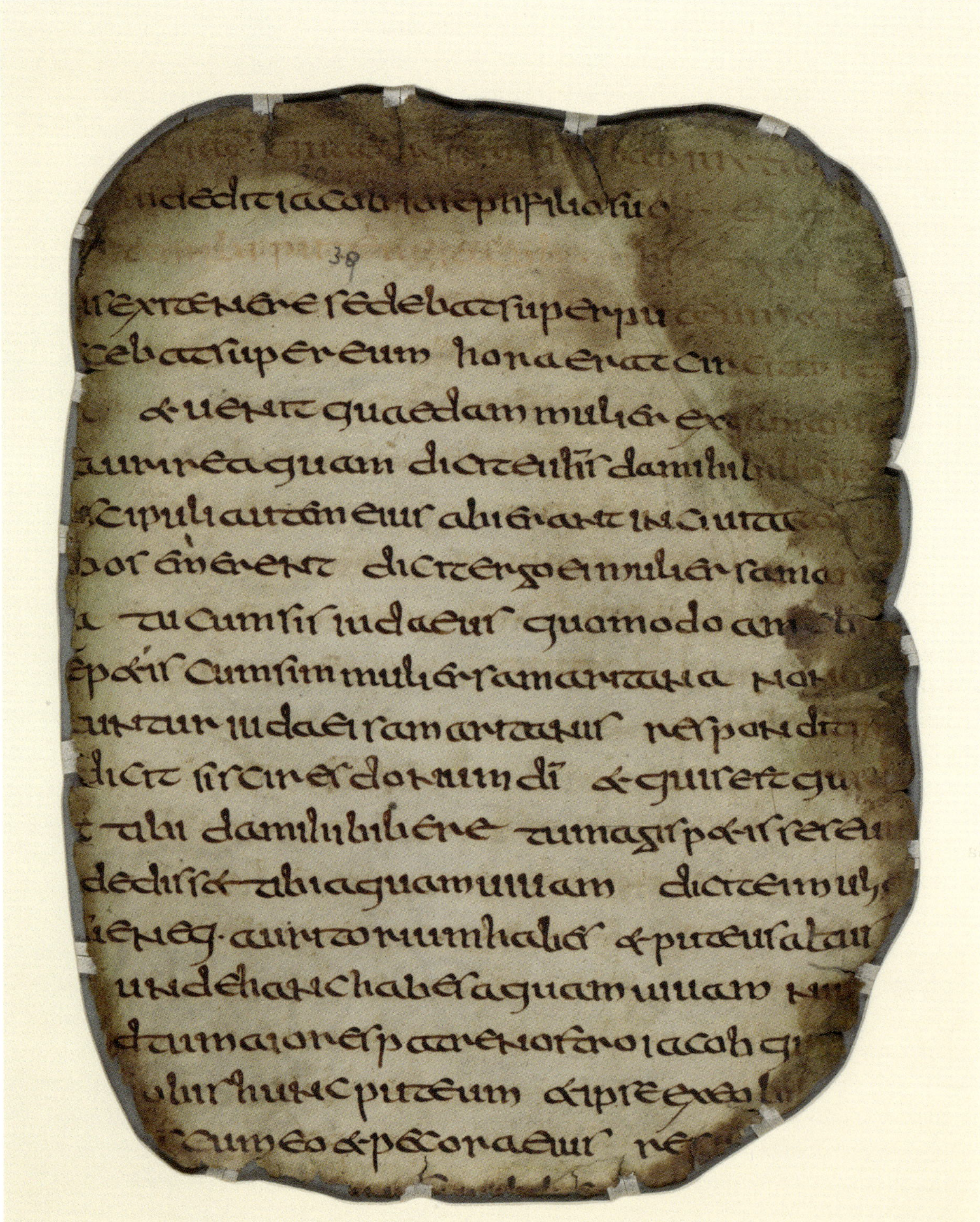

Fig. 2.1—TCD MS 55, Usserianus Primus, p. 30. © Trinity College Dublin

The argument is reinforced by the increase in mill construction at the beginning of the ninth century.[17] Regardless of any move away from cattle-farming, Irish manuscripts produced in scriptoria and later as secular commissions continued to use vellum as the substrate for their books. Examples such as the Stowe Missal (RIA MS D.ii.3), a composite manuscript dated to *c.* 800, the twelfth-century Book of Leinster (TCD MS 1339), and the Yellow Book of Lecan (TCD MS 1318) and the Red Book of Ossory (RCB Library D11/2/1), both dating from the fourteenth century, attest to this practice, continuing the tradition exercised by the maker of the FMP.

Vellum was not the only substrate employed for writing in early medieval Ireland. In common with the rest of the literate world, wooden tablets were also used for note-taking. Ink was sometimes written directly on the surface, but more typically a wax-filled recess on the surface of the timber provided a more user-friendly surface, which was inscribed with a pointed stylus. In Ireland these tablets had various names, including *taibhli filidh* (*taibhli* being derived from the Latin *tabula*) and *tamlorga filidh*.[18] Commonly described as *pólaire*, their use by ecclesiastics is documented, and Adomnán mentions Colgu recording the date and time on his tablet.[19] The Springmount Wax Tablets (from the late sixth century) mentioned in the Introduction are a rare and fortunate survival and provide material proof of their use in monastic centres.

Evidence is lacking that would allow any definitive dates to be assigned to the arrival of the first Latin texts in Ireland. No Christian codices survive from the time of the introduction of the religion, perhaps as early as the fourth century, to its formally established state by the sixth century, with the missions of Palladius and Patrick in between, a period which Dáibhí Ó Cróinín calls 'a no man's-land of two hundred years, as uncharted terrain in the areas of literacy and literature'.[20] This uncertainty as to when Christians in Ireland began to write by necessity also leaves unanswered the questions of when and by whom the first vellum skins were produced in Ireland. Given that the primary function of parchment was as a substrate for writing and that it was for that reason that it was produced, its genesis in Ireland coincides with the production of texts. It is possible that, by a process of trial and error, a variety of parchment could have been produced by adopting and modifying the skills already practised in the tanning of hides for leather, and this is perhaps the reason for the sometimes 'leather-like' qualities of 'Insular parchment'. Alternatively, perhaps the very first missionaries who arrived from Gaul and Britain prior to the arrival of Patrick and Palladius,[21] bringing with them the necessary books for conversion, were accompanied by monks who had the know-how to make parchment. Moreover, Irishmen who went to study in Britain at early monastic schools such as Candida Casa in Galloway in Scotland and Mynyw in Wales[22] would have returned with knowledge of Latin, theology and the sacred texts and perhaps with the skills to produce the parchment for making copies of the books that they brought back with them.

The earliest word for parchment in Irish is *mem(m)rum(m)*; this has an obvious root borrowing from the Latin *membrum*, used for *membrana*.[23] The use of the Irish word *memmrum* can be found in a copy of Cassiodorus's commentary on the psalms (Laon, Bibliothèque municipale MS 26), a manuscript

17 Ó Súillebháin *et al.* 2018, 129.

18 Joyce 1997, 482.

19 Sharpe 1995, 138.

20 The Tripartite Life of Patrick relates how, on entering the territory of Uí Maine, he founded Fidarta (in modern County Roscommon) and left there a deacon, Deacon Justus, and his book of ritual and baptism; Stokes 1887, 105; Ó Cróinín 1995, 171.

21 Ryan 1972, 380; Walsh and Bradley 2003, 9; T. Charles-Edwards 2000, 185.

22 De Paor and de Paor 1964, 49.

23 See http://dil.ie/31924, *Electronic Dictionary of the Irish Language* (accessed January 2018).

written by an Irish scribe in the early ninth century, either in Ireland or on the Continent.[24] In addition to the transcribed commentary there are a series of Old Irish glosses in the margins, some of which include observations by the scribe on the quality of his writing material:

8r:	*is lomm in membrum nacailne hísiu*	the parchment of this location is bare
21r:	*Isfinnach in membrumm hisiu im tra*	But this parchment is hairy once
23r:	*isém dúnn im in membrum hisiu*	But this parchment is thin for me

A second example is found in the margins of another ninth-century manuscript, now in St Gall (Cod. Sang. 904), a copy of *Institutiones Grammaticae* by the grammarian Priscian (sixth century). It includes over 9,000 glosses, including over 3,000 in Irish. It is believed to be a product of either Nendrum or Bangor in Northern Ireland,[25] although Castledermot in Kildare has also been proposed.[26] Further use of *memmrum* is observed among the Irish glosses, with disgruntled scribes bemoaning the standard of their writing material:

p. 195: *isgann in memr[umm] et ascribend'*	the parchment is rough and the writing
p. 217: *memmbrum naue droch dub ó ní epur na hail'*	New parchment, bad ink. O, I say nothing more (Fig. 2.2)
p. 228: *isgann membrumm*	The parchment is scanty

All the above examples significantly post-date the production of the first books in Ireland and demonstrate the commitment of scribes and scholars engaging with vellum as part of the Latin Christian culture, as well as, by this stage, their awareness of the variable quality of the material. The presence of these scribblings and their nature suggest a scribe working in isolation, restricted by the silence in the scriptorium or perhaps in his cell or outside, with nobody on whom to vent his frustrations concerning the quality of his vellum. In the Rule of Ailbe, written in the mid-eighth century but named after the saint who died over 200 years earlier, rule 2 states: 'Let his work be silently done, without speech. Let him not be garrulous, but rather a man of few words.'[27] The text of this Rule is found in a number of manuscripts, including RIA 23.N.10 and TCD MS 1285.

The fact that a loanword from a Latin root is used suggests that no word was available in the vernacular and, moreover, that both the material and the word were introduced from a Latin source, in the form of Christian pilgrims. If a word of Irish origin did exist, there would be no obvious reason for it to be supplanted by its Latin derivative. Caution is necessary with this hypothesis, however. Consider the example of the Irish word *pell*, meaning 'an animal's skin or fur', hence a rug or blanket, generally one for sleeping on.[28] The definition here dates from the ninth century and is located in Cormac's Glossary.[29] Like *memmrum*, it also has a Latin root, in *pellis*. It is hardly credible that the Irish had no alternative word prior to the adoption of *pell*, given the wide and varied use of rawhide products by the pre-Christian population.

Accepting that the monasteries of Ireland were the centres of book production, it follows that all aspects of that process and the necessary know-how were contained and valued within the monastic

24 McNamara 1973, 230.

25 See http://www.e-codices.unifr.ch/en/searchresult/list/one/csg/0904.

26 Byrne 2005b, 663.

27 Ó Maidín 1996, 17–27.

28 See http://dil.ie/34261, *Electronic Dictionary of the Irish Language* (accessed January 2018). I am indebted to Dr Aoibheann Nic Dhonnchadha, who carefully guided me to the correct sources in this area.

29 Meyer 1912b.

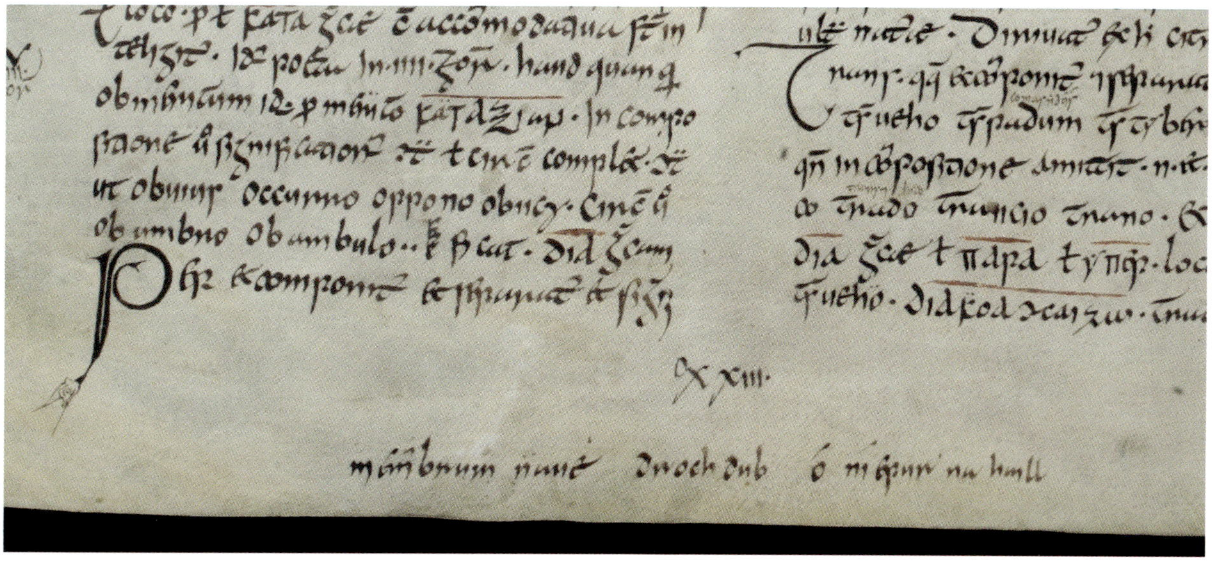

Fig. 2.2—St Gallen, Stiftsbibliothek MS 904, *Institutiones Grammaticae*, p. 217.

enclosures, at least during the early medieval period. This would have included the production of skins of vellum, a detailed and highly skilled task. Recent archaeology has provided compelling evidence for the production of vellum within a monastic community. On the Tarbat peninsula, on the north-east coast of Scotland, lies the coastal town of Portmahomack, and at the southern end of the village, standing above the beach, is St Colman's Church. Excavations by Martin Carver and his team between 1996 and 2007 in the church building and the surrounding land unearthed layers of earlier Christian activity, including evidence of nine previous churches, the earliest dating from the eighth century.[30] Several workshops were also discovered in the immediate location and were identified as associated with a monastic community. In the northern quarter, the excavation of building S9 revealed convincing evidence for the production of vellum during the eighth century. In addition to large quantities of cattle bones, the necessary tools identified included pumice rubbers, whetstones and, critically, a crescent-bladed knife (*lunellum*), the typical shape of the blade used for scraping the tensioned vellum on the frame. Pits containing winkles and dog whelks were also found. It is thought that these were reduced by burning to produce lime for making vellum, as no local limestone was available. Carver believes that the Pictish monastery was established in the sixth century and was destroyed in the late eighth as a result of Viking raids.[31] The likelihood of an Irish connection with the monastery and its foundation is based on the rationale that the St Colman after whom the standing church was named is Colman of Lindisfarne, the Irish monk who began his career on Iona and returned to Ireland and Inisbofin after the Synod of Whitby settled differences between the 'Celtic Church' and the Roman, coming down firmly on the side of the latter.[32] The discoveries from Portmahomack are highly significant in preserving the only material evidence of early medieval Insular vellum production within the confines of the monastic community.

The literary sources are equally scant and the example here comes from beyond this island. St Leobard of Marmoutier (*c.* 583), the son of noble parents from Auvergne in central France, whose life

30 Carver 2008, 49.

31 *Ibid.*, 124.

32 Hughes 2008, 325–6.

was recorded in the martyrology of St Gregory of Tours (538–94), renounced the world and joined a hermit named Alaric, who spent his time making parchment and writing Holy Scripture. Leobard continued the same tasks for twenty years.[33] Illustrated evidence is available from the twelfth century in the form of a series of miniature roundels in a full-page illustration at the beginning of a German manuscript (Bamberg, Staatsbibliothek MSC Patr. 5, f. 1v), depicting specialised monks engaged in the various stages of book production but, curiously, not writing (Fig. 2.3).

The source of vellum for medieval manuscript production was, of course, calves. Matthew Stout believes that pastoral farming within the monastic settlement in Ireland was frowned upon and avoided if at all possible, the monks preferring to base their economy on 'tillage activity'. He remarks on the greater number of tillage-based miracles compared to pastoral examples, and notes that the monastic focus on crop-growing would not have clashed with the secular cattle-based system.[34] Given the monastic requirement for vellum, a by-product of cattle-rearing, the argument needs to be reconsidered. In the early Christian period, up to the ninth century, the prime consumer of vellum was the monastic scribe. It has already been proposed that, given the specific use of vellum, secular society in Ireland at this time would have had little use for the material. The quality of early Irish vellum implies a profound understanding of the material by its makers. It required a concerted and determined effort to consistently produce books from the same source animal. There was certainly no manufacturing or economic advantage to be found in choosing calfskins over those of either sheep or goats, both of which would have been available. The hide of an adult sheep or goat can be successfully converted into parchment, whereas the hide of a calf older than six or eight weeks is too thick to produce folios for writing; only very young, newborn animals can produce vellum suitable for the scribe's pen. In addition, the hides of these calves are quite narrow in comparison with those of sheep or goats and, as such, less economical.

The many comments found in the marginalia of extant Irish manuscripts, usually disparaging references to the quality of the skin (see above), further confirm this in-depth knowledge. Finally, considering that this cattle-derived product was to be the carrier of the Word of God (and the source of knowledge and veneration on the altar), it is difficult to imagine the cow being 'undesirable' in the monastic context. Furthermore, cattle and calves appear in saints' Lives, and St Brigid of Kildare (d. 524) is said to have performed a miracle by milking cows three times in one day.[35] It seems probable that the rearing of cattle and the production of vellum would have been the work of the larger monastic centres, which may have supplied the smaller churches with vellum and books.

Surviving manuscripts demonstrate that Irish scribes, in addition to learning the Latin language and letters, developed a script of their own, using the books brought by the missionaries, most likely written in some form of half-uncial, as a template.[36] O'Neill points to exemplars from North Africa and the prototype of the initial letter employed in the fifth century that would influence the Irish style.[37] The early adoption of the decorated capital by Irish scribes led Françoise Henry to suggest an Italian source of inspiration owing to their use of the same feature from an early date.[38] This Insular hand was distinctive enough to have been identifiable abroad as early as the ninth century, as evidenced by an entry written in rustic capitals in the library catalogue of the monastery of St Gallen in Switzerland: '*LIBRI SCOTTICE SCRIPTI*' (Fig. 2.4). In keeping with the inventive tradition of 'doing it their own

---

33 Baring-Gould 1882, 279.

34 Stout 1998, 75–80.

35 Ó Riain 2011, 120.

36 O'Neill 2014, 3; Ó Cróinín 1995, chapter 7, in which Ó Cróinín discusses what the Roman script that influenced the development of the Insular hand might have looked like; Diringer 1982, 469.

37 O'Neill 2017, 283.

38 Henry 1965, 25.

Fig. 2.3—Bamberg, Staatsbibliothek MSC Patr. 5, f. 1v.

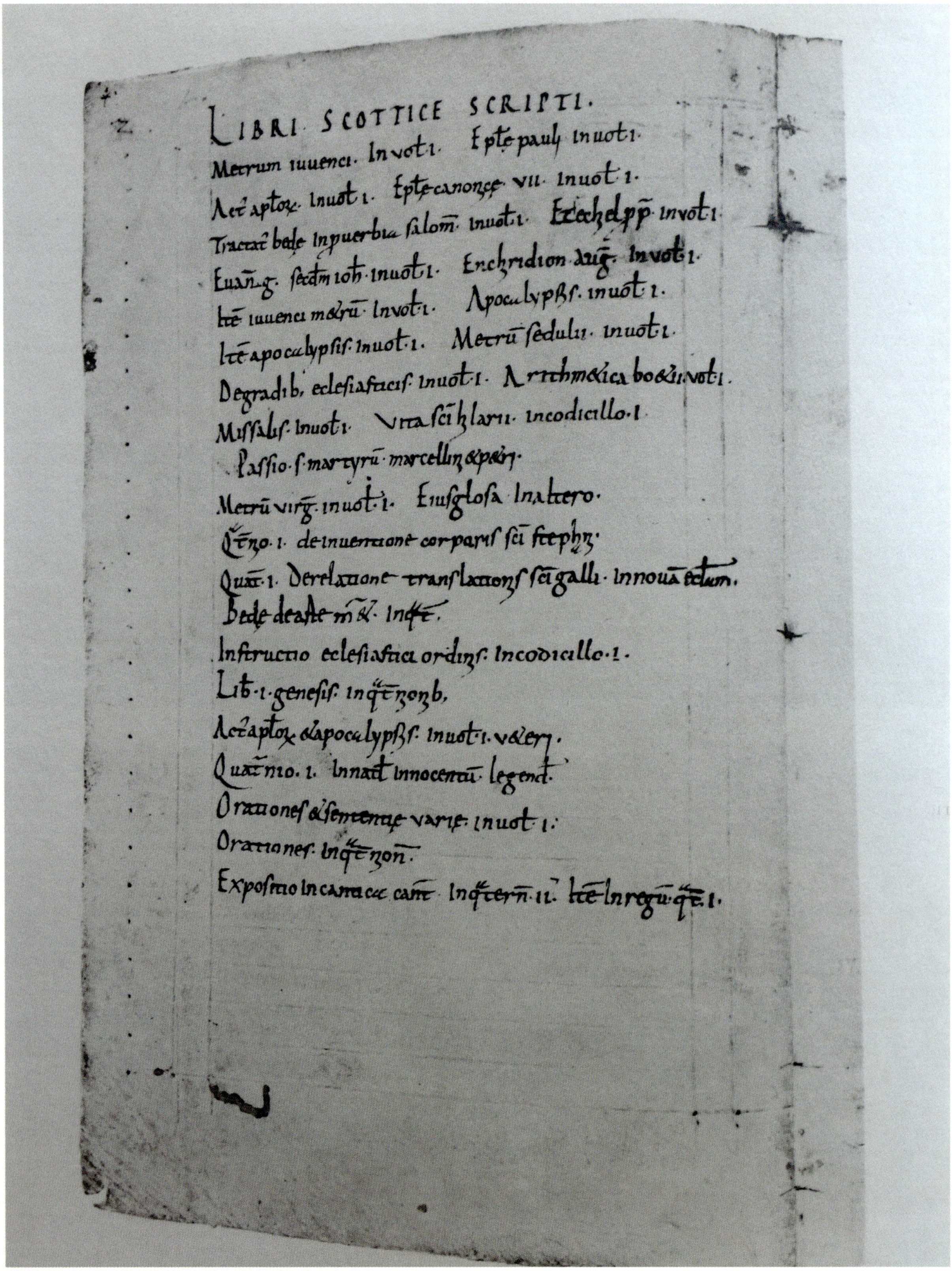
LIBRI SCOTTICE SCRIPTI.
Metrum iuuenci. In uol. i. Eptę pauli in uol. i.
Act. aptor. in uol. i. Eptę canonicę vii. in uol. i.
Tractat. bedę in puerbia salom. in uol. i. Ezechel pp. in uol. i.
Euang. sedm ioh. in uol. i. Enchiridion aug. in uol. i.
Itē iuuenci metru. in uol. i. Apocalypsis. in uol. i.
Itē apocalypsis. in uol. i. Metru sedulii. in uol. i.
De gradib. ecclesiasticis. in uol. i. Arithmetica boetii. in uol. i.
Missalis. in uol. i. Vita sci hilarii. in codicillo. i.
Passio s. martyru marcellini et petri.
Metru virg. in uol. i. Eius glosa in altero.
Quatn. i. de inuentione corporis sci stephi.
Quat. i. De relatione translationis sci galli. in noua [illegible]
Bede de arte metr. in quat.
Instructio ecclesiastica ordinis. in codicillo. i.
Lib. i. genesis. in quaternionib.
Act. aptor. et apocalypsis. in uol. i. vetere.
Quaternio. i. in nat. innocentiu. legend.
Orationes et sententię varię. in uol. i.
Orationes. in quaternion.
Expositio in cantica canticorum in quatern. ii. Itē in [illegible] quat. i.

Fig. 2.4 – St Gallen library catalogue.

way', the Irish makers of vellum folios also developed a particular type of skin as an end-product. Reed believes that the peak of 'technical excellence' in the production of parchment was reached in the medieval period and that the skill, knowledge and experience had been lost by the sixteenth century.[39] Based on my experience with parchment, I suggest that a visible decline in quality by the end of the thirteenth century can be generally observed. It is worth considering again the vellum of the earliest extant Irish writing on this material, Usserianus Primus. If this sixth-century manuscript is a product of Ireland, the quality achieved is quite remarkable and can be considered the work of experienced and technically proficient parchment-makers.[40] This suggests that the production of vellum for folios was solidly established at the time of Usserianus Primus, along with, by inference, the making of books.

There are no extant instructions or descriptions of how the Insular skins were manufactured from young Irish calves during what must have been a feverish period of book production. This lack of documentary evidence is not unexpected from the late and post-Roman world. No account of the process has come down to us prior to the text from a manuscript written in a monastery in northern Italy in the eighth century, a millennium after its refinement in Pergamum: 'Place [the skin] in lime water and leave it there for three days. Then extend it on a frame and scrape it on both sides with a sharp knife and leave it to dry.'[41] Later in the tenth century a more detailed description appears in an English manuscript (Exeter Cathedral Library MS 3501) in the form of a riddle. The following is included for preparing the skins in the description of the making of a book:

> *An enemy came and took away my life*
> *and my strength also in the word; then wetted me,*
> *dipped me in water; then took me thence;*
> *placed me in the sun, where I lost all my hair.*
> *The knife's edge cut me— its impurities ground away;*
> *fingers folded me.*[42]

Although it would be impossible to produce a finished product based on the scant instructions in these early recipes, they do provide clues, in some fashion by what they do not say. In the Exeter riddle there is no mention of the use of a lime liquor as a depilatory to remove hair from the pelt; rather it was 'placed in the sun'. It is known that lime was (and is) widely used to de-hair pelts prior to their conversion into parchment, but it is not certain who was responsible for its introduction or, more specifically, whether it was an Islamic or a European source. The Arabs, who by the eighth century were occupying parts of Europe and were known for their work with alkalis, may have adopted it for their own use.[43]

It is reasonable to state that manuscripts produced across Europe by the end of the eighth century were composed of skins of varying species de-haired by lime liquors. Byzantine parchment was similarly produced possibly as early as the sixth century[44] but the practice might not have been widely adopted in Britain and Ireland, although no specific research has been conducted to substantiate this. Greek

39 Reed 1972, 118.

40 I worked closely with this manuscript over an eighteen-month period, during which I handled and examined every folio fragment. A particular feature was the thinness of the skins and their consistency in 'feel'. This would not fit the category of the later 'Insular vellum'.

41 Codex 490 (Bib. Cap. Lucca), ff 21–25.

42 Baum 1963, Book 43, K-D 26.

43 Haran 1991.

44 Wächter 1962.

and Roman practices at the beginning of the fifth century AD list dove dung, urine from camels and humans, and plant infusions of bryony and mulberry in depilation recipes.[45] Other recipes based on infusions of fresh vegetable matter would have introduced tannins to the parchment.

Reed observed that, under controlled conditions and with the use of an ultraviolet light source at a wavelength of 2537 A.U., the presence of tannin in parchment will suppress any fluorescence, whereas those skins prepared by the use of lime without the addition of tannins will show pronounced fluorescence.[46] This simple test method was carried out at different times on the two most significant, or at least most widely known, Insular manuscripts, and the findings suggest the use of an alternative mechanism to lime in the preparation of their folios. When a blank area of the Lindisfarne Gospels (BL Cotton MS Nero D.IV), a product of the Northumbrian priory on Holy Island around 700, was examined by Roosen-Runge and Warner, they noted the lack of fluorescence, which indicated the presence of tannins.[47] When Cains carried out a similar test on the Book of Kells (TCD MS 58), written and illuminated in an Irish monastic settlement around 800, he noted that the folios did fluoresce; nevertheless, his close examination of the nature of the vellum in Kells convinced him that no lime had been used to de-hair the pelts, but rather a method of controlled putrefaction, or puering, using farinaceous materials such as dung and urine.[48]

The 'feel' of the skin is an overall impression when its physical nature and characteristics combine to define it in some manner. An example of this would be the slower or less violent reaction of Insular vellum to changes in relative humidity, particularly when those values drop.[49] The folios of Kells typify as closely as can be defined the nature of Insular vellum, although in reality this has no technical basis for definition. There was little merit in exposing the FMP folio fragments to an ultraviolet test since the effect of organic matter in the bog had introduced tannins to the vellum, as evidenced by the dramatic colour change to a 'leather brown'.

The question of what characterises Insular vellum was also posed by Julian Brown, who summed it up as follows: 'It is rather thick. It has a kind of suede-like finish. You can generally see the mark of the scraper on both hair and flesh side; and the hair-side and the flesh-side are very alike in surface as well as colour.'[50] He believed that its origin lay in a local variant developed in some Romano-British centre before the usual method of manufacture was established. Lowe was reluctant to venture far into the subject but did proffer the idea that many of the differences noted between Continental and Insular skins were related to the 'manner of preparation'.[51] Bischoff describes Insular vellum as 'roughened on both sides with pumice stone, with the result that hair- and flesh-sides become indistinguishable from one another'. Bischoff also notes that the missionaries took their distinctive vellum with them, as is evidenced by the extant Carolingian manuscripts from Fulda and Mainz in Germany.[52] De Hamel does not hold the Insular parchment used to produce early Irish manuscripts in high regard, referring to it as 'poor-quality vellum, consistent with the primitive nature of the communities'.[53]

The survival condition of the vellum from the FMP restricts any substantial descriptive analysis of

45 Reed 1972, 90.

46 *Ibid.*, 253.

47 Roosen-Runge and Warner 1960, 263–77.

48 Cains 1990, 180.

49 This would be observed as the curling of a folio on dry days, especially in winter. It would suggest that the preparation of Insular skins resulted in a property that made them less hygroscopic than skins de-haired with lime.

50 J. Brown 1993, 126.

51 Lowe 1935, viii.

52 Bischoff 1990, 9.

53 De Hamel 1994, 22.

Fig. 2.5—Faddan More Psalter, head of f. 10v.

how it might fit with the criteria of Insular vellum. Thickness measurements taken during the four-year conservation process recorded values from 0.19mm to 0.37mm. This is comparable with the measurements of from 0.08mm to 0.39mm that Cains recorded in his examination of the folios of the Book of Kells[54] and my own recordings across a selection of folios in the eighth-century gospel-book of Durrow (TCD MS 57), which gave values ranging from 0.08mm to 0.28mm. A selection of thicknesses taken during the conservation of Usserianus Primus also delivered similar results: 0.09–0.44mm with variations occurring on single folio fragments, for example 0.12–0.19mm, 0.14–0.18mm and 0.18–0.44mm. In the case of the FMP it is necessary to take into consideration the extreme conditions in which the text block lay and the effect that saturation over such an extended period might have had on the fibre structure of the vellum; nonetheless, the values recorded (dry) represent an accurate mean of the FMP vellum.

The folio size of the FMP is approximately 305mm x 226mm, a height-to-width ratio of 1.35:1; this is based on the only (almost) intact bifolio, ff 29–32.[55] The edges of the folios of the FMP have been trimmed in a haphazard manner with a generally short cutting stroke, followed by a second stroke, often with a slight change in angle. This would suggest that a blade without the guide of a straight-edge was typically employed for trimming. When describing the extant edges, it is not possible to be definitive about the stage at which trimming took place, whether after the manuscript was produced or as a later attempt to 'clean up edges' after the psalter had been in use for some period of time. Double cuts are also present, indicating a failed attempt to trim. These appear as incisions in the vellum close to the cut edge but do not penetrate the full thickness of the skin. One such example is seen at the head of folio 10v, where the cut is very close to the rough trimmed edge and is 20mm in length. The trueness of the cut indicates that a straight-edge was also involved, at odds with the otherwise chaotic edge work. Looking into the incision, the 'walls' have a smooth dark appearance, consistent with long-term wear and tear, similar to the original extant edges of the folios. The indicators here suggest that this incision has some age in the working life of the psalter (Fig. 2.5). There are no corresponding incisions on adjacent folios in the quire and the position of the incision on the verso allows for the trimming or attempted trimming to be carried out with the quire folded. The margins for a manuscript of this format are tight, with typically only 20mm at the head and fore-edge. This favours the argument for a second trimming of the edges. The practice of balancing the width of the inner text margin to half the

54 Cains 1990, 178.

55 Gillis 2012, 138.

width of the fore-edge margin, creating a homogeneous appearance to all borders when the manuscript is open and the two back-to-back inner margins are on view, needs to be considered, however. The inner margin on the FMP is quite narrow, not the ideal 10mm (half the fore-edge width) but close, at approximately 13–15mm. It is possible to identify from which side the edge trimming was carried out, as the incision side has a clean edge which becomes somewhat jagged as the blade fails to cut cleanly all the way through. Examining the cut edges of the bifolio 29–32, the same short strokes are evident. An additional detail at the centrefold of the tail provides further clues to the trimming procedure of the folios. Here the short cut stroke matches on either side of the centrefold, indicating that trimming was carried out when the bifolio was folded. Further evidence to support this is seen when comparing the two fore-edges of the bifolio; folio 29 has a clean-cut edge all the way through, while the edge of folio 32 has the same clean edge for two-thirds of its thickness and then becomes jagged and hairy, indicating that the knife failed to cut through both thicknesses cleanly. Unfortunately, no sequence of edges has survived to indicate whether the folded and assembled quire was edge-trimmed *in situ*, but I suggest that this was the case. As was mentioned in the Introduction, the FMP has an indiscriminate layout in relation to the orientation of the hair side and flesh side of the folios, and as such complies with the *modus operandi* of the early medieval Irish scribe and book-maker.[56] The collation map of the FMP shows equal disregard for regularity in the make-up of the quire numbers.

It is evident from this comparison of the methods of working and the materials used that the FMP sits comfortably with those other books of the same period and, despite its appearance today, it is not difficult to imagine the source of vellum used for the FMP also supplying the skins for the Book of Dimma (TCD MS 59) or the MacRegol Gospels (Bodleian Library MS Auct. D.2.19), all three being local products and written in the same epoch. The same can be said of the scribe who prepared the FMP for writing. The writing itself is the subject of the next chapter.

PRICKING AND RULING

The physical preparation of medieval manuscript folios for writing has long been included in the descriptions of palaeographers and codicologists alike. Although some conclusions can be drawn based on the execution of pricking and ruling, the variety of patterns and possible combinations prevent definitive deductions based solely on these features. Rather, when combined with reliable traits such as a colophon or a distinctive hand, they can reinforce an argument for placing a manuscript in a time or place. Pricking and ruling were used to guide the scribe in his writing and to ensure a consistent and uniform appearance of the page. Aesthetics were considered by the scribe, who did not want anything to distract from the visual impact of his written word. Ruling was carried out with a 'metal point' or 'hard point' that was clear enough to guide the writing but less visible afterwards. In addition to the horizontal lines, vertical bounding lines created a framework within which the writing could be contained. These lines could be single or double and allowances were, on occasion, made for the addition of illumination or decorated capitals, more typically—but not exclusively—in the de luxe manuscript. By the twelfth century the hard point was being replaced by graphic lines produced with plummet, a form of metallic lead. From the thirteenth century writing ink was also used to rule the folio.[57] Interestingly, Irish scribes were slow to adopt graphic ruling and manuscripts with hard-point ruling were produced until the end of the medieval period; examples include *Leabhar Uí Mhaine* (RIA MS D.ii.I, late fourteenth century), the Book of Ballymote (RIA MS 23.P.12, *c.* 1400), the Book

56 O'Sullivan 2005, 516; O'Neill 2014, xiii.

57 De Hamel 2009, 23.

of Lecan (RIA MS 23.P.2, early fifteenth century) and the Book of Lismore (RIA MS 12.M.11, late fifteenth century).

This practice is typically included in the codicological study of manuscripts. In this section the conventions are discussed and compared against the evidence surviving on the FMP. As a means of guiding the ruling, small punctures were made in the skin against which a straight-edge could be lined up before scribing the line. The position, the shape of the puncture and the method of operation have come under the scrutiny of many scholars, and hence a range of conventions have been established that attempt to draw some conclusions in relation to the period and place of production of a manuscript, and on occasion even the exact location, usually reinforced by additional material evidence. Leslie Webber Jones identified seven different methods of pricking which he used to indicate date and place, though by his own admission the study was not conclusive, as access to particular manuscripts was hindered by the Second World War. Jones did manage to examine some 800 manuscripts, both originals and through secondary sources, including *CLA* I, II and III[58] (the seminal palaeographical study of surviving Latin manuscripts before AD 900, printed in eleven volumes). He identified prickings in the centre of the folio as originating in 'very ancient times'. This system only works as a guide for the straight-edge if there is a second set of prickings on the conjoint folio and the bifolio is laid out flat. Jones identifies this as a fourth-century practice and cites Codex Sinaiticus (BL Add. MS 43725) and Codex Vaticanus (Bibl. Vat. gr. 1209), both of which he identified from *CLA* II.[59] Because both these manuscripts are written with four and three columns per folio respectively, the pricking can be placed between columns. He does, however, identify single-column manuscripts that also have their prickings down the centre of the folio, in what he terms 'inside-text' pricking.[60] Jones produced a number of publications on the subject and in 1946 he wrote an article that attempted to identify the instrument employed to generate the prickings on medieval manuscript folios by studying the shape and size of the resulting punctures in the parchment. The discussion, assisted by reproductions of the varying types, also speculates on the working practice of the scribe.[61] The tools under scrutiny were the awl, the dividers, the knife and the toothed wheel. Additionally, the angle of the hole and its 'trueness' indicated whether the pricking was guided by a straight-edge. E.A. Lowe offered a brief observation on prickings in his introduction to *CLA* II, mirroring Jones's observation on the ancient nature of a central pricking and adding the Insular practice of pricking in both the inner and outer margins.[62] Bischoff repeats this information, which by the 1980s was standard palaeographical information for the student of manuscript studies.[63] James Harmon carried out a detailed study of the subject, focusing on the collection of manuscripts produced in the scriptorium of the Court School of Charlemagne. The comprehensive study revealed an in-house style which evolved over time but also compared influences from pricking, ruling and folding conventions outside the Court School.[64]

I have applied Jones's principle to the prickings that survive on the FMP. Pricking was carried out after folding and with the quire assembled, as the corresponding holes on each bifolio line up. This demanded that the awl, compass or knife tip be pushed through all of the folios in a single action. It also

58 Jones 1944, 73.

59 Lowe 1935.

60 Jones 1944, 73.

61 Jones 1946.

62 Lowe 1935.

63 Bischoff 1990, 22.

64 Harmon 1984. With detailed measurements and ratios across a range of early medieval manuscripts, this publication is a useful tool in placing the examined features of western manuscripts, including the FMP.

necessitated pricking on the inner margins of the writing space in addition to the outer margin, a feature of many Insular manuscripts. Examples are observed over a considerable time-span, from the *Cathach*, the fragmented psalter dating from as early as the end of the sixth century,[65] to the eleventh-century Ricemarch Psalter (TCD MS 50), produced in Wales under Irish influence. Given the typically thick nature of Insular vellum, I doubt the possibility of driving a tool through as many as ten skins to puncture the final folio. The tool, whether awl or compass, needs a tapered shaft for strength and rigidity, with the resulting perforations leaving a larger hole on the first folio and decreasing as it makes its way through the following leaves. My findings across the early medieval Insular manuscripts that I have examined (although with some variation) demonstrate that the perforations are generally uniform in size and shape. I believe that the scribe would more typically, when attempting to pierce through a quire of ten folios, initially push through perhaps three skins, leaving an indent on the fourth. He would then repeat the exercise, starting from the indented folio and pushing through another three skins. In this scenario it would require three attempts before a pricking point or station was visible on all the folios in the quire.

Ruling was, as in the Continental practice, carried out in hard point, employing a purpose-made tool. Again, adopting the same principle as pricking, the ruling of the first outer folio would simultaneously impart ruling lines on the folios beneath. And, again, it must have been necessary to repeat the ruling, as it became ever fainter further into the quire, probably even more so than the pricking. Harmon agrees in relation to the likelihood of successfully ruling a quaternion in a single operation but we differ in his opinion that the pricking could be achieved as a single action.[66]

The effect of ruling in hard point was to leave a furrow on the tool side and a ridge on the other. This particular feature is often difficult to discern with the passage of time, and in some instances no trace whatsoever of ruling survives, with only the pricking holes and straight lines of text to indicate its presence. The consensus is that ruling generally took place on the hair side, but again I have seen numerous exceptions to this.[67] There was a further refinement in the Continental method, which came about early in the ninth century, whereby four bifolios were pricked and ruled on the hair side before folding (with the furrow on the hair side). Two bifolios were folded with the hair side out and two with the flesh side out. The quire was then assembled by gathering alternating bifolios from the two sets. The effect was in addition to having like facing like for the hair and flesh sides; the ridges and furrows also faced each other to complete the homogeneous appearance. Edward Rand noticed this feature on his examination of the manuscripts originating in Tours but now dispersed through France and further afield.[68] It requires considerable detective work to identify this feature; such a refinement has yet to be seen in an Insular context and it is one that would be categorically impossible to identify on the FMP.

Surviving evidence of the 'tools of the trade', combined with secondary evidence from contemporaneous illustrations of these tools in use, facilitates a better understanding of the processes involved in writing books in the early medieval period. Examples of scribes at work from the folios of medieval manuscripts over a 300-year period from the early eighth century can be seen in Figs 2.22–2.27. Although no positively identified parchment-prickers (*punctoria*) dating from the period of the FMP have been recovered, a collection of five objects that can be described as fit for purpose have been identified. The earliest of the five, discovered in Winchester, dates from the twelfth century and is constructed from bone, with a metal point inserted at one end and the other end shaped into a spherical knob. The metal pins are either of iron or of copper alloy. Although variously identified in the past as pins, bodkins or

65 Ó Cróinín 2009, 3.

66 Harmon 1984, 22.

67 Brown 1993, 235; Harmon 1984, 20.

68 Rand 1929, 13–14.

Fig. 2.6—Biblioteca Apostolica Vaticana Barb. Lat. 570 (Barberini Gospels), f. 11v. © Biblioteca Apostolica Vaticana

Fig. 2.7—Barb. Lat. 570, Barberini Gospels, f. 124v. © Biblioteca Apostolica Vaticana

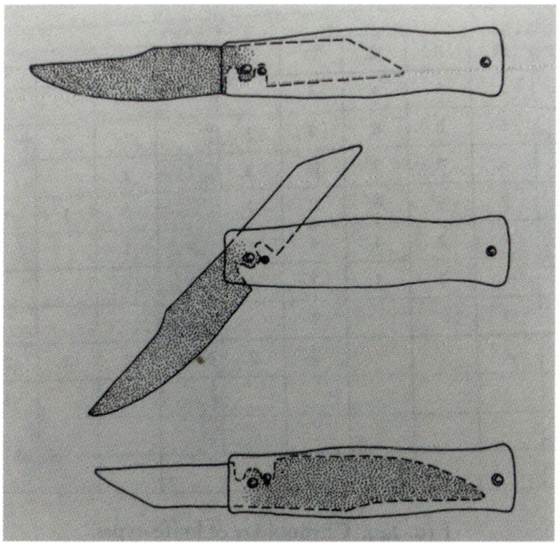

Fig. 2.8a—Reconstruction of pivoting knife (Winchester Excavations Committee).

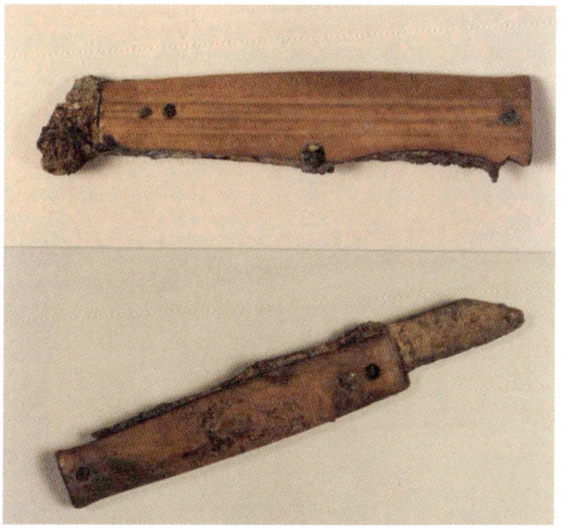

Fig. 2.8b—Dublin pivoting penknife.

styli, more recent research has suggested that they are parchment-prickers.[69] In addition to the pricker, one of the other tools used to mark up for ruling was the knife. The shape of the puncture marks in several Insular manuscripts strongly suggests that the knife was the scribe's tool of choice. Its multi-functional purpose must have made it an essential tool for the writer of medieval books. Uses would include the erasure of errors in writing or illumination by scraping the surface with its edge, as well as the preparation of the quill, or 'nibbing' as it dulled through use, which required both a sharp cutting blade and a paring action. Apart from the quill, the knife is the scribal tool most frequently illustrated in medieval manuscripts. The scribe is often depicted with quill in one hand and knife in the other, as seen in the late eighth-century Barberini Gospels (Figs 2.6 and 2.7). Like the prickers, no positively identified example is known in the archaeological record. Biddle suggests that a collection of pivoting knives from Winchester meet the requirements. These contain two blades which swivel, with one blade exposed while the other is housed inside the handle. The blades are of different shapes, one straight and the other curved, to facilitate different tasks. The knives were recovered from contexts ranging in date from the late ninth century. Some had decorative inlays on the bone handle. A rivet passes through the bone scale and through the centre of the double blade before exiting on the opposite bone scale, where it is peened over, allowing for a pivoting action (Fig. 2.8, a and b). Biddle's argument for scribal use is valid, although he does concede that penknives, as they are today, were an 'all-purpose' tool rather than a specialised one.[70]

The skills required for penknife manufacture would have been found within the monastic community and there is documented evidence to support this. Adomnán's Life of Columba tells of a monk named Molua Ua Briúin who asked St Columba for a blessing for the implement he held in his hand, a knife. When he later tried to slaughter a bullock (a further reference to cattle), the knife failed; Columba added that 'the implement I have blessed will not harm man or beast'. On discovering this, the monks who knew the blacksmith's craft melted down the iron of that knife and then used it to coat all the other iron tools in the monastery.[71] There is an allegorical element

69 Biddle 1990, 734.

70 *Ibid.*, 734.

71 Sharpe 1995, 177.

Fig. 2.9—Faddan More Psalter, f. 29v.

to the story, as iron-smelting did not arrive in Ireland until the introduction of the blast furnace at the end of the sixteenth century and prior to this iron was worked in the solid state.[72] It does, however, give a clear indication of the craft skill available within the monastic community.

Interpreting the surviving evidence of pricking and ruling on the folio fragments of the FMP is considerably more challenging than carrying out the same investigation on any contemporary or even earlier manuscript folios. In addition to the notable change in the physical appearance of the surviving folio fragments, the swollen state of the collagen fibres over such an extended period has had a disguising effect on any imprints, intentional or accidental, on the topography of the skin. This, combined with the fragmented nature of the manuscript, makes the definitive identification of specific modes of working somewhat speculative. What has been identified fits within the Insular approach for preparing a manuscript for writing. Pricking perforations survive on a small number of the folio fragments, and again the fortunate almost-intact survival of bifolio 29–32 has provided the best evidence. A series of prickings is observed along the inner margins of this only intact backfold. They are wedge-shaped horizontal slits up to 3mm in length; the 'fatter' end of the wedge faces the backfold. The perforation shape suggests the tip of a penknife blade as the tool (Fig. 2.9). There are no corresponding prickings visible on the fore-edge, lost no doubt to edge trimming; any prickings for the vertical bounding lines have also been trimmed off. The prickings on the FMP correlate with Jones's type H,[73] in which 'horizontal slits are made away from a ruler in an irregular line'. His example for type H is based on examination of Cod. Sang. 904, the manuscript

72 Scott 1981.

73 Jones 1946.

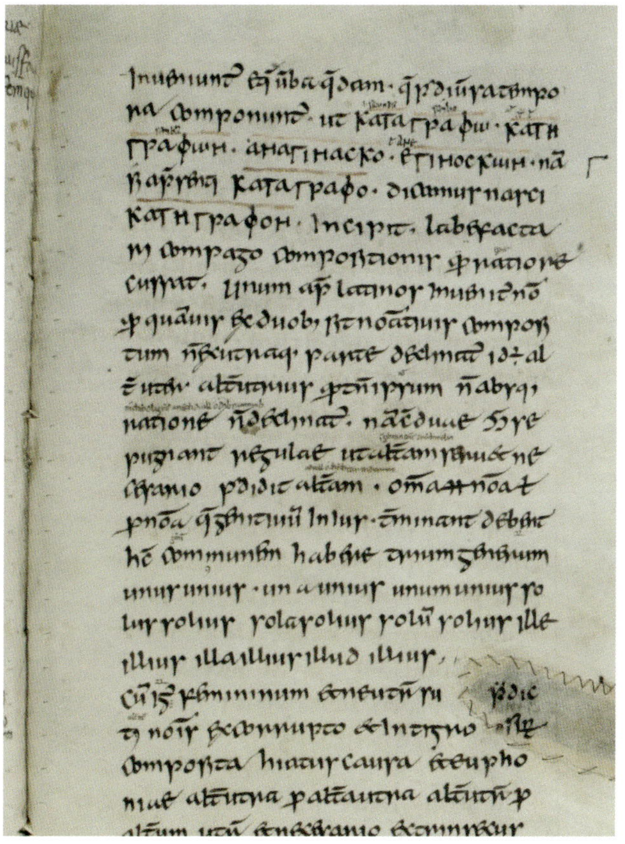

Fig. 2.10—St Gallen, Stiftsbibliothek MS 904, *Institutiones Grammaticae*, p. 75.

Fig. 2.11—Faddan More Psalter, f. 7v.

Fig. 2.12—Faddan More Psalter, f. 55v.

referred to above for its Irish glosses (Fig. 2.10).[74] Other surviving prickings on the FMP are seen on folio 7, in this instance on the fore-edge, and again the perforations are slit-shaped (Fig. 2.11).

I identified the evidence for ruling on the psalter in two forms: either a faint furrow line under the text, where the hard-point ruling has imparted an impression, or more typically a graphic line in a silver/grey colour. Unsurprisingly, any evidence of a ridge on the opposing side of any surviving furrow was not found. Studying the surviving furrows shows that ruling was carried out in typical random fashion with little regard as to which side of the skin was chosen. An excellent example is observed on bifolio 55–56. The centre bifolio of the ultimate fifth quire displays definite furrows on folio 55r, a flesh side, and equally well-defined furrows on 55v, a hair side. Identification is assisted here by the thinning out of the vellum fragment through deterioration, which had the effect of enhancing the work of the scribe's point (Fig. 2.12). No ruling can be seen on either side of folio 56. On the tail fragment of bifolio 27–34 a furrow runs across the vellum approximately 5mm from the bottom edge. The scribed impression crosses the backfold area in a continuous line, indicating that in this instance the ruling was executed before folding. There is some question regarding the purpose of the line, given its proximity to the bottom edge of the bifolio. Perhaps it served a different function, such as a trimming guide as seen in modern-day books, a feature which would naturally be lost after the manuscript was completed (Fig. 2.13).

The bifolio fragment 4–9 from the first quire retains interesting details with regard to its ruling. While it was in a saturated state prior to the de-watering process, what appeared to be graphic lines were visible as both horizontal and vertical bounding lines. These were grey/silver in colour and were executed on the flesh side (Fig. 2.14). As already mentioned, it was not the intention of the scribe to graphically rule his bifolios, as this practice did not commence in earnest until the late eleventh century (when lead or

74 Jones 1946.

Fig. 2.13—Faddan More Psalter, ff 27v–34r.

Fig. 2.14—Faddan More Psalter, f. 4v.

plummet was introduced).[75] The grey/silver line is probably the result of trace elements from the scribing tool which became deposited on the surface and were revealed by the particular conditions in which the FMP rested. The colour would indicate deposition from a tool of lead or silver. Dr Paul Mullarkey of the Conservation Department in the National Museum of Ireland carried out XRF analysis on one site of this line, which returned graph peaks indicating the presence of lead. After the drying of the vellum, the lines were still visible but now appeared more like a line ruled with a hard point, as expected. Under low magnification, the horizontal lines show evidence of more than one pass of the scribing tool, with double lines running side by side in places—most likely the result of a need to re-scribe lines that were too faint after the first attempt, as mentioned earlier. This would fit that pattern, as this bifolio is the fourth of five plus a singleton in the first quire. With eight folios above it, the folio, 9r in this quire, is unlikely to have been effectively ruled at the first attempt. Moreover, it is noteworthy that the trace elements visible in the wet state confirm that the tool was in direct contact with the surface rather than being the result of an indirect impression. Folios 4v and 9r would not, in the Insular tradition of ruling, have had direct contact with the scribe's point. On the reverse of this bifolio fragment, i.e. 9v and 4r, faint ruling is in evidence, but much less so; this is the hair side, where deterioration is generally at higher levels, so indistinct lines are to be expected. In the top corner of 4v, running parallel with the fore-edge of the folio, is a partial double vertical bounding line. As with the horizontal ruling, in its wet state this appeared as a graphic line with the same grey/silver colour, and the associated pricking is just evident. The survival of fore-edges throughout the manuscript is minimal, making this a key piece of evidence.

Throughout the manuscript faint rulings appear randomly, not owing to inadequate preparation but because of the extreme conditions in which they survived. To establish some pattern to the ruling throughout the FMP, quire five (chosen because it retained the largest folio fragments) was examined in its folio sequence. The quire commences with folio 51r; this hair side shows no trace of any ruling but the verso flesh side has clear ruling under the extant writing. Folio 52r is a hair side with considerable damage to the surface layer, but where writing has survived no evidence of ruling is visible. The verso flesh side, 52v, has clear ruling. Folio 53r is in a poor state of survival, but this flesh side does display evidence of ruling while the verso hair side does not. Folio 54r, a flesh side, is similar to folio 53; although in poor condition, ruling can again be detected, while the verso hair side has one partial and now faint line. The verso of folio 55r—which, as already mentioned, displays not only its ruling lines but also the furrow on the flesh side of the vellum—also displays ruling on the hair side and confirms the practice of re-ruling or 'double ruling', with two thin lines running closely in parallel in places. The second half of quire five commences with folio 56r, also previously mentioned in relation to the clear furrows on its hair side. The verso flesh side does not show any extant ruling, perhaps because the degree of deterioration here is high. Folio 57r is a hair side with no visible ruling; the verso flesh side, 57v, is equally lacking in any visible ruling, and again the degree of deterioration is significant. Folio 58r is a hair side and no ruling is discernible under the text, but the verso flesh side has faint evidence in places. Folio 59 is one of the larger surviving folio fragments in the psalter and the recto flesh side has clear ruling lines in evidence, both on the major surviving fragment and on the relocated additional fragment at the bottom corner of the folio. The verso hair side shows the faintest trace of ruling in places. The last folio of the manuscript, folio 60, is blank on both recto and verso and no ruling lines are present. The detached bottom corner of this folio also survives and likewise displays no evidence of ruling. As stated, the conjoint folio 51 has clear ruling on its verso flesh side.

In the Insular system of preparing vellum folios, the quires were pre-ruled ready for the scribe's quill; accordingly, folio 60 of the FMP should display ruling lines, even if not required. Careful pre-planning could result in calculating exactly how many of the folios would require ruling, with the necessary spaces left for any illumination, although the random make-up of the FMP folios, with the inclusion of

75 M. Brown 1994, 111.

Fig. 2.15a—Faddan More Psalter, ff 32v–29r.

Fig. 2.15b—Faddan More Psalter, f. 32v.

singletons, suggests that this was not the case. If the re-ruling was carried out by the scribe as he wrote, this would explain the blank final folio, which would have no trace of the initial ruling process, as it was at the bottom of a pile of eight and the scribe had reached the end of the psalter on the previous folio. On folio 32v, a set of parallel lines runs in an ad hoc fashion from the head down three-quarters of the page. Examination of the marking under video microscope with raking light reveals a dark black pigment in the almost incision-like grooves (Fig. 2.15, a and b). These markings were produced with a single tool in one event, as the lines remain parallel regardless of any change in direction. The nature of the line and its incursion into the text indicate that it was not an intentional addition to the psalter but was more likely a secondary event at some later date. Similar track lines are found on the leather cover.

In conclusion, it can be stated that the folios of the FMP were ruled following the Insular practice of ruling in hard point after folding, but the pricking and ruling were carried out from the flesh side rather than the more typical hair side. Vertical bounding lines were included, and these were narrow double lines. Without doubt, secondary ruling was carried out as required to clarify faint impressions. The spacing between lines is approximately 8mm. Owing to the erratic trimming and the lack of extant text margins, the fore-edge margin is estimated at between 20mm and 25mm. The same applies to the head margins and 12–18mm would be a mean value. These data were hard won, given the condition and survival of the folios of the FMP. In the following section the survival condition of each quire is described and the codicological features observed are noted.

COLLATION OF THE TEXT BLOCK

The description of the five quires of the FMP is included in the Introduction; it notes 60 folios of vellum measuring originally 305mm x 226mm and without any evidence of flyleaves. The difficulty encountered in establishing the collation and the methodology employed to do so have been addressed in Chapter 1. Many of the generally accepted conventions regarding the Insular method of preparation of parchment for writing are represented in the FMP: for example, the folio count favoured per quire was the quinion,[76] whereas in the Latin West from the fourth century onwards the eight-leaved quaternion was the popular choice, probably because it produces a balanced quire, is not too thick and produces a stable binding structure when it is combined in a text block. The use of singletons often suggests planning that has gone awry or a shortage of parchment. My own experience, however, based on dealing with Irish material from the early medieval period over several years, is that no particular convention was followed and that random quire counts are typically found between the boards of a single manuscript, including in the FMP. Nonetheless, I would point out that quires three and five, the only two quires in the FMP that have not been adjusted by the addition of singletons or bifolios, are both quinions. The Insular arrangement by tradition displayed the hair and flesh sides alternating on facing pages as a result of the bifolios being assembled with the hair side on the outside of the fold. The Continental preference was to face like to like for a more homogeneous appearance, as previously observed. Again, I have not detected Irish scribes following one of these conventions with any real conviction; rather, in most instances they appear to have been blissfully unaware of either. This includes the scribes of some of our 'high-profile' Insular manuscripts such as the Book of Dimma, the Book of Mulling (TCD MS 60) and even the eleventh-century Ricemarch Psalter (TCD MS 50).

Studying the collation map (Fig. 2.28, p. 71) reveals the random nature of assembly. The notion of the medieval Irish practitioner ignoring protocol does not go unnoticed. H.V. Morton, in his enlightening publication based on his travels in Ireland, comments on a range of medieval church

76 A quire consisting of five bifolios, resulting in ten folios and twenty pages.

Fig. 2.16—Faddan More Psalter, ff 29v–32r.

features: 'there seems to be no limit to the indifference to the "rules of the game" which the Irish architects display when designing Gothic churches …'.[77]

OBSERVATIONS ON THE INDIVIDUAL QUIRES OF THE FMP

Quire one, 1–12

This has twelve folios with two singletons, folios 5 and 8, which sit on either side of the central bifolio. Although there is minimal survival of the backfold area, enough survives to confirm that both folios were singletons. Under magnification, a clean edge to the folded areas that hook around the next bifolio indicates that they were trimmed in this fashion rather than lost through deterioration or removal. The continuation in the sequence of the psalms with adjacent folios affirms the collation. Folios 2, 3, 10, 11 and 12 survive only as outer margins with only a few lines of text from the psalms, and folios 11 and 12 are lacking any of the written space. This quire lay inside the leather cover while buried, with folio 1 in direct contact with its inside surface. Folio 1r displayed Psalm 1:1, *Beatus vir*, executed in display capitals (see Chapter 3). Deterioration levels were high, but several detached fragments were identified and repositioned using the character count calculations (see Chapter 1). Apart from the singleton, the hair/flesh orientation follows the Insular practice, with the hair side on the outside of the bifolio.

Quire two, 13–25

This has thirteen folios; folio 15 is a singleton on the same evidence noted above. Folio 13 has a skin defect near the head which the scribe, in typical fashion, has written around. Folios 18, 19 and 20 are lacking any written space, with only the extremities surviving. Folio 22v has the beginning of Psalm 51 and the enlarged and decorated lettering associated with the tripartite division of the psalms. Some additional fragments of text were relocated in this quire, particularly on folios 23, 24 and 25. The skin orientation follows Insular practice, including on the singleton.

77 Morton 1930, 88.

Quire three, 26–35

This quire is a quinion of ten folios (five bifolios, with no singletons). The percentage of survival is generally poor, with any text areas located near the head. This quire, however, contains the almost complete bifolio of 29–32, which has supplied the key codicological evidence for the FMP. The reason for this survival is not clear, given the level of loss of all other bifolios within the quire. One explanation may be that the skin for this bifolio was chosen from a different batch of vellum, a batch that was prepared with a modified recipe. Alternatively, there may have been some post-manufacture solution applied to the surface of the skin by the scribe.

At the head of folios 34 and 35, vertical incisions have been made in the vellum which encroach on the text. The cuts do not align and were made individually. The incision on folio 34 was made from the recto; it has a change of direction halfway through, and a faint cut line can be seen on the vellum where the blade continued beyond the incision. Although the bifolio 29–32 is for the most part intact, it has a horizontal split running across the entire skin, dividing it into two separate pieces (Fig. 2.16). The two halves were retrieved from different locations within the mass of fragments and bog material and have individual grid references in the database (see Chapter 1). It was presumed that the trauma event suffered by this bifolio was the result of its unearthing, when it was damaged by the backhoe of the mechanical digger. Examining the two halves of the skin, however, it is notable that the level of deterioration is at a more advanced state on the lower half of the bifolio. This is manifest in perforations and losses, in addition to tears and splits, which are not in evidence to the same degree of severity on its upper half. This can only be the result of both halves inhabiting different micro-climatic conditions over an extended period of time. The explanation, therefore, is that the trauma occurred at a much earlier stage in the psalter's existence, either prior to deposition, during it or as a result of impact from an implement while buried. Every folio in quire three has some surviving and identifiable text. The hair/flesh orientation resembles the Continental system, with like facing like, and the hair side is on the outside of the first bifolio, 26–35.

Quire four, 36–50

This is the most perplexing quire in the psalter. It contains two singletons, folios 37 and 39; in addition, inserted before the last folio, f. 50, is a bifolio with a singleton inserted inside it, making up folios 47–49. There is no extant writing on these three folios or on the last folio, as they consist only of the head margins and the start of the fore-edge and do not include any of the writing space. The psalm number and chapter have been estimated based on the character count formula. The unusual format in quire four was identified by studying the fragments while they were still *in situ* and observing the backfolds as they lay in position. Post-conservation analysis provided further evidence, using the fixed-focus high-resolution images of the FMP folio fragments that made it possible to virtually overlay two edges and match up their form, indicating that they were the subject of the same trimming action. This was the method used to establish that the singleton was inserted into the bifolio despite this being an unlikely arrangement. With this layout, any sewing, apart from a side-stabbing, would not secure these three folios (Fig. 2.17). Of the remainder of the folios in quire four there is a reasonable amount surviving,

Fig. 2.17—Faddan More Psalter, head margins ff 47v–48r–49r.

Fig. 2.18—Faddan More Psalter, ff 40v–45r.

Fig. 2.19—Faddan More Psalter, ff 60v–51r.

with all the writing space located at the top of each folio, typically nine partial lines of text on each. Folio 40v now contains the relocated interlace fragment inside a frame. This is associated with Psalm 101 and could be a component of a decorated D from *Domine exaudi orationem meam* at the beginning of the psalm (Fig. 2.18). The hair/flesh arrangement adopts a more typical Irish random selection with no apparent order.

Quire five, 51–60

The last quire of the psalter is again a quinion, with indiscriminate layout of hair and flesh orientation. As with previous quires, the area of survival is from the head down, and in some instances in this quire partial lines of writing remain in the bottom corner of selected folios. Identified text is seen on each of the ten folios apart from folio 60. As mentioned earlier, this folio is blank because the final psalm concludes on folio 59, finishing halfway down on the verso (Fig. 2.19).

The random make-up of the five quires fails to follow any of the assembly traditions of medieval manuscripts; in this regard what can be said is that the FMP maintains the Irish tradition as expected. The use of singletons might hint at corrections or additions to the text; equally, a shortage of vellum may have resulted in their use. The principal obstacle to a definitive description of the text block is the level of survival at a 'guesstimated' 12–15%, and in particular the lack of backfold areas of the folios. The particularly disjointed assembly of quire four and how—or whether—the three additional folios were attached to the remainder of the quire remain unresolved. It is evident, however, that some form of sewing was employed, and this is discussed below.

SEWING

Although the sewing of a manuscript is an expected aspect of the binding process, this was not a foregone conclusion with the FMP. The only conclusive evidence was the discovery of two short and very degraded fragments of vegetable fibre threads, without which it could not be assumed that any sewing had ever existed; indeed, a 'loose collection of leaves inside a leather cover' would have been an equally plausible interpretation. Even with the evidence of mechanical attachment of the quires, however, there are several possible types of sewing that could have held the text block together.

Any codicological study of a manuscript that endeavours to establish the chronology, methods or materials of previous sewings will use the backfolds of the bifolios as the primary source of evidence. The 2016 study of the Book of Dimma (TCD MS 59) included such analysis,[78] but the lack of this feature in the surviving folio fragments of the FMP greatly reduced the possibility of definitive deductions. As a result, all analysis and conclusions in this field are drawn from a single bifolio, 29–32, the sole surviving backfold in the entire manuscript containing this single piece of evidence that indicates some form of sewing, subsequently identified as linen threads, located between two enlarged and distorted holes 35mm apart, with the two thread fragments lying side by side. This is a clear indication of some form of stitching, employed as part of a sewing system for the manuscript or as a means of keeping the individual quire together, in the form of a quire tacket. The linen thread fragments were in the upper half of the horizontally split bifolio, where the level of survival was higher. It would be expected that a corresponding set of holes and thread fragments would be found in the lower half of the backfold, but the poorer condition of the vellum makes positive identification difficult (Fig. 2.20). There are several holes in this area—some deliberate, identified as such by their form, and others caused by the deterioration of the vellum. Two purposely produced holes have been identified, a similar

78 Gillis and Meehan 2017.

Fig. 2.20 — Faddan More Psalter, sewing threads ff 29v–32r.

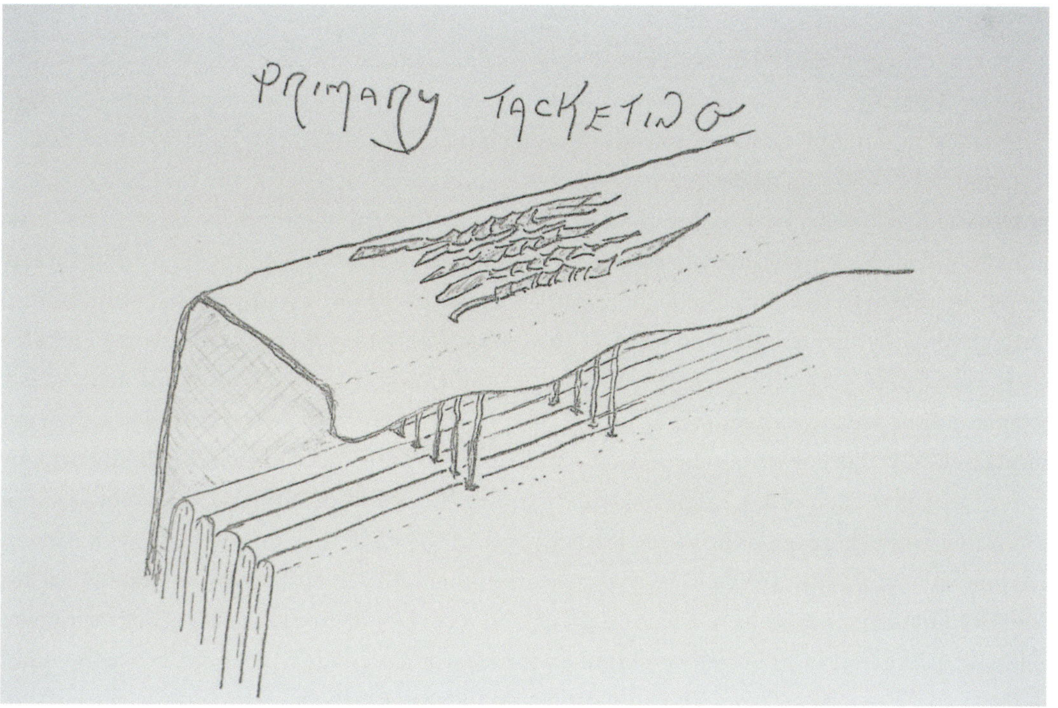

Fig. 2.21 — Illustration of direct tacketing.

Fig. 2.22—Florence, Biblioteca Medicea Laurenziana MS Amiatino 1 (Codex Amiatinus, early eighth century), f. 5r.

distance apart to those in the upper half, but in this case no evidence of any thread fragments is seen between them. This does not rule out the possibility of their use in this location, as fragile material such as linen thread would not be expected to endure in the harsh environment of Faddan More Bog.

According to the surviving evidence, there are two possibilities as regards the function of the sewing of the FMP. The first is a primary tacket. This method of containing the folios of a codex belongs to the evolution of the codex itself (see Introduction). It requires individual lengths of cord or thread to be passed from the centre of the quire through two holes in the backfold, exiting the backfold of the outer bifolio and passing on through aligning holes in the cover, where they were simply twisted together (Fig. 2.21). This would generally be repeated in a second location. In its inception this method was used for the single-quire codex, resulting in a structure akin to the modern-day copybook with wire staples. Later, multi-quired codices were handled in the same fashion, with each quire individually attached to the cover but not to each other.[79] The evidence from the backfold of bifolio 29–32 would support this method, but while there are holes in the leather cover of the FMP they do not align with those in the backfold. An explanation for this could be that the extant thread fragments emanate from an earlier cover or that the five individual quires were never attached to the cover—or to each other—but rather were individually secured gatherings. I briefly entertained the idea of a secondary support, typically of leather, to which the five quires were tacketed; this support would then be attached by stitching or glueing it to the

79 Szirmai 1999, 10.

Fig. 2.23—Codex Eyckensis, Church of St Catherine Maaseik, f. 1v.

Fig. 2.24—St Gallen, Stiftsbibliothek Cod. Sang. 1395, ninth century, p. 418.

Fig. 2.25—Paris, BnF, the Godescalc Evangelistary (MS nouv. acq. lat. 1203), late eighth century, f. 1r.

Fig. 2.26—Gospel-book (Bodleian MS Auct. D.2.16), early tenth century, f. 71v.

inside of the leather cover. The Nag Hammadi codices employ such a system, but the lack of any trace of this support in the FMP rules it out. The second possibility is that the extant evidence represents the paltry remains of an unsupported link-stitch sewing system. There are a number of variations of this early method of securing a multi-quire codex, but some speculation is required to establish which of these best fits the features surviving in the FMP. With an unsupported sewing, regardless of type, the threads, in addition to securing the bifolios in the quire, also link the quires together, thereby constructing the text block of a multi-quired codex. The sewing threads have the additional function of lacing into and attaching the two binding boards, thus completing the structure. One particular form of link-stitch sewing is what Szirmai refers to as 'paired sewing stations'.[80] The method is typically executed with two or more needles, and its appearance in the centre of the quire is of two or multiple threads running between two locations or sewing stations. There is no change-over point, or kettle stitch, at the head and tail where the thread would exit and enter from one quire to the next; instead, at each end of the station each set of threads would climb up into the next quire. The two threads lying between what could be a sewing station in the backfold of bifolio 29–32 match the criteria for the system. The caveat, however, is that the threads did not also attach the cover to the FMP text block, as typically the system utilises individual boards of cartonage or timber. Again, there is the possibility that the link-stitch sewing is a remnant of an earlier binding structure, replaced by the leather cover and flap at a later date. It is of interest that this Near Eastern sewing method is to be found in three Insular

80 Szirmai 1999, 10.

Fig. 2.27—Byzantine Gospels (Bodleian MS Cromwell 16), mid-tenth century, f. 30v.

manuscripts from the early medieval epoch which retain their original bindings, namely the St Cuthbert Gospel (*c*. 700; BL Add. MS 89000), the Cadmug Gospels (eighth century; Landesbibliothek Codex Bonifatianus 3) and the Stowe Missal (*c*. 800; RIA MS D.ii.3). Given that these account for the majority of Insular manuscripts in original structures from this period, it can be said to be representative of a typical sewing despite its Oriental origins. If the FMP was originally sewn in a similar fashion, it fits comfortably with its surviving contemporaries.

An overview of the text block of the FMP points to a book being made in the early medieval period and by a book-maker and/or scribe using the Insular conventions, as well as some particular Irish conventions such as the random nature of assembly of the quires. The text block is a good fit among the corpus of extant Insular manuscripts of the period. Because, untypically, the text block preserves its original or perhaps first trim of its edges (which, given the deposition date in the early ninth century, were also representative of contemporary edge-trimming methods), it retains a feature more usually lost on medieval manuscripts owing to later rebindings and subsequent edge trimming. The technique involved short knife strokes against a straight-edge. I have not encountered this method either on manuscripts of the same period or in the literature, although of course the fact that the vast majority of comparative manuscripts have been re-trimmed as a result of later binding events is a major factor here. More typically, although research is lacking on the subject, there is mention of the draw-knife, which was clearly not employed for the FMP text block.[81] One possibility for this atypical edge treatment might be the trimming by the scribe as he folded, pricked and ruled his bifolios prior to writing; the operation may also have included a 'first trimming', carried out with the scribe's penknife. This would be lost as the binder applied his craft but, as will be seen in Chapter 4, the nature of the binding for the FMP suggests a simplified structure, lacking the refinements of the more typical hard-board bindings.

81 *Ibid*., 219.

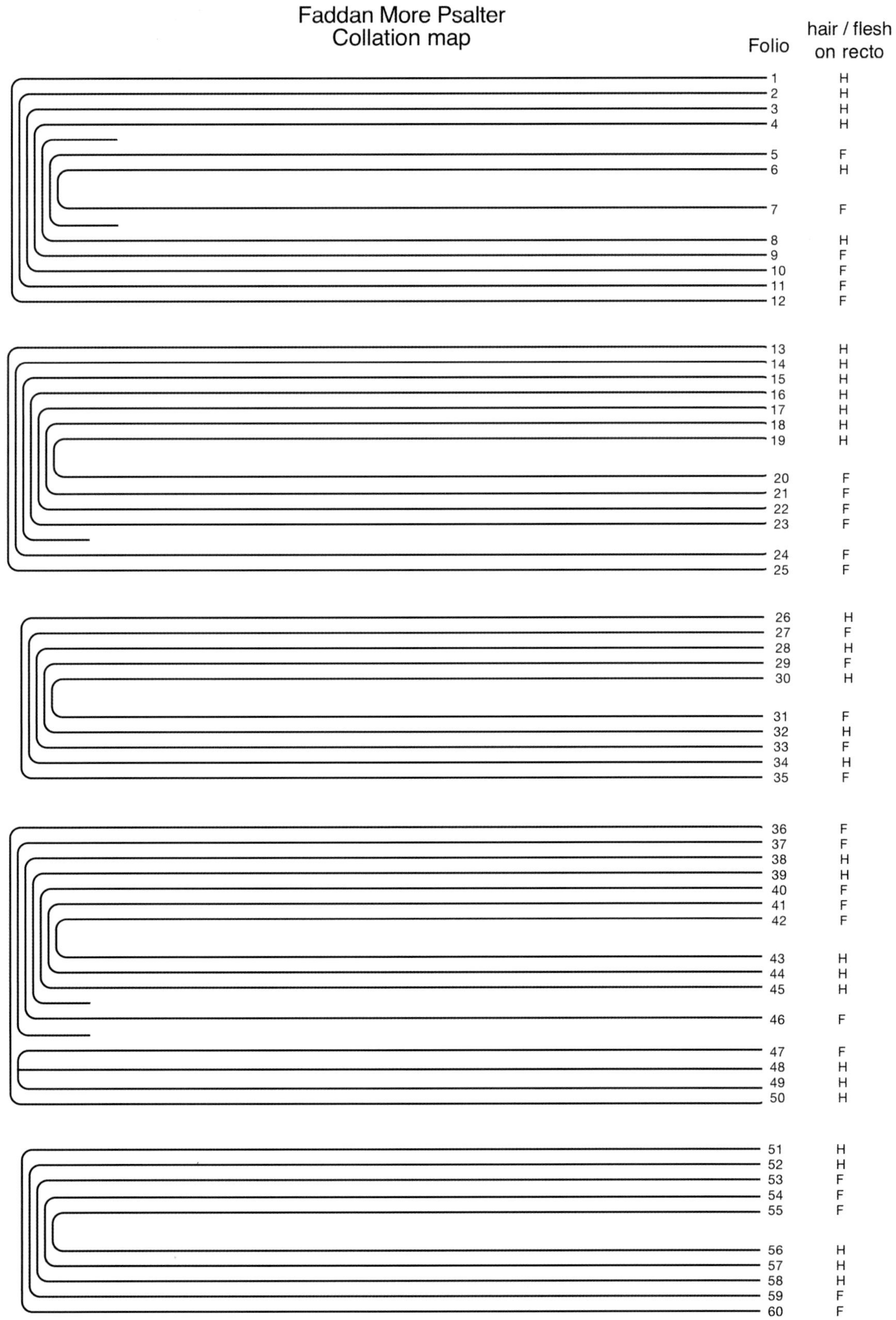

Fig. 2.28—Collation map of the Faddan More Psalter.

CHAPTER 3

Writing and decoration in the Faddan More Psalter

CHAPTER 3

Writing and decoration in the Faddan More Psalter

When the remaining folio fragments of the FMP were slowly separated out, unravelled and dried, it was little surprise to find display lettering of divergent types employed with typical purpose among the Insular majuscule or half-uncial script.[1] The development and refinement of enlarged and decorated lettering as a visual aid to the separation of sections of scripture, while drawing the reader's attention to specific openings, chapters and verses, were achievements of the Insular scribe.[2] This was combined with another initiative of the Irish scribe: canonical separation, or the process of spaces after every word[3] and part of what Malcolm Parkes termed the 'grammar of legibility'.[4] Latin always remained a 'foreign language' in Ireland, hence aids to reading and understanding it were introduced and practised. The psalms, as part of the liturgy, were especially suited to clear visual division in their written form as one of the most critical of Christian texts and as part of the monastic requirement to commit all 150 to memory in order to achieve the level of *psalteratus*. In the first instance the beginning of each psalm required marking; furthermore, various psalms were selected for particular attention, augmenting the liturgical division of groups of psalms, including the tripartite division—or 'three fifties'—which was the earliest division of the psalms and known in Ireland from an early stage.[5] In time this practice became common beyond Ireland.[6] Whereas enlarged and decorated lettering assisted with the division of scripture,[7] the use of word separation or 'aeration' of the text allowed for easier reading and subsequently for copying from

1 M. Brown 2016, 83.

2 M. Brown 2012, 129.

3 Saenger 1997, 34.

4 Parkes 1991.

5 McNamara 1973, 269.

6 Toswell 2016, 474.

7 McGurk 1994, 13; M. Brown 2012, 135.

exemplars.[8] An additional visual factor was the layout of the text; this could be arranged in one long line or in two or even three columns of writing. According to Patrick McGurk, the majority of psalters were written in long lines,[9] the eleventh-century Harley Psalter and its exemplar, the Utrecht Psalter of *c*. 825, being notable exceptions. McGurk also points out that most Irish books were written in long lines, as are the FMP and the *Cathach* (RIA MS 12.R.33), Ireland's earliest surviving codex and psalter. This clear division and decoration of the psalms would continue in later centuries.[10]

The aim of this chapter is to examine the scribal activity in the FMP and, by identifying features among the initial letters and sparse decoration, to draw comparisons with the body of Insular manuscripts that are considered to have an established provenance. The archaeological evidence suggests that the FMP is a local product, but the transient nature of medieval books requires collateral evidence from palaeographical and art-historical observations to support or question any presumptions. Additional extant writing in the psalter text has also been noted, as has the use of punctuation. Contractions are unsurprisingly found throughout the surviving writing of the FMP and are listed in Appendix 6. Additional material relating to this chapter can also be found in the appendices, including a location guide identifying each folio fragment and its psalm, indicating the extant text from the Vulgate psalter in the FMP and noting known and unknown variants, as well as evidence of the scribe's errors and a full listing of extant initials used to indicate the beginning of the psalms.

INSULAR SCRIPT

Accompanying the arrival of Christianity in Ireland in the fifth century was Latin writing in both formal and cursive forms. The half-uncial is the most likely script from which the Irish converts learned their letters.[11] The Springmount tablets, dated to *c*. 600 and containing segments of the psalms, are written in this hand using a pointed stylus. According to Timothy O'Neill, the fragmented Usserianus Primus (TCD MS 55), containing similarly dated gospels on the more conventional writing surface of vellum, is also in what he describes as a calligraphic version of the same Roman hand executed with a quill.[12] According to Dáibhí Ó Cróinín, there must have been writing in Ireland (long) before 600, quite possibly an unbroken tradition going all the way back to the missionary period (late fourth/early fifth century), and perhaps even beyond in the pre-Christian era through Roman contact.[13] Within 75 years the Irish scribes developed from this precedent a distinctive and influential version of their own.[14] This Insular half-uncial or Irish majuscule had as its defining feature wedge serifs, a decorative element that also had the effect of slowing down writing and thereby maintaining the quality of the finished work. Nicolete Gray describes the writing as 'majestic, rivalled only by Textura many centuries later'.[15] The earliest example of this hand is seen in the *Cathach* (RIA MS 12.R.3), also dated to *c*. 600. Irish majuscule was employed for most major works of Irish monastic writings, including the Book of Durrow (TCD MS 57) and the Book of Kells (TCD MS 58).[16] The text of the FMP is also written in Irish majuscule to a high standard.

---

8 Saenger 1997, 49.

9 McGurk 2009, 9.

10 Cleaver 2015, 32.

11 M. Brown 2007, 48.

12 Pers. comm., January 2019.

13 Pers. comm., 22 October 2020.

14 Bischoff 1990, 84.

15 Gray 1986, 55.

16 O'Neill 2014, 76–7.

An additional feature accompanying the Irish written hand was the use of enlarged initials and the effect of reducing the following text incrementally down to the standard letter size, known as diminuendo; this features throughout the writing of the FMP. The Anglo-Saxons were introduced to this hand through Irish missionaries to Britain and Anglo-Saxon monks who studied in Ireland. The Lindisfarne Gospels are written in an adapted form called Insular Phase II.[17] According to Bischoff, the rise of Irish monastic activity resulted in the development of an alternative hand derived from the Irish majuscule. This hand is seen fully developed in the writing of the Antiphonary of Bangor (Bib. Ambr. C.5.Inf.), securely dated to between 680 and 691, and is described as Insular minuscule, which is notable for being more compressed and thus more economical, allowing more words per folio. According to O'Neill, the sharper angle of the minuscule allows faster writing, but the serifs were maintained to control quality.[18]

CATALOGUE OF INITIAL LETTERS OF THE PSALMS

In addition to the standard Insular majuscule script in which the FMP is written, embellishment in the form of enlarged lettering occurs at the beginning of each psalm. The average size of the standard letter is about 3mm; this accounts for letters without ascenders or descenders, such as *m* or *e*. The first extant beginning of a psalm (omitting Psalm 1, which is dealt with separately below) is Psalm 6.2 on folio 3r. Scraps of text survive from Psalms 1, 2 and 4 but not from their initial verses. Psalm 6.2 commences with an enlarged *D* from *Domine ne in furore*. It should be noted that the FMP does not display any of the psalm headings or titles employed by the Latin Church.[19] This observation and many of those that follow are issued with the caveat that fewer than one third of the first and second verses of the 150 psalms has survived. As is the case with much of the FMP's surviving text, it is difficult to decipher the writing at the beginning of Psalm 6; the *D* survives almost alone on this folio, hanging precariously from the top margin, accompanied by what appears to be an *n* or *m* (Fig. 3.1). This most likely represents a contraction of one of the *nomina sacra*, the commonly used abbreviations of sacred names—in this case *Dn(e)* for *Domine.* [20] The enlarged *D* is three lines in height and can be described as Insular majuscule with wedged serif letter forms similar to those seen in the Echternach Gospels (Paris, Bib. MS lat. 9389), the Lindisfarne Gospels (London, BL, Cotton MS Nero D.IV) and the Book of Durrow (Dublin, TCD MS 57). The additional decorative element in the letter consists of two half-circles facing back to back inside the bow of the *D*. There is no use of colour here and the letter is written in the same ink (iron gall) as the standard text. A stylistically similar letter-form can be seen in Ireland's oldest surviving manuscript written entirely in the Irish language,[21] *Lebor na hUidre* (RIA MS 23.E.25), which dates from the beginning of the twelfth century and is historically linked with the monastery at Clonmacnoise.[22] On page 55 of this manuscript an enlarged *D* is penned halfway down the left-hand column. The similar Insular letter-form also contains the two half-circles inside the bow, albeit in slightly different positions and with the space inside the half-circles filled in (Fig. 3.2a). This untypical embellishment is also to be found in an Anglo-Saxon manuscript of the early ninth century,

17 M. Brown 2007, 50.

18 Pers. comm., January 2019.

19 McNamara 1973, 214.

20 Bischoff 1990, 152.

21 O'Neill 2014, 38.

22 Carey 2009, 17.

Fig. 3.1—Faddan More Psalter, detail of f. 3r.

likely a product of Canterbury. On f. 2 of the collection of Saints' Lives (BnF MS latin 10861), the enlarged and highly decorated *P* introduces the account of the life of *Philippus apostolus*. Included in the smaller capitals on the two-column folio are three examples of the back-to-back half-circles and, similar to *Lebor na hUidre*, they are coloured in (Fig. 3.2b).

Examination of the initial *D* from Psalm 6.2 in the FMP reveals that additional 'standard'-size letters are also visible, one attached to the bottom of the letter. In this instance, however, this is one of the 'floating letters' freed from its correct location as the substrate dissolved and deposited it out of place as a result of the fluid conditions in the Tipperary bog; this unique feature must always be considered whenever the writing of this psalter is under scrutiny.

The form of *D* employed for Psalm 6.2 does not remain constant in this psalter, as is evidenced on folio 6r, the beginning of Psalm 13, located at the top of the folio. *Dixit insipiens* survives but is very faint. The *D* is about two lines in height and is an Insular majuscule form of what Bischoff calls a 'round *D*', more resembling an 'o' with the minim (the upright stroke) leaning over the top of the bow and terminating in a wedged serif.[23] Examples of this form can be seen in both the Book of Kells and the Lindisfarne Gospels.

Yet another form of initial D makes an appearance at the beginning of Psalm 20, with *Domine in virtut[e]* on line ten of folio 9r. *Domine* is presented as *Dne*. The *D* is approximately two lines in height. It is a square format, with the two upright strokes slightly concave; the head stroke has a well-defined wedge-shaped serif at one end, the base stroke enclosing the space. Within the square are two half-circles facing back to back, as seen inside the *D* of *Domine* at the beginning of Psalm 6, and although the form of the letter itself is very different the common element of the half-circles suggests the same scribe. Additional double graphic lines in a light colour are barely visible following the contours of the letter (Fig. 3.3).

The free-flowing writing by the scribe carries the final verse of Psalm 20 onto folio 9v; here a third form of *D* occurs. The second line commences Psalm 21.2, *Deus Deus [m]eus respice in me*. The

23 Bischoff 1990, 85.

Fig. 3.2a—RIA MS 23.E.25, *Lebor na hUidre*, p. 55.

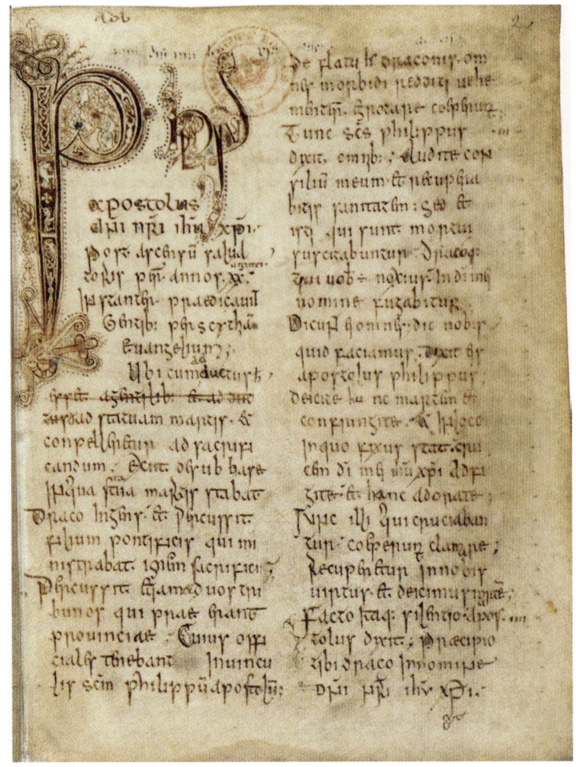

Fig. 3.2ab—BnF MS latin 10861, f. 2.

Fig. 3.3—Faddan More Psalter, f. 9r.

Fig. 3.4—Faddan More Psalter, f. 9v.

abbreviation has been employed and the first *Deus* is almost heart-shaped (with what would be the minim leaning over the top of the letter and terminating in a wedge serif), and the *S* is inside the bow of the *D*. The letter is three lines in height. The second *Deus* is similar, but owing to deterioration the *S* has 'dropped out'. This *D* is about half the size of the first (Fig. 3.4). A similar form and construction can be seen in another Insular manuscript with its origins in the centre of Ireland, the Book of Dimma (TCD MS 59), *c*. 750–800, likely from the same geographic region as the FMP. On page 106 in St John's Gospel, at the top of the page, the *nomen sacrum DM* is written with the same heart-shaped *D* and the *M* inside the bow. It could be argued that both scribes were exposed to similar scribal practices or had seen the same exemplars from which they borrowed the design (Fig. 3.5).

The deterioration and level of loss increase after Psalm 20 and, although identified text fragments do survive, it is not until Psalm 37.2 on folio 16v (quire two) that an initial letter is identified. As before, this is a lone survivor, a single letter fragment, having been located in the area of this quire

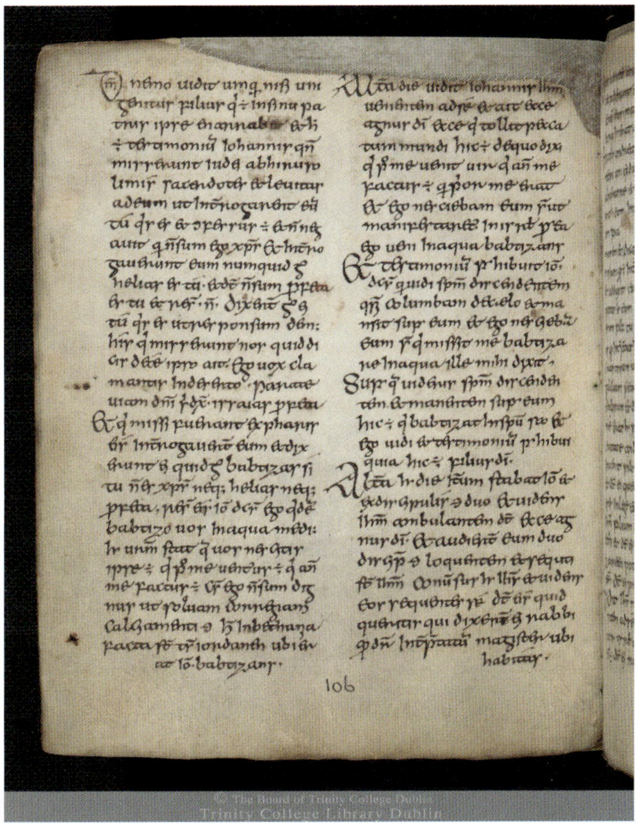

Fig. 3.5—TCD MS 59 (the Book of Dimma), p. 106.

Fig. 3.6—Faddan More Psalter, dislocated 'D'.

during conservation and placed in position on the first line of the folio after identification. The *D* is from *D[omine ne in furore]*... and is likely to have been abbreviated, but this cannot be confirmed. The initial is over two lines in height and commences with a wedged serif. Inside the bow the two back-to-back half-circles are again present (Fig. 3.6).

On the top of folio 34v, quite close to the head, Psalm 82 commences *Deus quis [similis] erit*. The *nomen sacrum* is employed and an Insular *D*, again with the minim leaning over the top of the bow and terminating in a well-formed wedge serif, stands at three lines in height. The *s* is placed inside the bow in its initial form. The *D* mimics the survivors from Psalm 6.2 and 37.2 but it differs from the *D* in *Deus* from Psalm 21.2, which also has the *s* inserted inside the bow, but is heart-shaped. Because the heart-shaped *D* falls between the more standard Insular types of *D* practised in the FMP, it appears that the same scribe was competent in both forms. An additional thin line of colour has been worked on top of the *D* letter-form and possibly also the *s* (Fig. 3.7). Three other examples of this form of *Ds* are found within the loose letters rescued from the floating debris within the mass of material taken from inside the cover (see Chapter 1). Their positional location was recorded but was not precise enough to allow their identification of specific psalm beginnings with confidence. There is an excellent if somewhat obscure parallel to this letter-form within the contents of a composite manuscript brought together in the nineteenth century by Pater Ildefons von Arx (1755–1833) and dedicated to his former supervisor, Pater Johann Nepomuk

Fig. 3.7—Faddan More Psalter, f. 34v.

Hauntinger, Abbey Librarian. Held in St Gallen, Cod. Sang. 1394 contains fragments from the fourth century to the fifteenth century and includes, among the variety of material fragments from the *Aeneid* and the *Georgics* by Virgil, fragments of Hebrew script and—of interest here—an Irish missal fragment (pp 95–8). Previously used as a binding component, the heavily trimmed bifolio now measures 230mm x 220mm. It is written in long line, with 22 lines surviving in both expert Insular majuscule and minuscule. There are several enlarged three-line initials, including a *nomen sacrum* for *Deus* in *Deus placatus accipire* (Fig. 3.8). A drawn *D* is presented with a wedged serif on the terminal of the minim, similar in form to Psalm 82. The wedge has additional flourishes in the form of two circles. The initial *s* is also inside the bow of the *D* but, unlike Psalm 82, it is formed as a continuation of the closing bow of the *D*. This forms a spiral shape for the top half of the *s*, while the bottom half is augmented with a wedged serif and a flourish at its tip. There is no over-drawing with an additional colour as seen on Psalm 82 (Fig. 3.9). The St Gallen catalogue entry for the fragment makes the closing comment: 'Origin of manuscript: written doubtless in Ireland'.[24] Textual similarities in the form of a Eucharistic antiphon used by Columbanus during the liturgy have been noted between this manuscript and the Stowe Missal, which might be a product of Lorrha, Co. Tipperary (see Chapter 6), although the author does not associate the two manuscripts.[25]

Beginning a third of the way down the page on line nine of folio 4r is Psalm 9.2. Without its heading, it begins *Confiteor tibi Domine*. The *tibi* has been inserted above and between *Confiteor* and *Domine*, having been omitted during the original copying of the psalter. Of interest here is *Confiteor*. The *C* is enlarged, written in ink and displays a similar decorative element to the *D* from Psalm 6.2; a half-circle sits inside the bow of the *C*, with its terminal ends attached to the inside face. The wedged serif, a feature of Insular majuscule, is atypically employed at both terminals of the *C* with the addition of flourishes, which are both unusual and well executed (Fig. 3.10). The same use of two wedge serifs is employed on folio 6v with the beginning of Psalm 15, *Conserva me Domine quoniam* (Fig. 3.11). Both examples of the oversized *C* are followed by a few letters of decreasing size

24 I am grateful to Tim O'Neill for bringing this manuscript to my attention.

25 Stevenson 1997, 212.

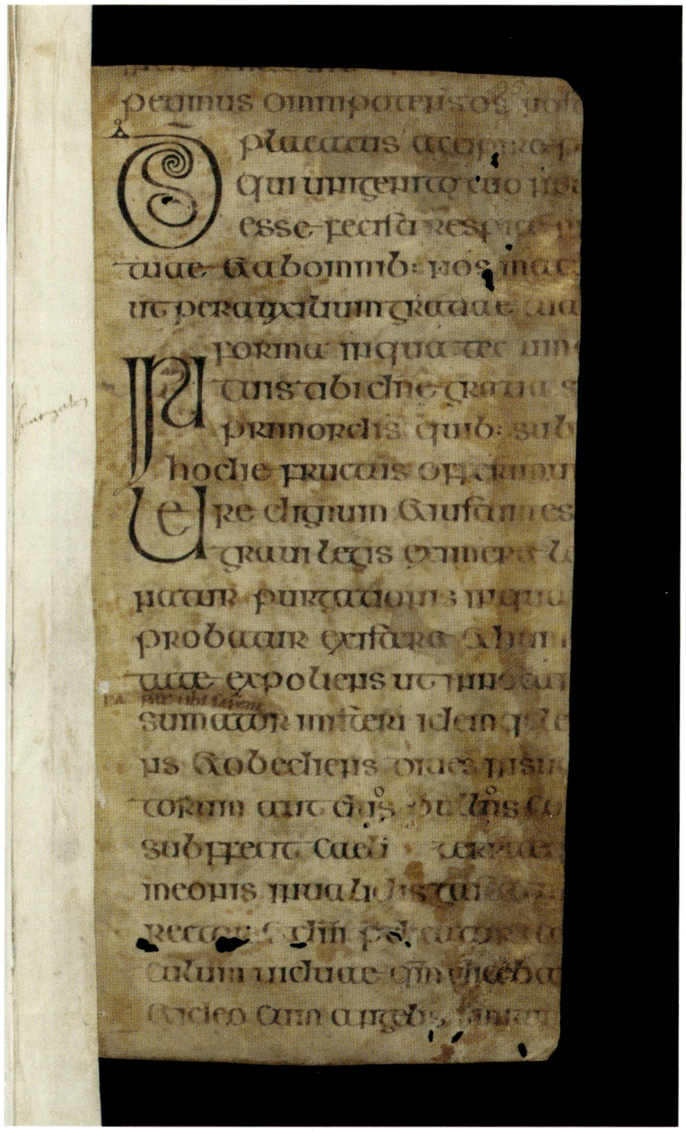

Fig. 3.8—St Gallen, Stiftsbibliothek Cod. Sang. 1394, f. 95.

Fig. 3.9—St Gallen, Stiftsbibliothek Cod. Sang. 1394, f. 95, detail.

Fig. 3.10—Faddan More Psalter, ff 9v-4r.

Fig. 3.11—Faddan More Psalter, f. 6v.

Fig. 3.12—Faddan More Psalter, f. 6v, detail.

until the standard letter-form is reached (Fig. 3.12). This is a 'gentle' form of diminuendo, the Insular convention of the script taking the reader from an enlarged initial letter back to the standard writing.[26] The *Cathach* displays the same feature with more dramatic effect, as can be observed on folio 48r and the beginning of Psalm 90, *Qui habitat in adiutorio altissimi*. The *Q* begins at the height of five lines, followed by the *u*, *i* and *h*, all decreasing incrementally to the *b* at the standard letter size.

A different treatment of the terminals can be seen at the beginning of Psalm 18 on the fourth line of folio 8v. At *Caeli enarrant glor[iam] Dei* the first two words survive intact. The three-lines-high *C* has trumpet terminals with the following *A* placed inside the bow. The left minim extends through the back of the *C* and terminates in a trumpet-like form. The right-hand stroke is vertical, with a wedge-shaped serif at its head. The cross-stroke of the *A* also extends beyond the bow of the *C*, a convention often employed in Insular writing. At the time of examining these letters prior to de-watering the vellum, it was possible to see thin graphic lines inside the body of both letters following their contours (Fig. 3.13). This was either additional decoration or the marking of an area to receive colour—or perhaps evidence of 'building up' the initials.

Another Insular scribal tradition is found at the start of Psalm 11.2. *Salvum me fac Domine* is located on folio 5v. Here there is an elongated *S* with trumpet terminals. The much-enlarged letter extends along the inside edge of the following three lines of text. There is a vertical stroke behind the *S*, matching its length, with a wedged serif at the top. Although the vellum is lost behind this area, it is identifiable as an element of the *S* and what Timothy O'Neill describes as a 'split initial', a double-stemmed letter joining at the base, with the space between the minims left blank; the join is no longer visible in this occurrence[27] (Fig. 3.14). The Book of Dimma, thought to have been produced in Roscrea, less than 20km from Faddan More, displays several examples of the 'split initial'.[28]

26 O'Neill 2014, 12.

27 O'Neill 2017, 290.

28 Gillis and Meehan 2017, 86.

Fig. 3.13—Faddan More Psalter, f. 8v.

Other multiple examples can be seen in Insular manuscripts from the same epoch, including the St Gall Gospels (St Gallen Cod. Sang. 51) and the Stowe Missal. According to O'Neill, this is an evolution of the double-stemmed initials employed in the *Cathach*. An example is seen in Psalm 75.2 (*Notus in Iudaea*), where both minims of the black-inked *N* are split, with the uncoloured vellum as the central line (Fig. 3.15). Another example of diminuendo is seen on the same folio. The remaining letters in *Salvum* quickly drop to standard size, with only the *a* slightly larger.

I had hoped to compare another capital *S* in the FMP, but the only survivor is in very poor condition—located in the third quire, where typically the folios from this part of the manuscript exist as narrow ribbons of vellum at the head, with even narrower occasional strips below the writing space of the page at the tail. On folio 27 the beginning of a psalm is available for scrutiny. Psalm 68.2, *S[al]vum me [fac Deus]*, is located on the first line of folio 27v. The surface is much abraded, and suspended from the head margin is an enlarged capital *S* with wedge terminals. Little else survives of the psalm and the condition of the letter itself limits any descriptive analysis, except to say that it is not the split *S* seen in Psalm 11.2, which again demonstrates the scribe's use of variations of the same letter (Fig. 3.16).

On the verso of folio 29, at the start of line 22, Psalm 73 commences *Ut qui[d] Deus*. The drawn enlarged letter *U* is over two lines in height. Two wedge serifs and a wedge-shaped terminal at the

Fig. 3.14—Faddan More Psalter, f. 5v.

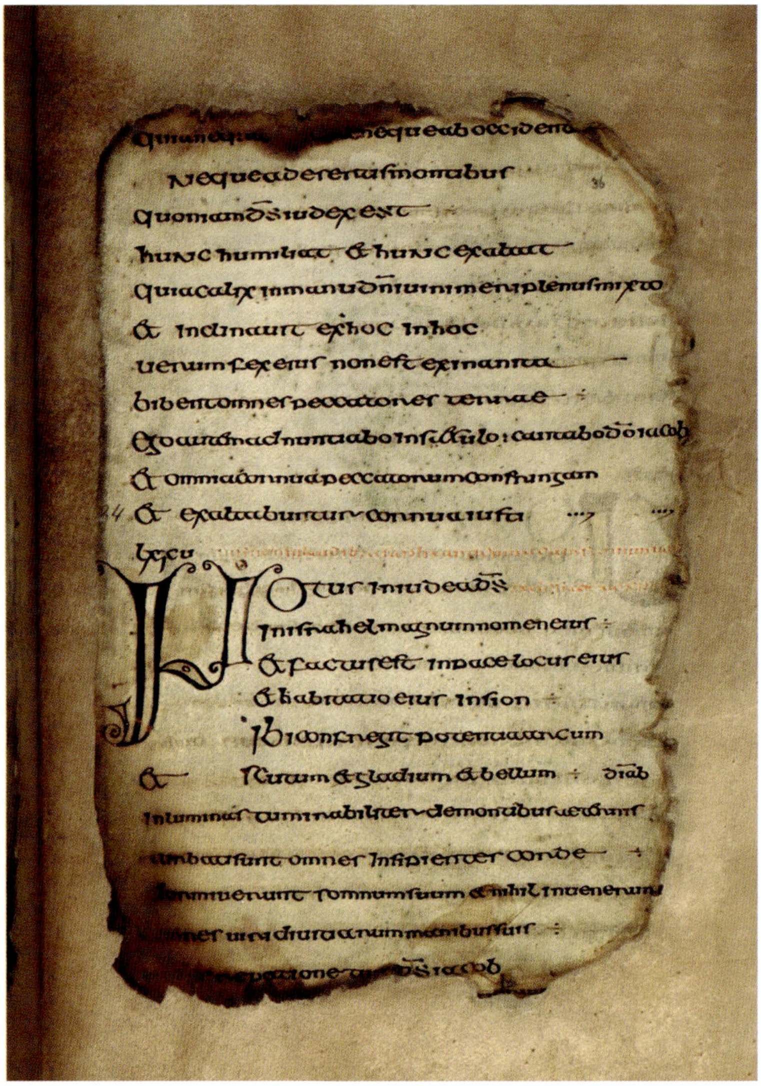

Fig. 3.15—RIA MS D.ii.3, the *Cathach*, p. 36.

Fig. 3.16—Faddan More Psalter, head of f. 27v.

Fig. 3.17—Faddan More Psalter, f. 29v.

base of the right-hand minim are employed. The letter is unremarkable apart from the decorative addition between the two minims: a vertical line of lozenges fills the space, quite crudely executed and worked in the same writing ink (Fig. 3.17). On folio 1r of the FMP the remains of a decorated border running along the head display a similar run of lozenges as part of the decorative infill. In this instance they are filled in with a black pigment and they are discussed later in this chapter. A further example of connected lozenges can be seen carved in stone on one of the 72 surviving early medieval cross-slabs at St Berrihert's Kyle in Ardane, Co. Tipperary. Among the many simple carved Latin crosses there is a slim rectangular slab with a set of vertical connecting lozenges. They differ only from the infill in the *U* on Psalm 73 by virtue of being a double set and placed inside a simple line border (Fig. 3.18). Representations of the technique in metalwork are also available for comparison, such as the eighth-century Helgö crozier terminal (Statens Historiska Museum, Stockholm, Z5075:1000), likely to be of Irish origin but found in Helgö, Sweden, a trading and manufacturing centre.[29] The socket is of copper alloy inlaid with yellow enamel patterns, including vertical rows of lozenges tip to tip, mirroring those on folio 1r but, like the cross-slab, in a vertical orientation (Fig. 3.19).

One of only two surviving examples of an enlarged *B* is found at the bottom of folio 17v. With only the *B* extant from the beginning of Psalm 40.2, *B[eatus qui]*, the Insular majuscule letter displays a wedge serif at the top; the bow does not quite close and ends in a point. As in previous examples, this is a relocated fragment, with other surviving word fragments allowing positive identification and the estimated character count guiding its correct position on the folio (Fig. 3.20). The following 25

29 Murray 2015, 113–14.

Fig. 3.18—Cross-slabs at St Berrihert's Kyle in Ardane, Co. Tipperary.

Fig. 3.19—Statens Historiska Museum, Stockholm, Z5075:1000, Helgö crozier terminal.

folio fragments do not reveal any psalm beginnings, but the surviving text does allow almost all the psalms after Psalm 80 to be identified through small extant fragments of verse. The second *B* is located at the first line of folio 58r in the final fifth quire, from Psalm 143.1, *Benedictus Dominus Deus meus*. The insular *B* has an unclosed bow similar to that of Psalm 40.2, with a wedge serif on both terminals, which could be considered a decorative flourish and not typical in the Insular corpus of manuscripts from this period. The letter is almost three lines in height, with the following *e* about twice the size of a standard letter (Fig. 3.21).

An interesting combination of initials for comparison is provided by Psalm 80.2, *Ex[ultate Deo adiutori]*. Only the first two letters survive, and these only as isolated fragments relocated through an estimation of their position on folio 33v, which is preserved as a fragment of the head margin and the first six lines of text. The insular *e* and *x* are over two lines in height; one minim of the *x* extends under the *e* and makes contact with the bottom of the preceding letter and terminates with a wedge serif. This is mirrored on folio 25r with the beginning of Psalm 60.2, *Exaudi Deus*, seen here while the folio was saturated and the writing easier to decipher (Fig. 3.22, a and b). Similar examples are not difficult to locate in the corpus of Insular manuscripts from the same epoch. One example can be identified by returning to Cod. Sang. 51, where on page 8 a similar execution is seen starting the words *ex surtens*; the '*ex*' is slightly enlarged, and the serif on the *x* is smaller and less defined than in the FMP example

Fig. 3.20—Faddan More Psalter, dislocated 'B'.

Fig. 3.21 — Faddan More Psalter, folio fragment, f. 58r.

(Fig. 3.23). Subtle variations on the Insular majuscule execution of these two letters can be seen in the text of the Book of Kells, the Book of Durrow and the Lindisfarne Gospels.

Another noteworthy—but in this instance difficult to decipher—combination of initials is located on folio 25r. It is the relocated fragment from the beginning of Psalm 61.2, *Nonne Deo subiect[a]*. The writing here is particularly faint and identification was only possible through manipulating the high-resolution digital image by selecting a particular colour value of the faint ink and artificially enhancing any area of this colour. Both vertical bars of the two-line enlarged *N* show well-defined wedge serifs. The second and smaller *N* is placed between the vertical bars of the first as an abbreviation of the word. The application and end-product here suggest a scribe confident in his skills (Fig. 3.24).

Located halfway down 29r, on the only complete bifolio in the manuscript (29–32), line sixteen begins with *Quam bonus Israhel Deus* from Psalm 72.1. The *Q* is almost three lines in height, with a well-defined wedge serif on the termination of the minim. The upper part of the bow is more U-shaped, with a thin crossbar across the top to close the top of the letter. The letter appears to have additional tram lines inside the bow (Fig. 3.25). The execution of this form of Insular *Q* can be seen with the same thin-line crossbar in the mid-eighth-century gospel-book written by Irish monks in Ireland or in the monastery at St Gall in Switzerland. Throughout the long-line text of St Gallen MS 51, slightly enlarged initials mark the start of passages, typically with the addition of some colour. Page 42 gives two examples of the FMP-type *Q*, albeit without the wedge serif (Fig. 3.26).

There is a consistency to the writing in what is available for examination in the FMP, but too little survives to be definitive on how many scribes were involved, if indeed there was more than one. The change in form of most of the initials suggests a certain freedom of choice, with the scribe displaying a breadth of knowledge of the Insular hand and its variations. This is clearly not the work of a novice scribe or a pupil under instruction but rather of a well-practised exponent of the craft. The ease in locating comparisons to letter-forms and letter combinations reinforces the 'good fit' of the FMP among early medieval Irish manuscripts.

Fig. 3.22a—Faddan More Psalter, folio fragment, f. 33v.

Fig. 3.22b—Faddan More Psalter, folio fragment, f. 25r.

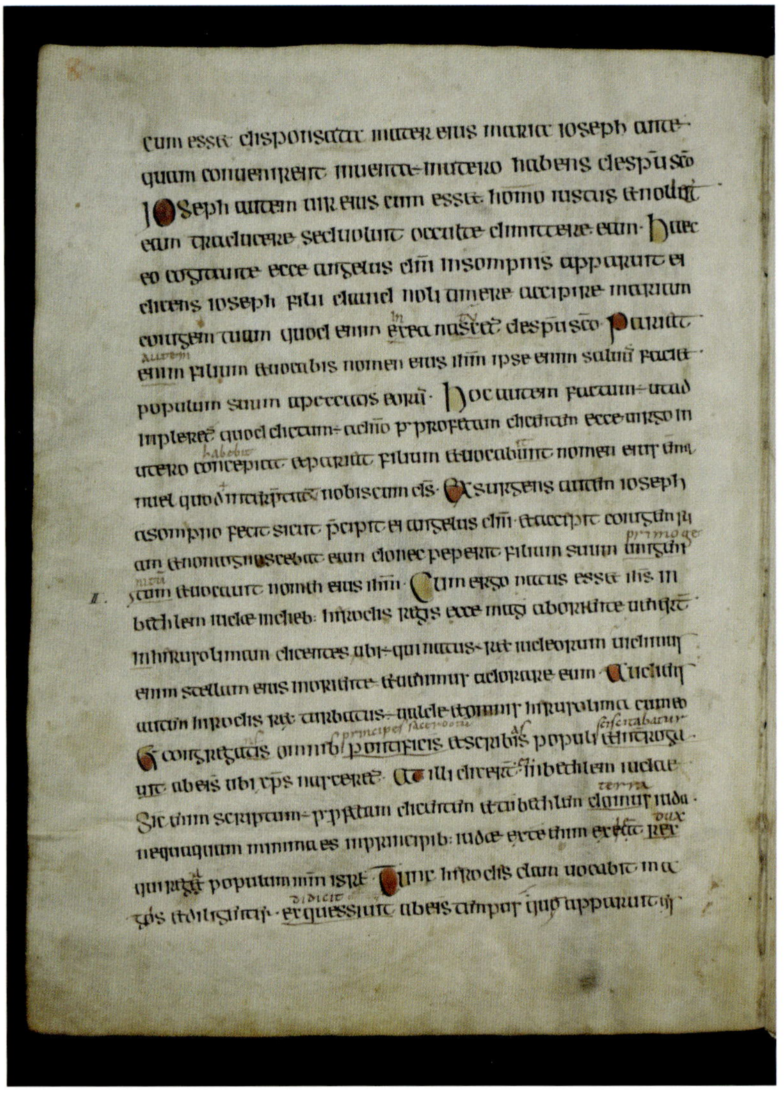

Fig. 3.23—St Gallen, Stiftsbibliothek Cod. Sang. 51, p. 8.

Fig. 3.24—Faddan More Psalter, fragment, f. 25r.

Fig. 3.25—Faddan More Psalter, detail of f. 29r.

DISPLAY LETTERING

Despite the fragmentary and incomplete condition of the FMP, it can be stated with some conviction that the 150 psalms had been divided into three 50s in the Insular tradition and, as was typical for this tradition, the divisions were clearly marked. Psalms 1, 50 and 101 mark the tripartite division of the FMP, with each displaying much-enlarged and decorated lettering at the beginning of the verse. In the case of Psalm 101, however, small fragments of interlace decoration and some oversized dismembered letter-forms are the only extant evidence of the once-elaborate design.

Folio 1r is the first folio in the manuscript, as no flyleaves were included as part of its construction. As such, this folio was directly facing the inside of the leather cover. This layout was not conducive to the survival of the vellum folio, which had deteriorated badly over time (see Chapter 1). The surviving remains are fragmented and disjointed but sufficient to confirm that Psalm 1.1 was presented in a form of display script described as 'geometric display capitals' or 'calligraphic display script'[30] (Fig. 3.27). It is suggested that this form of lettering may have evolved for practical reasons, as it was first used by the stonecutter or the woodcutter for engraving crosses on their respective materials.[31] It is unquestionably easier to engrave in a series of straight lines than in the curved letter-forms of the Insular majuscule hand. This differs from the display lettering for Psalm 51, which, in addition to geometric letters, includes a curvilinear form often employed in Insular gospel-books from the time of the FMP. The combination of both styles of display capitals on the one page, and

30 Higgitt 1994, 210; G. Charles-Edwards 2007, 228.

31 G. Charles-Edwards 2001, 116.

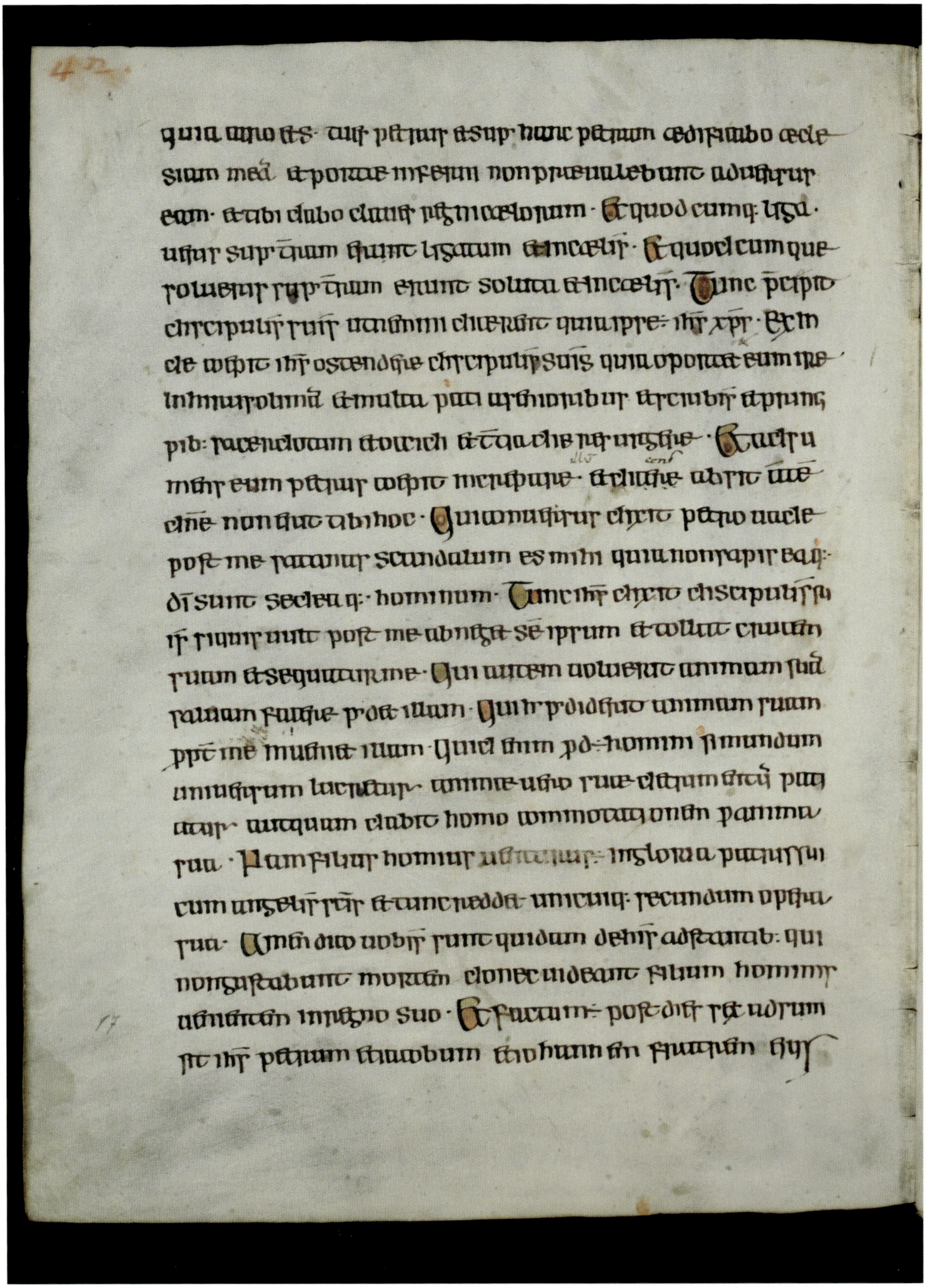

Fig. 3.26—St Gallen, Stiftsbibliothek Cod. Sang. 51, p. 42.

Fig. 3.27—Faddan More Psalter, f. 1r.

even in the one line of text, is mirrored in two pinnacles of Insular manuscript production, the Book of Kells and the Lindisfarne Gospels, and has been a feature considered noteworthy by scholars.[32] Its appearance in the FMP is significant in placing it within a particular corpus of manuscripts that were products of a distinctive tradition of Insular lettering.

Only the first word from the opening verse of Psalm 1.1, *Beatus vir qui non abiit in consilio impiorum*, survives, with the *B* of *Beatus* fragmented and difficult to decipher. It is presented in slim geometric form, with well-defined wedge serifs at the terminals of the minims. The body of the letters is built up with the same ink utilised for the text and would have required more than one stroke of the pen. There is a fine outline following the contour of each letter, with evidence of colour used to fill the space between. The much-enlarged letters occupy four lines of space on the folio (Fig. 3.28).

The origin of this geometric Insular display script has been much discussed and the influence of epigraphy in wood and stone is thought to have influenced its development. The greatest number of geometric Insular inscriptions are to be found in Northumbria, suggesting the region as a possible source for the spread of this decorative display lettering, influenced by the Anglo-Saxon use of the runic alphabet and an earlier exposure to Roman letter-forms prior to Rome's abandonment of its most westerly outpost in the early fifth century.[33] The acceptance of a Northumbrian origin is questioned by more current research, however, and influences from epigraphy and, in the case of Irish-produced books such as the FMP, ogham are suggested as having played a role in the development of geometric lettering.[34] The Book of Durrow is considered to be one of the earliest

32 Higgitt 1994, 210; M. Brown 2012, 134.

33 Higgitt 1994, 217; G. Charles-Edwards 2007, 228.

34 G. Charles-Edwards 2006; Gray 1986, 62.

Fig. 3.28—Faddan More Psalter, detail of f. 1r.

manuscripts to employ the Insular geometric letter-form, albeit in limited quantity.[35] The Book of Kells and the Lindisfarne Gospels have already been cited as examples, and it can also be found in later manuscripts, including the MacRegol Gospels and the Book of Armagh (TCD MS 52), both of which were written in Ireland in the first part of the ninth century.

Extant examples of this letter-form outside the pages of manuscripts also survive in both metal and stone. The eighth-century Ardagh Chalice, discovered in 1868 as part of a hoard of buried objects in County Limerick, has inscribed in outline the names of eleven Apostles and St Paul against a stippled background beneath a girdle of gold filigree on its silver bowl. Higgitt compares the inscription type to the Book of Kells capitals, including matching up some of the letter-forms[36] (Fig. 3.29). The epigraphic application of this letter-form can be seen at Toureen Peakaun, a monastic site in south County Tipperary founded by St Alban in the seventh century. Here, among a number of cross-slabs and cross fragments, is a free-standing cross shaft, 200cm of which is above ground. On the west face of the shaft there is an equal-armed cross with square expanded terminals. Immediately above the cross, a lapidary inscription of six lines of Insular geometric capitals is inscribed, mostly between borders, mimicking the ruling of the manuscript page. Not unlike the FMP, the current condition makes reading and interpretation difficult; it is thought, however, that the text is either partially or wholly in Irish.[37] Carved Insular crosses with inscriptions from the early medieval period employed an Insular majuscule script in most extant examples. The use of geometric lettering at Toureen Peakaun is unusual, despite the epigraphic history of the letter-form. A noticeable and typical feature of geometric lettering is its placement between well-defined borders and those borders containing the letters with little in the way of ascenders or descenders. Although the few surviving letters on folio 1r of the FMP are much disturbed and the surrounding areas of the folio are for the most part lacking, there is enough extant evidence to suggest that the geometric Insular capitals were not contained, at least at their base, with the descenders of the *A* and *T* from *BEATUS* extending well below their companion letters. Furthermore, study of the badly fragmented *B* prior to the dismantling

35 Higgitt 1994, 214.

36 *Ibid.*, 216.

37 Okasha and Forsyth 2001, 292.

Fig. 3.29—National Museum of Ireland, Ardagh Chalice inscription.

of the fragmented text block revealed, in addition to its interlace pattern, that the outline of the letter sits above that of its companions at the head, which are most unusual executions for this form of geometric lettering, since as a general rule the letters maintain the same height. Again, the extreme and unique disturbance of the FMP text and the possibility of distorted or misplaced letter fragments must be taken into account, but in this instance I believe that there is a variation in letter heights.

Examining the extant letters individually, a very close comparison is identified for the *A*, in which the right minim is vertical with a left-facing wedge serif at the top and a trumpet form at the bottom. The left-hand minim is set at an angle and commences about a third of the way down the vertical right-hand minim. The cross-stroke is also placed at an acute angle between the two. This 'tilted' *A* is similar to one illustrated on folio 130r of the Book of Kells, the incipit of St Mark's Gospel and the word *evangelii*; here the vertical right-hand minim is part of the ligature with *N* (Fig. 3.30). Another example is available in the Lindisfarne Gospels on folio 27r, although the similarities are less striking. The *T* has an elongated minim with a short horizontal stroke at the top, the right side of which is not visible, as the space is filled by the wedge serif on the adjacent *U*. At the foot of the minim there is a line projecting at right angles to the right. This resembles the *T* from *Initium*, also on the incipit page of St Mark's Gospel in Cod. Sang. 51, p. 79, which has a right-facing projection at the foot of the minim, albeit shorter than in the FMP (Fig. 3.31). It is also possible that this projection in the FMP example might be part of a now-lost border decoration for *BEATUS*. The *U* has two closely spaced minims joined at the base of the letter. The top of each minim displays well-defined left-facing wedge serifs. Comparative examples are not difficult to find as an archetypal geometric Insular display letter; for instance, in the Lichfield Gospels (Lichfield Cathedral Library MS 1), p. 221, the incipit of Luke has similar *U* letter-forms among the *Quoniam*

Fig. 3.30—TCD MS 58, Book of Kells, incipit of St Mark's Gospel.

Fig. 3.31 — St Gallen, Stiftsbibliothek Cod. Sang. 51, incipit of St Mark's Gospel, p. 79.

quidem multi conati (Fig. 3.32). In the Book of Kells, f. 114v, Matthew 26:31, *Tunc dicit illis Iesus omnes vos scan[dalum]*, the *v* is a good match with the same left-facing wedge serifs.

The *S* in the *BEATUS* of the FMP has a very simple form with a vertical minim and no noticeable horizontal terminals. These parts of the letter-form are represented by a wedged terminal at each end of the vertical, although the bottom one is now detached and no doubt faced in the opposite direction to the wedge at the top. A similar form can be seen in the display script of the word *Peccavimus* on p. 426 of the composite manuscript in St Gallen, Switzerland (Cod. Sang. 1395), which contains several Irish fragments dating from the seventh to ninth centuries. The *e* is in majuscule form rather than the more typical capital employed for the geometrical Insular script (Fig. 3.33). Similarities between this folio and the aforementioned Stowe Missal have been noted.[38]

The *B* of *BEATUS* has survived in a poor state, being somewhat fragmented and 'floating' free. It is difficult to be certain of its original form and some speculation is required. What can be confirmed is the use of an interlace pattern inside the bow of the capital *B* as part of its construction. There are other fragmented minims and letter parts located on this folio which are awaiting further work and identification in the near future.

On folio 22r in the second quire, Psalm 51 commences on the sixth line, *Quid g[loriatur]*. The *q*

38 Ó Cróinín 2018, 22.

Fig. 3.32—Lichfield Cathedral Library MS 1, Lichfield Gospels, incipit of St Luke's Gospel, p. 221.

Fig. 3.33—St Gallen, Stiftsbibliothek Cod. Sang. 1395, p. 426.

is presented as the largest letter of those that survive, standing to a height of eleven lines (Fig. 3.34). This example of Insular display script combines Higgitt's type (i) and type (ii), with both 'freer curvilinear lettering that is coloured and usually zoomorphic in form' and 'a more rigid, calligraphic and frequently angular capitals'.[39] This is no great surprise, as the FMP uses the stylistic format employed on the pages of other Insular manuscripts of the era, the mixture apparently being derived from Insular half-uncial (Insular majuscule) and Roman capitals. The treatment of this lettering does not, however, follow the more typical framing of the letters within decorated borders; instead, it is simply inserted into the line structure of the text, with no special treatment or isolation of the display lettering for visual impact. Michelle Brown identifies this particular treatment of Insular display capitals in other manuscripts and expresses the opinion that it is a development from the calligraphic

39 Higgitt 1994, 210.

Fig. 3.34—Faddan More Psalter, Psalm 51, f. 22r.

diminuendo lettering of the *Cathach* of Columcille, 'evolving into the monumental display openings of the great insular Gospelbooks'.[40] Brown cites Durham Cathedral Library MS A.II.10, the Book of Durrow and the Echternach Gospels as transitional manuscripts with more elaborate display lettering that occupies greater space on the page. Although it would be tempting, therefore, to apply this principle to the incipit of Psalm 51 in order to place the FMP chronologically among the corpus of Irish/Insular manuscripts, Brown cautions that the continuing use of smaller unframed lettering continued throughout the eighth century.[41]

The *q* is dominated by the very large bow, formed with a narrow-drawn outline in proportion to its size and using what appears to be the same ink employed for the text. At the centre of the bow is a small square, with an equal-armed cross further dividing the square into four equal-sized segments. The four arms of the cross extend out to the inner parameters of the bow, dividing the bow into four sections. There are expanded terminals on each arm of the cross where it contacts the inside of the bow, forming a small square with a cross inside. Each of the four quadrants of the bow is subdivided by another thin-armed cross. In the two lower quadrants there is a central square with an equal-armed cross placed inside. The centre of the two upper quadrants displays a geometric pattern forming a squat equal-armed cross. The divided spaces within all the quadrants are defined with an outline and blocks of contrasting colours. The yellow, which has been identified as orpiment, is manifest.[42]

40 M. Brown 2003, 238.

41 *Ibid.*, 240.

42 XRF analysis was carried out in the National Museum's Conservation Department by Dr Paul Mullarkey on a small fragment of the vellum with the yellow pigment present. It displayed the signature peak of arsenic sulphide.

Fig. 3.35—Oseberg no. 157, the Oseberg enamelled mount.

Other colours are present but are difficult to distinguish, although a typical Insular palette is expected, with red, blue, purple and green all likely candidates. The geometric divisions within the bow of the *q* and the use of blocks of vivid colour are reminiscent of contemporary enamelwork, and the same geometric division and infill can be seen in elements of the Moylough belt-shrine (NMI 1945:81), found in County Sligo and dated to the eighth century. Particular pieces of the Staffordshire hoard, a collection of seventh-century decorative objects bearing both Christian and pagan symbolism, display similar treatment. A sword pyramid (Staffordshire Hoard Cat. 752) employing *cloisonné* methods with garnets and blue glass surrounded by gold geometric borders is but one example. The Oseberg enamelled mount (Oseberg no. 157) displays geometric patterns around a central cruciform shape. The vivid yellow glass of the latter makes for a particularly interesting comparison to the FMP *q*. The mount, dating from the eighth or ninth century, was discovered in the furnished grave of a Viking noblewoman, possibly one of the spoils of a raid on an Irish settlement (Fig. 3.35).[43] The influence of Insular metalwork on the artists who decorated the gospel-books and psalters of the era is well attested.[44] Stylistic similarities to the decorated *q* can also be found on the vellum folios of Insular manuscripts and the cross carpet-page on folio 1v of the eighth-century Book of Durrow, which employs geometric blocks of colour forming a series of crosses, here combined with intricate interlace work (Fig. 3.36). The FMP displays an interesting mark/addition in the top expanded terminal of the cross: in the top left division of the square there is a pen stroke creating a curve suggestive of the *chi-rho* symbol, X and P (a monogram of Christ's name when written in Greek). When clearly depicted, the P intersects the X, but it was also represented

43 Youngs 1989, 61.

44 Netzer 2011, 9; Ryan 1989, 127; L. de Paor 1977, 101; Moss 2014b, 107; Gleeson 2014, 107.

Fig. 3.36—TCD MS 57, Book of Durrow, carpet-page, f. 1v.

Fig. 3.37—TCD MS 55, Usserianus Primus, *chi-rho* cross, f. 149v.

more subtly by using an illustrated or carved cross as the *chi*, with the *rho* depicted as a loop at the top of the cross. An example can be seen in Codex Usserianus Primus (TCD MS 55), the pre-Vulgate gospel-book produced in Ireland or abroad under Irish influence (Fig. 3.37). The same interpretation can be seen on the small grave-marker found at Inis Cealtra, Co. Clare, and dated to the mid-seventh century.[45] It is evident that the *rho* stroke or curve in the FMP *q* is intentional; the only caveat is its left-side (as opposed to right-side) application to represent the bow of the P, a scribal error perhaps.

The descender of the FMP *q* has a zoomorphic aspect in the form of a bird head in profile. The long, hooked beak is well defined below a round eye with an almond-shaped outline. The head of the bird appears to have some form of plumage, which flows back in a zigzag pattern and was highlighted with colour. The body of the bird is represented by the curved stroke of the letter under the bow. Beneath the bird's head is a single zigzag pattern, starting under the beak and continuing back until loss of the vellum terminates it. Identification of the bird as a hawk, peacock or other species with Christian symbolic meaning is not obvious. The zigzag plumage and the pattern are unusual and do not appear to be repeated in any Insular illuminated manuscripts of the same epoch.

The remaining letters of *Quid* drop down one line and are reduced in size to five lines in height. The letter-form returns to the sharp geometric type. The letters are drawn with broad minims outlined with a thinner line that encases the letter. The *U* and *I* are combined by inserting the *I* into the centre of the *U*, which resembles a 'V' shape with serifs on the two minims. There is a cross-bar at the base of the *U* with short upright strokes and serifs at the end of each stroke. This is similar to Higgitt's type V3 and he cites examples in the Book of Kells, the Book of Armagh and the Leningrad Gospels (Cod. F. v.I.8).[46] Graphically, the FMP example differs in having the serifs attached to the upright strokes as opposed to directly to the cross-bar. Examples of the FMP-type cross-bar can be observed, albeit rotated 180° and resting precariously on the top of an *A*, on the symbol page of Matthew in the Echternach Gospels (f. 18v) and likewise on the John symbol page (f. 176v). In addition, on the same page an example of a 'V'-shaped *U* with an *I* inserted inside is executed. The Echternach Gospels are considered to date from the late eighth or early ninth century and are possibly a product of one of the monasteries in Northumbria or of Iona or Ecternach (Fig. 3.38).[47] The Ardagh Chalice, employing geometric letters, also uses the cross-bar *U* on its inscription. On the opening page of Cod. Sang. 15, a psalter dating from the ninth

45 De Paor and de Paor 1964, 63; L. de Paor 1977, 99.

46 Higgitt 1994, 232.

47 J. Brown 1993, 130; Meehan 2018, 111.

Fig. 3.38—Paris, Bib. MS lat. 9389, Echternach Gospels, symbol of John, f. 176v.

century and possibly produced in France, the *Beatus vir* page from Psalm 1.1 displays lettering and illumination 'heavily influenced by Irish models', according to the library's catalogue entry.[48] In the framed panel of text, both the *V* and the *U* are presented with the *I* inserted inside (Fig. 3.39). Based on the parallels of geometric letter types used in the FMP, the scribe or artist is patently aware of and exposed to the current practice in this form of decorated writing.

The geometric *D* is adopted from the uncial type and, as executed in the FMP, is a basic rectangle; as such, it replicates many of the Insular geometric examples in manuscripts from the same period. Blocks of varying colour inside thin drawn frames are inserted between the letters of *Quid*, filling the spaces of blank vellum and creating a closer visual coherence with the multi-coloured core of the *q*. A similar approach of creating a backdrop for the enlarged illuminated opening words to parts of the canonical text was widely practised among the scribes and artists producing manuscripts in the early medieval period. The use of different blocks of colour, shaped to fit between the letters, similar to the *Quid* in

48 See https://www.e-codices.unifr.ch/en/searchresult/list/one/csg/0015 (accessed 1 April 2018).

Fig. 3.39—Cod. Sang. 15, Psalm 1.1, *Beatus vir*, p. 1.

the FMP, can be seen to good effect on folio 78 of the Leningrad gospel-book at the opening to Mark. Adjudged as an Insular work of the late eighth century, E.A. Lowe attributes it to Northumbria.[49] A similar treatment of the geometric letters with a less-refined execution is displayed in the already mentioned Cod. Sang. 51 on p. 7, the 'Xpi' illuminated page (Fig. 3.40, a and b).

Only the *g* of *gloriatur* has survived on the fragment of folio 22r of the FMP, and here there is a return to an Insular majuscule letter-form at the same five-line height as the preceding letters. The left-hand upward-pointing serif on the cross-bar of the letter *g* is of a type practised in the standard text of the Book of Kells, the Book of Durrow, the Lichfield Gospels and others. No text has survived below this line on folio 22, but on the verso of the same folio the first line starts with Psalm 52.3. Applying the calculated character count per line of text, it is possible to estimate the space required on folio 22r to fit from *gloriatur* in Psalm 51.3 to *requirens Deum* in 52.3. In order to achieve this, the writing would have dropped to standard size after *gloriatur*. Tim O'Neill's reproduction on vellum of this psalm expertly demonstrates how the pristine folio would have looked (Fig. 3.41).

49 Lowe 1966, 1621.

Fig. 3.40a–Cod. F. v.I.8, Leningrad Gospel, incipit of St Mark's Gospel, p. 78.

Fig. 3.40b–Cod. Sang. 51, 'Xpi' illuminated page, p. 7.

The expected location for Psalm 101 and its treatment as the beginning of the last of the 'three fifties' was folio 40v, but the surviving fragment of this folio terminated at the end of Psalm 100. The removal of this quire fragment from the mass of material inside the open leather cover also brought with it other fragments of the vellum folios in a more advanced stage of deterioration (see Chapter 1). Among this material was a collection of individual enlarged majuscule letters with blocks of yellow painted into blank spaces and one piece of square interlace inside a narrow double border (Figs 3.42 and 3.43). Writing on the recto of this fragment was identified after scrutiny as two fragmentary lines from Psalm 98.4/5, *d[i]r[e]ctiones iu[dicium]* and *[sca]billum* (Fig. 3.44). This allowed accurate positioning and orientation of the piece, using the surviving text from Psalm 98 on folio 40r. Without the psalm headings, as is the practice in the FMP, Psalm 101 would commence *Domine exaudi orationem meam*. Examining the enlarged majuscule letter fragments, it might be tentatively possible to identify a *D* and an *M*. It would be expected, even in the case of enlarged decorated lettering, for *Dominum* to be abbreviated to *DM*. Other fragmented and distorted letters survive, but identification is speculative at best.

Similar to the ordinary writing in the FMP, the decoration and decorated lettering confirm a stylistic knowledge of current practice, attested by the close parallels available in typical media of the period. Clearly the work of the artist does not match that of the Book of Kells or the Lindisfarne Gospels, or even of his close neighbour MacRegol, but it still sits comfortably in the framework of early medieval Insular manuscript-making by a proficient exponent. It also displays what I believe to be a most unusual treatment of the geometric lettering by allowing certain minims to break through the typical framing used to contain the word or words. The unfortunate aspect is the poor condition of the vellum whereon this feature is employed, making it difficult to be definitive. The use of geometric lettering without a border for Psalm 51 tentatively suggests an earlier use of the letter-form and could assist in placing the manuscript in the eighth century from an art-historical perspective.

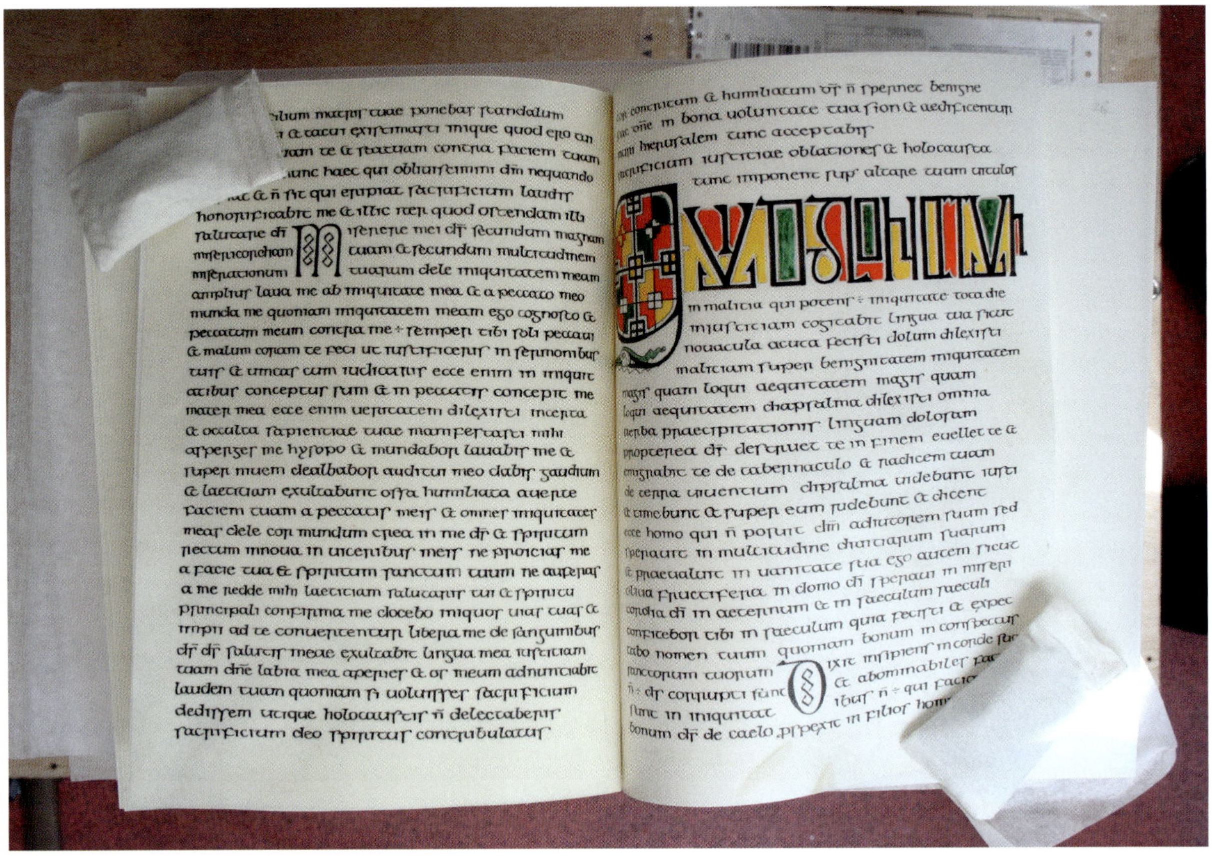

Fig. 3.41 — Psalm 51.3, reproduction by Timothy O'Neill.

Fig. 3.42 — Faddan More Psalter, initial letter fragments.

Fig. 3.43—Faddan More Psalter, initial letter and decoration fragments.

OTHER EXTANT DECORATION IN THE FADDAN MORE PSALTER

In addition to the decorated letter-forms, one distinct area of illumination has survived on folio 1r: a broad border, which probably enclosed the text of Psalm 1 but now survives only along the top edge and as it turns 90° down the fore-edge. The construction is quite intricate: the outer margins of the border consist of two narrow drawn parallel lines, with the space between coloured. Between these lines, individual panels with their own borders contain the elements of decoration and make up the overall pattern. A single panel is employed as the border turns the corner from head to fore-edge. It contains a multi-coloured interlace pattern, with which the practitioner appears to have had some difficulty navigating the turn, a stray ribbon not following the expected pattern (Fig. 3.27). Errors like this, where a clear understanding of the architecture behind interlace is lacking, appear in other manuscripts of the period. Mildred Budny points out 'the botched version of interlaced animals in an initial P in the ninth-century Antwerp Sedulius'.[50] The ribbon interlace in the FMP border displays the use of at least two colours, a yellow and perhaps a red; stylistically, where a strand comes to the end of its frame, a U-bend system has been practised, employing Budny's diagnostics.[51]

The use of interlace is ubiquitous among all media of Insular art forms in the early Middle Ages and is nowhere more prolific than on the pages of gospel-books and psalters, particularly as a form of border. The origin of this complex and structured design element and its enthusiastic adoption by Insular artisans are much discussed and often written about by scholars. Mark Van Stone examines and explains the basic methods used to produce what he calls 'knotwork' across several Insular manuscripts. The premise revolves around the use of a frame and a series of dots which guide the pen to quickly build up a pattern.[52] These guiding dots can sometimes still be seen, particularly with the help of magnification, such as in the portrait of St John in Cod. Sang. 51 (p. 201), which places the evangelist inside a border of interlace, and close examination reveals the guiding dots as the artist's aid.

50 Budny 2001, 191.

51 *Ibid.*, 185.

52 Van Stone 1994, 240.

Fig. 3.44—Faddan More Psalter, text from Psalm 98.4.

At the top of the border a series of dark lozenges with the spaces between filled with two alternating colours, yellow and red(?), run across the folio. Within each lozenge, four small squares sit against the four sides of the form. Although not as prolific as interlace, the geometric lozenge pattern makes a regular appearance on the decorated pages of Insular manuscripts of the same epoch, including the carpet-page of the eighth-century Barberini Gospels (Vatican City, Biblioteca Apostolica Vaticana Barb. Lat. 570), f. 2v, and on the opening of John, f. 211r. A run of three plain lozenges tip to tip are placed in the columns of the arch enclosing King David and musicians in the Vespasian Psalter (British Library Cotton MS Vespasian A.I), f. 30v, a ninth-century product from southern England displaying Mediterranean influences. The feature appears several times in the Book of Kells, including a principal role in the decoration of the four symbols page, f. 290v, where one lozenge sits inside a larger lozenge to form the crossing point of the saltire cross that divides the page into four. Its use extended beyond the vellum of manuscripts and was practised by the artisans of both stone and metalwork. A lozenge panel sits high up on the west face of the shaft of the Moone High Cross above a number of religious iconographic scenes from both the Old and the New Testament (Fig. 3.45).[53] In metalwork, lozenges can be found on early medieval artefacts, both liturgical and secular; examples are seen on such high-status artefacts as the Tara Brooch, the Cross of Cong and the Derrynaflan Chalice (Fig. 3.46). The lozenge as a Christian symbol is believed to represent the Second Person of the Trinity, the *Logos* or Word of God.[54]

Beneath the border pattern at the head of folio 1, the figure of a bird in profile looks out towards the edge of the page. Although the species cannot be identified with absolute certainty, it displays the distinguishing features of a predatory bird, including the large round eye and hooked beak. These features are typically accompanied by sharp talons but this expected trait is lacking, along with the

---

53 The granite cross, like many high crosses, is difficult to date with accuracy and anywhere from the eighth to the tenth century has been proposed. It is a ringed cross in three sections, standing to a height of 7.65m. The site of the cross is believed to be that of an early Columban monastery. The base is a tall rectangular block with a truncated pyramid on top. It was discovered originally without the shaft, which was located buried in Moone Abbey churchyard, Co. Kildare. In modern times it has been moved inside the ruin of the nearby church, which had a glass roof added to offer protection from the weather. See Powell 2007, 36–45; de Bhaldraithe 2009.

54 Richardson 1996; Meehan 2012, 125.

Fig. 3.45—Moone High Cross, Co. Kildare, west face.

Fig. 3.46—National Museum of Ireland, Tara Brooch, detail.

tail, owing to the loss of vellum in these areas (Fig. 3.47). Comparisons are not difficult to locate in the lexicon of Insular manuscripts from the same era and similar forms are seen in the same profile view. I draw attention to two examples here. On folio 176v of the Echternach Gospels, the full-page image of the eagle with all the requisite features stands on a perch surrounded by the description *Imago Aquile* (Fig. 3.38). Perhaps a more relevant example is to be found in one of the Irish pocket gospels, the Book of Dimma, which, as we have seen, was likely produced close to the location of Faddan More. On p. 104, John's eagle is again displayed as a full-page image, in this instance holding an FMP-type cover in its talons (see Chapter 4) (Fig. 3.48). The well-defined beak of the FMP bird is yellow and closed with an exaggerated hook at its end, which is rather rounded at the tip. The black pupil is clearly visible, but any other feature of the eye is difficult to make out. Yellow segments form the bird's neck in a collar-like manner. The front of the body is drawn as two

Fig. 3.47—Faddan More Psalter, bird, f. 1r.

interlocking curves, one yellow and the other a darker colour, possibly red. There is further detail inside the darker curve, now difficult to see. The wings and the rear part of the body display two arches reaching backwards; the upper is again coloured in yellow, with the lower in the darker colour. Beneath is a panel that originally contained some decorative detail but survives only as a 'shadow'. Continuing use of digital enhancement will hopefully bring more clarity to this prevalent issue in the FMP as research continues.

As a zoomorphic feature in the FMP, the eagle on folio 1 represents one of two surviving examples (the other as described as a feature of the 'Q' in Psalm 51). Different species of birds were well established in the repertoire of animal decoration in Insular manuscripts at the time of the FMP (Fig. 3.34). The adoption of animal figures from pagan Anglo-Saxon metalwork onto the pages of early medieval Irish gospel-books and psalters is a regular feature (Figs 3.38, 3.48, 3.49a, 3.49b, 3.49c).[55] The Irish artists avoided lifelike interpretations of their subjects, often resulting in strange limb angles and extravagant polychrome garments, plumage or fur. It is commonly believed that many of the animals depicted had Christian symbolic significance—none more so than the eagle of St John the Evangelist. The FMP is not a gospel-book, however, and the bird on folio 1 may hold a different symbolic meaning, or none whatsoever.[56]

Although now very faint, a chain of dots can be observed closely outlining the figure of the bird (Fig. 3.47). The use of dots, most typically red, as an element of decoration in early Insular manuscripts is ubiquitous and the FMP is no exception. The adaption of this technique has links with metalwork. Inga Morris, while discussing the appearance of dots in Carolingian manuscripts and the influence of Irish manuscripts of the seventh century, suggests that Irish artists may possibly have been inspired by metalworkers of the same period, and that these might in fact have been the same individuals.[57] The use of dots in metalwork is seen to great decorative effect on the Ardagh Chalice, dated to the first half of the eighth century,[58] as a background to the display script listing the names of the Apostles (Fig. 3.29). Dots used in decorative metalwork can also be found on pre-Christian Celtic bronze, applied to the surface of domestic objects dating from 300–100 BC.[59] Dotting on Irish manuscripts is first seen employed around the cross in the undated but clearly early Usserianus Primus (TCD MS 55) (Fig. 3.37). Scholars have over time also pointed towards a Coptic influence for the use of dots.[60] Examples of early Coptic textiles show the use of dots in the fourth century AD (Fig. 3.50). Alexander also suggests the influence of Christian decorated texts from the late antique period, citing the Greek Dioscorides manuscript.[61] Of the many Irish manuscripts from the period of the FMP employing the use of dots as

55 De Paor and de Paor 1964, 114; Laing 2010, 115; Moss 2014a, 63.

56 Herman 2017, 118.

57 Morris 1965, 26.

58 Rynne 1987.

59 Willingham 2003, 306.

60 De Paor and de Paor 1964, 112.

61 Alexander 1978a, 10.

Fig. 3.48—TCD MS 59, Book of Dimma, incipit of St John's Gospel, p. 104.

part of their repertoire, the Book of Dimma, already highlighted because of its close geographic and production date, is again illustrated. The use of red dots around the head of the eagle of St John is a noteworthy comparison, given the same subject-matter chosen for this treatment as in the FMP (Fig. 3.48). It is interesting how this small manuscript suggests itself for comparison across various features present in the FMP. Although written in an Insular minuscule hand by several scribes, features of the decoration and initials match up closely, and if a mid-eighth-century date for Dimma is accepted it could push the making of the FMP back to that period.[62]

62 Gillis and Meehan 2017, 88.

Fig. 3.49a—St Gallen, Stiftsbibliothek Cod. Sang. 60, incipit of St John's Gospel, p. 4.

Fig. 3.49b—St Gallen, Stiftsbibliothek Cod. Sang. 51, incipit of St John's Gospel, p. 208.

Fig. 3.49c—RIA MS D.ii.3, Stowe Missal, portrait of St John, f. 11v.

Fig. 3.50—Coptic textile (https://quizlet.com/23335957/textile-history-test-2-flash-cards/).

In the same way that the initials and decorated lettering display a knowledge of current practices, the use of the decorative elements reinforces this and indicates an awareness of developments beyond the monastic midland location. The decorative elements in particular seem to me to have the qualities found in the MacRegol Gospels, produced 6km from Faddan More and approximately half a century later.

ADDITIONAL TEXT

A noteworthy palaeographical feature of the FMP is that, unlike the majority of extant early medieval manuscripts, it lacks any additional writing, such as marginalia, colophons or interlinear glosses, and also has very few corrections. This augments the significance of what additional material is to be found. The lack of this characteristic is interesting and prompts a comparison with a miracle of St Columba as recorded by Adomnán. When Baithéne came to St Columba and asked him to help with any corrections for a psalter that he had copied, the saint replied: 'Why do you bring this trouble on us when there is no need? For in your copy of the psalter there is no mistake—neither one letter too many, nor one too few—except that in one place the letter I is missing.'[63] In the case of the FMP, however, it must be remembered that all evidence is based on less than a third of the complete text.

Located along the head margin of folio 40r are five letters in an Insular majuscule hand: *a b* (*c* or *e*) *e* and *e* (Fig. 3.51). The letters are undoubtedly a pen trial, a device used by the scribe to test a newly trimmed quill, or alternatively for a novice scribe to practise his letter-forms. *Lebor na hUidre* or the Book of the Dun Cow (RIA MS 23.E.25), the late eleventh-century manuscript of Irish sagas, historical and spiritual tracts and the legends of Irish kings, written in the monastery at Clonmacnoise, Co. Offaly, displays on the top of page 55 *Probatio pennae Maelmuiri* ('a trial of pen by Mael Muire'), the principal scribe of the manuscript. Although he wrote the text in Irish, this trial was in Latin and was probably an exercise that Mael Muire had learned and repeated many times as a novice monk being instructed in Latin and writing. Monastic instruction in writing included at its base level the transcribing of the alphabet,[64] *abecedarium*, and this is reflected in the letters with which the Faddan More scribe chose to test his pen. An inscribed slate fragment from the monastic site at Nendrum on Strangford Lough, Co. Down, is believed to be a practice piece and is an interesting parallel to the letters on folio 40r, bearing the same opening alphabet letters *b* and *c* (Fig. 3.52).

Fig. 3.51—Faddan More Psalter, detail at head of f. 40r.

On the last extant line of folio 4v, Psalm 9.21 reads: *super eos sciant gentes quoniam homines sunt*. The scribe omitted the word *gentes* and it was inserted above the line in its intended position. The writing is fainter and lighter in colour—possibly the work of the master scribe in his corrections of the text. Further up the folio on line seven, the word *cognoscetur* is written with

63 Sharpe 1995, 129, I:23.

64 Bischoff 1990, 39; McGrath 1979, 68.

Fig. 3.52—Nendrum, Co. Down, slate fragment.

Fig. 3.53—Faddan More Psalter, saturated folio, f. 4v.

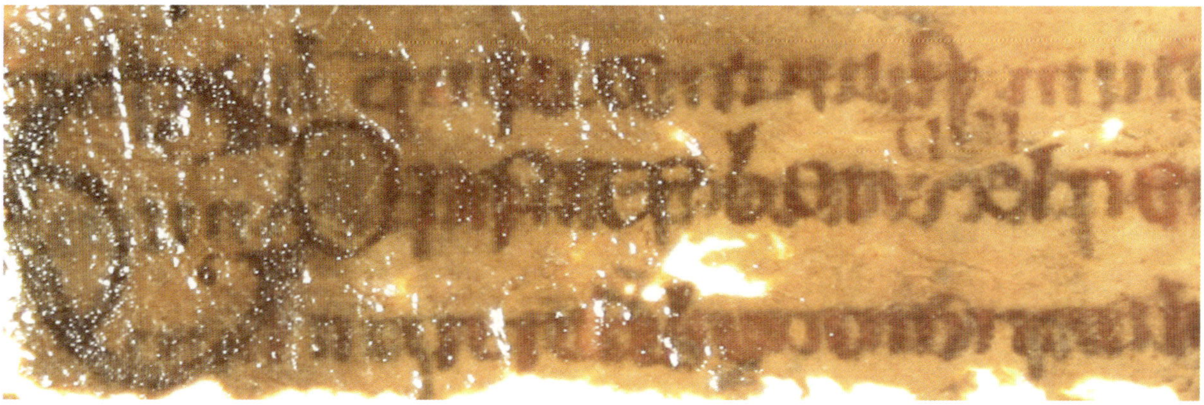

Fig. 3.54—Faddan More Psalter, detail of f. 4r.

the *n* omitted and inserted above the word in a reduced size (Fig. 3.53). The trouble that was taken to correct the FMP text is another indicator that the manuscript was the product of a structured monastic community, where the correction of texts was an integral aspect of the production process.[65]

On the recto of the same folio is the beginning of Psalm 9.2, *Confitebor tibi Domine in corde meo*. The scribe omitted *tibi* and again it is inserted above the line in the correct position (Fig. 3.54). The observation here is that all the interlinear corrections found in the surviving folio fragments of the FMP are on the one folio, namely folio 4. There are additional scribal errors present throughout the text, mostly relating to misspellings (see Appendix 4). This does not suggest an incompetent scribe at work and the FMP displays a typical array of mistakes seen in the majority of early medieval manuscripts. It is possible that the correcting of the remaining psalms never took place owing to the psalter's premature deposition in the bog—examined in detail in Chapter 7—or as a result of structural damage and subsequent disposal (see Chapter 2).

In addition to the *nomina sacra* employed throughout and consistently, other words have been abbreviated in the FMP. In combination with abbreviations or *sigla*, the expected use of ligatures is found in the Insular tradition.[66] The vast majority of the abbreviations employed for both whole words and syllables can be considered pan-Insular and are listed as being in use in Insular script before AD 850.[67] The list given in Appendix 6 is not likely to be complete owing to the fact that the writing is often difficult to decipher in its current condition.

DATING THE FMP

Like most Irish early medieval manuscripts, it is difficult to establish accurately when the FMP was written. Any definitive dating depends on a colophon providing either a date or the mention of a historically recorded individual as scribe or patron. A manuscript generally held to have been produced in close proximity to Faddan More, the MacRegol Gospels, is an example of the latter, being linked to the abbot of Birr who died in 822. An inscription on the final folio asks for prayers for the scribe of the manuscript, MacRegol. Interestingly, the inscription was not identified until the nineteenth century, when the link was made with the Birr MacRegol.[68] Caution is required with such

65 Bischoff 1990, 43.

66 *Ibid.*, 86.

67 Dumville 2004.

68 Meehan 2018, 211.

additions, as colophons are often altered, and examples of this are to be found in the Book of Durrow and in another midland manuscript from near the find-spot, the Book of Dimma. The FMP, however, contains no such clues regarding scribes or patrons; indeed, as already noted, there is little or nothing in the way of text apart from the psalms.

In the absence of direct evidence, comparing features such as script and decoration with other extant manuscripts already dated with some degree of accuracy by scholarly study may be of some help. If we accept the deposition date to be *c.* 800 (see Chapter 7) and consider a production period during the eighth century, this provides a chronological window in which to work. As was demonstrated in this chapter, the decorative features of the FMP are sparse, and interlace, the main element, is so commonplace, with its application spanning the Middle Ages, that it is of limited use for accurate dating.

The Insular display capitals in the FMP are, however, a more productive indicator. As discussed, their combination of the curvilinear and geometric letters is represented in many early Insular manuscripts. Charles-Edwards considers their use to be an eighth-century practice but also tracks their evolution and decline, placing the examples in the MacRegol Gospels in the last phase.[69] As was illustrated above, comparisons for the more geometric types similar to those in the FMP were found in the Book of Kells, the gospel-book Cod. Sang. 51 and the Echternach Gospels, among others, and this in general terms places the FMP in the second half of the eighth century. Although difficult to decipher clearly, I would suggest that, untypically, the geometric lettering on folio 1, *Beatus vir*, is not constrained inside a frame but is apparently governed by a head line. Higgitt observes this aspect of the geometric letters and, comparing the Lindisfarne Gospels with the Book of Kells, states: 'Again in both the lines of lettering obey ruled head and foot lines. In Lindisfarne the letters float with some freedom between lines of red dots; in Kells letters are held rigidly in place by the frames.'[70] In this instance, I suggest that the FMP *Beatus* better fits the Lindisfarne model, the earlier of the two manuscripts. Gray lists a number of Insular manuscripts that display this geometric form, again for the most part dating from the eighth century. She makes the additional observation that by this time 'the round letter forms had been eliminated or squared up'.[71] In the FMP's *Quid gloriatur* (Psalm 51) we see a combination of the geometric and enlarged majuscule lettering. Higgitt uses the quality of the geometric lettering as a date indicator, drawing attention to its decline, and also points to the MacRegol Gospels, describing the display capitals therein as 'ponderous and unimaginative',[72] whereas O'Neill in his assessment of the FMP's drawn letters comments on their quality, referring to 'some finely-drawn examples [that] follow a large initial'.[73] Based on these criteria, the FMP may be placed before the MacRegol Gospels, which are dated to before 822.

Since it has been established that the cover is a distinct object from the text block, it cannot be used in dating the book. Nevertheless, because of the unique circumstances of its discovery, a dating method hitherto inapplicable to manuscripts may be applied to the FMP. As mentioned in the Introduction, radiocarbon dating was carried out on a selection of components related to the archaeology of the book. The earliest dated material was from the vellum folios (see Appendix 7), with a calendar range of AD 677–883.[74] Unfortunately, the science could not provide tighter

69 G. Charles-Edwards 2007.

70 Higgitt 1994, 211.

71 Gray 1986, 63.

72 Higgitt 1994, 215.

73 O'Neill 2017, 289.

74 It is important to note that with radiocarbon dating no mean can be extracted from the two projected dates, and either extreme as well as any date between the two all have the same probability.

parameters, although I understand that improved methods are currently providing a narrower range. Therefore, if we consider a deposition date of *c.* 800[75] and allow for the manuscript to have been in use for some reasonable period of time—it would be logical to expect that the intentional disposal or deposition would be related to the usefulness of the psalter—then a production date in the mid-eighth century is realistic. This would place the FMP somewhere between the Book of Durrow and the Book of Kells.

CONCLUSIONS

What can be deduced by examining the surviving contents of the FMP is how this early medieval manuscript is a 'good fit' in the corpus of Insular books of the same epoch. It follows the conventions in relation to both palaeographical practice and decorative techniques, while also displaying some unusual elements to the script. As previously stated, scrutiny of this manuscript is hampered by the aggressive deterioration of the substrate of the vellum as a result of its prolonged submersion in the bog, but this does not prevent in-depth study of its characteristics, albeit requiring higher levels of concentration aided by some technology to enhance the heavily faded ink and pigments. The scribe of the FMP was clearly accomplished, and particular drawn initials demonstrate this well. *Caeli* at the beginning of Psalm 18, for example, shows a sophisticated and well-balanced execution of the first two letters. This skill is again manifest in *Nonne* from the start of Psalm 61.2, with a neat insertion of one N inside the other. The *Quid gloriatur* of Psalm 51 suggests awareness of the methods practised in other Insular manuscripts from a similar orbit, with the combined use of both Insular and geometric letter-forms in the one line of text. The untypical use of the half-circle additions inside the bow of letters suggests a short-lived convention of the scriptorium or a personal decorative feature of the scribe, as it is not seen elsewhere in extant Irish texts until the twelfth century in *Lebor na hUidre*, over three centuries later. Taking an overview of the initial letters, there appears to be a lack of homogeneity, with variation in letter size; although a height of two lines is the chosen dimension for the majority, heights of three lines, five lines and values in between are also employed for the opening text of psalms. Moreover, there are random stylistic appearances of particular features, such as diminuendo and the use of additional colour overlying the ink of the drawn letter. When compared to manuscripts such as the Stowe Missal or the St Gallen gospel-book, the element of 'randomness' in the FMP is even more apparent. The drawing of the initials for the most part involves only the use of the same ink employed for writing the text, apart from the marking of the 'three fifties'. In this respect parallels could be drawn with the Book of Armagh or another manuscript that displays this feature and, in addition, good parallels in its initial letter-forms, viz. Ambrosiana C.301 inf., the so-called Milan Commentary, a commentary on the psalms with old Irish glosses. The manuscript, similar in format to the FMP, was at one time in the library at Bobbio at the foot of Monte Penice in northern Italy. It was either written there by an Irish scribe or was brought from Ireland, possibly being a product of Bangor or Leinster in the late eighth or early ninth century.[76]

All extant initials in the FMP fit Gumbert's definition of an initial: 'it occurs at the left-hand edge of the text area, and this makes it possible to give it a size of more than one unit of ruling'.[77] The FMP initials also fit his criteria for an 'instant initial', i.e. the initial was written as the text was

75 Plunkett *et al.* 2009.

76 Lowe 1966, Part III, 136–7.

77 Gumbert 2009, 305.

transcribed, not delayed to be filled in later with a space left vacant. Gumbert is convinced that this is a feature of the earlier manuscripts. A further observation of the FMP initials is that the continuing text is not in line with the top of the initial but rather more usually halfway down its length and, as such, atypical.

It is evident that there was access to a standard palette of pigments to execute the additional decorative elements. These, too, followed Insular convention, as seen in the use of colour infills between letter spaces in Psalm 51. The use of interlace and lozenges inside framed borders as seen on folio 1 reinforces these credentials. The two surviving bird figures are well drawn, with the bird form as part of the *Q* in Psalm 51 displaying an unusual zigzag element, which has no known parallels. The body of the text is well spaced out on equally well-spaced-out hard-point ruled lines on a generous-sized folio, albeit with narrow margins (see Chapter 2), all of which suggests a considered production with the resources made available to ensure quality, despite its outward appearance, lacking as it does any form of elaborate decorative binding or enclosure.

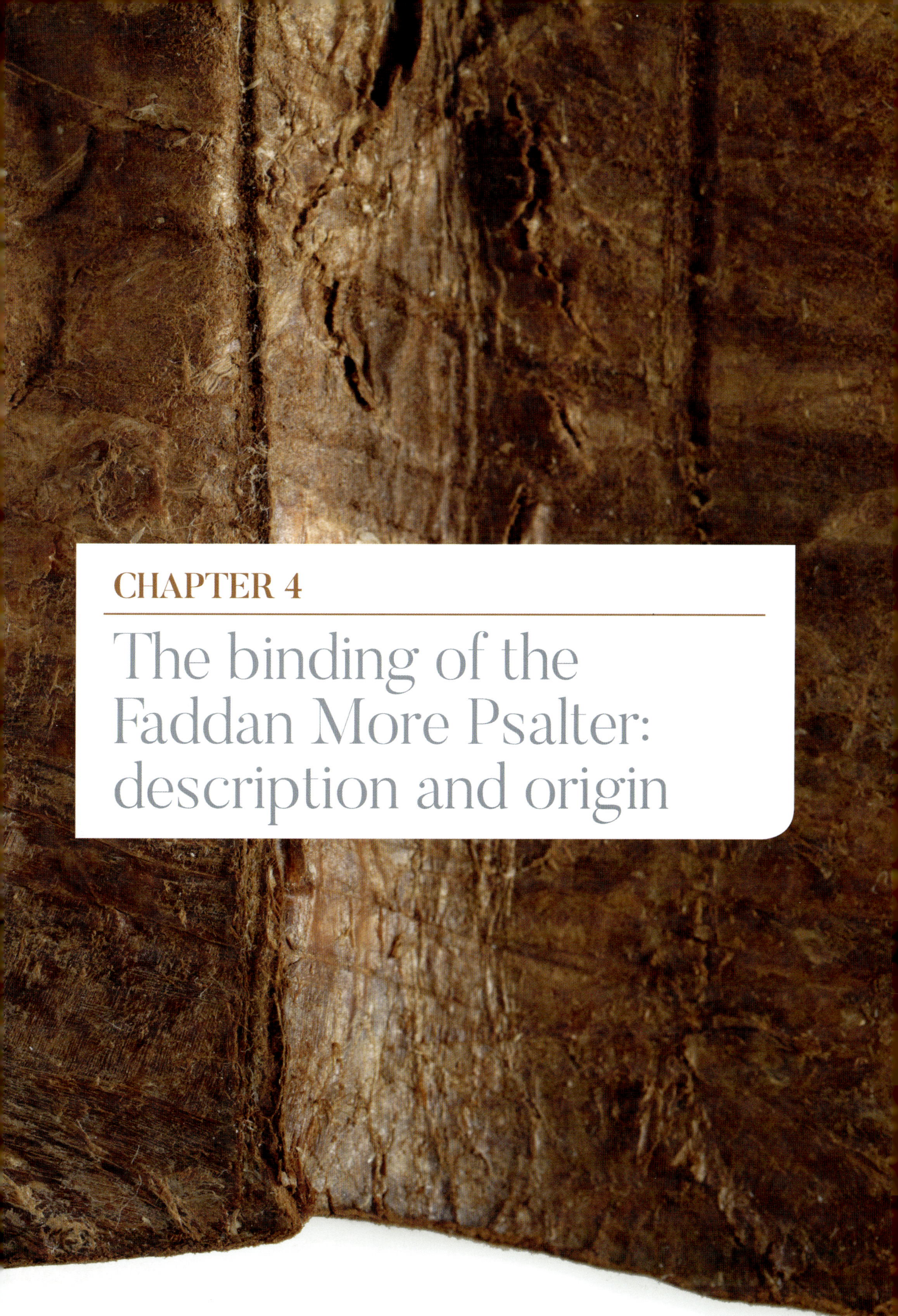

CHAPTER 4

The binding of the Faddan More Psalter: description and origin

CHAPTER 4

The binding of the Faddan More Psalter: description and origin

The assessment process began almost immediately upon the retrieval of the manuscript from Faddan More Bog by staff from the National Museum of Ireland. It was transported to the Conservation Department in Collins Barracks, Dublin, and over the following weeks the NMI invited experts from different disciplines to examine the still-saturated mound of manuscript and bog matter. One observation of particular interest was the nature of the binding enclosing the manuscript. Although it lay beneath the contents of the retrieved material, enough of it was exposed to allow some preliminary remarks. There was a consensus of opinion that the structure was not in any way typical of an Insular binding from the early medieval period. This was premised on accepting the binding as being contemporary with the text block, as initial examination had placed the psalter in the eighth or early ninth century (this dating is still considered to be accurate). The nature of the binding employed on the FMP has prompted broad speculation in relation to the origin of the manuscript. The similarity to structures more typically found in the early Christian period of the eastern Mediterranean was for some unexpected but no great surprise to those more informed: the majority of extant early medieval manuscripts that have come down to us in their original bindings (and this is a minute percentage of what existed originally) also display distinct technical features of the Coptic and Byzantine tradition.

DESCRIPTION OF THE BINDING

The cover of the Faddan More Psalter is a semi-limp structure consisting of a single piece of vegetable-tanned leather, measuring 330mm x 530mm, about 1.5mm thick and from young cattle stock (Fig. 4.1). I identified the species under magnification and this was later confirmed by Dr Roy Thompson, formerly of the Leather Conservation Centre in Northampton, England, who added that, based on common historical animal husbandry practice, the animal had been born in the spring and slaughtered

Fig. 4.1—The conserved binding of the FMP.

in the autumn of the same year.[1] This is supported by archaeological evidence from monastic sites and by monastic rules, in which meat is considered 'winter food'.[2] The conversion of raw animal hides to a stable, versatile end-product was highly developed by the time the binding of the FMP was produced. Vegetable-tanning was one of the three widely employed methods, the other two being tawing and chamoising. The process involved immersing the prepared pelt—which would already have gone through de-hairing by either chemical or mechanical means—in pits of an aqueous solution interspersed with layers of bark (often oak), leaves and other plant matter.[3] The production of vellum and parchment cannot be considered a tanning method because the skin remains vulnerable to putrefaction if re-wetted, as is evidenced by the condition of the vellum folios of the FMP. Excavation of the FMP find-spot also revealed additional material deposited around the general area. Among this material were fragments of a flat whitish substance, which analysis revealed to be the degraded collagen of an animal pelt with hair roots and hair.[4] Because the production of pelts with the hair still intact for items such as clothing and blankets did not involve tanning, the pelt, like the vellum, could not survive the saturated conditions of the bog. A true leather, on the other hand, will withstand exposure to wet conditions—on occasion over extended periods of time. This, too, is evidenced by the survival of the FMP binding.

The leather cover has been scored vertically at four points, from top to bottom on both sides, employing a blunt-edged tool and a straight-edge, as is evidenced by the regularity of the score lines. The effect was to create a simple wrap or portfolio. The binding in its closed form measures 330mm x 224mm, giving a height-to-width ratio of 1.47:1. The lower cover extends and is folded to form a flap that rests on the upper cover. The papillary layer or hair side of the leather is on the outside of the binding. This format is similar to the Islamic codex, albeit in a less refined and undecorated form. The adoption of the codex by the Arabs was strongly influenced by their conquest of Byzantium, Egypt and northern Africa in the mid-seventh century.[5] It is interesting to note that the first observed comparison for the binding of the FMP was provided by the Nag Hammadi codices from Egypt. This collection of thirteen manuscripts dated to the mid-fourth century AD contains works of the Gnostic Gospels within twelve codices and their bindings.

In the centre of the spine area of the FMP cover are two punched holes, approximately 3mm in diameter, both equidistant from the head and tail respectively at 85mm. The holes were punched from the inside using a tool that produced a Y-shaped hole, which is confirmed by the orientation of the walls of the aperture. It is interesting to compare this feature to an observation made by Esther Cameron: 'Awls for piercing leather are traditionally shaped in cross section'.[6] The holes themselves have an unused appearance, with no evidence of 'drag' from any form of thong or tacket being passed through, as evidenced by all three edges of the aperture still coming together when compressed (Fig. 4.2). This supports the possibility that the five quires of the book block might not have been mechanically attached to the cover by any form of direct tacketing and that the cover served instead like a modern-day wallet-type folder, helping to keep the leaves together.

Both of the punched spine holes have four accompanying holes, forming a square with the punched hole in the centre. The surrounding holes are much smaller and are positioned along the crease lines of the spine; their function, like that of the larger holes, is unclear to date but could be considered as a form of primary tacketing. Similar 'X' tacket systems are employed in later limp binding structures,

1 Roy Thompson, unpublished report for the National Museum of Ireland, 2008.

2 De Paor and de Paor 1964, 90.

3 Waterer 1972, 6.

4 Walton Rogers 2008, 2.

5 Szirmai 1999, 51; Avrin 1991, 261.

6 Cameron 2000, 5.

Fig. 4.2—Punched hole in the spine of the cover.

Fig. 4.3—Secondary holes in the spine of the FMP cover.

with examples extant and housed in the Vatican Library.[7] The method creates an 'X' pattern with the threads running diagonally across the spine at two stations. On the cover of the FMP most of the four holes appear to show a slight 'drag' in a similar diagonal direction (Fig. 4.3). I have not as yet had the opportunity to examine these other surviving manuscripts to establish the method employed, but Monica Langwe studied two examples dating from the eighteenth century and described the use of the holes to attach the cover to the text block independent of the sewing.[8] I would caution against drawing any definitive conclusions, given the time-lapse between the Vatican manuscripts and the FMP, until earlier examples of the practice can be found. I have sketched a possible thread path to illustrate how this system might attach the text block to the cover. The use of diagonal stitching such as this served to attach an already sewn text block to the cover by catching the first and last quires with independent stitches, forming the 'X' pattern on the spine of the cover (Fig. 4.4). There is a good alignment between these smaller holes and the text block from the only surviving backfold and the sewing evidence in bifolio 29–32. This, however, is part of the third quire of five, and as such would not be employed for this method of attachment. While the suggestion of a disconnection between the text block and the cover remains the most likely arrangement, the X-pattern holes might offer evidence to the contrary. The examples I have found of its use are not a good fit for the reasons mentioned above; furthermore, the date of their manufacture is later, adding a need to err on the side of caution. Nevertheless, because of the good alignment of the holes in both bifolio and cover, I shall keep an open mind and an open eye for examples that might be a better fit.

The edges of the cover are cut as opposed to having turn-ins (a feature whereby the leather is turned over on itself and stuck down on the inner face, presenting a folded edge, common on bindings today). This is untypical; turn-ins on the covers of books are a feature extending back to the development of the codex itself and continuing to appear even on the most basic limp and semi-limp bindings. Its absence from the FMP cover must be considered a modification carried out later in its use. The outer surface of the leather has been coloured with a black pigment, some of which survived. After analysis, this was shown to be a vegetable charcoal or carbon black with a casein binder (milk proteins).[9] Production of this deep black colour was known since ancient times, as it was used not only as a pigment but also as a writing ink.[10] More typically, the binder would be a form of gum, such as gum arabic. This ink/pigment does not fix itself permanently to its substrate and in effect sits on the surface, hence it is usually lacking on archaeologically retrieved leather. Its partial survival on the cover of the FMP was unexpected.

Attached to the extending flap of the binding are three buttons made of horn, each held in place by a tanned leather thong passing through four holes in the button and knotted on the inside (Fig. 4.5). As a readily available material from both domestic and native wild animals, horn has a long history of use in Ireland, often for domestic wares such as utensils and cups which took advantage of the natural shape and form. It is a non-shedding cuticle composed of keratin and is naturally hollow, forming a sheath over a horn-core which projects from the skull of the animal.[11] In order to produce the flat disc shape for the buttons, either the tip of the horn would be used, as it is solid and could be cut and then easily shaped, or else a sheet of horn would be produced by heating, cutting and flattening out the horn from its cylindrical shape.[12] The disc shapes can be cut from the sheet after it has cooled.

7 Rome, Biblioteca Apostolica Vaticana, Arch. Cap. S. Pietro, Campomorto, libri di grani e bestiame 10.

8 Langwe 2013, 37.

9 Singer 2008.

10 Avrin 1991, 214.

11 MacGregor 1985, 20.

12 *Ibid.*, 66.

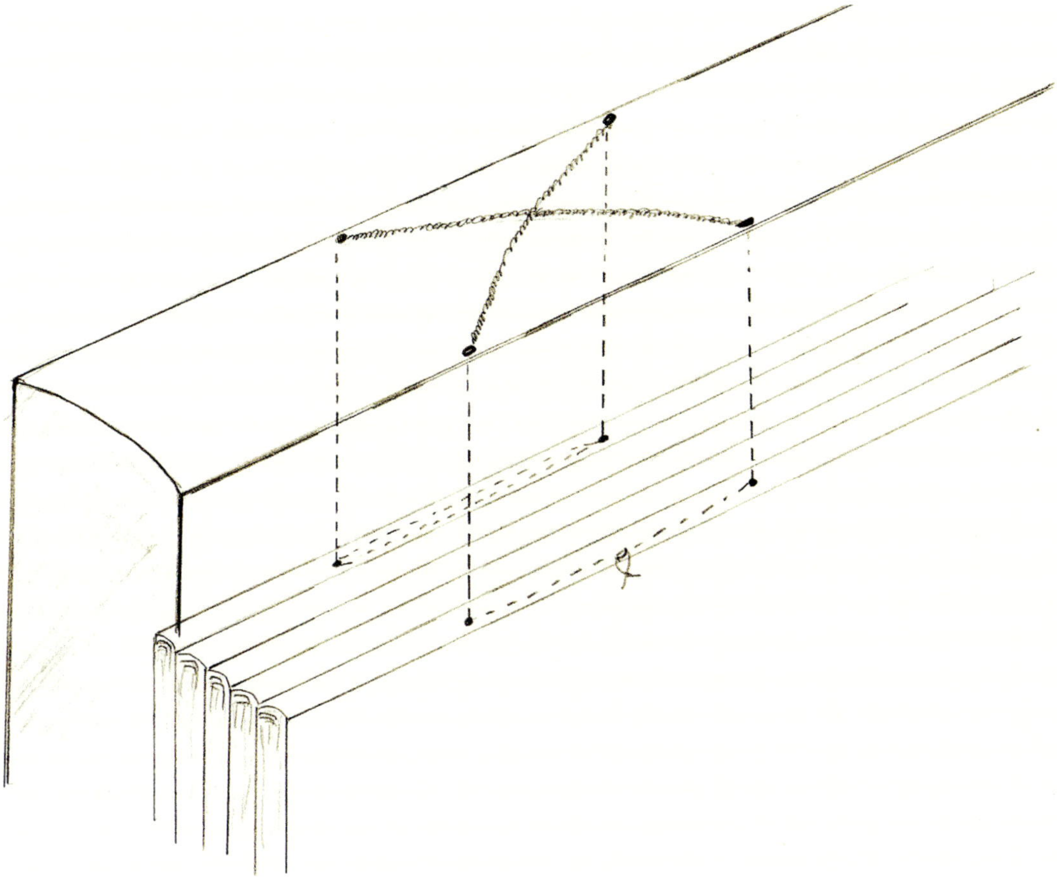

Fig. 4.4—Sketch of 'X' stitch pattern.

Fig. 4.5—Central horn button attached to the flap of the FMP cover.

Fig. 4.6—Replica button, underside, detailing the knot.

The location of the buttons on the flap is unusual; other examples of this style of binding from later centuries tend to have the buttons located on the spine or on the upper cover. Typically for this system, the button acts as an anchor point for a strap or thong which has one end fixed to the cover and functions by being wrapped around the book, often more than once, and fastened on the button.[13] One might also expect some space between the underside of the button and the cover to allow a thong or strap, often of leather, to be secured beneath. The buttons on the FMP, however, are tight to the cover. Even allowing for some swelling during its extended wet state, the most that could be accommodated would be a thin thread. There is no evidence of this system; there are no visible marks on the cover that might represent the impression of a thread, cord or thong. Given the format of this codex, the use of three closing straps seems excessive, leading to the conclusion that the buttons are decorative rather than functional. The knotting on the underside of the leather flap holding the buttons in position is consistent for all three and remains intact; the central button is pointed while the other two are round, as demonstrated by a model I made (Fig. 4.6). This appears to be deliberate and is thus a design feature. Though its meaning is uncertain, the number three is one of the more significant numbers in Christian numerology: the Trinity of the three Divine Persons in one God, for example. The number three is the first of the four perfect numbers and is said to denote divine perfection.

The inside surface of the cover is in a more advanced stage of deterioration, as the exposed flesh side of the skin lacks the protection of the more tightly packed fibres on the top surface of the dermal layer. A certain degree of delamination had taken place over time, leaving the surface uneven and varying in thickness. At the period of its manufacture, this inner surface was lined with at least one layer of papyrus, employing an adhesive, either starch-based or an animal glue. The intention here

13 Medieval examples of this style can be found in the Herzog August Bibliothek in Wolfenbüttel, Germany, HAB Cod. Guelf. 29.4. Aug. 4°, HAB Cod. Guelf 931 Helmst.

Fig. 4.7—Writing on the inside surface of the FMP cover.

was to produce a stiffer material that would allow it to be folded in order to produce semi-rigid covers to protect the contents within. The examination of the inner surface of the cover resulted not only in the discovery of fragments of a papyrus lining but also of three random lines of writing in the same majuscule hand used for the text block. These were examined by some members of the Faddan More Steering Committee while the cover was still in its saturated state and the writing was clearer.[14] Unfortunately, the highly degraded condition of both the substrate and the ink made any positive deciphering impossible. There was a consensus that one word was likely to be *filium*, but the identification of whose son was frustratingly illegible (Fig. 4.7). Equally intriguing is the fact that the writing is directly on the degraded flesh surface of the leather. This indicates that the papyrus lining was stripped off while the cover was still in use rather than dissolving away in the bog.

The general appearance of the cover is that of a much-used item and one that had a multi-functional purpose in the monastery, its most likely home. One of its uses appears to have been as a support for the creasing, ruling and even cutting of the vellum folios for the production of manuscripts. The evidence for this is in the form of a random series of impressed lines on the outer surface produced with an appropriate tool and a straight-edge. Their appearance is enhanced owing to the survival of the black pigment in the trough of the impression. It appears that these lines are the 'shadow' from the process of ruling and perhaps folding the vellum folios in preparation for writing the text (Fig. 4.8). The leather cover would have been used as a base beneath the prepared skins. In an Insular tradition, several skins at a time were often ruled by stacking them in a pile (see Chapter 2).[15] In practical terms, the leather acted as a surface that allowed heavy pressure to indent down to the bottom skin without damage. Some of these lines appear as a set of close parallel lines and may be the result of ruling the

14 Mr Raghnall Ó Floinn, Dr Bernard Meehan and Mr Eamonn Kelly.

15 Harmon 1984, 21.

Fig. 4.8—'Tram lines' on the outer surface of the cover of the FMP.

vertical bounding lines, which were sometimes double, although they are closer together than would be expected. Incisions on the surface indicate the use of a cutting tool, with the aid of a straight-edge, and do not penetrate the full thickness of the leather. The cuts are most likely the result of the cover's position at the bottom of a pile of vellum folios being trimmed before writing (Fig. 4.9).

Further illustrating the apparent multi-functional nature of the cover, several randomly placed incised trial motifs can be seen across its outer surface. The patterns were created by a sharp instrument being drawn over the surface, both freehand and with the aid of instruments such as a straight-edge, particularly for borders but not exclusively so. This work had the effect of marking the surface but also of removing the colour layer and exposing the natural leather colour beneath. In many instances the drawing line cuts through the grain layer of the leather; the cut is very fine and almost scalpel-like (this unexpected feature is examined separately in Chapter 5). There are several curved striations on both sides of the skin; these are related to its manufacture and the scraping process called 'scudding' to de-hair the skin on the upper surface and remove any fatty substances from the flesh side. A two-handed blunt-edged knife is thought to have been the tool of choice; an example of such a knife was excavated at Pompeii.[16]

On the outer/hair side a number of blemishes are visible, circular in shape with a diameter of 3–5mm

16 Goldman 2001, 104; Thompson 2006b, 68.

Fig. 4.9—Incisions on the inner surface of the cover of the FMP.

and slightly raised off the surface. Roy Thomson has identified these defects as likely to be a form of wart.[17] This type of infection was caused by a strain of virus and may be passed on to the cattle in a number of ways, including by insects.[18] It is interesting to note that young cattle are particularly vulnerable, which agrees with Thomson's observation on the age of the FMP leather.

In addition to the warts, a series of holes in the skin, with diameters up to 5mm, were identified as the 'exit holes' of the warble fly, a typical infestation of cattle up to the present day. The adult female lays her eggs on the leg of the animal during summer. When hatched, the larvae burrow through the skin layers of the host and over several months make their way up to the spine area. During this process they produce a lump with a hole which is used for breathing, and these are identified as the smaller holes in the leather. When fully developed, the grub emerges and drops to the ground to pupate for over a month before a new adult emerges.

There are several long splits in the leather, most of them corresponding to the creasing lines of the cover, this being the hinging area and thus subject to a higher degree of wear and tear. The creasing line between the flap and the front cover is split for over 50% of its length. There are other, shorter splits, not related to the creasing lines; these start at the edges of the cover and are mostly, but not entirely, at the head. Other trauma on the body of the cover includes a large crescent-shaped split, rather jagged in form, on the front cover and a smaller jagged split on the back. It appears that the jagged splits are recent and occurred during the unintentional unearthing of the manuscript by the backhoe bucket.

17 Roy Thomson, unpublished report for the National Museum of Ireland, 2008.

18 'Warts in Cattle' (29 July 2014): http://www.thecattlesite.com/articles/3999/warts-in-cattle-cause-and-cure/.

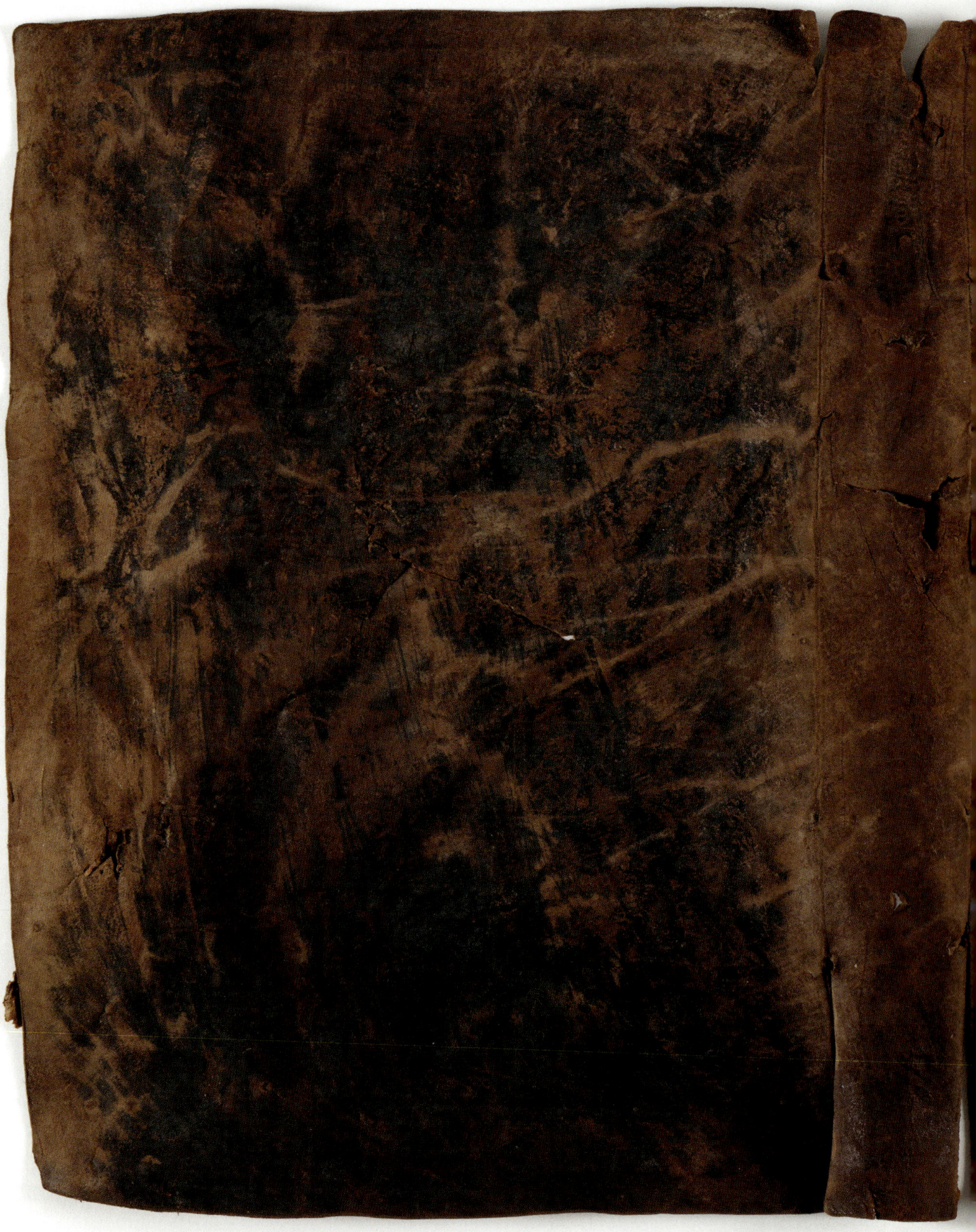

Fig. 4.10—Outer surface features of the FMP cover.

The vast majority of the remaining splits are of some age, however, and their appearance suggests their presence long before deposition of the manuscript in the bog, as evidenced by the worn and rounded edges at the start of the splits, indicating that the area has been exposed to contact and abrasion over a long period. Overall, the cover displays signs of heavy and extensive use prior to its long immersion in the bog. The surviving pigment also indicates considerable use of the cover: strategic wear on the pigment and the leather beneath correspond with the typical handling and carrying of a book of this format (Fig. 4.10). This typical 'grip' is illustrated on the pages of another Irish manuscript from almost the same period, the Mac Durnan Gospels (London, Lambeth Palace MS 1370), in which St Luke is depicted holding a manuscript. Here Luke's hand is in the same location as the wear pattern on the FMP cover, and his book cover also has a flap and three buttons (Fig. 4.11).[19] A more detailed description is given in the following section.

Given the Irish location of the FMP and its cover, its place of origin notwithstanding, mention must be made of another iconic keeper of the Irish manuscript, namely the book-satchel or budget. Owing to similarities in the basic form of construction and in the materials employed to produce them it is interesting to make a comparison. A single piece of material, tanned leather, is creased and folded to complete the construction, although this is a more complex exercise in the case of the satchel. Three extant Irish satchels typically referenced in this regard are the *Breac Moedóic*, the Corpus Christi budget and the Armagh Satchel. The first two date from the eighth to tenth centuries, while the Armagh Satchel may post-date its contents by 600 years, placing it in the fifteenth century (Fig. 4.12).[20] Comparisons with the cover of the FMP were promptly identified and Mark Clark drew attention to similarities in 2008, not long after conservation had begun.[21]

During the early stages of the conservation process, I produced a close facsimile of the leather cover of the FMP, complete with surface dyeing, folding creases, papyrus lining and horn buttons; in addition, an accurate tracing of all the surviving vellum fragments were drawn onto a heavy paper representative of the five quires of the original intact text block (Fig. 4.13). Over the past eight years I have carried this model to numerous talks and lectures, and have encouraged its handling by the audience, while at the same time deliberately avoiding any particular care in its handling, storage or transport. The aim was to observe how this structure stood up to the rigours of everyday life and in particular with its ill-fitting contents, mimicking that of the original manuscript. The results so far confirm a similar bowing on the spine of the cover as a result of the leaves within not filling the form. No splits or weakening along crease lines have occurred thus far, suggesting that it would require considerable time and use to produce those present on the cover of the FMP. I will continue to use and abuse my copy and observe developments.

The literary sources also inform us of the use of satchels, with a mention in the *Hisperica Famina*, as referenced in the Introduction. The text includes a typical day's activity, describing a wealth of social events of the time. Lines 262–4 instruct: 'Hang your white booksacks on the wall, set your lovely satchels in a straight line, so that they will be deemed a grand sight by the rustics'. Line 508 describes the adornments of individuals, noting that they '... carry bright booksacks around their necks'.[22] Despite the identical function of both the satchel and the semi-limp cover of the FMP, there are clear structural differences between these items. The complexity of manufacturing the book-satchel, as expertly demonstrated by John Waterer,[23] displays the level of craft skills necessary and how at variance

19 Mac Durnan Gospels, f. 115v.

20 Meehan 2014, 276; 2005.

21 Clarke 2008.

22 Herren 1974, 85, 104.

23 Waterer 1968.

Fig. 4.11 — London, Lambeth Palace Library, MS 1370, f. 115v.

Fig. 4.12—The Book of Armagh Satchel (TCD MS 52).

this is with the making of the cover of the FMP. It nonetheless demonstrates the high degree of skill and craft in leather-working at that time in Ireland. I did, however, note a common factor in another detailed description of a book-satchel in *Hesperica*, although its meaning is not entirely clear. It reads: '... a single opening, which is closed by a tight covering with many-angled turning knobs, then bound with twelve cords'.[24] This prompts the drawing of parallels with the three buttons on the cover of the FMP and the speculation that if they had a function it would be to lock leather cords in position after being wrapped around the cover. Perhaps the non-functioning buttons/knobs of the FMP were attached to mimic the look of a book-satchel.

COMPARISONS FOR THE BINDING OF THE FADDAN MORE PSALTER

This section examines bookbindings or covers similar to the FMP and will endeavour to draw comparisons regarding form and context. Intentionally, medieval manuscripts originating in the West that are for the most part bound in parchment and defined as 'limp' or 'semi-limp' bindings have been excluded from scrutiny here. This is because the western limp structure developed from the tenth century onward[25] and was not directly influenced by the Near Orient, which was the inspiration and possible origin of the FMP cover. Although the term 'limp' has been applied to the FMP cover, it is a term of convenience; not all comparable material with a similar definition but different chronology can be considered a homogeneous classification. It becomes noteworthy that the dearth of western limp structures from the time of the FMP to the beginning of their use in the tenth century further suggests a lack of continuity. Comparative material has been selected from the ninth century at the latest in

24 Herren 1974, 105.

25 Szirmai 1999, 286.

Fig. 4.13a—Model of the FMP.

Fig. 4.13b—Model of the FMP.

relation to western structures; here caution is required, as many ninth-century texts are not within ninth-century covers, a fact not always conveyed in library catalogues. Mention of later material is brief and chosen for particular codicological similarities to the FMP.

The Nag Hammadi Library consists of thirteen codices, eleven of which retain their original bindings. The manuscripts were discovered in a jar at the foot of the Jabal al-Tarif site in the cliffs along the Nile in northern Upper Egypt by Mohammed Ali al-Samman in December 1945.[26] The content of the Coptic manuscripts includes a large number of Gnostic scriptures, from a complex religious and heretical movement of the second century AD. The theological content has both Christian and non-Christian elements, and scholars date the 'Library' to the second half of the fourth century. The bindings are often reported as being mostly 'sheepskin and some goatskin'.[27] This identification is open to doubt, as codicological examination of the Nag Hammadi bindings has been scant and the identification of sheep and goat is historically difficult owing to their similar follicle pattern. The situation is further complicated by the cross-breeding of the two species in this part of the world for many centuries and the existence of a breed of sheep known as hair sheep.[28] All but three of the bindings are made from a single piece of leather and all but two employ a fore-edge flap as an extension of the lower cover which is brought around and rests on the upper cover. To each flap is attached a long strip of leather which wraps horizontally around the book. Additional straps attached at the head and tail wrap vertically around the book, keeping it tightly closed. Some straps are attached to the cover by a running stitch, while others appear to be inserted into a slot in the leather and are presumably glued down on the inside surface. The flaps are either triangular or rectangular, the latter matching the format on the FMP's cover. All the bindings employ generous turn-ins, a feature lacking on the FMP. Beneath the turn-ins a lining of papyrus was adhered in place, although all have now been stripped out. These multi-layered sheets were manuscript waste, and scholars were quick to remove them for study after their discovery, without any proper recording taking place. The remaining fragments bear evidence of their crude removal. The outer surface of some of the covers has been decorated with simple blind line tooling, apart from one (Codex II) which displays a more complex pattern and the use of colour. All covers housed single-quire codices of papyrus, apart from Codex I, which has three quires. Their attachment generally consisted of two rolled leather thongs passing through the central fold of the quire and through a secondary strip of leather which was stuck down on the inside along the spine of the cover. The thongs would either pass on through the spine of the cover itself and be knotted on the outside or, for a more aesthetically pleasing effect, stitched only to the secondary strip of leather, resulting in no knots being visible on the outside of the cover. Because the quires of the Nag Hammadi are written on papyrus, additional stays of leather were placed in the centre of the quire to prevent the flax thread from pulling through the brittle material; this becomes unnecessary when the quires are of parchment (Fig. 4.14). Interestingly, this kind of stay reinforcement would return with the introduction of paper manuscripts and incunabula in the fifteenth century, with the bookbinder not quite trusting the strength of the new material. Szirmai attempted to group the bindings into different classifications based on their technical details. His second group, Codices VI, IX, X and possibly II, best fits the FMP binding type, having rectangular flaps and a lack of decoration (apart from Codex II).[29] The Nag Hammadi codices may be considered the antecedent of all similar structures by which the lineage of this format is traced, and this now includes the binding of the FMP.

26 Meyer 2005, 15.

27 Needham 1979, 55.

28 Ryder 1983, 108.

29 Szirmai 1999, 11.

Fig. 4.14—Cairo, Coptic Museum Codex X: inside surface of one of the Nag Hammadi covers, showing secondary strip and fragments of papyrus lining.

With so few binding structures surviving from the first centuries of Christianity, it is helpful to find another example outside the Nag Hammadi Library but with a similar date range, location and structural features. One such example is the leather cover of a manuscript known as the Philo Codex (BnF MS suppl. Gr. 1120) after Philo of Alexandria (20 BC–AD 40), a Hellenistic Jewish philosopher and prolific writer from a wealthy family.[30] The manuscript contains two of his texts and additional material, used as flyleaves, containing parts of the gospels of Matthew and Luke, pre-dating the codex itself, possibly from the late second or early third century. The manuscript was discovered in a niche in a wall in Coptos in Upper Egypt in the late nineteenth century and is currently thought to date from the third century.[31] It is a multi-quired papyrus book with additional papyrus waste, believed to have been employed as a lining. Measuring 178mm x 165mm, with a height to width ratio of 1.07:1, it is in an almost square format. This is to be expected, as the early codices tended to echo the square format of the *rotuli* which they were for the most part replacing. The constructional details are identical to the majority of the Nag Hammadi Library codices—and, by extension, the FMP binding—in that they are constructed from a single piece of vegetable-tanned leather folded with a flap as an extension of the back cover that folds onto the front and is secured by a leather strap, still extant in the case of the Philo Codex. The manuscript housed four quires, with evidence of the sewing structure remaining (Fig. 4.15).

The next extant example comes from the first quarter of the eighth century and thus is closer in date to the binding of the FMP. British Library Papyrus 1442 is an imperfect codex containing a tax register from Arab Egypt, written for the most part in Greek but with Coptic place-names. Although the use

30 Sly 1996, 4.

31 Gathercole 2012, 223.

Fig. 4.15—Paris, BnF NS suppl. Gr. 1120, cover of the Philo Codex with flap and strap.

Fig. 4.16—London, BL Papyrus 1442: opened-out leather cover with now-fragmented flap.

of Greek declined after the Arab conquest of Egypt in 642, the Greek language continued, particularly for administrative purposes.[32] The extant text block consists of 33 folios and fragments; additional leaves from the codex are preserved in Berlin (P. Berol. Inv. 25006). The material is papyrus and the format is 340mm x 250mm, a ratio of 1.36:1. Much of the original binding for this codex survives, albeit detached from the text block. It is a single piece of leather designated as goatskin but with the same caveat as with the Nag Hammadi covers. It constitutes a front cover, a narrow spine, a back cover and a flap. The narrow spine and the single set of direct tacket holes indicate a single-quire codex. The flap as an extension of the back cover differs from both the Nag Hammadi codices and the FMP in its form. The profile is stepped, narrowing to the front edge. Unlike the FMP binding, the leather does not appear to have been scored to define the different components of the cover and to assist with hinging during use. Instead, it has been folded, resulting in more rounded hinging points. The edges have turn-ins similar

32 Gabra 2002, 122.

to those of the Nag Hammadi bindings with generous margins. The inner surface is lined with papyrus in what appears to be two separate pieces, leaving the area of the spine unlined. This mirrors some but not all of the Nag Hammadi structures and would have been an intentional decision by the bookbinder, allowing more flexibility in the spine region, where it is most critical. The spine area displays a series of holes related to the attachment of the single papyrus quire by direct tacketing. The original number of holes can only be estimated, owing to a large missing area at the tail and a smaller loss at the head of the cover. The eight extant holes are quite consistent in size and shape, and, interestingly, they appear similar to the two holes in the spine of the FMP cover, with three sides to the aperture. Unlike the FMP holes, however, they show signs of use, with the edges pushed up and out as a result of the thongs—most likely strips of tanned leather—being passed through the cover from the centre of the quire and knotted on the outside. The groupings of the holes suggest repairs over the years as perhaps more folios were added, a likely probability for a tax register, or as a result of the papyri leaves detaching and being resewn through a new set of tacket holes. The grouping consists of four holes on a vertical axis separated by a few centimetres; above this, on the same axis, the remaining four holes are in two groupings, with the holes in each group only a few millimetres apart. The surface of the covers is decorated by drawing with ink or dye that appears to be black in colour. For each cover the decorative pattern consists of three double-lined panels of decreasing size placed inside each other. The space between the panels is filled with loose spiral patterns and dots. In the centre of the panel on the front or left-hand cover is a six-pointed star inside a double-lined circle, the space between the points of the star being decorated with dots. There may have been similar decoration on the back or right-hand cover, but severe damage has blackened and distorted the leather, making it impossible to clarify. The leather surface of the cover has a red/brown colour and this could be the natural colour of the skin as a result of the ingredients of the tanning infusion (Fig. 4.16).

In seventh-century Egypt, before the Arab invasion of 641, Egyptian monasticism was the basis of the Coptic Church. During the early stages of Arab rule, the Copts enjoyed greater religious freedom than they had known under the Byzantines. They were no longer considered heretics but were now *dhimmis*, protected non-Muslims; they were still a subject people, however, and were assessed for an annual poll tax as non-Muslims.[33] During the eighth and ninth centuries, owing to the combination of many conversions of Copts to Islam and intensive Arab migration to Egypt, the Copts became a minority people and were considered second-class citizens. Two revolts sparked by their treatment were put down in the early ninth century, and a decline in their religion and language gathered momentum in the centuries that followed. It is highly plausible that British Library Papyrus 1442 was registering taxes collected from the Copts and the Coptic Church during its use in the early eighth century.

Because of the geographical area of interest and some technical features matching the cover of the FMP, the following additional extant material is offered. Although it consists of fragmentary pieces, it is relevant in strengthening the argument that a flap-type cover was typical and widespread in Coptic Egypt over an extended period of time. Several book cover fragments were identified during archaeological investigation of the leather finds from the Coptic monastery of Deir el-Bachit, which stands on the hilltop of Dra' Abu el-Naga in Qurna (West Bank of Luxor).[34] The collection consisted of 63 pieces, undated but believed to be from between the sixth and ninth centuries, matching the active period of the monastery. All but the very small pieces display some form of decoration, which mostly takes the form of parallel impressed lines. The arrangement of the lines confirms them to be intentional decorative features. The majority of the fragments also have remnants of papyrus adhering to the inner, flesh-side surface. In the few cases where edges have survived, the bindings have turn-ins, the feature notably lacking on the FMP cover. One of the larger pieces (Cat. No. 120, Find No. DB2146) includes a flap-type arrangement and a

33 Gabra 2002, 16.

34 Veldmeijer 2012, 41.

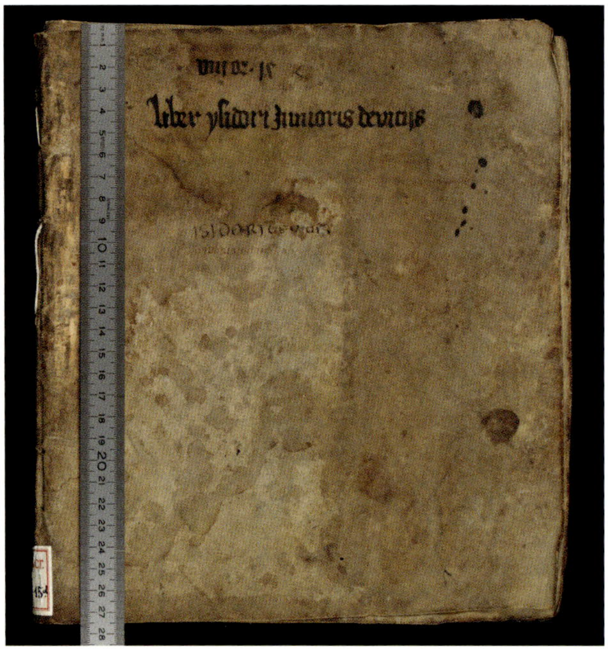

Fig. 4.17—Basel, Universitätsbibliothek F.III.15d: the contemporary outside cover of the manuscript.

leather strap attached with a running stitch. The piece is described as 'a thin semi-circular fragment that is black on the obverse (outside) and brown on the reverse (inner side)', which matches the colouring on the FMP. Veldmeijer observes that 'The book cover leather has not been identified, but possibly is calfskin judging by the thickness of some',[35] again matching the FMP cover.

The next manuscript scrutinised confirms knowledge of limp binding structures in Ireland in the eighth century. *Isidorus iunior Hispalensis, De vitiis. Consentius, De barbarismis et metaplasmis. Victorinus, De soloecismo et barbarism* (Basel, Universitätsbibliothek F.III.15d) is a manuscript of Fulda provenance but likely to be of Irish origin. The grammatical manuscript is written in an Insular minuscule hand in two columns per folio and presents as its main text *De vitiis (linguae)*, which it attributes to an *Isidorus iunior*. The Anglo-Saxon monastery founded in the mid-eighth century by St Sturm under instruction of St Boniface in Fulda, located in the modern German state of Hesse, is known to have hosted Irish *peregrini* monks[36] and this is affirmed by the presence of the manuscript. It measures 275mm x 245mm, with a height-to-width ratio of 1.12:1. There are two quires, a quinion and a ternion, with a total of sixteen folios; there is no back flyleaf and the front flyleaf is the first folio of the first quire. The Irish tradition of ignoring the conventions in assembling their quires even manifests itself in a simple two-quire arrangement of sixteen folios. The contemporary cover is a single piece of vellum, probably calfskin; the skin displays 'insular characteristics' and is thick, with a leather-like quality, more flexible than Continental vellum and slightly brownish in colour (Fig. 4.17). The covering material of the manuscript corresponds to Ronald Reed's description of early vellum-making and the quality of the end-product:

> *'Where the medieval parchment makers were greatly superior to their modern counterparts was in the control and modification of the ground substance in the pelt, before the latter was stretched and dried. The inclusion of oils, fats, aluminium salts and vegetable tannins in the pelt*

35 Veldmeijer 2012, 15.

36 Schutz 2004, 164.

> *structure, coupled with a more deliberate control of the drying rate, meant that the dried ground substance had different water-absorption properties in the final parchment. The fats and oils also had tanning, fat-liquoring and lubricative action on the pelt fibres so that limp and more flexible forms of stable vellum, such as are ideal for book covers were produced.'*[37]

This structure is the simplest of affairs and in effect is a 'wrap' for the two quires. There is no scoring of the surface to distinguish the two covers from the spine area. The dimensions are barely sufficient to enclose the text block, with resulting damage to the edges of many of the folios within. There are no turn-ins, as in the FMP structure, with the cut edges to view. The spine area displays at least six and possibly more holes, some of which have extended into slits as a result of the primary tacket material cutting through the vellum. The two extant vegetable fibre threads visible on the spine are not contemporary with either the cover or the text block. This attachment method is best described as a basic form of primary tacketing. Berthe Van Regemorter included a description of the structure in an article she wrote for *Scriptorium* in 1957:

> *'La couture passe en même temps dans l'interieur des cahiers et dans la couvrure. Les deux fils sont visibles sur une distance d'environ 30mm et se trouvent à peu près à 55mm de la tête et de la queue. Travail assez primitif.'*[38]

The cover lacks any decoration and is clearly a utilitarian structure, which perhaps was never intended to be a permanent housing for the manuscript, a theory that has also been postulated for the binding of the FMP. The relevance of this cover as a comparison for the binding of the FMP lies in its provenance as an Irish composition of a similar date, manufactured from a single piece of material and entirely utilitarian in its function.

Another manuscript present in the Fulda library at that time may be noted: the Cadmug Gospels (Fulda, Landesbibliothek Codex Bonifatianus 3), a 'pocket gospel'[39] of the late eighth century with Irish glosses and colophon of the scribe, '*cadmug scripsit*'. It is uncertain where this manuscript was written, whether in Fulda or in Ireland, but it does present us with a relevant technical feature.[40] The Cadmug Gospels is thought to be in a contemporary binding[41] and, although structurally it has little in common with the FMP, it does mimic a 'Coptic' binding system, particularly in relation to the sewing method employed.

The next example is again from Fulda. *Admonitio generalis* (Cod. Guelf. 496a Helmst) is a late eighth- or early ninth-century manuscript. Its contents include, as part of the 'General advice', interpretation of the Lord's Prayer and a strong emphasis on order, uniformity and proper discipline within the church, as well as on learning and literacy. It is one of the earliest books copied at Fulda. [42] The manuscript contains three quires with a total of 26 folios. The inner face of the back cover forms part of the manuscript text block as a fully written folio and is in effect folio 27r. The generously spaced long-line text is written in an Anglo-Saxon minuscule but the marginalia and glosses, considered contemporary, are in an Insular minuscule hand and include

37 Reed 1972, 124.

38 Van Regemorter 1957, 255.

39 Meehan 2015, 83.

40 *Ibid.*, 86–90; Alexander 1978a, 70.

41 Szirmai 1999, 97.

42 Raaijmakers 2012, 82.

Insular abbreviation symbols. The vellum is described as 'prepared in the insular fashion'.[43] The binding is a single piece of material, in this instance calfskin vellum, and appears to have been creased at the hinging points or joints rather than deliberately scored. The front joint now forms a defined hinging point through use; the rear joint, however, has a more rounded form, as typically there is minimum flexing here with normal use of the manuscript. It measures 260mm x 160mm, with a height-to-width ratio of 1.62:1. The binding, as in the Basel manuscript, is economic in its format and is more or less the same size as the text block. There are no turn-ins and no fore-edge flap. Missing areas and modern repairs to damage are visible, particularly at the top corner of the front cover. The three quires are attached to the binding, employing a type of primary sewing (Fig. 4.18). This style is defined by Szirmai as 'limp binding structures where the cover attachment has been carried out simultaneously with the sewing of the book block'.[44] Judging by the thickness and brightness of the sewing threads, it may be surmised that they are not contemporary with the manuscript, although the original sewing holes/stations have been reused.

The relevance of the *Admonitio generalis* in relation to the FMP binding, apart from the limp structure and the similar date of manufacture, lies in the attachment exit holes on the spine of the binding. Here there are three sets of four holes, one set more or less in the centre of the spine and the other two outboard of this, approximately equidistant but away from the head and tail. The layout of each set of three holes places them along the hinging or joint of the cover, two on the front joint and two on the rear joint and facing each other, forming a rectangle. The threads from the current sewing exit and enter two holes diagonally, forming an 'X' pattern across the spine. It cannot be certain that this is the original method employed, but the positioning and number of each set of holes does mirror the two sets of smaller holes found on the spine of the FMP binding, as was discussed earlier. Given that there are no additional holes on the spine of the *Admonitio generalis* manuscript, it is reasonable to assume that they are original and were a result of the first primary sewing or primary tacketing of the text block to the cover. This in turn offers a plausible explanation for the seemingly redundant holes on the binding of the FMP.

The final comparable manuscript is Bodleian Library MS Marshall 19, written in the ninth century, most likely at the Benedictine Abbey of St Médard at Soissons in northern France. Although the manuscript dates from the late ninth century, there are additions to the text from the tenth and early thirteenth centuries, when it was first at St Aldhelm's at Malmesbury and later at St Augustine's in Canterbury. It is thought, however, that it may have been imported from France into Anglo-Saxon England. The manuscript contains Jerome's Latin translation of a treatise by Philo Judeus, *Interpretatio nominum Hebraicorum*. There are 42 folios in six quires of four quaternions and two ternions, written in two columns. The covering, which is generally accepted to be contemporary with the manuscript, is a single piece of thick tawed leather described in the Marshall catalogue as 'rough sheepskin'.[45] The binding style is in the same fashion as the FMP cover; the lower cover is extended and forms a rectangular flap that covers the fore-edge and rests on the upper cover. The closed manuscript measures 290mm x 200mm, giving a height-to-width ratio of 1.45:1, very similar to the FMP. The flap of MS Marshall 19 is not sculpted, again mirroring the FMP. The outer surface lacks any decoration, apart from a label with a later shelf-mark which adheres to the bottom of the spine. A feature of this limp binding not seen in other examples are the remains of a tab, or extension of the leather, at the head of the spine, reminiscent of Carolingian hard-board binding structures but without their functional purpose, given that the edges of the cover are flush with the text block. There

43 Lowe 1959, 41.

44 Szirmai 1999, 291.

45 Madan and Craster 1922, 996; Szirmai 1999, 294–5.

Fig. 4.18—Wolfenbüttel, Herzog August Bibliothek Cod. Guelf. 496a Helmst: spine displaying X-pattern sewing.

Fig. 4.19—Bodleian Libraries, University of Oxford, MS Marshall 19.

is no tab at the tail, presumably lost owing to contact with the bookshelf (Fig. 4.19). Three braided cords are attached to the flap, all of which have been cut back to their attachment points. Attachment of each cord to the flap was achieved by what appears to be a widely spaced running stitch using a thinner version of the cord tie. The function of the cords was to secure the closure of the book by fastening around three aligned buttons located on the front cover about two thirds of the way across. All three buttons are now lost, but a clear imprint of their form remains, as does a four-hole pattern where each button was sewn to the leather cover. The diamond-shaped pattern is identical to the attachment system employed for the FMP buttons. The impression left in the surface of the leather suggests slightly smaller buttons than those on the FMP (Fig. 4.20).

The proportions of flap to cover on both the FMP and MS Marshall 19 are very similar, with the flap accounting for about one third of the width of the front cover. The attachment of the six quires to the cover is by primary sewing. The link-stitch sewing uses five equally spaced stations, which are visible on the spine of the limp binding; the change-over stations at the head and tail are not visible, as they do not penetrate the spine leather. There is mention of unused holes located in the centre of the quires,[46] most likely as a result of quire tackets, used to keep a quire together while awaiting sewing. On examining this binding in 1982, Jean Vezin (Directeur d'Études à l'École Pratique des Hautes Études, Paris) made the following summary in relation to the study of limp bindings:

> '*Nos bibliothèques conservent actuellement en assez grand nombre des reliures souples des XV et XVI siècles, dont certaines sont construites suivant une technique analogue à celle qui est employée dans le manuscrit d'Oxford. Pour les époques antérieures, seuls quelques spécimens subsistent, ce qui rend leur recherche d'autant plus importante, car il est vraisemblable qui cette méthode* économique *de couvrir les livres a* été *beaucoup plus utilisée que ne le laisseraient supposer les rares examples que nous connaissons.*'[47]

Unsurprisingly, my efforts to locate early medieval bindings with similar structural features to the FMP did not unearth a plethora of semi-limp covers with fore-edge flaps. The ephemeral nature of this form of binding no doubt encouraged its replacement with the more elaborate western hard-board structures which developed and gained popularity from the ninth century onward.[48] This circumstance further emphasises the codicological importance of the FMP cover. There can be little doubt, however, that these bindings did exist in much greater numbers and, as evidenced by the examples here, were geographically spread across the literate world.

ICONOGRAPHICAL EXAMPLES OF THE FMP-STYLE BINDING

In addition to identifying extant examples of the type of semi-limp binding with some or all of the features of the FMP structure, an attempt can be made to identify this structure through illustrations in contemporary media as an additional source of collateral evidence. Representations of the FMP-type cover can be seen in depictions of the book as an artefact in early medieval art, in iconographic images on the pages of manuscripts. This is particularly significant because it connects the contents of the FMP as an essential Christian text to the specific type of cover depicted on the folios of Christian books, therefore putting both the image and the FMP in context.

46 Vezin 1982, 239.

47 *Ibid.*, 241.

48 Szirmai 1999, 100; Agati 2017, 380.

Fig. 4.20—Bodleian Libraries, University of Oxford, MS Marshall 19: indent from button and hole pattern.

It is likely that the use of vellum for the folios of manuscripts throughout the medieval period prompted the inclusion of methods to keep the contents under pressure between the covers. Vellum and parchment are hygroscopic and will react, often dramatically, to a rise or drop in humidity, distorting and curling, usually towards the hair side, and, as we have seen, those who worked with the material had an in-depth understanding of its nature. It is clear that these manuscripts were for the most part working texts as part of the liturgy or with a didactic function. They would not have been stored in the highly controlled conditions in which the surviving manuscripts of today find themselves. As a result, there would be a need to restrain movement within the text block, particularly with the larger-format manuscripts. The use of these fore-edge flaps and later metalwork clasps would help to achieve this.

The first illustrated example comes from an Irish manuscript dating from the late ninth or early tenth century, the Mac Durnan Gospels (Lambeth Palace MS 1370). An inscription on one folio (f. 3v) informs us that Máel Brigte mac Tornáin (Mac Durnan), who either commissioned or wrote the manuscript, dedicated this book to God. Mac Durnan was abbot of Armagh from *c.* 888 until his death in 927.[49] The inscription also records that the manuscript was given to King Athelstan of England, possibly as a gift, and Athelstan in turn bequeathed the manuscript to Christ Church, Canterbury.[50] The Latin Vulgate gospel measures 159mm x 110mm and therefore falls into the category of a 'pocket gospel'. It is written in an Irish minuscule hand with some decorated pages. In addition to the four Evangelist portrait pages, other illumination includes an introductory cross page with the Evangelist symbols. Of interest in the context of the FMP is the portrait of St Luke (f. 115v). Standing inside a broad frame with L-shaped interlace panels at each corner and two fretwork panels at each side, Luke holds a white crozier in his right hand and a

49 W. O'Sullivan 2005, 537; Moss 2014c, 243.

50 Dodwell 1993, 92.

book in his left hand, held by the spine with very long fingers and facing out towards the viewer. Gripping the book by the spine would be a natural way to support it. The front of the book, facing outward, displays three large black dots aligning with the fore-edge, depicting three buttons on a flap. The flap itself differs from the FMP version in that the edge is profiled around the form of each button, resulting in a scalloped edge. On closer examination of the three buttons on Luke's book, it can be seen that the central button comes to a point while the other two have a round form (Fig. 4.11). This resembles the form of the FMP buttons, as mentioned earlier. It can also be noted that the size of the book depicted in the Luke portrait is a large-format manuscript on the same scale as the FMP.

The second manuscript of interest is the Cadmug Gospels (Landesbibliothek Codex Bonifatianus 3), another Vulgate gospel of the 'pocket' type, measuring *c.* 125mm x 112mm. It is written in both single and double columns in an Irish minuscule hand and contains old Irish glosses believed to be contemporary with the main text.[51] An inscription on folio 65r, *Do gratias ago cadmug scribsit*, gives the manuscript its name. It is not certain whether the colophon of this Irish scribe was transferred from its exemplar or relates specifically to the manuscript. There is some notion that it was written before the death of St Boniface (d. 754), after whom it is named.[52] The manuscript is dated to the second half of the eighth century.[53] Illumination of the Cadmug Gospels includes four Evangelist portraits and their incipit pages opposite. The portraits look very similar, with not much distinction between the four. There are no symbols; rather the Evangelist's name is written beside each portrait as an aid to identification. In matching stylised dress, the four figures are presented facing forward and standing inside a decorated frame with their feet extending beyond the lower end of the frame. Each holds a sceptre in his right hand and a book in his left. The book is gripped at the tail with the same distinctive long fingers as seen in Mac Durnan's Luke portrait, again orientating the book with the spine down and the fore-edge up. In all four images there is the same sculpted type of flap observed in Mac Durnan, and in three of the four the three buttons are also illustrated. An inner frame of three sides runs close to the head, fore-edge and tail of the book, which might be an attempt to give a three-dimensional aspect to the drawing. The absence of buttons from Luke's book may be an oversight rather than something intentional, as there is a considered effort to match all four portraits in every other detail (Fig. 4.21). The Cadmug Gospels in effect provide four examples of the style of binding represented by the FMP.

A third example is provided by another Irish pocket gospel-book, measuring *c.* 175mm x 142mm, the Book of Dimma (TCD MS 59), named after the scribe whose colophon appears a number of times in the margins of the folios; these, however, are later additions, erasing the original scribe in an attempt to associate the manuscript with an early seventh-century scribe named Dimma, whose fame rests on the fact that St Crónán (d. 619), who founded a monastery in Roscrea, Co. Tipperary, asked him to write a gospel in one day. Dimma set to it and wrote from sunrise to sunset; the sun did not set for 40 days, allowing him to complete his task.[54] It is likely that the forging of his name in the folios was an attempt to link this manuscript to the miracle. It is believed that the manuscript was a product of Roscrea and dates from the second half of the eighth century.[55]

The manuscript is written by a number of scribes in what O'Neill describes as an 'economical insular minuscule hand'.[56] There is a consensus among scholars that St John's Gospel is of a better

51 Meyer 1912a.

52 J. Brown 1972, 242.

53 Alexander 1978a, 70.

54 Diringer 1982, 468.

55 Meehan 2015, 87.

56 O'Neill 2014, 26.

Fig. 4.21 — Fulda, Landesbibliothek Codex Bonifatianus 3: the four matching Evangelists.

Fig. 4.22—TCD MS 59, f. 104: the eagle of St John.

standard and by a separate scribe, and it is this gospel that is relevant here. Each incipit page of the four gospels is preceded by an author portrait. Matthew, Mark and Luke are each presented looking out at the reader, dressed in highly stylised garments. Matthew and Luke stand, while Mark is seated. All are presented holding books. The presentation of John differs in all respects from the preceding three. The quality of writing is more disciplined and the incipit page of John is written in long lines with large display lettering for *'In p'*, employing dots and a bird-head figure at the base of the *I*. The portrait page, in contrast to the other Evangelist pages, displays the symbol of John as the eagle. He stands with two sets of wings, a haloed head looking towards his incipit page, with matching colours and dots generously distributed within the figure, all inside a decorated frame of interlace and fretwork. Held in John's talons but positioned behind them is a book, and here again is a representation of the FMP style of binding, with the flap uppermost and the three buttons in view. Similar to the Cadmug Gospels, the flap following the profile of the buttons shows a sculpted edge. The slightly awkward depiction of the book behind the leg of the eagle required the artist to offset the left-hand button and flap profile to ensure that it would not be obscured from the viewer. The artist painted two rather awkward V-shaped shadows at the head and tail of the book, referencing the same portfolio-type form as the FMP cover (Fig. 4.22). It should be noted that the association with Roscrea places this manuscript in the same general geographical location as Faddan More, in the centre of Ireland.

The next manuscript displaying an FMP-type cover within its pages comes from St Gallen in Switzerland (Cod. Sang. 1395). This is a collection of fragments from the Abbey Library dating from the fifth to the tenth century and including a large number of Irish fragments from the seventh to the ninth century. The manuscript appears to have been bound in this form in the sixteenth or seventeenth

Fig. 4.23—St Gallen, Stiftsbibliothek Cod. Sang. 1395, f. 418.

century, with a full tanned leather binding over wooden boards and brass furniture still extant, although no longer attached to the manuscript. Currently the book is in modern half-vellum binding with marble paper sides. Of interest is pp 418–19, the singleton measuring *c.* 219mm x 178mm which is stitched for the length of its back edge to a vellum guard. The recto shows a full-page miniature of St Matthew, while the verso lists charms against illness written in Old Irish and Latin dating from the ninth century.[57]

Matthew is presented seated and facing the reader, with the tools of book-writing in his hands; the pen in his right hand is dipped into a cone-shaped ink-well which appears attached to the back of the chair, and the knife in his left hand rests on a book, more or less in his lap. A figure facing him also holds a book. The scene is set inside a polychrome frame of orange, purple and blue, with fret patterns and corner pieces. Beneath the chair is additional material related to book-making: a number of scrolls of parchment tied around the centre, awaiting folding, marking up and writing. Two other objects beneath the chair take the form of broad 'S' shapes, narrowing slightly at each end and widest in the centre, which is marked by two parallel lines running across the body of the shapes. At the top of each form there is a projecting tab and beneath it a filled-in circular shape. One of the two forms has an additional inner border line following the profile. Carol Farr has suggested that these forms represent the FMP-type binding. Given the general stylised nature of the miniature, and examining both forms in detail, they appear to display the essential features of the binding style of the FMP, with the spine area defined by the close parallel lines and the tabs representing the flap, while the

57 Dora 2019, 83; Farr 2017, 188–9.

filled-in circles correspond to the buttons.[58] I noted while studying a digital image of this folio that it is presented reversed from its intended orientation. This is evidenced by a series of sewing holes along the fore-edge of what was originally a backfold. The correct order would place Matthew on the verso, facing the incipit page of his gospel (Fig. 4.23).

Although the following manuscript appears removed from the milieu of previous examples both in date and geographically, it is included as a demonstration of the longevity of this type of structure from its source. This manuscript (Cairo, Coptic Museum No. 94), dating from 1250, contains the letters of St Paul and the Acts of the Apostles. The full-page miniature on folio 131v shows four Apostles standing facing the reader in a line, identified from left to right as James, Peter, John and Jude. All are haloed and all but John have beards. They are identified by name, written below each figure in Arabic and above in Coptic. In the background is a pair of opened curtains, and above them the space is filled by decoration that is clearly heavily influenced by Islamic art. The Coptic-Arabic nature of the manuscript can be expected after centuries of Arabic rule. During the period of manuscript No. 94, Egypt witnessed a growth in Coptic-Arabic literature, which declined thereafter as conversion of the population to Islam increased, as mentioned previously.[59] Each Apostle holds a book in his hand (or hands, in the case of Peter). All four books represent a slightly different form of the FMP-style binding. The defining feature of the flap is visible in each. On James's book it is rectangular, in the same fashion as the FMP, but encroaches less onto the outer cover. Peter obscures the flap of his book with his hands, but enough detail is visible to make out an envelope-type flap, which appears to terminate about halfway across the front cover. John holds his book by the fore-edge and again obscures the view, though an abbreviated envelope-type flap is just discernible. In addition, John's book also displays the only decoration on any of the four, in the form of an equal-armed cross on the front cover. Finally, Jude holds a book with a more substantial envelope-type flap, with the tip terminating at least two thirds of the way across the front cover. There may also be a button depicted in the centre of the flap (Fig. 4.24).

The final examples documented here come not from the folios of medieval manuscripts but from the Byzantine mosaics decorating the interior of two medieval buildings in Ravenna, located in Emilia-Romagna in central Italy. Among the profuse mosaics on the walls of the Basilica of San Vitale is a portrait of the Evangelist Luke. He stands on a rocky outcrop, holding an open book in his left hand. The format of the manuscript depicted here is somewhat different from the other examples presented above that employ the use of an extending flap in the same manner as the FMP cover; instead, the illustrated binding in San Vitale displays either a three-loop or three-button closing system which extends from the fore-edge on the back/right-hand board. The corresponding tying straps are visible on the front/left-hand board. These mosaics date from the sixth century and serve to remind us that closing systems for manuscripts were employed throughout the medieval period in several guises. The second example comes from the Mausoleum of Galla Placidia, with its portrait of St Lawrence, who was martyred in the third century and is depicted here with the large gridiron on which he was burnt. In his right hand he holds an open book, with what appear to be page-markers and an abbreviated fore-edge flap on the back or right-hand board. This flap does not run the full length of the cover but rather extends out from the centre for about two thirds of the length. It seems to display a single button in the centre of the flap (Figs 4.25 and 4.26).

It is noteworthy that those comparative examples above that are presented between the folios of medieval manuscripts from the same period as the FMP all emanate from Ireland or were produced under Irish influence abroad. I found no contemporary images from manuscripts produced under the Anglo-Saxon or Carolingian dynasties or from a brief trawl through Mozarabic manuscripts from Spain

58 Pers. comm., 23 March 2016.

59 Gabra 2002, 17.

Fig. 4.24—Cairo, Coptic Museum No. 94, f. 131v.

Fig. 4.25—Basilica of San Vitale, Ravenna: portrait of St Luke the Evangelist.

Fig. 4.26—Mausoleum of Galla Placidia, Ravenna: portrait of St Lawrence.

in the same period. The example noted from further east, in Cairo, post-dates the FMP by anything up to half a century. Furthermore, those illustrated all display the feature of buttons on the flap.

WIDER INFLUENCE OF THE COPTIC FLAP BINDING

Accepting Egypt, and more specifically the early Coptic Church, as the place of origin for the binding style whose main features are a cover manufactured from a single piece of material, typically leather, with an extension to the lower cover forming a fore-edge flap, the Nag Hammadi Library can be put forward as an exemplar of this style. It can reasonably be argued that this format not only was adopted within the Christian churches, including what has been commonly called the Celtic Church, as the FMP demonstrates, but also represents the prototype for bindings in non-Christian traditions.

The Manichaean religion traces its origins to third-century Mesopotamia, where its founder, Mani, having been exposed to Christian and Buddhist teachings, formed his own philosophy and at the age of 24 founded a new religion. Missionary disciples spread the 'Religion of Light' westward into the Roman Empire and eastward into India and Central Asia. The discovery of a large collection of Manichaean Coptic papyri buried in the sands of Dāḵla oasis, about 230 miles west of Luxor, provides a clear indication that the Manichaean religion was establishing itself in Roman Egypt in the fourth century and in co-existence with Christianity. The material now in the Chester Beatty Library, Dublin, includes a psalter (CBL Pma 3 Psalmbook, Part I, CBL Pma 3 Psalmbook Part II) dating from the early fifth century.

Another find of Manichaean manuscript material was excavated from a ruined medieval city near the oasis town of Turfan, also known as Turpan, located today in the Xinjiang region of north-west China. The material, approximately dated to between the mid-eighth and early eleventh centuries, is mostly fragmentary and includes scraps of book covers and fragments of illuminated manuscripts. One of these illuminations shows one of the elect beside a low table on which is a book (Berlin State Museums MIK III 8260). The dating of this particular fragment is the subject of some discussion but the first quarter of the tenth century is suggested.[60] Zsuzsanna Gulácsi, who surveyed the collection with the aim of establishing the codicological characteristics of Manichaean books, describes the book illustrated in this fragment as a 'different kind of book cover' and she goes on to draw comparisons with the Nag Hammadi style of cover.[61] Examination of the illustration reveals a square-format book cover with a large curved flap extending two thirds of the way across the cover and with a button just forward of the flap. There appears to be a decorative element to the flap, with an inner curved line following the profile of the flap's edge.

The religion of Islam, which post-dates both Christianity and Manichaeism by over half a millennium, was to be influenced by both in book-making. Evidence of this can be observed when examining what is considered to be the 'classic Islamic book cover'. This particular style was identified as early as the 1700s, when John Bagford (1650–1716), a British antiquarian, writer and bibliographer, discussing the distinguishing features of the books of the Turks and Persians, noted that:

> *'Their books are not bound as the Europeans', theirs are set together with a sort of paste on the back of books, and over that they cover it with a piece of linen cloth, and with the headband the book is fastened to the cover, and all their books have flaps that cover the fore-edge of the book, not unlike our vellum pocket book and almanacs, but they have no clasps to them.'*[62]

60 Gulácsi 2005, 54.

61 *Ibid.*, 87.

62 Davenport 1904, 19.

With the Arab invasion of Egypt in 641 and the conversion of its population to Islam over the following centuries, the assimilation of the Coptic book-making techniques is no surprise, particularly given the restricted use of the book in Islam, in which there was early disapproval for any books other than the Qur'an.[63] The distinguishing features mentioned by Bagford perhaps drew their inspiration from the Nag Hammadi tradition of Coptic book-making but developed it to a far more sophisticated and highly decorated level, in no small part owing to the technology, ingenuity and skills of their craftspeople. Extant binding fragments mirroring the Islamic models were found among the archaeological discoveries of the Manichaean manuscript material from Turfan, and here, when reconstructed,[64] we see an almost identical appearance to the Islamic book. The Manichaeans tried to integrate their religion with Islam in the Arab Islamic empires but also suffered persecution at the hands of their would-be religious partners.[65] Although this would have restricted the number of Manichaean books in circulation, supporters of Mansūr al-Ḥallāj, the Persian revolutionary writer (executed in 922), imitated the lavish books of the Manichaeans, and the decoration and religious status of the book became an important factor in Islam.[66]

THE TREASURE BINDING

As a contemporaneous alternative to the semi-limp structure of the FMP and at the other end of the scale to what was achievable in the early medieval milieu, 'treasure bindings' are closely associated with Christianity and display a complex level of decoration, where typically the decorated panel or plate is produced separately from the book and is attached when complete, as opposed to being an integral part of the materials used for the structure of the binding. Evidence of these de luxe structures is to be found in both rare extant examples and in the written sources, where they are described in both a positive and a negative light.

Magnus Aurelius Cassiodorus (485–585), a Roman nobleman holding high office in the mid-fifth century, retired from public life and travelled to Constantinople, where he studied Christian writings. After twenty years he returned to Italy, abandoned the secular world and established two monasteries, Vivarium and Castellum, on his estate in Calabria, southern Italy.[67] Cassiodorus's passion for producing books is clearly demonstrated in the guide that he produced for his monks, *Institutiones*, in which he includes provision for decorated bindings:

> *'We have supplied artists well trained in bookbinding, so that the beauty of the sacred writings should have a comely outward appearance—In addition to these things we have provided workers skilled in bookbinding, in order that a handsome external form may clothe the beauty of the sacred letters; in some measure, perhaps, we imitate the example in the parable of the Lord, who amid the glory of the heavenly banquet has clothed in wedding garments those whom He judges worthy of being invited to the table. And for the binders, in fitting manner, unless I err, we have represented various styles of binding in a single codex, that he who so desires may choose for himself the type of cover he prefers.'*[68]

---

63 Bell 1937, 382.

64 Gulácsi 2005, 84.

65 Rippin 2013, 73.

66 Mez 1937, 175.

67 Brown 2006b, 65.

68 Cassiodorus, *Institutiones*, I.xxx.3 (Mynors 1937, 77).

Cassiodorus's instructions say much about the emphasis placed on the visual impact of sacred writings and about the level of skill and artistry that was demanded when producing the words and illustration for the great Gospel and other liturgical works. It is logical that the structure employed to house such monumental books should equal their contents in artistic endeavour. The text tells of the existence of a specialised group of trained individuals who were in effect bookbinders, although it is plausible that these artisans were also skilled in other crafts, such as leather- or woodworking, or possibly metalworking. It can also be deduced that the profession was well enough advanced to have had a selection of styles from which to choose, and that the mechanical criteria of how a book was put together were standardised and understood by this period. If only Cassiodorus's 'sample codex' had survived we would be much better informed about sixth-century European bookbinding. Although it is evident that similar skills and resources were available in the monastic midlands of Ireland, with extant metalwork in particular testifying to this, no such treatment of the FMP was carried out and it was presented in a far more modest and practical housing, most likely intended as a temporary arrangement.

There is illustrated evidence of the products of Vivarium passed down from an exemplar (now lost), the Codex Grandior, a sixth-century bible which Ceolfrid (d. 716), abbot of Monkwearmouth-Jarrow, brought back from Vivarium or Rome and of which he had three copies made, one of which, the Codex Amiatinus (Biblioteca Medicea Laurenziana MS Amiatinus 1), survives. Produced in the early years of the eighth century as a copy of its exemplar, the Codex Grandior, it contains a full-page portrait of Ezra (f. 5r) wearing the breastplate and headdress of a Jewish priest and transcribing a manuscript on his lap while seated. He is surrounded by the apparatus needed for manuscript production. Behind him is a cupboard with the doors open and containing a nine-volume bible, clearly displaying examples of the types of binding mentioned by Cassiodorus. The simple line-drawings of the cover decoration employed on the shelved manuscripts were reproduced by Haseloff, presumably working from the source manuscript. We see a selection of geometric patterns as part of the cover decoration, with the lozenge shape featuring prominently; this same design is included in the collection of trial motifs on the cover of the FMP and will be discussed in the next chapter. A further observation concerning the volumes on the shelves of the *armarium* is that no sewing supports are visible on the spines, which if illustrated would appear as a number of spaced raised bands running across the spine, an image associated with western binding structures from the medieval period. Instead, the spines appear smooth, and this suggests that an unsupported sewing system was employed for all the manuscripts (Fig. 4.27). This method of link-stitch sewing is of Coptic origin, yet it is not surprising to find this style of binding in southern Italy, as there is strong evidence to support the theory that the Coptic method of sewing was widely employed in the Mediterranean and further west. This can be supported by an examination of some of the early medieval western manuscripts still in their contemporary or near-contemporary bindings, where considerable influence from an eastern Mediterranean book-making tradition is evident, both stylistically and in the methodologies employed to assemble the components. The St Cuthbert Gospels (British Library Add. MS 89000) is a good example; besides an unsupported sewing, it exhibits elements of eastern motifs on the decorated cover. Another small Insular gospel-book, the Cadmug Gospels (Fulda, Landesbibliothek Codex Bonifatianus 3), is also bound using Coptic techniques, although the sewing has been repaired at some stage in the past. The cover of the FMP strongly follows this trend and is unique in also employing one of the materials only found on actual Coptic or eastern structures, namely papyrus.

Returning to the portrait of Ezra, it is worth considering the possibility that the visible volumes do not represent 'a comely outward appearance' of manuscripts produced at Vivarium in the sixth century but rather are more representative of the 'house style' of a northern Anglo-Saxon monastery in the late seventh century. I believe that the artist would have adapted the portrait to some degree

Fig. 4.27—Codex Amiatinus (Bib. Med. Laurenziana MS Amiatinus 1), f. 5r.

during his copying from the Codex Grandior in order to make it current for a late seventh-century audience. Otto Pächt observes that, '... as far as pictorial element is concerned, the assumption of absolute fidelity to the original will certainly create problems and can no more be taken as an absolute'. He continues: 'Even the most unadventurous copyist will always interpret his copy according to his preconceptions. Thus a *deliberate misunderstanding* resides in any new form, in the sense of having to speak in the language of one's own generation.'[69] As an example of this in relation to medieval bindings, the limited-edition facsimile copies of the Book of Kells produced by Faksimile Verlag of Luzern in 1990 can be cited. These are now in many library collections around the world. In order to complement the high-quality reproduction of the folios, including holes in the skin, a lavish medieval-style binding was commissioned to accompany the contents, using traditional materials and methods and executed by hand. It is, however, clear to anyone with an understanding of book structures that the product is far from its robust and structurally sound medieval exemplars and is more accurately described as a pastiche, with many modern adaptations of traditional features. This was not an attempt by Faksimile Verlag to deceive the would-be purchaser of this not-inexpensive volume with poor workmanship; it was simply a modern interpretation with current influences at play, including the influence of time. Today, 'time' plays a major role and is an important factor in most manufacturing processes, even when it comes to the production of a high-

69 Pächt 1986, 24.

value, handmade medieval-style binding. 'Time' would not have exercised the same influence on the production of a book in ninth-century monastic Ireland, as evidenced in surviving examples by the quality of the materials employed and the complexity with which they were worked in order to reach the high standard of the early medieval codex.

Closer to the environs in which the FMP was produced, the Annals of the Four Masters[70] record that in AD 1006 'The Great Gospel of Columb Cille was stolen at night from the western erdamh of the great church of Ceannaus. This was the principal relic of the western world on account of its singular cover; and it was found after twenty nights and two months, its gold having been stolen off it, and a sod over it.'[71] This is generally accepted to describe the looting of the *cumdach,* or book-box, housing the Book of Kells. Paul Mullarkey argues that a box rather than a shrine would have been used for such a precious symbol of the Columban community, as access to the manuscript would have been required, rather than its being kept solely as a relic of the saint.[72] The tradition of housing sacred writings in shrines as venerated relics of the saints associated with the manuscripts within—links that are often tenuous—is a particular Irish practice. Given the loss of folios from the beginning and end of this pinnacle of Insular manuscripts, however, possibly during its theft from the church at Kells, it can also be surmised that this was a result of the violent stripping of the precious bejewelled covers. Unlike a shrine, covers would have been mechanically attached to the manuscript and considerable force would have been needed to remove them, given the robust nature of book structures in the early medieval period. The practice of that time of pasting down the first and last folios of the quires to the inside of the binding boards would also have resulted in detachment of the adjacent folios in the event of a forceful removal. Bernard Meehan states that 'around 10 leaves are missing from the start';[73] this would equate with a typical quire.

There is direct reference to the production of decorated covers, or perhaps a book-shrine, by Tírechán, a seventh-century Irish bishop and biographer of St Patrick. In his Life of the saint transcribed in the Book of Armagh, he lists the many disciples of St Patrick, including St Asicus, bishop of Elphin. Asicus was also a skilled coppersmith and produced liturgical vessels and instruments for Patrick. Tírechán states that 'he made altars and book-cases, which he made in plates, for the honour of Patrick the bishop, and also the three square plates well finished, which I saw'.[74] In continuation of this tradition there is the case of St Dageaus, abbot of Inishcealtra (d. 587), who is described as '... equally skilful in making covers for books, which he adorned with gold silver and jewels'.[75]

Across the water, the Lindisfarne Gospels (British Library Cotton MS Nero D.iv) displays among its pages a tenth-century reference to its own treasure binding, written by a priest called Aldred, who glossed the manuscript, 'and Ethelwald, Bishop of the Lindisfarne Islanders, impressed it on the outside and covered it as he well knew how to do. And Billfrith, the Anchorite, forged the ornaments which are on it on the outside and adorned it with gold and with gems and also with silver over silver—pure metal.'[76] It is not surprising that references to book-making found in the documented sources should focus on these bejewelled, important, high-status gospel-books and psalters, with little

70 Mícheál Ó Cléirigh *et al.*, Annals of the Four Masters, Royal Irish Academy, MS C.iii.3, a seventeenth-century paper manuscript, of which copies are also held in Trinity College Dublin and University College Dublin.

71 Meehan 1994, 14.

72 Mullarkey 2000, 68.

73 Meehan 2012, 32.

74 Betham 1827, 348–402; Ó Riain 2011, 570.

75 Kenney 1929, 383–4.

76 M. Brown 2003, 118.

Fig. 4.28—Caherlehillan, Iveragh Peninsula, Co. Kerry, cross-slab.

or no mention of the simple utilitarian type such as the cover of the FMP. That is not to say that the latter were not produced in significant numbers but that they were regarded as ordinary everyday items, not worth recording.

The majority of the medieval Christian texts that have survived into the present day have done so because of their status at that time, originally adorned in complex and elaborate bindings and well cared for; many then became relics and were enshrined, thus improving their chances of survival even further. The FMP survived for no better reason than that it was buried in a bog and was thus removed from the influences of time and repurposing; as such, it potentially provides insights into the more 'ordinary' type of book circulating in the eighth-century Insular world.

The treasure or highly decorated manuscript was not always well received: St Jerome (347–420) wrote a diatribe in 384 against wealthy Christian women 'whose books are written in gold on purple vellum, and clothed with gems'.[77] This fits the character of the saint, who was a strict ascetic and was generally critical of all excess and creature comforts. No doubt he would have approved of the unadorned and simple binding of the FMP.

Finally, although not strictly in the realm of treasure bindings, it is worth mentioning the St John's (Rinnagan) Crucifixion Plaque (National Museum of Ireland R554.H.20), a thin sheet of copper alloy which was worked into its form and then engraved with Insular patterns. It displays a typical representation of the crucifixion of Christ, with angels above, resting on the outstretched arms of Christ, while Stephaton and Longinus stand beneath. The format of the plaque and the nail hole in each corner suggest that it may well have adorned the cover of an Irish gospel-book of the late eighth or early ninth century; it hints that Ireland had kept pace with the development and elaborate nature of European bindings of the period and that it was not a lack of know-how that placed the FMP in its more utilitarian binding.

CONCLUSION

Much of the preference for monasticism in sixth-century Ireland, and the adoption of many practices of the Egyptian prototype model (albeit modified as it passed through Europe and on to Ireland from France and Britain), derived from the influential writings of John Cassian, introducing Coptic asceticism to the West.[78] It might not be surprising that the materiality of later Egyptian monasticism, now the Coptic Church, would also be embraced with some degree of enthusiasm in Ireland, perhaps more so than elsewhere in the Christian Europe of the seventh and eighth centuries. The early monastic (fifth- or sixth-century) site at Caherlehillan on the Iveragh Peninsula, Co. Kerry, supports this idea, with evidence to suggest that it was a small cenobitic community similar to what was to be found in the deserts of Egypt. The site has produced archaeological fragments of eastern Mediterranean amphorae (Bii ware[79]), and two cross-slabs display what appear to be symbols of the Eastern Church's stylised peacock, a symbol of the Resurrection, and a flabellum, the liturgical fan used on the altar of the Eastern Church (Fig. 4.28).[80] Father Gregory Telepneff tentatively goes so far as to suggest direct Celtic–Oriental contact, basing much of his argument on differences between Irish and Gallic monastic practices and a better Irish alignment with Coptic monasteries, and he cautiously concludes the likelihood of the presence of a few Coptic monks in Ireland in the

77 Migne, PLXXII col. 418 (Ep. 22 to Eustochium).

78 Endres 2017, 218.

79 Kelly 2010.

80 Sheehan 2014, 132.

early sixth century.[81] Reversing the direction of travel, we have contemporary reports, *c.* 700, by Adomnán in his *De locis sanctis* of the travels of the Frankish Bishop Arculf,[82] who spent time in the Holy Land, Alexandria, Constantinople and Rome.[83]

Were it not for the papyrus cartonnage that originally lined the inside cover of the FMP I would suggest that it was a local product constructed from a model or exemplar; the exotic nature of the lining, however, supports the argument for its being an import. This hypothesis is reinforced by the meagre writing discovered on the inside of the cover, which is on the leather surface and therefore applied after the papyrus lining was removed. It occurs to me that perhaps the papyrus lining was stripped from the inside because, like the linings of the Nag Hammadi codices, the FMP lining was also made from manuscript waste and would have been of immense interest to the Irish monastic scholars, even if they could not have deciphered the language, emanating as it did from Coptic Egypt, home of the inspirational Desert Fathers. Although, as already mentioned, it is known that papyrus continued in use in isolated settings such as papal bulls, it is unlikely that such a document would find itself as the lining of a bookbinding cover.

I believe that the extant examples of similar structures, and especially the illustrated images of the FMP-type cover in manuscripts, indicate that what was an unexpected discovery from a codicological and binding history viewpoint was most probably a reasonably abundant form of protection for early medieval Insular—or perhaps more specifically Irish—manuscripts. The artists producing the images of saints and apostles in liturgical writings were aware that their work, in addition to venerating the word of God, had a didactic role for the audience. If a book was to be depicted in the hand of an Evangelist, then it had to be recognised as such, and in the same way as the shoes on their feet are considered an accurate historical record of early medieval footwear, so too should their representation of a book be considered 'typical'. The cover of the FMP might well be our only extant example, thus far, of what was once the standard binding in the eighth-century Insular world.

81 Telepneff 2008.

82 The authenticity—and even the existence—of Arculf has come under scrutiny in recent times, but as there is no scholarly consensus on the matter it remains a valid historical reference. Woods 2016.

83 Sharpe 1995, 54.

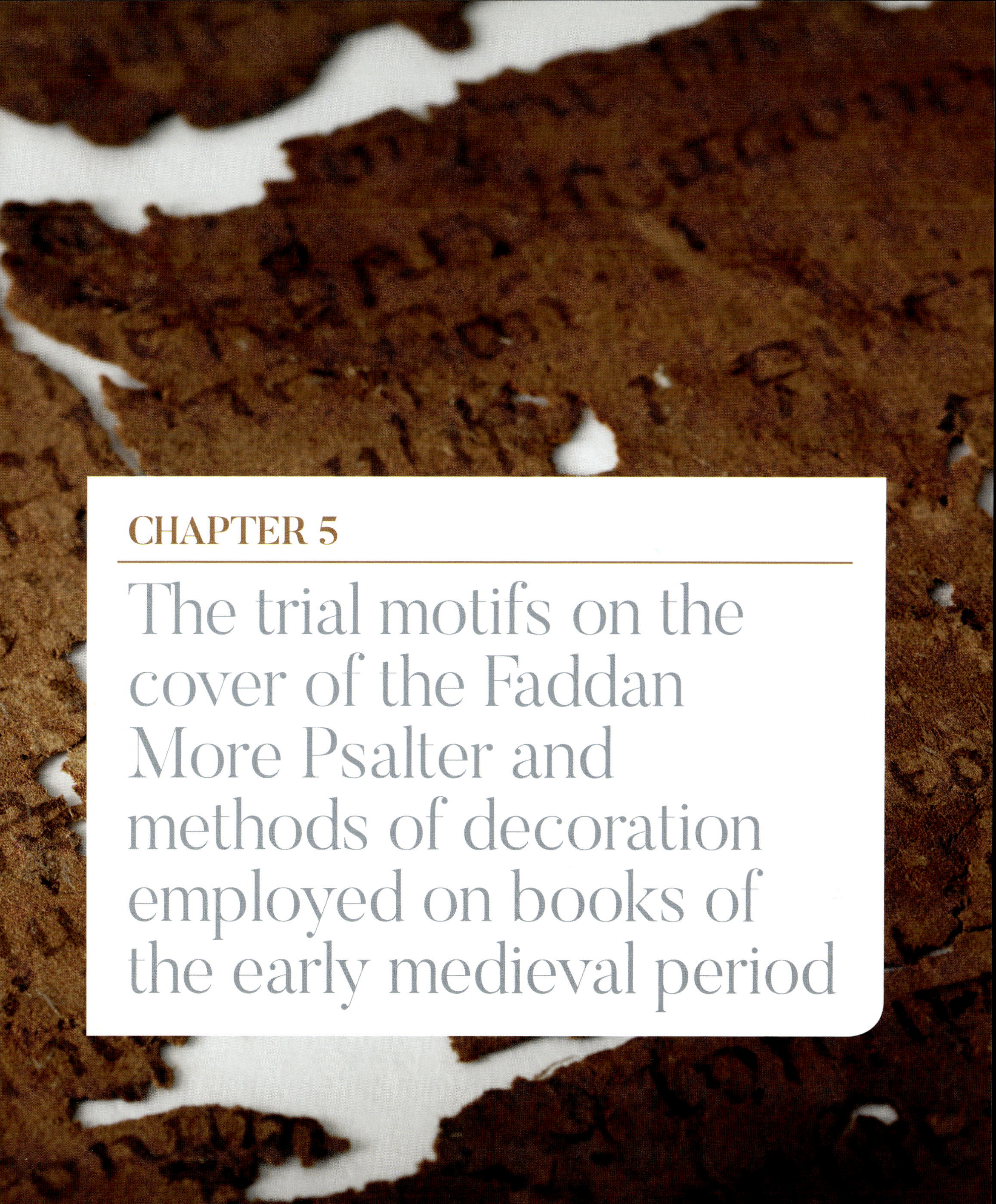

CHAPTER 5

The trial motifs on the cover of the Faddan More Psalter and methods of decoration employed on books of the early medieval period

CHAPTER 5

The trial motifs on the cover of the Faddan More Psalter and methods of decoration employed on books of the early medieval period

One of the many complex and challenging tasks faced while conserving the FMP was the preparation of the tanned leather cover for drying. In the same manner as the rest of the manuscript, the cover or binding of the psalter had been lost in a watery hollow beneath the peat bog at Faddan More for over a millennium. A particularly time-consuming aspect of this preparation work was the surface-cleaning of the leather. The process involved working under magnification (0.75x) to remove, by various means, the array of organic bog material adhering to the leather, none more challenging than the plethora of seed pods, which numbered in the thousands and took on a transparent appearance while wet (see Chapter 1). It was during this close-up work that several ultra-fine incised lines became evident. They appeared in random zones across the entire outer surface with the exception of the spine area. Given what appeared to be the intentional application of these markings, it was critical that the incisions be recorded and mapped in the 'wet state', as I could not be certain of their behaviour during and after the drying process. In addition to the incised forms, unassociated markings were identified as a series of 'tram lines', likely to be the result of the cover being employed as a support for hard-point ruling of the vellum folios; this is discussed in detail in Chapter 4.

The investigation on the cover of the FMP mapped and identified 31 trial motifs. The decoration matches all the criteria of Uaininn O'Meadhra's definition of a trial piece. In a motif there are always two distinct aspects: the pattern(s) and the piece, where the patterns are of primary importance and the piece of secondary importance (meaning that the patterns do not 'decorate' the piece but 'use' the piece as a support for their representation). This best describes the rudimentary results of the artist(s). I am guided here by Uaininn O'Meadhra for the descriptive terminology of the patterns that follows.[1] The patterns appear to have been created with an extremely sharp-edged tool, 'scalpel-like' in its execution; indeed, in a number of instances the keen edge has almost cut through the tanned leather surface (Fig. 5.1). The patterns can for the most part be described as incomplete, where the field line or field, in the case of the curvilinear patterns, does not close. In other examples, the motif itself is unfinished. The quality of both

1 O'Meadhra 1979, II, 8.

Fig. 5.1 — Deep incisions in the surface of the leather.

the finished and the unfinished patterns, the difficult working surface of the substrate notwithstanding, would be best described as naïve—perhaps the efforts of someone at the early stages of instruction in manuscript or metalwork decoration. Using O'Meadhra's classification,[2] the motifs on the cover of the FMP fall into either Category 2 (apprentice artisans, learning attempts, copying exercises, test pieces (samplers)) or Category 3 (artisans' trial sketches and working drawings for testing pattern composition and technique). The former seems to provide more appropriate comparisons.

Both inscribed and impressed decoration were employed on the surface of leather bindings from an early point, as demonstrated by some of the Nag Hammadi bindings and nicely illustrated in an eighth-century legal manuscript from Leon, now in St Gallen in Switzerland, in which a figure standing inside an interlace frame holds a staff and a book, the surface of which displays a simple repeated pattern in orange and black (Fig. 5.2). The trial motifs on the cover of the FMP, however, were not intended as part of its decoration. Their random layout, poor quality and general disarray point to a well-established tradition in early medieval Ireland of trying out and doodling patterns on surplus pieces of a range of materials. According to Peter Harbison, the practice is rare outside Ireland.[3] More typically the substrate would be bone, wood or even stone. Archaeology has unearthed a large and varied quantity of this material throughout the country, with a high percentage from Dublin. Some well-recorded examples include a piece of green slate found at Lissue ringfort, Co. Antrim, in 1946, now in the Ulster Museum (J228632), bearing a combination of patterns, including zoomorphic motifs. A partial long bone, highly polished and displaying incised patterns down its length (NMI W.29/Wk12), was excavated in the 1930s from the Early Christian crannog at Lagore, Co. Meath.[4]

Although the incising of patterns on the tanned leather of an early medieval book cover, Insular or otherwise, was not a typical method of decoration, everyday items of leather such as shoes, belts and sheaths were commonly incised for decorative purposes. There are examples of incised decoration on

2 *Ibid.*, 91.

3 Harbison 1999, 261.

4 Raghnall Ó Floinn, in Youngs 1989, 176.

Fig. 5.2—St Gallen, Stiftsbibliothek Cod. 731, f. 234.

leather shoes taken from a bog in County Derry, now in the National Museum (W10, WII), where they are described as 'covered with incised ladder-patterns and irregular and curvilinear motifs'. The type of shoe, 'Type 2' according to Lucas, dates from the early medieval period.[5] There are also two scabbard fragments from Dublin excavations, displaying an incomplete human figure in a tunic (DLS 283) and the incised image of a running animal (DLS 308).[6] Needless to say, the practice of incised decoration is not exclusive to Ireland; the mineralised remains of substantial leather sheaths in which a weapon called a seaxe was housed, displaying incised decoration and metal studs, have been unearthed in Saxon cemetery sites in Britain dating from the seventh century.[7]

In the context of the trial motifs it is important to examine the substrate or platform employed. In this instance it is the tanned leather cover of the FMP. This is a unique combination, and no other example is known to the author, where the cover of a manuscript has been utilised as a surface for the production of trial motifs. It is the nature of the FMP cover that allows the work to be carried out, presenting as it does a flat and yielding surface receptive to engraving with the appropriate tool. A survey of extant early medieval book covers demonstrates that the simple wrap of lined leather was only one of a variety of styles of bindings employed during this prolific period of manuscript production. The intentional marking of book covers as a form of decoration can be seen on the earliest surviving book structures in a codex form, on which patterns were impressed with blunt, pallet-like tools of metal, or possibly bone, and surfaces inscribed with simple strands forming motifs, typically of a cross or panelled borders. Such decoration is to be found on the covers of the Nag Hammadi codices,[8] which have also been discussed in relation to their structural similarities to the FMP binding. The later and more sophisticated decoration employed metal dies, allowing the pattern to be repeated over the surface of the leather. This blind stamping was probably carried out after heating the tool.

Considered to be the earliest evidence of tooling on a binding,[9] the fifth-century Glazier Codex of Acts (New York, Morgan Library G.67) displays simple roundels blind-stamped into the leather. As book structures became more technically advanced, so too did the decoration of their covers. The use of more complex patterns, the employment of colour to emphasise backgrounds and the addition of different materials to create impressive visual effects all became part of the book-makers' repertoire. Also in the Morgan Library, the seventh- or eighth-century copy of the gospels discovered in the early twentieth century in the Coptic monastery of St Michael of the Desert in southern Fayum, Egypt, exhibits all of the above techniques to great effect, displaying a well-balanced and visually satisfying pattern.[10] To achieve this, different layers were laid down; the first was of gilded leather, over which red-dyed goatskin with openwork patterns was applied, revealing the gilded surface beneath. The openwork itself was further worked with the threading of strips of vellum in both a large circular form in the centre and frames outside the circle. This upper piece was stitched to the gilded leather below. As indicated in Chapter 4, the binding of the FMP owes its origins to the same geographical area, yet it does not display the advancement in design and manufacture seen in this Morgan Library gospel-book but rather reflects the fourth-century archetype model. That is not to say that there was no awareness of sophisticated binding and decoration techniques in monastic Ireland during the era of the FMP. In Trinity College Dublin, there are two oak binding boards with the scant remains of a crimson alum-tawed covering which have long been associated

5 Lucas 1956.

6 Cameron 2007, 56.

7 Cameron 1998, 54.

8 M. Meyer 2005, 15–32. The collection comprises thirteen manuscripts dated to the mid-fourth century AD and containing works of the Gnostic gospels. Twelve of the codices had bindings.

9 Needham 1979, 10.

10 Four Gospels, Coptic, illuminated manuscript on vellum, Egypt, seventh or eighth century, Morgan Library M.569.

with the Book of Armagh (*c.* 807). The codicological examination of the boards suggests a Carolingian binding structure, as reported by Berth Van Regemorter (1879–1964), the Belgian-born bookbinder who examined them in the British Museum in 1961.[11] Despite the fragmented and very worn surface of the covering material, faint traces of blind-stamped tooling remain, with evidence of three different complex motifs and of interlace patterns. It would be fair to surmise that the Book of Armagh in its original red-stained binding would not have looked out of place in Ezra's *armarium*.

THE TRIAL MOTIFS ON THE FMP COVER: DESCRIPTION AND PARALLELS

Using the identifying key on Fig. 5.3, the 31 trial pieces on the cover of the FMP can be subdivided as follows.

A1–A4: Curvilinear patterns, two of which are penannular as a result of being basic unfinished outlines. One of the remaining two displays attempted interlace. The second pattern appears to be four double triquetras dividing the space inside the field equally. The background shows fine hatching of both the diagonal and the cross type.

B1–B6: Rectangular or square field lines containing patterns that can be identified as an attempt at plaitwork, all interlaced. Three of the patterns have double field lines. One pattern shows hatching in the field behind the motif. All six appear incomplete.

C1: Square pattern employing double field lines creating a narrow border, filled with a diagonal layout of key patterns.

D1: Square pattern; the field lines overshoot at three of the four intersections and the field is filled with diagonal strands in two directions, to form a series of square patterns. Possibly the guidework for the key pattern, which is situated just above it. This theory is reinforced by J. Romilly Allen's publication on the early Christian monuments of Scotland,[12] in which he discusses the setting out of key patterns by dividing up the space into squares; this, he says, was only occasionally used in Celtic art, the Celtic designer having a marked preference for the setting out of the squares in a diagonal 'where the setting-out lines cut the border at an angle of 45° instead of 90°'. This accurately matches the motif (D1).

E1–E2: Square patterns, inside which the field lines are divided by a double-strand cross creating four inner squares, each of which contains an 'X'.

F1–F6: Square patterns whose main feature is a single 'X' figure terminating in each corner of the pattern. Four of the patterns display an 'X' of a double-strand type; the other two are single-strand. The fields behind the 'X' show hatching and single and double strands to various degrees in four cases. One pattern (F1) employs double field lines and the addition of a central diamond shape. This could be considered a loose interpretation of the Four Evangelist symbols page on f. 290v in the Book of Kells. One pattern may be an attempt at a duplex. Examining similar patterns found in contemporary manuscripts and stonework, it appears that, where an 'X' pattern is displayed inside a square field, in

11 TCD MS 10525/1/286.

12 Romilly Allen 1903, 325.

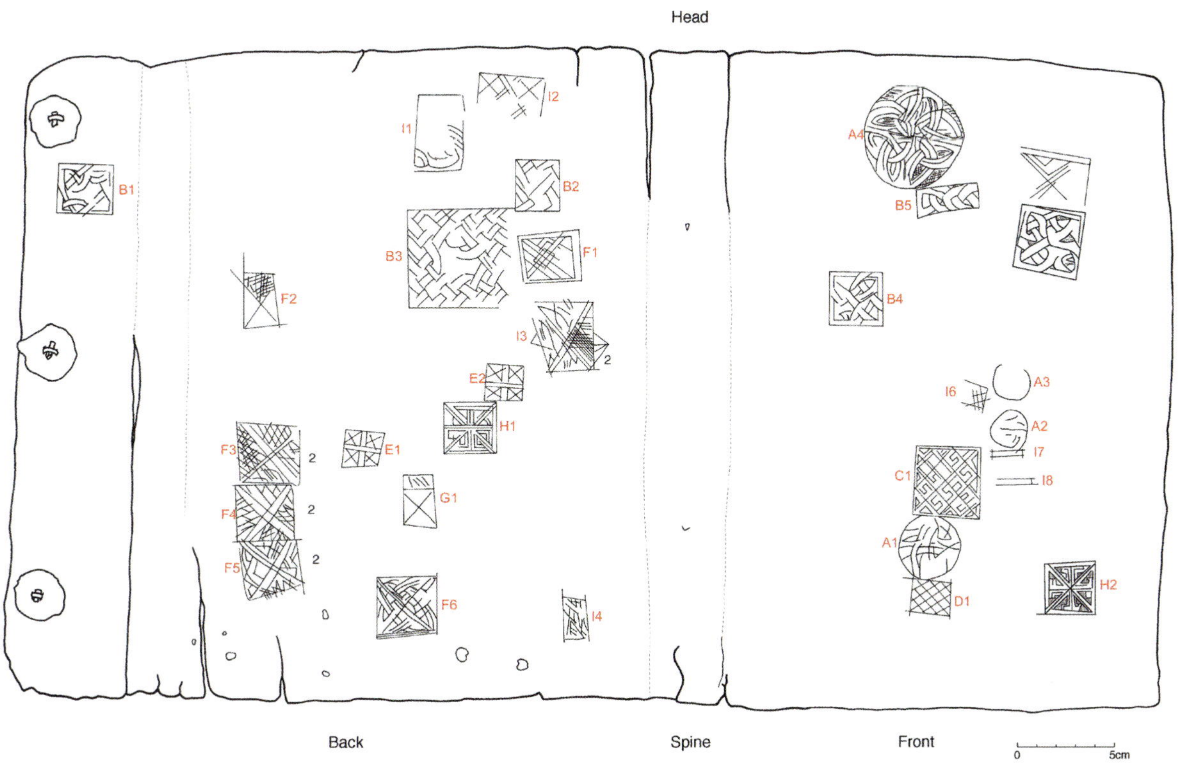

Fig. 5.3—Traced motif identification system.

most cases the 'X' is formed by placing four triangular motifs of some description inside the square, dividing it into quarters. The space between the triangles forms an 'X' from the background. In the motifs displayed on the cover of the FMP, the 'X' appears to be in the foreground and is itself a motif, as opposed to a consequence of the alignment of a repeated set of motifs.

G1: Rectangular pattern; a single strand runs horizontally inside, about one third of the way from the top, creating two panels of uneven size. The larger lower panel displays an 'X' terminating in each corner. The smaller top panel includes 'loose' hatching.

H1–H2: Square patterns with double field lines; both contain an 'X' of the double-strand type terminating in the corners of the pattern. One of the patterns displays a double-strand cross behind the 'X'. Single and double strands and curvilinear lines can be seen in the spaces between the motifs. The second pattern is the most accomplished and complete of all 31 pieces; it also displays an 'X' of the double-strand type with a single-strand type running inside it. Behind is a multi-strand cross with expanded terminals. The background has fine hatching.

I1–I8: The remaining motifs, all intended to be either rectangular or square, are fragments of patterns abandoned at such an early stage that it is impossible to determine the artist's intent. Five of the eight are missing one, and in one case two, of the frame lines. Two of the smallest rectangular pieces are devoid of decoration. Three pieces appear to display 'X' patterns in one form or another. One shows some diagonal strands crossing inside the field lines, resulting in an unfinished grid pattern. Two contain what appear to be random strands with no cohesive motif obvious.

It is useful to reinforce here what was stated at the beginning of this chapter, namely that the above description should not suggest that any of the motifs—apart from two—show indications of expert execution or indeed, in many cases, the required knowledge to complete any given pattern. They appear to be in a real sense 'trials' without ever achieving an end-product. The use of square and rectangular motifs outweighs the curvilinear at a ratio of 6.75:1. Perhaps dividers, a base tool employed for executing curvilinear motifs, were not readily available for use. Stevick demonstrates clearly the use of this tool as an aid for the production of curvilinear decoration in stonework and manuscript illumination.[13] The suggestion that there were no dividers available to the practising artist is contradicted, however, by direct evidence of their use, observed under magnification during the Optical Coherence Tomography scanning of the cover. Dr Haida Liang and her team from Nottingham Trent University mapped selected areas of the trial motifs through a process that renders an image in slices and slightly below the surface. I was able to identify a compass point not visible to the naked eye on one of the curvilinear motifs (A4) (Fig. 5.4).

The hatching of the field in a number of the patterns is not a feature that transfers easily to manuscript illumination when the medium changes from incising tool to pigment and dyes. More typically, this is a technique to introduce shading or to highlight the foreground motif in metalwork engraving. Françoise Henry notes that the technique was employed among Irish metalworkers in the early medieval period.[14] It can be seen put to good use on the field of Ultimate La Tène decoration worked on a gilt and silvered cast-bronze piece thought to be the crest of a bell-shrine.[15] Another example can be observed on the first phase of the late eighth- or early ninth-century *Domnach Airgid* shrine.[16] On one of the short sides an original decorated plate is still visible, others having been obscured by later additions and mounts. Ó Floinn observes that 'These plates are ornamented with crudely engraved broad ribbon interlace surrounded by a border of fretwork and is executed against a hatched ground. The covering may be dated to around 800 AD, when engraving of this kind was common on Irish metalwork.'[17] Ryan observes that 'Background hatching became a standard feature on tinned and engraved Irish and other Insular eighth-/ninth-century objects and may also have an Iron Age origin'.[18] Paul Mullarkey, Senior Conservator in the National Museum of Ireland, has suggested to me that it also seems to be associated with tinned surfaces, so that when the metal is incised a colour contrast is set up, with the golden-bronze metal revealed against the tinning.[19] The use of hatching is found as a feature in manuscript illumination when that illumination is more accurately described as drawing, typically in monochrome. There is an excellent example of this from the beginning of the ninth century in the Book of Armagh, where on the Evangelist symbol page (f. 32v) hatching is used particularly on the wings of the four figures in separate panels to create contrast. Interestingly, the Utrecht Psalter (Utrecht, Universiteitsbibliothek MS Bibl. Rhenotraiectinae I Nr 32), a ninth-century manuscript believed to have been produced near Reims,[20] is highly illuminated also in a monochrome style, depicting a range of scenes from the psalms and the New Testament. Rather than hatching, a subtle shading method is employed to good effect.

---

13 Stevick 2000.

14 Henry 1965, 98.

15 NMI 1920:37, ninth century AD.

16 NMI R.2834, late eighth–early ninth century, with fifteenth-century remodelling.

17 Raghnall Ó Floinn, 'Catalogue entry 85: Domnach Airgid shrine', in M. Ryan (ed.), *Treasures of Ireland: Irish art 3000 BC–1500 AD* (Dublin, 1983), 177.

18 Ryan 1989, 127.

19 Pers. comm., November 2014.

20 Alexander 1978a, 35.

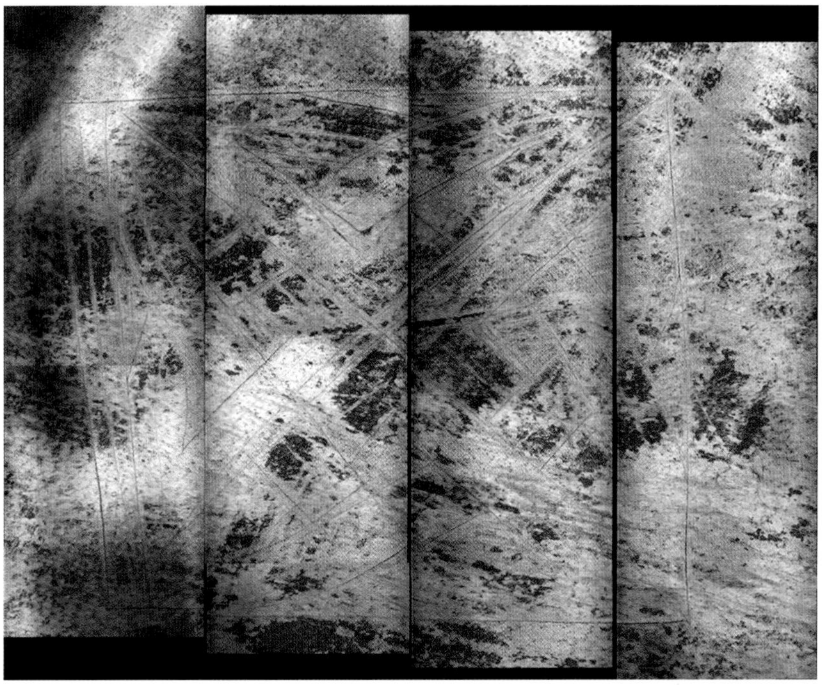

Fig. 5.4—Optical Coherence Tomography scanning of the cover.

Moving to the foreground and examining the patterns typically executed on trial motifs of Insular origin, it appears that the illustration of the cross does not feature as a central symbol. Does this indicate that trial motifs were for the most part produced by the secular population, either inside or outside the monastery? A range of patterns can be observed with plaitwork, interlace, duplex, triquetra, trumpet and zoomorphic features, while other pieces display the influence of Norse settlement in the ninth century.[21] Throughout a trawl of hundreds of images of recorded trial motifs, for the most part from Uaininn O'Meadhra's *Early Christian, Viking and Romanesque art motif-pieces from Ireland*, no obvious depiction of the cross was observed. Among the motifs located on the FMP we can identify four cruciform motifs; in this respect the work is atypical and, combined with the nature of the substrate, it may be strongly suggested that it was carried out inside the confines of a monastery.

It is no great surprise that parallels to the trial motifs on the cover of the FMP can be identified on metalwork and in manuscript illumination, the crossover being part of the scholarly narrative.[22] The motif described above as 'Six square patterns whose main feature is a single "X" figure, terminating in each corner of the pattern' (F1–F6) is particularly well represented in Insular manuscripts. It can be found as a corner motif in the border of illuminated folios in several manuscripts of the period. Here follows a selection where clear parallels can be seen between motif and decoration.

The Chronicon of Paulus Orosius (MS D.23.sup.), an early seventh-century Insular manuscript produced possibly in Bobbio, the monastery founded by St Columbanus in 614, and now in Milan Biblioteca Ambrosiana, displays on folio 1v what may be the earliest Insular carpet-page. The top and bottom border areas for the large central rosette display a continuous line of square fields, each with a multi-strand 'X' filling the space. The background field is coloured pink and yellow (Fig. 5.5).

The Lichfield Gospels (Book of Chad), produced around 730, is a manuscript whose origin is

21 Laing 2010, 127.

22 Ryan 1983, 37, and Laing 2010, 99, *inter alia*.

Fig. 5.5—Milan, Biblioteca Ambrosiana MS D.23.sup., f. 1v.

much discussed, with scholars suggesting Iona, Mercia, Northumbria, Ireland or even Lichfield.[23] It displays eight illuminated pages, the first of which is the incipit page for St Matthew's Gospel.[24] It is also the first folio of the manuscript and had clearly been exposed without the protection of a binding for an extended period, resulting in considerable erosion of the pigment. Among the badly damaged decorated lettering and illumination there are two dark, possibly black, roundel fields, one of which displays a double field line 'X' and behind a double field line cross with expanded terminals. Other than the roundel format, this is the closest example to the motif category H on the back cover of the FMP containing the cross.

In the Stiftsbibliothek of St Gall, Switzerland, is a composite manuscript (MS 1395) with fragments from the Abbey Library of St Gall. Among them are Irish fragments dating from the seventh to the ninth centuries.[25] One of these, a single folio, displays an initial *P* (*Peccavimus*) and continuation capitals housed inside a decorated frame of interlace and zoomorphic features. In each corner of the frame there is a square pattern, two of which (diagonally facing each other) display a double field line border, one coloured yellow and the other left with the vellum colour. Inside each there is a central field line 'X' with key patterns between the arms. The background field is coloured

23 Henry 1965, 162; M. Brown 2011, 35; Meehan 2018, 142.

24 Alexander 1978a, 48.

25 *Ibid.*, 261.

Fig. 5.6—St Gall, Stiftsbibliothek Cod. 1395, f. 426.

in black (Fig. 5.6). This folio is dated to the second half of the eighth century.

The Insular gospel-book in the Russian National Library in St Petersburg (Cod. F. v.I.8) dates from the late eighth century and is thought to have been produced in Northumbria under Irish influence.[26] On the incipit page to St Mark's Gospel, f. 78r, the enlarged decorated initial lettering *Initium evangelii Ih[es]u p[ist]i filii d[e]i sicut scriptu[m] est* is accompanied by a broad decorated frame. The bottom corner of the frame displays a square pattern of double field lines, inside which

26 *Ibid.*, 64.

Fig. 5.7—Leningrad Gospels (Cod. F. v.I.8), f. 78r.

there is a central field line 'X' and behind a closed band outlining the 'X' (Fig. 5.7).

Among the early medieval manuscript collection in the Bodleian Library, Oxford, is the already mentioned MacRegol Gospels, written and illuminated sometime before 822. Both geographically and chronologically this gospel-book is close to the FMP. On folio 126v, the portrait of St John, two rectangles are centred at the top and bottom of the broad outer border of the St John miniature, while two squares are centred on the left and right of the broad inner border framing St John (Fig. 5.8). All four display a repeated pattern of an 'X' inside a square. The 'X' is a narrow single strand inside a band of the background vellum. The spaces between the arms of the 'X' are filled with black triangles. The examples on the St John page make for a good comparison to the repeated pattern of the motifs

Fig. 5.8—Oxford, Bodleian Library MS Auct. D.2.19 (MacRegol Gospels), f. 126v.

F3, F4 and F5 (see Fig. 5.3). Also in England, in Lambeth Palace Library, is the aforementioned Mac Durnan Gospels, dating from the second half of the ninth century and possibly written in Armagh by Máel Brigte mac Tornáin (Mac Durnan).[27] This manuscript falls into the category of 'pocket' gospel, albeit produced to the standard of a decorated altar book. On folio 4v is the Evangelist portrait of St Matthew, framed by a broad decorated border. In each corner of the frame there is a square pattern, two of which (diagonally facing each other) display a double field line border with a central 'X' filling

27 Alexander 1978a, 86.

Fig. 5.9—London, Lambeth Palace Library, MS 1370 (Mac Durnan Gospels), f. 4v, portrait of St Matthew.

Fig. 5.10—Cambridge University Library MS Ii.6.32 (Book of Deer), f. 16v, portrait of St Mark.

the square. Behind the 'X' there is a central square, flanked at each corner by four smaller squares. Between the spaces there is closed-band outlining. Dots have been applied inside the larger central square (Fig. 5.9).

For a comparison observed in a manuscript produced outside Ireland, the Book of Deer (MS Ii.6.32) can be cited. Held in Cambridge University Library, it dates from the ninth or tenth century and was written in Scotland.[28] On folio 16v is the Evangelist portrait of St Mark, presented as a highly stylised figure of the saint standing inside a frame, holding a book or perhaps a satchel suspended from his neck (Fig. 5.10). The panel is a double-strand square pattern coloured to form a narrow border, inside which a multi-strand 'X' fills the space. Behind is open bandwork forming eight triangles to fill the field. There is a dot in the centre of the 'X'. Also in Cambridge, at St John's College, there is the early eleventh-century Southampton Psalter (MS C.9 (59)). Produced in Ireland, this manuscript, like the FMP, adopts the tripartite division of the psalms.[29] On folio 4v there is a full-page illumination of David fighting a lion. The miniature is framed by a broad decorated border with roundels dividing all four sides. In each corner of the frame there is a square pattern, two of which (diagonally facing each other) display a

28 Alexander 1978a, 87.

29 *Ibid.*, 88.

Fig. 5.11 – Cambridge, St John's College MS C.9 (59) (Southampton Psalter), f. 1v, David and the Lion.

double field line border, coloured in a pinkish red with a multi-strand 'X' filling the square (Fig. 5.11). Behind this is a single-strand cross and between the arms are four equal squares with single field lines. This pattern is repeated with slight variation on folio 72, the initial *D* page.

The 'youngest' manuscript from which parallels were drawn with the trial motifs on the FMP is the Gospel of Maelbrigte (British Library Harley MS 1802). This is another of the pocket gospel series, measuring only 165mm x 120mm, and is most likely to have been made for personal use. It dates from the early twelfth century and was probably written in Armagh. On folio 60v and folio 86v, two Evangelist symbol pages of St Mark and St Luke are displayed (Fig. 5.12). Both illuminations are housed in broad,

Fig. 5.12—London, British Library Harley MS 1802 (Gospel of Maelbrigte), f. 60v, Evangelist symbol of St Mark.

Fig. 5.13—St Gallen, Stiftsbibliothek Cod. Sang. 51, f. 209r, and London, Lambeth Palace MS 1370 (Mac Durnan Gospels), f. 4v.

double-stranded frames. Within the frames is a series of uninterrupted square patterns and single square patterns. Each displays a single field line border, with a multi-strand 'X' filling the square. Behind, there is a single-strand cross. Between the arms are four equal squares with single field lines.

During the research into this pattern, I became aware of what amounts to two almost identical designs appearing in different manuscripts spanning over a century. The first pattern is the one I describe as a square pattern with a double field line border, housing a central 'X' terminating in each corner. Behind the 'X' there is a central square, flanked at each corner by four smaller squares. In the spaces in between there is closed-band outlining. This appears in two manuscripts: St Gallen, Stiftsbibliothek MS 51,[30] p. 209, the initial page of St John's Gospel, the 'I' from *'in principio'*, about AD 750, and Lambeth Palace MS 1370, the Mac Durnan Gospels,[31] f. 4v, the Evangelist portrait of St Matthew, second half of the ninth century (Fig. 5.13).

I describe the second pattern as a double field line border with a multi-strand 'X' terminating in each corner. Behind there is a single-strand cross. Between the arms are four equal squares with single field lines. This also appears in two manuscripts: St John's College MS C.9 (59),[32] the Southampton Psalter, folio 4v (David and the Lion), of the early eleventh century, and British Library Harley MS 1802,[33] the Gospel of Maelbrigte, folios 60v and 86v, two Evangelist symbol pages of St Mark and St Luke, of the early twelfth century. This demonstrates the standardisation of Insular design motifs employed in the decoration of ecclesiastical ware and the longevity of such patterns. In context, I cannot imagine a graphic designer today producing a book cover and using composition and layouts from a post-World War I publication. It is also evident that pattern-books must have been circulating among monasteries, allowing the motifs to be practised and mastered before being committed to the folios of a gospel-book. Just as an experienced scribe would instruct his pupil in the minuscule and majuscule letters, the artist would pass on the designs and techniques of the patterns that we see repeated over the majority of our extant Insular manuscripts, these covering a time-span of 200 years with impressive consistency.

In relation to the broad interlaced plaitwork motif in a rectangular frame (B5) on the back cover of the FMP, many comparisons can be drawn, given the widespread use of this form of decoration in Insular manuscripts and metalwork. A motif similar in its proportions can be seen in the border decoration on the Evangelist portrait of St Luke in the Mac Durnan Gospels, folio 115v. Here it is presented as an L-shaped corner piece inside a double field line frame. The plait is interlaced with a double field outline which is coloured 'off-white'; the inside displays pink and yellow, and there are four dots in each corner of the terminal end of the motif, perhaps mimicking nails from its metalwork exemplar.

The almost complete square field on the back cover of the FMP displaying a key pattern inside a double field border (C1) is similar to that seen on the cross carpet-page of the Lindisfarne Gospels, folio 138v, albeit without a field border and presented diagonally repeated over the background field (Fig. 5.14). More interesting, however, is another comparative example of this key pattern, found in the broad decorated border of the incipit page to St Matthew's Gospel, folio 1 of the

30 Alexander 1978a, 66.

31 *Ibid.*, 86.

32 *Ibid.*, 88.

33 *Ibid.*, 89.

Fig. 5.14—London, British Library Cotton MS Nero D.IV (Lindisfarne Gospels), f. 138v, cross carpet-page.

MacRegol Gospels. A similar pattern can also be seen in the borders of the Evangelist page of St Mark, folio 51v (Fig. 5.15), and of St Luke, folio 84v. As in the Lindisfarne Gospels, it is presented diagonally and in this case as sets of stepped blocks of alternating colours. The geography and chronology make this an interesting and relevant study. The monastery of Birr, of which MacRegol was abbot, is the closest recorded monastery to the find-spot of the FMP, a distance of 7.5km (see Chapter 6). Both manuscripts fall into a similar period at the end of the eighth and beginning of the ninth century, but additional codicological and palaeographical comparison of the two manuscripts does not thus far point towards MacRegol's involvement with the FMP.

Fig. 5.15—Oxford, Bodleian Library MS Auct. D.2.19 (MacRegol Gospels), f. 51v, Evangelist page of St Mark.

As regards parallels to be found in other media for this pattern, an example worked in stone is seen on one of the Pictish cross-slabs (no. 23, back) from St Andrews Church in Fife, on the east coast of Scotland.[34] Here the carved 'X' is inside a square border, with the pattern repeated above and below the arms of a central cross. Looking at this cross-slab, it could be suggested that the FMP trial motifs F3, F4 and F5 are not individual attempts but rather a repeated pattern of the one design.

Studying the spread of the 31 patterns across the surface of the leather cover of the FMP, two features become apparent: there are no patterns on the spine area of the cover and there is only one on the extended flap of the back cover. This strongly suggests that, as a substrate, the cover was not laid out flat but rather was worked while in its normal 'book shape', i.e. closed and, if so, likely to contain its contents. The spine does not display any motifs, as this would be a vertical surface, and the flap would be more difficult to incise since it offered a smaller and less stable working area.

Examining the theory that the trial motifs are the workings of apprentice artisans in their learning attempts, there is visual evidence to support this. Two, or maybe three, of the 31 pieces could be described as competent and as displaying an understanding of the intended end-product. The contrast in level of competency between these pieces and the remainder is considerable, and they are unlikely to be the work of the same individual. This is highlighted by two motifs which appear to be attempts at the same design: the curvilinear motifs A1 and A4, the latter containing four double triquetras[35] with a cross-hatched field. Motif A1 shows a rudimentary attempt at the same design but probably not by the hand of the same person; a teacher/pupil scenario is likely in this case. Examining motif H2, described earlier as a square pattern with double field lines containing an 'X' of the multi-strand type terminating in the corners of the pattern, on front of a multi-stranded cross with expanded terminals, it can be seen that the background has fine hatching. Upon examination of any of the other F or H category motifs displaying an 'X' inside a square field, it becomes evident that they are not simply unfinished versions of H2 but poorly executed versions of whatever was the intended end-product. With field lines overshooting, untrue lines in the motif and a generally untidy interpretation, they are unlikely to be the attempts of a skilled individual. Examining the historical backdrop against which the FMP was made, it can be observed that secular families lived within the more developed monastic settlements to provide services and products for the abbot and his monks.[36] It has already been stated that these trial pieces are likely to be the work of a monk or monks rather than a secular craftsman. This is based on the fact that the motifs are on the cover of a psalter and, although personal devotional books were produced for the small percentage of literate lay people, the large format of the Faddan More Psalter makes it unlikely to be an example of such a book.

EXAMINATION OF THE SURFACE

A small sample of the black pigment used to colour the outer surface of the leather cover of the FMP was sent to Dr Brian Singer at the University of Northumbria for analysis.[37] The pigment was identified as a carbon black. In addition, Singer discovered a minute fragment of extraneous material, which further analysis identified as gold leaf combined with alumino-silicates, a possible

34 Henderson and Henderson 2004, 183.

35 Interestingly, O'Meadhra lists as one of her criteria for identifying apprentice pieces the presence of the simplest designs, including triquetra.

36 Ryan 2002, 246–8.

37 Singer 2008. The sample was analysed by means of FTIR spectroscopy, GC-MS, scanning electron microscopy and energy dispersive X-ray analysis.

component of Armenian bole. Most typically bole was an addition (to give colour) to gilder's gesso, employed as a ground prior to the application of gold leaf, for which one historical recipe can be found in Cennino's fifteenth-century *Il Libro dell'Arte*.[38] The method, however, is much older, and the use of a thick plaster base on which to lay gold leaf has been practised since at least 2000 BC.[39] The plaster, combined with an adhesive, was typically employed on porous surfaces such as timber. The plaster could be moulded while wet or worked when dry to form three-dimensional patterns on which to lay the ultra-thin gold leaf. The Egyptians used these methods to great effect, evidence of which can be seen today on goods excavated from tombs.

The use of gold for the illumination of the earliest Irish manuscripts up to and beyond the period of the FMP is not known[40] and is very rare in any of the extant Insular manuscripts from the early medieval era.[41] As a reminder of anomalies, Janet Backhouse observed an exception to this dearth of precious metals on manuscripts of the period:

> *'It was in general not a feature of early insular manuscripts, though both gold and silver are used quite extensively in the Codex Amiatinus, to emulate an earlier book from Italy. This was no doubt a matter of taste rather than lack of raw materials.'*[42]

In addition, I have observed a more frequent use of gold applied directly onto the vellum, with some form of glue to fix it in place, in manuscripts from southern England, the Codex Aureus (Stockholm, Kungliga Biblioteket MS A.135) being a spectacular example. Dating from the mid-eighth century, it was likely made in Canterbury. Similarly, the Vespasian Psalter (British Library Cotton MS A.i), also from Canterbury, displays well-executed flat gilding. Perhaps, like its uncial script, this results from alignment with the Roman Church and from a greater exposure to Continental manuscripts.

Returning to the FMP's fragment of gold leaf, there is a strong possibility that this represents contamination from other activities in the workshop such as the gilding of metalwork, one of the skills practised by the Irish craftsman of the eighth century, which also included engraving, enamel work and gold filigree. Examples with gilt components include the Ardagh Chalice (Limerick, NMI 1874:99), dated to the eighth century, and a silver gilt pseudo-penannular brooch (the Cavan brooch, NMI W.43) dating from the later eighth or early ninth century.[43] During the first millennium, gold as a component of decoration, either for metalwork or illumination, was rare and hence employed sparingly. The practice of manufacturing gold leaf and foil would extend its use somewhat. Such was its scarcity in the early medieval period that the recycling of previously produced pieces appears to have been a typical supply source. There is a recorded event of the period related to St Moling (d. 697), when fishermen found a gold ring inside the stomach of a fish. The ring was divided into three and used for the benefit of the poor, to enshrine a relic and to finance labours and works.[44]

Nevertheless, the presence of bole (if this is the case) points towards decoration of manuscript pages, as it had no use in the gilding of metalwork but, as mentioned, was commonly employed when combined with gesso to build up the surface of the vellum (raised gilding). This provided a smooth substrate and helped to maintain the integrity of the ultra-thin gold sheet. It also allowed the gold to

---

38 Thompson 1954.

39 Whitley 2000, 10.

40 Stokes 1932, 46; Henry 1965, 194.

41 Pulliam 2011, 73.

42 Backhouse 1981, 32.

43 Frank Mitchell, 'Catalogue', in P. Cone (ed.), *Treasures of early Irish art, 1500 BC to 1500 AD* (New York, 1977), pp 138 and 141.

44 Wilde 1848.

be burnished, and in some cases tooled, ultimately creating an impressive and magical effect for the viewer. Armenian bole was not always added, and recipes varied geographically.[45] Clues to the type of gesso and any additives can be gleaned when examining a raised-gilt illuminated folio by observing areas where gold has detached, as it inevitably does owing to the flexing of the vellum or parchment folio. If a pinkish-brown colour is exposed, this indicates the presence of bole in the gesso. The issue in relation to the FMP is that its use is not recorded until around the twelfth century,[46] and then it is to be found for the most part on manuscripts produced outside the Insular orbit, with the exponents of Byzantine-influenced manuscripts being particularly enthusiastic about its application, followed by Carolingian illuminators.[47] Considering other uses for the bole clay, however, perhaps its presence may not be adjudged an aberration, and an early treatise on the use of gesso might offer an explanation.[48] Included in the text was a set of instructions for the manufacture of gold leaf. It reads: 'Take some Byzantine parchment, which is made from flax fibre, and rub it on both sides with the red pigment that is made by burning very finely ground and dried ocher'. This is the same basic material as bole, and this stage of the work is the preparation of the modern equivalent of gold-beater's skin, after which small, pre-flattened nuggets of gold are placed between the sheets and then beaten with a hammer—'cast from brass', according to the instructor. It is therefore plausible that the gold leaf fragment and the bole together, as found on the cover of the FMP, are indeed related to the preparation of gold leaf for the gilding of ecclesiastical metalwork. Perhaps a fragment was sitting in the receptacle containing the black carbon dye used to colour the cover. Taking into consideration the motifs with hatching more akin to metalwork, the use of the cross (untypical in trial motif work) and the gold leaf fragment, it can be surmised that the FMP was present in a major monastic settlement where metalworking and the use of precious metals were to be found and that the motifs were those of a metalworker rather than an illuminator, and probably a monk. Nevertheless, it can also be argued that the gold leaf and clay are extraneous products not of the location where the trial motifs were produced but rather of where the cover was produced. Accepting that the trial motifs are good Insular indicators, like the Irish majuscule hand of the manuscript, their place of production can be located with some confidence within Ireland. The cover, however, displays enough codicological features to entertain the hypothesis that it is a product of Near Eastern origin. It is not known what age the cover was when the trial motifs were executed, but it seems clear that gilding of Coptic leather book covers was practised in the eastern Mediterranean during this epoch, as was the use of gold in the illumination of their pages.

METALWORKING

One of the most enduring and visually impressive skills of the medieval Insular craftsman was that of metalworking. A single stylistic example of the metalworker's craft is the almost iconic penannular brooch, with a range of extant examples displayed in museum collections. This clothing accessory demonstrates that high-quality metalwork was not solely a product for the larger monasteries, and a healthy customer base existed in the secular world among the plethora of major and minor kings throughout Ireland. Fine metalwork required within the monastery would include the

45 M. Brown 1994, 58–9; de Hamel 1994, 124.

46 De Hamel 2009, 60; Pächt 1986, 140.

47 Robb 1973, 19.

48 Hawthorne and Stanley-Smith 1963, 29. The interesting aspect of this instruction manual is its origin; although the original manuscript is lost, a twelfth-century copy survives. It is believed that 'Theophilus' can be identified as a Benedictine monk and metalworker, Roger of Helmarshausen, who penned the manuscript between 1110 and 1140. Some of his work is extant, including a book cover held in Trier Cathedral Treasury.

supply of chalices and patens for liturgical services. Archaeology has on several occasions indicated that metalworking took place in dedicated spaces within the monastic settlement. Not surprisingly, this evidence comes from archaeological investigations at the larger, more important sites, including Armagh,[49] Nendrum on Mahee Island in Strangford Lough, Co. Down, and Clonmacnois in the monastic midlands. Henry refers to this evidence from Nendrum, observing that a great number of crucibles with traces of bronze had been found in the location of some huts on the site.[50] Documented evidence of metalwork within monastic settlements is considerably meagre for the period before 900, although some sources are referenced by Michael Ryan from the later Lives of the saints.[51]

The question arises as to who were the various craftsmen (and perhaps women) working within the monastic community. Were they specialists brought in from the lay community or, if they were monks, could they have been *conversi* who, unlike the novice or monkish boy, had already spent some of their adulthood in the secular world and could have acquired skills that were then employed inside the monastic settlement? Did these craftsmen have apprentices, and did the abbot assign a novice monk to be trained in metalwork? Monasteries are habitually linked with education and the training of the *oblatus* from a young age in the skills of reading, writing and learning of Scripture, an attribute that is heavily documented and often quoted.[52] According to O'Meadhra, however, there is little reference to education outside that of a spiritual and academic world. Henry comments that 'lay specialised craftsmen were probably employed when none was available among the [monastic] community'.[53] We have already mentioned a monk, St Asicus, who seems to have been appreciated specifically for his skills in metalwork, which he put to use in order to supply St Patrick with the necessary liturgical vessels and shrines.

If the trial motifs on the cover of the FMP are the work of an apprentice metalworker under the instruction of a master, perhaps copying designs from an illuminated psalter or gospel-book, then it is credible that at least one of them was a member of the monastic community—either the apprentice, who as a novice monk had been designated as a future metalworker for his community, with his required copy of the psalms, or the teacher, who had in his possession a psalter of which he found the cover convenient for instructing his pupil in the patterns that he would need to learn for his metalwork.

On a technical note, the question of the tool employed to create the trial motifs on the tanned leather surface of the cover is one worth considering. As part of the conservation process I included tracings (see Fig. 5.3) produced on clear Mylar® film. It was necessary to employ a purpose-made scribing tool, as no graphic pen could reproduce the required line width, which brought sharply into focus the refinement and keen edge of the implement available at the time. Attempts were made to reproduce the motif patterns on a similar piece of tanned leather using a Swan-Morton® 10A scalpel blade. This fine edge also failed to produce a line of similar width. More in keeping with the available medieval technology, a second attempt was made using a sliver of obsidian, a form of volcanic glass valued since prehistoric times for its naturally occurring razor-sharp edges. This produced something closer to the incisions of the FMP motifs. The profile of the tool was visible under specialised magnification[54] and displayed a 'V'-shaped cut consistent with the profile of knapped glass. I intend to research this further with the goal of establishing the tool likely to have been held by our monk while trying out his Insular motifs.

49 Gaskell-Brown and Harper 1984.

50 Henry 1965, 80.

51 Ryan 1988.

52 T. Charles-Edwards 2000, 180; de Paor and de Paor 1964, 49; McGrath 1979, 114; J. Ryan 1993, 33, 209, 215.

53 Henry 1965, 103.

54 Dr H. Liang, Nottingham Trent University (see Fig. 5.4).

The hypothesis that the 31 trial motifs represent the efforts of teacher and pupil in the art of manuscript illumination cannot be discounted, despite the presence of hatching, more akin to metalwork, in many of the pieces; the fact that stylistically a greater number of comparative examples were found on the pages of Insular manuscripts than on ecclesiastical metalwork of the same period is relevant. Perhaps a more thought-provoking question is why the cover of a psalter was chosen to carry out this work, and whether the fact that it was utilised in this fashion reveals anything about the cover itself. What was the mind-set of the individual(s) who decided that the cover of a psalter was a suitable surface on which to 'doodle' or to practise some current designs for whatever purpose? Does this, in turn, reflect on the status of the psalter itself or just its cover? To put this in context today, it is unlikely that many book-owners would take a tome off their shelf and start to sketch some cartoon figure on the dust-jacket or the cloth binding. Perhaps the association between the psalter and its cover was not considered a permanent one, and the presence of these motifs, in addition to evidence of other uses as a surface for a range of tasks in the scriptorium, tells us that this Coptic-style binding was a temporary housing while the manuscript awaited a more permanent structure. Finding little evidence to suggest that the five vellum quires were mechanically fixed into their protective cover reinforces this argument. Unlike other surviving early medieval manuscript bindings that inform us about 'themselves', the cover of the FMP offers a glimpse into the day-to-day activities inside a monastic scriptorium or school in early medieval Ireland.

CHAPTER 6

The monastic landscape around Faddan More

CHAPTER 6

The monastic landscape around Faddan More

Historically, the portability of medieval manuscripts has led to difficulties in identifying their place of origin. This is further complicated in the case of Insular manuscripts by the stylistic and scribal similarities in the texts produced on these islands and in connected/allied Continental monastic settlements. These overseas monasteries were established by *peregrini* who travelled from Ireland and Britain, bringing with them books produced at home; once they were established abroad, additional manuscript copies in the same Insular style were produced under their supervision. St Colum Cille (d. 597), St Columbanus (d. 615) and St Willibrord (d. 739) were responsible for the production of such material many miles from home. The physical format of books varied; some, such as the 'pocket gospels', were designed for ease of transport, in a format ideally suited for personal use (and more often than not with the addition of illumination, mirroring their higher-status and larger-format liturgical manuscripts). These are routinely written in a more rapid hand, bordering on cursive, in contrast to the Insular majuscule found in the larger liturgical books. Bernard Meehan lists a number of these small-format manuscripts, including the St Cuthbert Gospel (BL Add. 89000), the Stowe Missal (RIA MS D.ii.3), the Cadmug Gospels (Fulda, Landes. Codex Bonifatianus 3), the Book of Mulling (TCD MS 60) and the Book of Dimma (TCD MS 59).[1] Another manuscript fitting this category is BL Add. 40618, a small-format gospel-book written in Ireland in the mid-eighth century; some passages, remarkably, are in a tiny Insular majuscule hand, whereas typically the more compact Insular minuscule was the writing of choice for this format (an exception being the St Cuthbert Gospel, written in uncial, the formal Continental book hand). By the tenth century, however, BL Add. 40618 had found its way to southern England, possibly Canterbury, where it was updated by erasing the Insular initial letters and replacing them with the more austere classical forms in vogue in the England of the period. Additional defacing of this manuscript involved the removal of the eighth-century Evangelist portraits and their replacement with their tenth-century counterparts, this activity further blurring any clues as to its

1 Bernard Meehan, 'Appendix 3', in C. Breay and B. Meehan (eds), *The St Cuthbert Gospel: studies on the Insular manuscript of the Gospel of John* (London, 2015), 164–7.

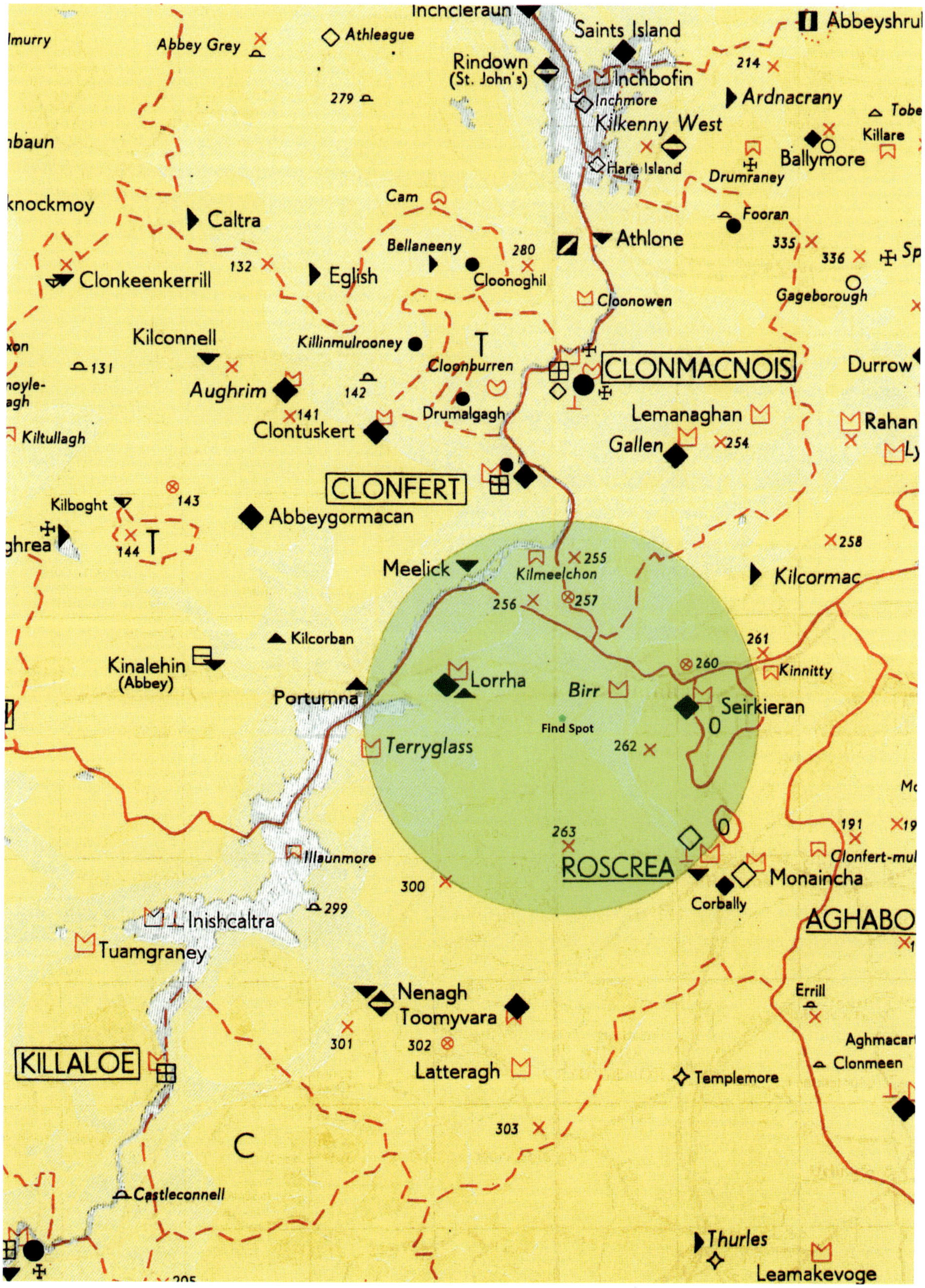

Fig. 6.1—Monastic sites in the midlands.

original place of production. Complexities such as these require alternative indicators in any attempt to establish exactly where such a manuscript from the Middle Ages was written. The fact that books produced across Europe at this period were for the most part products of the Christian Church—and, in the case of Britain and Ireland, a Christian monastic church—provides a 'target' from where to begin any search for the place of production of the FMP, mindful that the work was written in a style intended to be read by all literate contemporaries.

The site of the discovery of the FMP, buried deep in the inhospitable environment of a bog, might seem incongruous, but a consideration of the surrounding landscape presents several local possibilities for its origin. The townland of Faddan More in north County Tipperary is perfectly placed in the centre of what William O'Sullivan called the 'monastic midlands'.[2] Kathleen Hughes described the area as 'thick with major monasteries',[3] while Francis John Byrne somewhat poetically described the area as 'a flowering garden of monasteries' (Fig. 6.1).[4] From a political viewpoint, the area around Faddan More would have been considered an attractive location for ecclesiastical settlements in the early medieval period, being close to the interface between the territories of major dynasties whose patronage was key to developing an influential Christian base. Throughout Ireland monastic settlements varied in type, location and size; some were hermitages or small eremitical groups similar to models in the Christian Orient,[5] while others were consciously placed in populated areas close to major transport routes. From a geographical viewpoint, the monastic midlands, positioned in the centre of Ireland, are reasonably sheltered, with a combination of areas of well-drained soil, suitable for successful agriculture, and acres of raised peat bogs resulting from poor land drainage. Joseph Haughton views the latter as 'useless for settlement and a barrier to communications'.[6] As is the case with much of history, it is problematic to gauge people's tolerance for discomfort in times past, and it is likely to have been just such attributes that initially attracted some of the monastic settlements to these poorer, more isolated locations. John Feehan, in his foreword to George Cunningham's *The Anglo-Norman advance into the south-west midlands of Ireland*, talks of the monks 'whose mind and eye sought out the extraordinary deserts of the medieval midland landscape rather than the grazing plains that drew the Celtic dynasties'.[7] Referring to Munster's isolated parts, Byrne suggests that 'the wandering scholar, monk or craftsman could cheerfully brave the wilds where an army would starve'.[8] A nearby example can be found 19km north-east of the find-spot, where a Christian foundation was established by St Barrind in the sixth century, just over the border in the province of Mide. Known locally as Drumcullen church, it was positioned on the north bank of the River Camcor in a small area of bogland,[9] somewhat remote from any secular dwellings. It was likely chosen originally as a hermitage site but, like others, expanded into a monastic settlement over time. The site continued in use and later ruins, including a graveyard, are to be found at the location (Fig. 6.2).

Further examples of ecclesiastical settlements on bogland are found in nearby modern-day Offaly at Lemanaghan, where a monastic site, surrounded by boglands, was established in the seventh century. The founder of the monastery is recorded in the Annals of the Four Masters as Manchan of Maothla (Mohill, Co. Leitrim). Although he may have chosen the site because of its isolated location, the

2 O'Sullivan 2005, 533.

3 Hamlin and Hughes 2004, 25.

4 Byrne 2001, 170.

5 De Paor and de Paor 1964, 53.

6 Haughton 2005, 32.

7 Feehan 1987, xiv.

8 Byrne 2001, 170.

9 National Monuments database. Irish Transverse Mercator: Easting 61807, Northing 706118.

Fig. 6.2—Drumcullen, Co. Offaly: church ruins and graveyard.

discovery of toghers or timber pathways across the bog indicate that it was accessible soon after it was established. The saint died in 664 and his corporeal remains are held in a large twelfth-century house-shaped shrine with decorative metalwork over a core of yew wood, possibly made at Clonmacnoise but still kept at St Manchan's Church at Boher, Ballycumber, close to the original site of his monastery. The nineteenth-century church also includes a stained-glass window by Harry Clarke depicting the saint.[10] The monastery was linked by a bog road to St Mella's cell; Mella was, according to popular belief, St Manchan's mother. In both cases later structural ruins mark the location. Additional toghers dating from the late sixth and seventh centuries have been located in the Lemanaghan bogs.[11] The same bogs recently yielded a fragment of an eleventh-century crozier, now in the National Museum of Ireland.[12] Movement and travel were part of everyday medieval life, and for the most part on foot. With much of the country consisting of difficult terrain, it was necessary to find a way to navigate these areas successfully. The many raised bogs, similar to Faddan More, presented such a challenge. The discovery of wooden tracks in multiple bog sites throughout Ireland confirms that this solution was employed to cross this unstable topography. Many of these toghers had been constructed during the Bronze Age, and no doubt were maintained, repaired and rebuilt into the historic era.[13]

---

10 O'Brien 2006, 178–81.

11 Fitzpatrick and O'Brien 1988, 12.

12 Irish Archaeological Wetland Unit, 'Filling in the blanks: an archaeological survey of the Lemanaghan Bogs, Co. Offaly', *Archaeology Ireland* **11** (2), 22–5.

13 A. O'Sullivan 2007, 169–78.

About 50km south of St Manchan's church lies another important ecclesiastical settlement, on an island in the centre of a bog: the Holy Island of Loch Cré in Monaincha, close to Roscrea. The site was drained in the eighteenth century, improving access to the island.[14] The monastery was associated with a number of saints, including St Crónán of Roscrea and St Cainneach of Aghaboe; it was the former who commissioned Dimma to write a gospel-book for him.[15] Probably established in the sixth century as a hermitage, like many churches in the midlands of Ireland, it became a centre of the *Céli Dé* movement in the ninth century.[16] The annals mention an Elarius, anchorite and scribe of Loch Cré, who fell asleep in Christ in 807 (AU, AFM). At the close of the twelfth century the monastery came under the control of the Augustinians.[17] Today the ruins of the church include a finely decorated twelfth-century doorway and chancel arch in sandstone, as well as later architecture including thirteenth-century windows. Two twelfth-century high cross fragments, no longer in their original locations, stand to the west of the church (Fig. 6.3).[18] The prominence of this holy site suggests that the production of books would have been included among its activities. This is endorsed in the literary sources, which record the writing of a gospel-book on the island by St Cainneach—the now-lost *Glas Cainnigh*, the 'green book of Canice'.[19]

The townland of Faddan More is approximately 60m above sea level and is close to the border of modern County Offaly, with the town of Birr approximately 9km north-east of the find-spot.[20] Two-metre-long cores of peat were extracted from the find-spot for the purpose of establishing the palaeoenvironmental history of the locality. The time-span covered by the pollen analysis stretches from the late Bronze Age to the thirteenth century. In the period of interest here, AD 400–1010, human activity is evidenced in the area by a clearance of woodlands, particularly from the seventh century. By the end of the period, however, human activity had declined, as indicated by an increase in woodland growth. This is consistent with other Irish midland sites, though it is not until the late ninth century that more intensive woodland clearance was a feature of the area.[21] The nearest modern-day settlement is Carrig, 2km east of the bog on the main road (N52) back to Birr (Fig. 6.4).

There are two holy wells in close proximity to the find-spot. The first lies less than 2km to the north-west in the adjacent townland of Cloncorig (*Cluain-combraic*) and is marked on the 1843 Ordnance Survey map as *Toberbrandy*, probably referring to St Brendan of Birr. It is identified on the National Monuments database as TN008-002. The same distance to the south-east, near Loughkeen, the second holy well (TN008-12) is located in church grounds on poorly drained land. According to local tradition, it was used to cure sore eyes. There are several other archaeological features in the immediate area, including enclosures, barrows, ringforts and castles—evidence of activity and occupation before and after the deposition of the FMP. In addition, a wealth of decorated graveslabs and crosses related to the Christian sites of the area are extant, some still *in situ* and recorded on the National Monuments database.

The find-spot of the manuscript is almost 14km east of Terryglass on Lough Derg and 30km south of the *Slige Mór*, the great highway that crossed the centre of the country from east to west on an esker. This was a product of retreating glaciers, formed in melt-water tunnels inside the glacier; when the

---

14 Cunningham 2012.

15 Meehan 2014, 238.

16 Cunningham 2012; Leask 1920.

17 Hamlin and Hughes 2004, 106.

18 Harbison 1992, 310–11.

19 Plummer 1910, I, 152–69; Leask 1920, 21; Ó Riain 2011, 139.

20 I have allocated the following coordinates for the location of the find-spot. The visual identification was established using the NMI preliminary account of the excavation of the FMP; I transferred this to the National Monuments database and established the coordinates from here. Irish Transverse Mercator: Easting 600063, Northing 700460.

21 Plunkett *et al.* 2009.

Fig. 6.3—Church ruins and high cross at Loch Cré, Co. Tipperary.

Fig. 6.4—The find-spot at Faddan More Bog.

ice finally receded, the deposit of sand and gravel remained in the form of a ridge.[22] This raised land mass was ideally suited to provide a trackway across the boggy midlands. At Clonmacnoise it crossed the River Shannon, which provided an alternative mode of transport from north to south. Modern underwater archaeology has led to the discovery of a substantial oaken bridge, 120m in length, 5m wide and 10m high, that traversed the river at the monastic site in the early ninth century.[23] To the south-east at Roscrea, 17.5km from the find-spot, another ancient esker road, the *Slige Dála*, terminated. This road, travelling from Tara through Naas and the seat of the early kings of Leinster,[24] provided the third transport route within striking distance of Faddan More.

It is necessary to ignore the county borders of modern times, as they had no relevance in the period of interest here. In the eighth century the midlands, like the rest of the country, were divided into small kingdoms or *tuatha* (*tuath* loosely translated as 'tribe' or 'people'). Before the Norman invasion there were as many as 150 of these petty kingdoms.[25] The ever-increasing desire for the control of territories and the consequently greater power saw the rise of provincial kings and the expansion of their dynasties. Modern Ireland retains the geographical imprint of this consolidation in the current four provinces. The area around Faddan More was under the control of the Éile Tuaisceart, who were subject to the Eóganachta, the Munster overkings.[26] This federation of dynasties had their seat of power in Cashel. Faddan More lies close to the boundary with the even more powerful Southern Uí Néill, and violent encounters between the two are recorded in the eighth century. In 721, Cathal mac Finguine from the Eóganacht of Glendamnach took his seat as king of Cashel and began a campaign to stem the rising power of the Uí Néill dynasty. After some success he suffered a series of defeats, and in 737 the annals record a meeting (*dáil*) with the Uí Néill high-king Áed Allán at Terryglass, close to Faddan More.[27] No details are recorded but the following entry in the annals records that 'the law of Patrick was enforced throughout Ireland' (*Lex Patricii tenuit Hiberniam*). This probably marked a form of truce between the two dynasties.[28] The volatile nature of Irish kingship ensured, however, that any truce was likely to be breached; less than 40 years after the *dáil* at Terryglass, Dunnchad mac Domnall of the Southern Uí Néill, Clann Cholmáin, and then 'high-king' invaded Munster in 775 and again three years later, with the assistance of men from the monastery of Durrow.[29]

In the early part of the ninth century, the presence of another Munster king had a direct impact on the monastic landscape around Faddan More. Feidlimid Mac Crimthann had seized the kingship of Cashel in 819 (AU) or 820 (AI) and, although named in the annals as an ecclesiastic, scribe and member of the *Céli Dé*, he raided and destroyed churches throughout Ireland, including parts of the Clonmacnoise lands. He also sacked the monastery of Gailline of the Britons (Gallen, Co. Offaly) in 822.[30] Three years later he attacked and burned Dealbhna Beatha, in the same area. In 831 he burned the sanctuary land in Clonmacnoise and again the land of Dealbhna Beatha. Recorded in the annals as 'the great burner of churches and monasteries',[31] he was the first of the Irish high-kings to introduce this destructive practice. One of Mac Crimthann's churches, Derrynaflan, possessed a wealth of altarware,

22 Mitchell and Ryan 2003, 49.

23 O'Sullivan and Boland 1998.

24 O'Sullivan and Downey 2015, 17.

25 Stout 2017, 54; Thomas 1971, 84.

26 Fitzpatrick 1998, 93.

27 Byrne 2005b, 657; Stout 2017, 108.

28 Ó Cróinín 2005, 227; Stout 2017, 108.

29 Stout 2017, 115; Ó Cróinín 1995, 57.

30 Annals of the Four Masters.

31 Ó Corráin 1980, 86.

no doubt the spoils of his violent exploits.[32] He died in 847, and the Annals of Clonmacnoise suggest that his death was brought about by St Ciarán in retribution for the plundering of the monastery of which he was patron. These historical accounts demonstrate the unstable nature of life in early medieval Ireland and emphasise that a monastery or church did not in any way provide sanctuary from destruction and violence; indeed, Christian centres were often the specific target of an ambitious king, including those from the same dynasty. Moreover, in what appears at variance with the high ideals of monasticism, monasteries were known to attack other monasteries, and their battles were recorded in the annals with no more sense of consternation than those of any warring kings.[33]

The raiding and destruction of monasteries were not exclusive to local warring petty kings and high-kings. During the period under examination here, it is necessary to consider the devastation wrought by the hands and weapons of foreigners, in the form of invasions by the Northmen of Scandinavia, and more specifically Norway. Viking attacks, which commenced at the end of the eighth century, were not unsurprisingly focused on locations along the Irish coastline, particularly those on inlets or situated on offshore islands like Lambay, close to modern-day Dublin, which would become a permanent Viking settlement.[34] The Lambay raid was one of the earliest recorded Viking attacks, noted in the Annals of Ulster as 'The burning of Rechru by the heathens'. The island was the site of a Columban foundation. Initially these incursions were in the form of raids and, given that Irish social structure did not include towns or cities in the Roman sense, the marauders were denied concentrated targets. By the beginning of the ninth century, however, some monastic settlements had developed into structured communities with a commercial life and a secular community, functioning like a market town or city. In Irish-Latin, the term *civitates* was used to indicate larger monastic sites. The monastery at Clonmacnoise, founded in 544, was identified as one of the great 'monastic cities',[35] inevitably paying the price through multiple raids during the ninth century, the Shannon providing the Vikings with an easy route inland directly to the midland monasteries and churches.

It is evident that these attacks were not primarily motivated by hostility towards the Christian religion, although elaborate metalwork, including gold and silver, was part of the booty, substantiated by the archaeological evidence found in Norse graves.[36] The more practical and immediate reasons would have been the availability of provisions, stock and, particularly, slaves. This argument is reinforced in view of the practice of using monastic settlements as a place of safe keeping for lay property.[37] It would not require many repeat raids before it became apparent to the aggressors that within the enclosure a 'one-stop shop' of spoils was available for the taking, with the possible bonus of some trinkets. Anthony Lucas indicated that 'the bullion value of the great bulk of Irish metalwork of the time was exceedingly small'.[38] Although much documented and often discussed, the Viking raids on ecclesiastical settlements around Ireland are easily outnumbered by native Irish attacks, though the former caught the headlines and imaginations of early historians. Statistics from the annals suggest that Irish attacks outnumbered those of the Vikings during the first wave of foreign incursions.[39] The second wave of attacks later in the ninth century included battles between those Vikings who had settled here and fleets arriving from their Scandinavian homeland. The area around Faddan More in Munster also saw an increase in violence, as a local chronicler in the twelfth century described:

32 Bhreathnach 2014, 189; Stout 2017, 131; O'Dwyer 1981, 41.

33 Hughes 2008, 317; Lucas 1967, 178.

34 De Paor and de Paor 1964, 131; Stopford Green 1925, 314.

35 Woolf 2018, 112; Byrne 2005a, 619.

36 Johnson 2014, 45.

37 Lucas 1967, 199.

38 *Ibid.*, 208.

39 Ó Corráin 1980, 83.

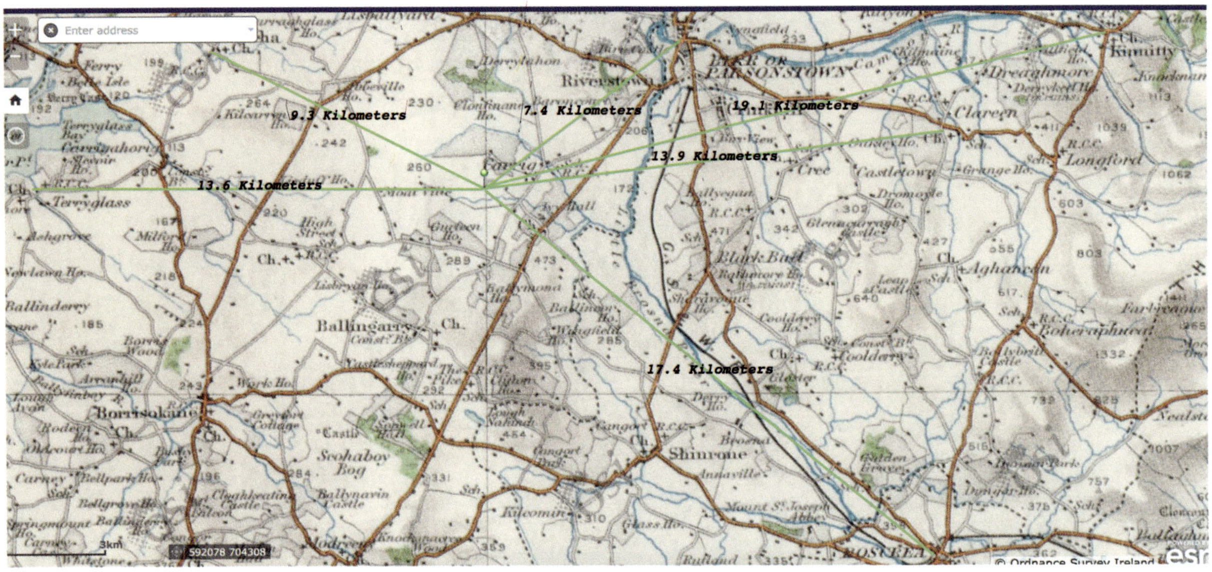

Fig. 6.5—Monastic locations within a day's walk of the find-spot.

'The whole of Mumhain became filled with immense floods and countless sea-vomitings of ship and boats and fleets so that there was not a harbour nor a land-port nor a Dún (all signify a fort or fortress) nor a fortress nor a fastness in all of Mumhain without floods of Danes and pirates, so that they made spoil-land and sword-land of her throughout her breadth and generally; and they ravaged her chieftainries and her privileged churches and her sanctuaries; and they rent her shrines and her reliquaries and her books.'[40]

Another entry refers to an attack in the area: 'there came a fleet onto Loch Derg and they plundered Inis Celtra and they drowned its shrines and its books'.[41]

The collective attacks, plunderings and sackings of the monasteries of Ireland by both native and foreign aggressors, and the internal turmoil, fear and confusion this generated, must be considered in relation to the very specific circumstance that led to the deposition of the FMP in such an unlikely location. Although Lucas, referring to his examination of the annals, reports that any plundering (Irish: *argain*) is never attributed to Irish attackers,[42] this is hardly an accurate depiction, as the exploits of Mac Crimthann, mentioned earlier, confirm that the natives also indulged in this destructive practice. Penalties for such plundering are listed in the Old Irish Penitentials; specifically, the stealing of books from the monastery incurred a penance of seven years.[43] Arguably, if it was considered necessary to create a penance for this crime, it must have been a regular occurrence.

Examining the hypothesis that the FMP is a local artefact and a product of a nearby monastery—say, one that could be reached in a day's walk from the find-spot—there is merit in checking out some of the possible candidates (Fig. 6.5). Material evidence for many early Christian foundations in Ireland is typically scant, as monastic buildings and churches of the first phase—up to AD 800—were for the most

40 Todd 1867, 41.

41 *Ibid.*, 39–41.

42 Lucas 1967, 180.

43 Bieler and Binchy 1963, 267.

part built from perishable organic materials that left little trace. The literary sources and sometimes a later stone-built replacement on the same site can, however, provide tangible proof. Archaeologists have on occasion found trace evidence of post-holes marking the outline of original timber buildings. Oak was the timber of choice, with the addition of other organic materials such as reeds for roofing. One Irish term for church, *dairtheach*, translates as 'oak house' and emphasises the dominance of this construction method.[44]

Birr, a sixth-century foundation of St Bréanainn (d. 573?), is the closest of the major monastic settlements to the find-spot in Faddan More Bog. No documented Life survives for Bréanainn but traditionally it is held that he had close ties with St Colum Cille and Iona.[45] Likewise, archaeological evidence of the monastery's existence is scant, if not lacking altogether. The site of the ruin of St Brendan's Church, a mostly seventeenth-century structure and graveyard, north of the Camcor River in the kingdom of Éile Tuaisceart is favoured as the location of the original monastery. It is described in the ninth-century *Félire Óengusso* as a monastery 'on the brink of water' and in the 'confine of Eile and Fircell'.[46] The Synod of Birr that enacted Adomnán's *Lex Innocentium* (Law of Innocents) protecting women and children against violence as non-combatants was held there in 697.[47] Paradoxically, the annals record the monastery in a battle with Clonmacnoise at Móin Choise Blae in 760.[48] Further disruption is recorded when it was the target of a Viking raid in 841,[49] a date which could fit the time-line of the FMP deposition. The event is reliably documented in several Irish annals, including the Annals of Ulster (AU), the Annals of the Four Masters (AFM) and the *Chronicum Scotorum* (*CS*).

The MacRegol Gospels, much referenced above and a product of the monastery, again comes under scrutiny; on the last folio (169v) of this gospel-book there is a colophon written in the same Insular majuscule hand as the manuscript and contained in two panels of a six-panel frame:

> MACREGOL DIPINCXIT HOC EVANGELIUM. QUICUMQUE LEGERIT ET INTELLEGERIT ISTAM NARRATIONEM ORAT PRO MACREGUIL SCRIPTORI.
>
> *(MacRegol illuminated this gospel-book. Whoever reads and understands the narrative, let him pray for MacRegol the scribe.)*

The scribe can plausibly be associated with the MacRegol, scribe, bishop and abbot at Birr, whose death is recorded in the Annals of Ulster in 822.[50] The manuscript is a large-format gospel-book with the already trimmed folios measuring 350mm x 270mm. It contains the complete text of the four gospels, although the prefaces and the Matthew portrait are now missing from the front of the manuscript. The remaining decorated folios include the three Evangelist portraits and their incipit pages. In addition, other folios in the gospels have the text placed inside decorated borders. Plaitwork, interlace, step patterns, zoomorphic and geometric lettering are all present. The manuscript's decoration has been variously described as 'rough', 'irregular' and 'slap-dash'.[51] Samuel Hemphill went so far as to describe MacRegol's work as 'painfully rough' when referring to some decorative elements. By contrast, Hemphill is impressed by the geometric lettering, comparing it favourably to the Lindisfarne Gospels, the Book of Kells and the Ardagh

44 Ó Carragáin 2010, 15–55; de Paor and de Paor 1964, 54; Manning 1995, 5.

45 Ó Riain 2011, 114.

46 Fitzpatrick 1998, 115.

47 Fitzpatrick and O'Brien 1988, 3; see also Bhreathnach 2014, 189.

48 Annals of Ulster (TCD MS 1282).

49 Lucas 1967, 216.

50 Moss 2014c, 241.

51 O'Neill 2014, 24; Henry 1965, 199.

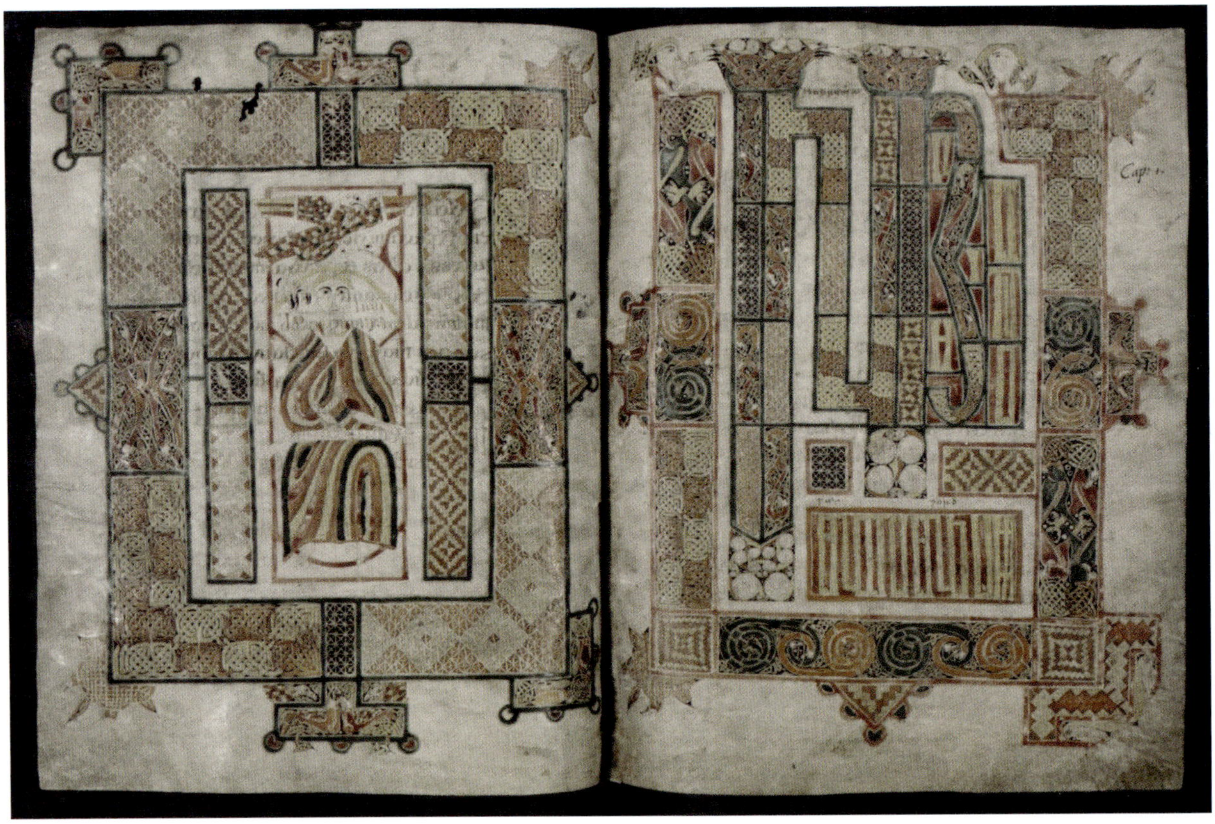

Fig. 6.6—Oxford, Bodleian Library MS Auct. D.2.19 (the MacRegol Gospels), f. 126v and f. 127r.

Chalice.[52] Tim O'Neill's observations on MacRegol's hand describe the writing as '… free, yet stately, Irish majuscule script'.[53] By the late tenth century the manuscript was in England in a place called Harawudu, thought to be Harewood, near Leeds, where the text was glossed by two Anglo-Saxon scribes named Farman and Owun, who followed MacRegol's example and left a colophon.[54]

Examining any parallel features between the FMP and the MacRegol Gospels is an obvious exercise. They are both large-format manuscripts with similar height-to-width ratio, calculated at 1.35:1 for the FMP (see Chapter 2) and at a similar 1.3:1 for the MacRegol Gospels. Although further similar features are unsurprising, they are documented here as a matter of record. Both manuscripts are produced on calfskin vellum. Geometric lettering and zoomorphic features are employed in the decoration, with a similar palette of colours, in particular a vivid yellow. MacRegol and the scribe of the FMP both wrote in an Insular majuscule hand, the standard for larger-format gospel-books from early medieval Ireland (Fig. 6.6). A palaeographical comparison would have merit, if only to eliminate MacRegol as the scribe of the psalter. Michelle Brown does comment on a similarity in the hands, in what she terms 'insular fractura' of the late Insular half-uncial. She places the FMP, the MacRegol Gospels, the St Gall Gospels and the Stowe Missal in this category, suggesting an Irish west midlands origin for all and a dating from the second half of the eighth century.[55] Codicological comparison with the Birr manuscript has not been possible thus far, as it would be necessary to investigate beyond—or, more accurately, behind—its current much-later binding.

Just over 12km east of the find-spot is the location of another early Christian monastery, Seir

52 Hemphill 1911, 5.

53 O'Neill 2014, 24.

54 *Ibid.*, 24; Alexander 1978a, 77; Moss 2014c, 241; Margaret Hogan 2007.

55 M. Brown 2016, 83.

Fig. 6.7—The present parish church at Saighir.

Kieran,[56] now located by the village of Clareen, Co. Offaly. It was founded by St Ciarán of Saighir, reputedly the first ordained bishop in Ireland—even before St Patrick, who directed Ciarán as to where he should place his church. His pre-Patrician status is now, however, believed to be propaganda.[57] As regards the choice of location, in addition to being an accessible water source the Fuarán River may also have had some significance in pagan times. Seir Kieran has a well now dedicated to the saint close to the monastic site; natural wells such as this were a focal point in both pre-Christian and Christian times. Close by, archaeologists have identified a bivallate hillfort and pre-Christian burial monuments. This repurposing of sacred sites for Christian use helped to smooth the transition from pagan worship during the initial conversion of the people. The strong traditions surrounding the well continue today; on 5 March, the feast day of St Ciarán, parishioners include the well as part of a pilgrimage, and locals are reputed to always keep some of the well water in their homes.[58] The monastery developed into a major settlement and had the support of local rulers, who granted it lands in this gently sloping valley. Like Clonmacnoise, Seir Kieran became the burial place of some of the supporting nobility,[59] including Cerball Mac Dúnlainge, the powerful king of Osraige, who died in 888.[60] Evidence of the monastic site remains within a substantial earthen enclosure *c.* 375m in diameter.[61] Examining the ringforts in modern County Offaly, Matthew Stout notes the location of a Cluster 3 ringfort, which denotes a high-

56 Irish Transverse Mercator: Easting 613887, Northing 7002255.

57 Ó Riain 2011, 172.

58 Ó Súilleabháin 1997.

59 O'Brien 2006, 17.

60 Byrne 2001, 162.

61 Stout 1998, 51.

status dwelling compatible with a royal location, close to the site of the monastery, and an area of 2km around the two sites without any other evidence of medieval habitation, emphasising both the isolation of the monastery and its support by local kings.[62] Typically later stone structures and a graveyard remain above ground. The base of a high cross, a small sandstone ring-headed cross and some graveslabs all attest to the high status of this Christian settlement (Fig. 6.7). It is reasonable to speculate that ecclesiastical metalwork and manuscript production would have been part of the repertoire of Seir Kieran. It was, after all, significant enough to warrant the attentions of the Vikings from Dublin, who according to the Annals of Ulster plundered here in 842.

Some 9km north-west of the find-spot in Faddan More Bog is the major ecclesiastical settlement at Lorrha, close to the current Tipperary/Galway border. It was founded in the sixth century by St Ruadhán (d. 583), a noted pupil of Finnian of Clonard and included as one of the 'twelve apostles of the Irish'.[63] The monastery flourished in the following centuries, and a chronology of archaeological evidence, mostly in the form of church ruins, can be found in and around the original site, including a late medieval Augustinian priory and a Dominican friary. Two ninth-century crosses within the enclosure are possibly commissions from Cerball mac Dúnlainge, king of Ossory. Additional evidence of the settlement includes a graveyard, a holy well and recumbent graveslabs within the priory.[64] The importance of this site is further enhanced by its close connection with the *Céli Dé* churches, in particular Tallaght,[65] and through the founder of the movement, Mael Ruain, who came from Lorrha.[66] Considering the prolonged existence and prominence of this monastic locus, liturgical books would surely have been produced here.

An extant manuscript associated with Lorrha is the small, pocket-sized book now popularly called the Stowe Missal, the name relating to a much later period in its life when it was in the possession of the Marquess of Buckingham at Stowe House; it should perhaps be more appropriately titled the Lorrha Missal. The manuscript and its book-shrine were reputedly rediscovered hidden in the walls of Lackeen Castle, close to Lorrha, in 1735 by John O'Kennedy while he was refurbishing the family estate.[67] Like many early Insular manuscripts, the date of its production is much discussed and somewhat fluid; the late eighth or early ninth century is the most widely accepted today, making it a close contemporary of the FMP. In addition to the liturgy of the Mass there are the rites for Baptism and for Visitation of the Sick. Written in Irish and in a different hand is a treatise on the mystical meaning of the Mass and three spells against loss of eyesight, injury by thorns and disease of the urine. The first eleven folios of the manuscript contain a partial Gospel of John, with his portrait included as a full page of decoration. This is considered to have been extracted from another manuscript and the two brought together as a matter of convenience, the common denominator being the same diminutive format (Fig. 6.8).[68] Associated with the manuscript is its *cumdach* or shrine, dating from the early eleventh century and, typically, altered substantially during later repairs. Despite the alterations, solid evidence of its provenance remains in two inscriptions, naming a local king, Find Ua Dúngalaig (d. 1033), and the abbot of Lorrha, Mathgamain Ua Cathail (d. 1037) (Fig. 6.9).[69] Unlike the shrine, the origin of the missal is less certain, and Tallaght is a popular choice, given the inclusion of Maél Ruain in a list of bishops at the end of the manuscript. Pádraig Ó Riain, however, suggests that 'Lorrha, which already demonstrably boasted a

62 Stout 1998, 51.

63 Ó Riain 2011, 542.

64 Bolger *et al.* 2012, 113.

65 Ó Riain 2014, 64.

66 Follett 2012, 13.

67 Ó Riain 2009, 11.

68 *Ibid.*, 11–14.

69 Mullarkey 2014, 301; M. de Paor 1977, 184.

Fig. 6.8—Dublin, RIA MS D.ii.3 (the Stowe Missal), f. 65v.

Fig. 6.9—Shrine of the Stowe Missal, National Museum of Ireland, no. 1883:614a.

scriptorium in the eighth century, has as good a claim as Tallaght to be the place of origin of the Stowe Missal'.[70] Supporting the hypothesis indirectly, William O'Sullivan compares the minuscule hand of the partial St John's Gospel bound with the Stowe manuscript with the same gospel in the Book of Dimma, a product of Roscrea, about 26km south-east of Lorrha. He describes the hands as 'very close' and suggests a 'local style' as a reason.[71]

Lorrha, as a well-established monastic site close to the Shannon, also suffered attacks from the Norsemen, as recorded by the annals in 843 (AFM), when Clonmacnoise and Terryglass were hit in the same raid. And in what appears to be an account of these attacks in the twelfth-century *Cogadh Gaedhel re Gallaibh* ('the War of the Gaedhil with the Gaill'), a work from the lower Shannon region, mention is made of the destruction of the shrine of Ruadhán.[72]

Directly west of the FMP find-spot, and on the shores of Lough Derg, lies the monastic settlement of Terryglass (*Tír Dá Ghlas*, 'land of the two streams'). The area is associated with a St Colum, who was buried there according to his own wishes (d. 552). Colum, like Ruadhán, was a pupil of Finnian of Clonard. After instruction in spiritual doctrine, he left Ireland and travelled to Rome and later to Tours before returning to Ireland with relics of St Martin.[73] He apparently established churches around Lough Derg before finally settling in Terryglass.[74] The church in Terryglass receives attention from Adomnán in his Life of Colum Cille, who was staying in Ireland and had travelled to visit the monks of Terryglass; on his arrival, the keys of the church door could not be found. Colum Cille announced that 'The Lord has the power to open his house to his servants even without keys', upon which the locked door sprang open.[75] The prominence of this ecclesiastical settlement and its likely association with Iona's *parochia* (hence its appearance as the only Munster church mentioned in Adomnán's Life of Colum Cille) would indicate that books would have been produced there from an early period. The mid-twelfth-century Book of Leinster is likely a later legacy of this tradition. The large-format manuscript is, for the most part, in Trinity College Dublin (TCD MS 1339), with the section containing the Martyrology of Tallaght held in the Archives Department of University College Dublin (UCD OFM A3). The manuscript contains Irish sagas, including the *Táin Bó Cuailnge*, and genealogies. Although several hands have been distinguished in the manuscript, the compiler identifies himself in a note: 'Áed Ua Crimthainn wrote this book and collected it from many books'. He is identified as a scholar of the twelfth century and coarb of St Colum of Terryglass.[76] Tim O'Neill describes the book as 'having the appearance of a scholar's compilation, from which scribes and illuminators could produce a fine manuscript'.[77] In support of this, I might add that its current appearance strongly suggests that the manuscript was never bound, or, if it was, that it spent a substantial period of its use as individual parts defined by the quires and subject-matter. Terryglass, like all the midland monasteries documented here, was raided by Vikings. One such attack is recorded in the Annals of Ulster in 845: 'Turgéis a Viking leader attacked from his base on Lough Ree and laid waste to Clonmacnoise, Clonfert, Terryglass and Lorrha'. His destructive activities were brought to an abrupt end when he was captured by the Uí Néill king Maél Sechlainn and drowned in Lough Owel, Co. Westmeath.[78]

70 Ó Riain 1991, 294.

71 W. O'Sullivan 2005, 533.

72 Todd 1867, 17.

73 Ó Riain 2011, 209–10.

74 *Ibid*., 210; Ó Riain 2014, 5–8.

75 Sharpe 1995, 184.

76 Moss 2014d, 421; O'Neill 2014, 24.

77 Moss 2014d, 421.

78 Ó Cróinín 1995, 246.

At over 19km north-east of the find-spot, Kinnitty is the furthest of the ecclesiastical sites examined here, but still within a day's walk for a dedicated monk. Just as at Birr, no above-ground evidence survives to locate the monastery and its exact location is not known, although it is likely to be in the vicinity of the current Church of Ireland church in the village. *Cenn-etig* was founded by St Fíonán Cam (Finian the Bent/Squint-eyed) in the sixth century. The saint is linked with Kinnitty through a liturgical text of the ninth-century Martyrology of Oengus but later accounts place him with churches in south Kerry, including the twelfth-century Martyrology of Gorman, which mentions Innisfallen.[79] The monastic settlement at Kinnitty became a significant site in the centuries following its construction and is thought to have been the principal legal centre for the Eóganacht dynasty in the ninth century.[80] An interesting graveslab discovered in the graveyard of the church is now housed in the porch of the Protestant church. The Kinnitty Stone is a large sandstone slab, over 1m tall, incised with pre-Christian spiral motifs in two parallel lines inside a curved border. The centre of the slab displays a cross terminating at the extremities of the stone. Within the cross and placed between the arms is a smaller cross with rounded terminals and spiral decoration, and at the base an even smaller outline cross. An additional cross and crozier are incised in the top right-hand panel (Fig. 6.10). The spiral forms could be compared to simplified versions of those found on one of the carpet-pages of the Book of Durrow (TCD MS 57, f. 3v) and the pre-Christian 'Ultimate La Tène' element of the decoration on that folio. Durrow is our earliest surviving decorated Insular gospel-book, produced in the late seventh or early eighth century (Fig. 6.11). Although the exact location of its production is not known and is often hotly debated, it was certainly located in the Columban foundation of Durrow by the late eleventh century, and plausibly considerably earlier.[81] It was in Durrow that the manuscript was placed in a shrine (now lost) as a relic of St Colum Cille. Durrow is approximately 35km north of Kinnitty on the modern R241.[82] The annals do not record any Viking raids on Kinnitty but there is little doubt that it too would have suffered and survived violent attacks from both foreign and native aggressors.

Fig. 6.10—The Kinnitty Stone, Co. Offaly.

The final church to come under scrutiny in this context is Roscrea, already mentioned in relation to its close proximity to the hermitage site of Monaincha and its founder St Crónán (d. 619). Crónán decided to move from the remote site of Monaincha, which was not suitable for a cenobitic monastic community, to establish Roscrea, located on *Slige Dála*, one of the principal travel routes. The impetus for the move may have been Mochuda of Lismore's refusal to accept hospitality at Monaincha.[83] Crónán's decision proved wise and by the ninth century Roscrea was under the influence of the successful *Céli Dé* movement, as indeed was Monaincha. Both were mentioned in a treatise of *Céli Dé* practice of the time. Additionally, Crónán is listed in the Martyrology of Tallaght (the calendar for *Céli Dé* saints).[84] Crónán's life is recorded in two recensions, one held in Marsh's Library, Dublin (MS Z.3.1.5), and the other in Trinity College Dublin (MS E.iii.11). Today nothing remains of the original monastery. The site is identified by the west façade of the twelfth-century Romanesque church on the side of the road. Above the rounded doorway is a figure of a bishop or abbot, probably St Crónán, and there is a high cross close by from the same period. On the other side of the modern road is a round tower, now greatly reduced in height.[85]

79 Ó Riain 2011, 328.

80 Fitzpatrick and O'Brien 1988, 3.

81 Moss 2018, 16.

82 Meehan 2000, 13.

83 Hamlin and Hughes 2004, 28; Ó Riain 2014, 21.

84 Follett 2012, 160–1.

85 Harbison 1992, 313.

Fig. 6.11—Dublin, TCD MS 57 (Book of Durrow), f. 3v, carpet-page. © Trinity College Dublin

Fig. 6.12—Dublin, TCD MS 59 (shrine of the Book of Dimma), upper face with substantial repairs.

Roscrea did not escape the attentions of the Vikings, and the *Cogadh Gaedhel re Gallaibh,* which recorded Norse plundering in Ireland, lists an attack in 845—the same year as attacks on its neighbours, as mentioned earlier. The ecclesiastical settlement at Roscrea has strong connections with an extant gospel, the Book of Dimma (TCD MS 59), the relevance of which to the FMP has been discussed earlier.[86] The manuscript was enshrined at Roscrea in the twelfth century, probably at the time of the construction of the Romanesque church and high cross and when Roscrea was established as an independent diocese. The shrine does not have the usual timber core; typically, however, it has been greatly altered over the centuries and it is possible that the original dimensions have changed, as indeed have those of the manuscript. The decorative metal openwork displays interlace patterns in silver on the back and partially surviving on the sides, representing the original craftwork.[87] Domnall Ua Cuanáin, mentioned in the inscription, is likely associated with the Ua Cuanáin family who were the hereditary coarbs of Roscrea and, as such, considered the spiritual heirs and successors of St Crónán (Fig. 6.12).

If, as mentioned in Chapter 2, it was no great surprise that a newly discovered early medieval manuscript should turn out to be a psalter, then the location of its discovery was equally expected. The wealth of monastic settlements reaching back to the earlier Christian period in Ireland and continuing beyond the burial date of the FMP indicates the richness of potential sources for this psalter. Accepting that the FMP is a local product, it provides material evidence of the knowledge and resources available in the midland monastic community. As demonstrated in Chapter 3, the writing and decoration are representative of what was being produced across the western Christian world. Equally, the binding shows historic influences and access to 'exotic' materials, conceivably through direct contact far beyond Irish shores. This short-listing of ecclesiastical sites within walking distance of the find-spot is by no means exhaustive, and other known centres such as Kilcolman, Churchland, Glebe and Graigue would also warrant consideration as a possible source of the FMP. In the period between the production of the FMP and its deposition in the bog—that is, sometime between 750 and 850—activity in Ireland's monastic midlands, while not perhaps at its zenith, remained influential and productive. Nevertheless, while it is reasonable to suggest that the psalter is a local product, the possibility that it comes from beyond the confines of Munster cannot be dismissed.

86 See Chapter 4, pp 00–00.

87 Ó Floinn 1982.

CHAPTER 7

The find-spot: intentional deposition or accidental loss?

CHAPTER 7

The find-spot: intentional deposition or accidental loss?

The turn of events that resulted in the burial of the FMP in a midlands bog can be considered intrinsic to the history of the manuscript, and the overriding question was whether the psalter was deposited, lost or hidden. Stepping back from the forensic investigation of the find-spot and viewing the topography and layout of the immediate area, it is easy to arrive at the conclusion that the FMP was simply lost by its owner or custodian as he navigated the difficult terrain of the Faddan More Bog. Looking at the evidence gathered during its excavation and later evidence that emerged during conservation, however, I am convinced that the manuscript was purposely deposited at this exact location and that a degree of preparation was involved in the event. The reasoning and evidence presented here are fundamental to this hypothesis, as the FMP has the potential to provide a contribution as a 'marker' from both art-historical and codicological viewpoints owing to its fixed location over most of its existence, an atypical situation for almost all of the manuscripts from this period, although the St Cuthbert Gospel has similar credentials. The aim in this chapter is to firmly link the find-spot with the manuscript and at the same time, albeit more speculatively, to reason why it was placed there.

It is worth bearing in mind that the bogland from which the FMP was retrieved displayed a similar topography in the early Middle Ages as it does now. The precise location where the manuscript was recovered is a natural hollow within the strata of the peat—or so it is presumed, since the dramatic unearthing of the find caused considerable disturbance in comparison to a controlled archaeological excavation (Fig. 7.1). This natural hollow is quite possibly the result of the removal of a tussock from the peat. Tussock is a compact grass or sedge that grows readily on bogs, its compact nature resulting in a hollow if intentionally removed. The palaeoenvironmental research carried out on the find-spot did locate such a tussock close by, evidenced by the discovery of *Eriophorum vaginatum*, confirmed by macrofossil analysis.[1] Typically the removal of a tussock and the creation of a hollow results in the development of a wet pool and such was the case in Faddan More. In effect, the FMP and associated

1 Plunkett *et al.* 2009, 14.

Fig. 7.1 — The hollow identified as the likely find-spot of the FMP.

finds were submerged in this defined space. The research, surprisingly, failed to locate *Eriophorum vaginatum* in or around the cavity itself, but according to the researchers this negative evidence does not rule out the suggestion of tussock removal. It does, however, present the alternative possibility that the 'cavity itself arose from the position of the psalter'. The same research reports that, broadly speaking, the peat in the strata of the find is contemporary with the date of the manuscript.[2] Given that neither the exact period of the strata in which the manuscript lay nor an accurate date for the production of the FMP is known, either of which could span anything from a decade to a century, any inferences drawn must be treated with caution unless and until dates can be narrowed down.

As demonstrated in Chapter 6, traversing and inhabiting areas of bog was not uncommon in the early medieval period and the use of toghers (wooden pathways) aided the process. No archaeological evidence of any pathways was found in the immediate area around the find-spot. This suggests that it was not an area of typical human activity and was 'off the beaten track'.

During the excavation of the site, clumps of what appeared to be animal hair were discovered, somewhat disturbed but clearly associated with the find.[3] Samples (#3) were sent to the Anglo-Saxon Laboratory in York; after initial identification as animal pelt with degraded collagen and surviving hairs, a subsample was sent to Dr Phil Greaves at Microtex International, a specialist in modern coat fibres. Although the results were not conclusive, 'white calfskin seems the best candidate at present, but this is far from certain'.[4] Owing to the disturbance at the find-spot it is difficult to be definitive about what lay where, but, given the evidence presented, it is certain that the manuscript and the calfskin pelt are associated with the same event, with the likelihood that the pelt was employed to cover the psalter after deposition. The other discovery of significance during the excavation was fragments of a leather bag, which will be discussed later in the chapter.

2 *Ibid.*, 15.

3 Sikora and Kelly 2009, 9.

4 Walton Rogers 2008, 2.

Having established that the find-spot contained not only the psalter but also two other objects clearly associated but evidently different in their function and, as such, separate items, it would be reasonable to suggest that, while a hapless monk might drop his psalter in the boggy terrain, it is most unlikely that he would have accidentally lost all three without noticing their absence. A more difficult question arises if deposition is accepted: were the items being disposed of or hidden with the intention of later retrieval? This leads to the consideration of a third scenario, albeit more speculative: that of deliberate deposition without any intention of later retrieval, i.e. that the items were part of a ceremonial burial or even a votive offering/deposition. This pagan tradition from antiquity was carried on into the Christian period at sites which had some particular significance, often close to a boundary between two territories. Developing this hypothesis leads the research to the subject of bog bodies and bog butter owing to the easily drawn parallels, most notably their shared location.[5] The intentional nature of the deposition could represent an event which was part of a ceremony, perhaps a deathbed request of their owner to have his most precious items interred at a location of some special personal significance. Although as a rule Christians were not buried with grave-goods,[6] a separate interment of a person's goods might have been an option.

The tradition of bog butter deposition and its broad time-line on either side of the FMP warrants consideration. By charting discovered bog butters, either in some form of container or simply compacted into a solid mass and buried in bogs or other wetland environments, Eamonn Kelly has observed that many were placed on or close to boundaries, either barony or parish. Proposing votive deposition as the most likely reason for the buried butter, Kelly suggests that the prehistoric practice might also apply to medieval deposits, as a number of the bog butters from this period were also located along a boundary, but he warns that 'other practices may have come to bear during the Christian era'.[7] The medieval population recognised bogs as a natural source of tanning agent for leather, so the insertion of a selection of collagen-based items into this environment would not necessarily have been considered detrimental to their survival, in the short term at least. In addition, Irish hagiography contains numerous accounts of books being retrieved from waterlogged environments and suffering no ill effects, typically owing to the saint with whom the book was associated. One account relating to St Columba tells of how a book of hymns written by the saint and housed in a satchel fell from the shoulder of a boy into a river and remained there for three months before being retrieved and returned by a woman; when opened, the book was dry and undamaged.[8]

Were the FMP and its associated artefacts hidden because of the threat of theft? If so, what was their worth as material goods? If the psalter had been housed in an elaborate bejewelled binding, like

5 In the case of bog bodies, most burials appear to comprise the final act of a ceremony—a sacrifice or offering placed into the bog. This can be embellished further by comparing the space in which interment took place. The FMP was most likely placed in a natural 'ready-made' space within the bog; this has also proven to be the case for more than one of the bog bodies discovered, with interment in ancient peat cuttings which, like the tussock space, have a tendency to flood with water. Two examples are Grauballe Man, found in Denmark at Nebelgaard Mose in 1952, and Old Tollund Man, found in central Jutland in 1950. Both date from the fourth century BC and both suffered violent deaths (see Aldhouse-Green 2015). Although there is an obvious time-gap between the later bog bodies, dating from the late Iron Age, and the eighth-century deposition of the FMP, I would propose that the practice itself presents examples from 2000–1600 BC (Cashel Man) to 400–100 BC (Gallagh Man), demonstrating a robust tradition that continued over centuries.

6 Well-documented exceptions include the coffin of St Cuthbert, bishop of Lindisfarne, the Irish-founded monastery of the English north-east coast. Included with the body of the saint was a portable altar and the St Cuthbert gospel-book (BL Add. MS 89000), dating from the late seventh or early eighth century. Another example of the ceremonial burial of a manuscript is the Mudil Psalter (LDAB 107731), a fourth-century Coptic book of psalms found 'under the head of a young girl' during excavations in a cemetery north of Oxyrhynchus in Egypt.

7 L. Downey, C. Synnott, E.P. Kelly and C. Stanton, 'Bog butter: dating profile and location', *Archaeology Ireland* **20** (1), 32–4.

8 Anderson and Anderson 1961, 107.

Fig. 7.2—Model of the FMP cover.

the gospel-book of Colum Cille, as discussed in Chapter 4, which was stolen from Kells in 1007 for the sole purpose of acquiring the precious covers,[9] then there would be a strong argument for hiding the FMP in the bog. This was not the case, however; though the manuscript itself was of value to the community who produced and used it, it would have meant little to a gang of marauding Vikings or warring locals. Although the ransoming of manuscripts is known to have taken place, the FMP would not make for an obvious target. The two other artefacts, the pelt covering and the leather bag, would have been equally if not even more modest in their appeal to opportunistic thieves.

As mentioned above, the unearthing and gathering up of the find by the accidental discoverers greatly disturbed the original intended position of the items. If the exact position and strata could be clarified, it might well give additional clues to the purpose of the deposition. During the conservation process, however, it was possible to establish some supporting evidence in relation to the leather cover of the psalter. I propose a haphazard placement of the manuscript in its hollow, based on two noteworthy features observed during conservation. First, in the course of wet cleaning of the folio fragments it was noticed that the final blank folio displayed a circular indent on the surface of the vellum near the fore-edge. Investigation revealed that this was an impression of one of the buttons on the flap of the leather cover. This indicates that the flap was tucked in behind the text block rather than being wrapped around it and resting on the front cover as was intended. Second, a constant feature of the cleaning process involved the removal of a profusion of seed pods distributed over every part of the manuscript remains. When removing these pods from the leather cover, I noticed a marked concentration of them running diagonally from the corner of the fore-edge to the corner of the spine.

9 As recorded in the Annals of Ulster, the manuscript was recovered two months later, found under a sod; it is generally accepted as being the extant Book of Kells, now bound in four separate volumes.

Fig. 7.3—The position of the psalter while buried.

This accumulation is the result of the cover not lying prone, or even upright as originally reported,[10] but rather folded to some degree, creating the diagonal trough in which the seed pods gathered over time. These features suggest a more haphazard approach to the deposition, or, alternatively, a possible disturbance of the items at some point after burial (Figs 7.2 and 7.3). In relation to this point, I have already noted (see Chapter 2) the variance in condition of the two halves of the horizontally split and singularly intact bifolio 29–32 and how this suggests historic trauma of the manuscript, as the bottom half of the bifolio is in a more advanced state of decay owing to being in a different micro-environment from the top half.

Supporting the evidence of historic damage to the vellum folios of the manuscript, it can be observed that, for all the remaining fragments, the survival from the head area is superior to that of the tail; in fact, there is practically no extant writing from the bottom half of any of the 60 folios, the material here consisting only of narrow strips of vellum from the tail edge (except for f. 29–32). If considerable damage occurred before deposition, in effect tearing the manuscript in two and rendering it worthless, difficult as this might be to achieve, then an act of disposal rather than careful deposition should be included as a possible motive. I suggest that it is unwise to make a definitive statement as to why the FMP was discovered in such an unlikely location other than to say that it was positively the result of a deposition rather than an accidental loss.

The fragmented pieces of leather found distributed over the find-spot indicate an artefact with a strong association to the FMP. The general form of what has been provisionally identified as a bag—a more accurate description might be a 'pouch'—appears to be unstructured, employing a single skin, stitched and then gathered. Around the resulting opening, a draw-string of thicker leather was introduced by turning over the bag leather to create a lip, and a thonging stitch was used to connect the strap (Fig. 7.4). There is a fragment of an additional leather strip, thicker and broader, perhaps part of a carrying strap similar to the type surviving on the Springmount Bog Tablets (NMI No. S.A. 1914:2) (Fig.7.5). Another structural feature appears as loops of thick leather attached by

10 Kelly 2006, 7.

Fig. 7.4—Larger fragment of the tanned leather bag or pouch in its wet state.

lacing through the bag, with the strap leather feeding through. Knots are also present in the leather strapping to lock the components in position (Fig. 7.6). Though the leather was identified as pigskin,[11] I am unconvinced of this, having had the opportunity more recently to work with the object, which remains in its saturated state.[12] There is a high degree of loss to the flesh side of the leather bag, which faced inwards, as might be expected. The delamination of archaeological leather is a known condition[13] and, while the more compact grain layer may survive, the flesh side can lose any structural integrity. This effect on the Faddan More bag results in the surviving grain layer displaying follicle holes

Fig. 7.5—The Springmount Bog Tablets (NMI No. S.A. 1914:2).

11 Cartwright 2010.

12 Carol Smith, conservator in the National Museum, and I spent two weeks in 2018 examining the wide range of fragments associated with the bag/pouch. The primary aim was to identify the additional materials present and to establish the inside and outside surfaces of the larger tanned leather fragments. Initial discussion about the future de-watering of the components was also included.

13 Cameron *et al.* 2006, 245.

Fig. 7.6—Loops of thicker leather wrapped around the bag.

Fig. 7.7—Dublin, Trinity College Library, TCD MS 52 (Book of Armagh Satchel).

through the full thickness, a feature of pigskin, but my examination under binocular microscope leads me to believe, based on follicle layout, that the leather is sourced from a calfskin.

It is difficult to be certain about the robustness of the bag, given the degradation of the leather, but I remain unconvinced that the manuscript was housed in the bag. For this I would expect a more structured and robust format, such as the Armagh Satchel (TCD MS 52*) (Fig. 7.7). Close examination during the recent assessment and treatment revealed small and minute fragments of additional organic materials, possibly the contents of the bag; these include textile, i.e. vegetable fibre, perhaps linen as found in the backfolds of the psalter's quire three, and papyrus. All these fragments were located on the flesh side (the inner surface of the bag), and thus it is reasonable to suggest that they were part of the contents. Interestingly, the vegetable fibre was wrapped into a ball, reflecting a convenient and contemporary method of storing linen thread. Could the bag therefore be a form of craft bag, carrying the materials required by a bookbinder monk to produce the manuscripts for his community?

Thus it may be surmised that a site was prepared, either by removing a tussock or by digging a hole in a remote area of the bog, and the three objects identified by the archaeological excavation were placed into the hollow, or possibly the bag and book were buried and then covered with the pelt, which would have been in the form of a blanket or cloak. The event was a conscious act for a purpose that is likely to remain unknown.

CHAPTER 8

Conclusion

CHAPTER 8

Conclusion

For many archaeological discoveries, it is the combination of a fortunate set of circumstances that results in their unearthing. In the case of the FMP, if the backhoe bucket which plucked the psalter from the saturated bog had been positioned 30cm in any other direction, the manuscript would have gone unnoticed and its contribution to early medieval monastic life would have been lost. I reminded myself of this constantly as I progressed through the many revelations it has yielded thus far.

The long and careful conservation of this archaeological artefact, followed by a thorough codicological study, has shed new light on aspects of medieval manuscript production. The circumstances surrounding almost every aspect of the FMP and its discovery in 2006 have generated interest and questions which, like many relating to early medieval manuscripts, cannot be definitively answered. Nevertheless, this volume addresses at least some of the more 'clue-laden' questions and adds to our understanding of this recently revealed manuscript, the first Insular book to be discovered in two centuries.

It has been noted that the five vellum quires of the FMP and its tanned leather cover are not what could be considered a 'good fit', and aspects of both components suggest makeshift bedfellows. A comparison of the dimensions of the text block and the cover is a primary indicator here, the approximated length of the folios measuring 1cm less than that of the cover from head to tail. In addition, the intentional creasings along the spine of the single-piece leather cover to accommodate its contents are over-generous when the thickness of the assembled vellum folios is calculated. These factors alone suggest that the cover of the FMP was a housing of convenience rather than an integral component of the manuscript. As a consequence, the FMP provides two discrete parts, both of which are valuable additions to the small corpus of extant early medieval books and the even smaller corpus of bindings. The cover in particular goes further, providing information beyond its function; the markings and trial motifs indicate day-to-day practices related to book-making inside the monastery.

The manuscript itself was originally a complete psalter of 150 psalms and cannot be considered a work in progress. Evidence of this was established by examination of the folio fragments during conservation. The text block lacks any flyleaves, commonly associated with medieval books, although it must be acknowledged that there is a dearth of early medieval text blocks still in their original form and format capable of indicating typical practice in this regard. The eighth-century St Cuthbert Gospel does retain its original flyleaves and shows the convention of employing the first and last leaves of the first and last quires as flyleaves and paste-downs,[1] while closer to home the binding boards of the Book of Armagh likewise retain evidence of this structural feature. It has been demonstrated that the cover of the FMP has the appearance of heavy and prolonged use, including the intriguing wear pattern on the spine area where it was gripped while being carried. These features are inconsistent with (the writing of) the text block fragments, uncluttered as they are by the addition of glosses or any corrections over time. This evidence and the suggestion of deposition having occurred not long (in relative terms) after the psalter was written lead to the conclusion that the cover represents a repurposing of what was a binding for another manuscript. Modifications might have included trimming of the edges closer to the size of its new occupant and thus removing the expected turn-ins (all the Nag Hammadi and comparative covers discussed in Chapter 4 display this feature).

I have proposed that there was no mechanical attachment between the five vellum quires and the tanned leather cover, while presenting evidence to suggest that the individual quires were held together as a text block with a form of quire tacket or an unsupported sewing, possibly a pair of sewing stations. Irrespective of which method was employed, the cover would have functioned as a 'wallet-type' folder for its contents. There are obvious advantages for portability in retaining a manuscript as a collection of unbound quires but also disadvantages as regards durability; the use of a lightweight container helps to protect without adding the bulk and weight of a medieval timber binding. Jonas, in his seventh-century *Life of St Columbanus*, writes of the second abbot of Bobbio, Athala, who, as he prepared for his own death, concerned himself with the preservation of the library, which included having the books bound.[2] This indicates that many early medieval manuscripts were in use, probably for extended periods after their production, without any solid structure in the form of a bookbinding. The options may have been to sew the text block, most likely using an unsupported sewing system or perhaps a side stabbing, and to house the folded quires in a satchel or FMP-type enclosure. An alternative possibility is that, rather than an integral text block, the psalter consisted of five individual quires, each held together with thread tackets. This would be a useful tool for the monastic scribe teaching his oblates, giving each student a quire from which he might copy the psalms. Within the oldest catalogue of the Library of the Abbey of St Gall there are additional catalogue titles of note, one of which reads *LIBRI SCOTTICE SCRIPTI*, followed by a list written in a minuscule hand (Fig. 8.1). I have already referenced this document in relation to the identification of Irish manuscripts in the monastery (Chapter 3). In addition to identifying Irish manuscripts in the library, the catalogue lists the books by their physical format: nineteen *volumina*, two *codicilli*, nine *quarterniones* and the term q*uarternionibus* in two of the nine entries. This clearly shows several codices not bound into books.[3] Corroborating evidence has been presented in Chapter 5, where the use of the FMP cover as a form of sketch-book could be considered an unlikely utilisation of a functioning bookbinding.

In presenting a counter-argument by considering features on the cover of the FMP that could suggest mechanical attachment to the quires, we may note the two 'star-shaped' holes in the centre of the spine and the two sets of four smaller holes positioned in pairs on the front and back crease lines of the cover. The central holes, as described, show very little (if any) use or wear and do not align with any holes in the backfold of bifolio 29–32 (the only extant backfold in the manuscript) and thus they can be

1 Pickwoad 2015, 46.

2 McGrath 1979, 88.

3 Duft and Meyer 1954, 40–1; Gullick 2012, 307; Szirmai 1999, 285; Dora and Schnoor 2018.

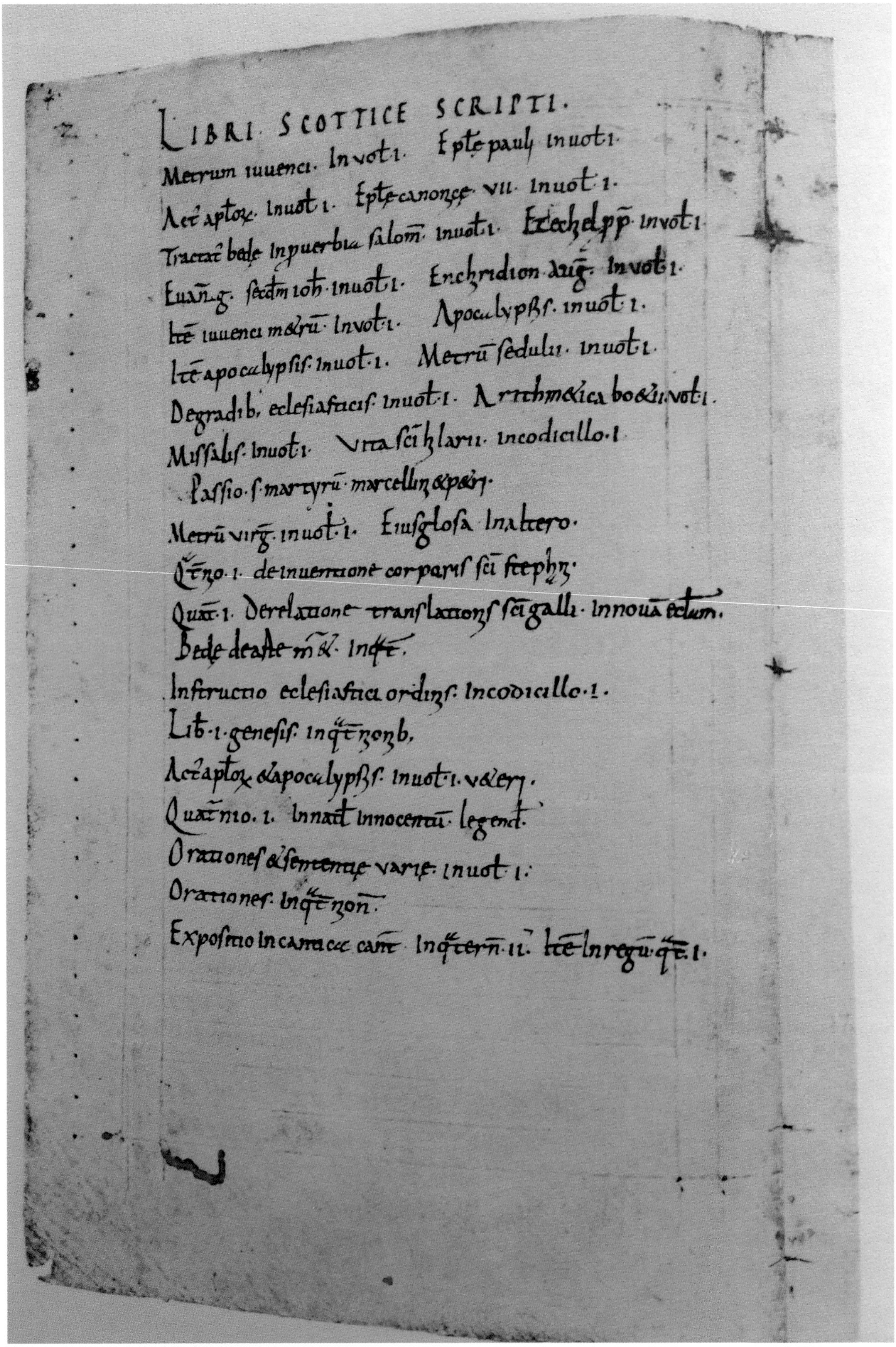

Fig. 8.1 – Catalogue entry in the Library of the Abbey of St Gallen.

discounted. The smaller sets of holes display positive evidence of use in the form of the diagonal exiting of a thread or cord, as examined in Chapter 4. These holes align with those that contained the vegetable fibre thread fragments in bifolio 29–32, but it is still not clear how this might have functioned as a primary tacket attachment system.

If it was no surprise that an early medieval manuscript pulled out of a bog in the monastic midlands of Ireland should be a psalter, the one-piece leather cover enclosing it provoked a different reaction as an exemplar of an early Irish bookbinding. The form, structure and even materials employed to produce the cover of the FMP all originate from eastern Mediterranean material culture under Roman influence. As illustrated in Chapter 4, the search for parallel extant structures all resulted in examples from outside the western European early medieval book-making tradition. Considering book-satchels as a historically recorded method of keeping manuscripts protected, with their stitched form and leather carrying straps, the format of the FMP cover would have appeared somewhat unfamiliar in an Irish setting. The representation of this 'flap'-style binding illustrated in iconographical images of the period demonstrates, however, a wider geographical spread back to its source in Egypt. My search for comparative imagery in western European art—and more specifically in illuminated gospel-books of the same epoch—involved studying illustrations from Irish, Anglo-Saxon and Carolingian source material. The research was restricted almost entirely to online resources, digital images, printed material and finally, in a few cases, actual examination of manuscripts themselves. The results detailed are interesting for what I consider to be semi-limp structures with flaps identified in a range of manuscripts, but I found no matching examples of the FMP-type cover, with its distinct flap with three buttons attached, depicted in any manuscripts other than those considered to be of Irish origin or produced under Irish influence abroad.[4] Any similar extant comparative models, such as the British Library Tax Register (BL Papyrus 1442) or the Nag Hammadi codices, lack the three-buttoned flap. Books illustrated on metalwork or stone provided no similar models. Additional, if somewhat less exhaustive, searches through Italian and Byzantine material failed to track the binding structure of the FMP from a source in North Africa to the island of Ireland. This leads to the hypothesis that the structural features, methods and materials employed in making the type of cover found with the Faddan More psalter, including the entirely decorative buttons, possibly related to Christian numerology, while the copying of monastic exemplars from the far-flung Orient was particular to Ireland and not uncommon; this sits comfortably with the Irish Christian alignment and the monastic traditions of Egypt during the sixth and seventh centuries.

Given the almost ephemeral nature of the FMP cover, it is no great surprise that it is the only known extant example from an Insular, or possibly European, context from the early medieval period. Contemplating again a comparison of the FMP binding and its Coptic features with extant early medieval bindings, such as the Cadmug Gospels and St Cuthbert's Gospel, it is important to note that the FMP preserves an intact structure that harks back to the very beginning of the Christian codex. Additionally and uniquely, unlike the two pocket gospels, in the manufacture of the FMP materials were used which were unlikely to be found locally but which are in fact common to the location of its Eastern model, suggesting that it is not based on a Coptic exemplar but rather is a product of its place of origin, albeit modified by its Irish owners. Bernard Meehan makes a similar observation.[5] Finally, this unique survival shows us that from the beginning of the Christian era the influence of eastern Mediterranean craft and technology extended beyond elaborate manuscripts to the everyday books employed in the didactic and spiritual life of monastic Ireland.

Unlike the cover/binding, the text block of the FMP leaves little doubt as to its place of origin.

---

4 The Mac Durnan Gospels (London, Lambeth Palace MS 1370), the Cadmug Gospels (Landesbibliothek Codex Bonifatianus 3) and the Book of Dimma (TCD MS 59).

5 Meehan 2014, 246.

Even if the manuscript had been discovered with text obliterated, the evidence of its physical nature and construction, i.e. its codicology, would have identified it as of Insular origin. As pointed out in Chapter 2, traits such as the assembly of the quires, the ruling methods employed and the nature of the skin firmly link the manuscript to the location where it was found in the monastic midlands of Ireland but, in so doing, put it at odds with its cover. In addition, the Insular majuscule hand, the decorative elements—scant as they are—and the geometric-style lettering further reinforce the Irish credentials of the text block and leave little doubt as to its place of production.

Initially I coined the phrase 'medieval paperback' to describe the quality of the FMP as an end-product, and a similar view is offered by Harry Gamble, who suggests that with the production of early Christian books 'the type of cover probably depended on the preferences of the owner and the value of the text'.[6] As my research progressed, however, it became evident that this was no hastily produced copy of the psalms for personal use but rather a manuscript for didactic purposes, for the singing of the liturgy or for assisting the efforts of novice monks in their attempts to become *psalterati*. While it is true to say that the FMP was not intended as a visual spectacle to impress its viewers with intricate knotwork, interlacing and hidden creatures lurking in the Insular majuscule text, it was a book carefully considered and produced by a skilled scribe or scribes. The FMP is unquestionably more comfortable in the company of the less elaborately produced manuscripts of the period, and even in its pristine state it would have appeared very plain and dour in the company of another presumed local product, the MacRegol Gospels (accepting that it was produced within the orbit in which it was discovered). Such divergence becomes even more apparent when it is placed side by side with the pinnacle of Irish manuscript production, the Book of Kells. Perhaps it is unfair to compare the FMP with such gospel-books, which would have been on display for liturgical ceremonies and feast-days in the church, with intended visual impact. The higher status of selected gospel-books is further evidenced by their association with or dedication to particular saints; examples include the Book of Dimma and the Book of Mulling, both linked with saints in an attempt to raise the status of the churches in which they were held and to increase the prestige of the books themselves. As a visual comparison, the FMP does sit comfortably with well-executed and professionally produced manuscripts such as the Book of Armagh, where either intentionally or because of a lack of resources a more sober spectacle was the result of the expert efforts of scribe and artist, although its later association with St Patrick changed this status. It has been demonstrated in the chapters discussing the text block that the writing and decoration of the FMP are wholly characteristic of the Irish traditions of book-making in the early medieval period. The choice of materials and the preparation of the folios both firmly locate the text block as an Irish product. The Insular majuscule writing and the geometric and interlace work, executed with a basic palette of colours, further anchor the psalter to home soil.

The conservation of the FMP may be considered a success and a testament to the value of collaborative work across disciplines. Reflecting on my own role and with the benefit of hindsight, I would, were I given the opportunity to start again, change little in my approach or in the techniques applied. I would, however, slow the project down somewhat and allocate more time to recording prior to using any treatment that might involve disturbing the fabric of the object. In turn, this would have produced more digital images and recorded a range of physical features present, some of which were to become more obscure in their dry state (see Chapter 1). It was inevitable that even such a culturally and historically significant discovery as the FMP would ultimately be subject to time restrictions. Nevertheless, the National Museum of Ireland provided the maximum resources and expertise at its disposal to ensure the highest standards at all stages of the work. It is hoped that the associated database will prove to be a useful tool and an aid to future research, as it maps to the best of our ability the movement and

6 Gamble 1997, 69.

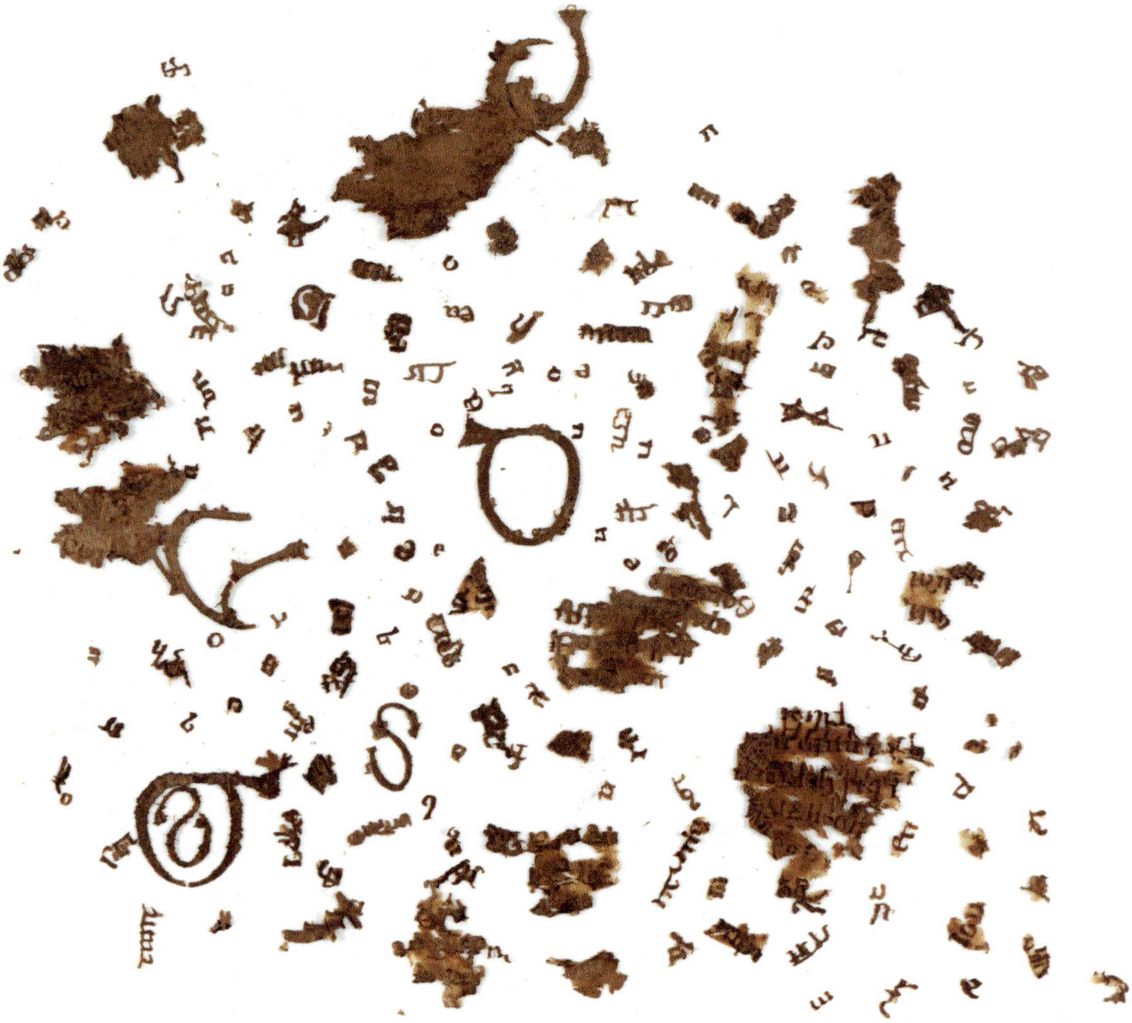

Fig. 8.2—Unplaced fragments of the Faddan More Psalter.

identification of the plethora of folio fragments of the psalter as conservation progressed. Anticipated scientific work might provide definitive analysis of both the vellum text block and the tanned calfskin cover. Protein and DNA testing has advanced greatly since the beginning of this project in 2006. Non-destructive and micro-sampling techniques might yet confirm not only the species—although I am convinced of my identification here—but also the geographic region in which both cover and text block originated. This would definitively answer the question as to where the cover of the FMP was produced and consequently add supporting physical evidence of craft practice, material culture and the much-discussed occidental–oriental connections in the monastic Ireland of the early medieval period.

As was established and discussed in Chapter 7, the FMP was the subject of deliberate deposition rather than an accidental loss. I found it difficult to come to terms with the notion of this manuscript being disposed of—discarded as no longer useful—but perhaps this scenario needs to be considered. There is a tendency in modern times to regard the few survivors of scribal achievement as symbolic and material witnesses to the dedication of the people who wrote and studied their contents. Books were an essential part of the monastic environment and as familiar as the buildings or church furnishings. As products of organic materials, like the wooden buildings that housed them, they are vulnerable to decay and cannot have been considered permanent. It is reasonable to suggest that the contemporary users of

these books understood this and, according to Richard Sharpe, did not necessarily regard them as possessing an unlimited lifespan. Sharpe sums up the situation in the medieval monasteries of Ireland by stating that '... books were being destroyed by overuse, or neglect, or being scrapped'.[7] It has to be argued, of course, that dedicated volumes held a different status in the consciousness of their custodians and that some were viewed as beyond mere material objects, having acquired relic status because of their associations with founding saints.

One ongoing aspect of this project (as of November 2018) is the relocation of disjointed smaller text fragments. This time-consuming and eye-straining but highly rewarding task should add additional text to the assembly of the Vulgate psalter, where extant writing has been highlighted and variants noted (see Appendix 4). It is hoped that this will assist in a future full transcription of the FMP. Once complete, the psalter will add not only to the materiality of medieval Irish book-making but also to the corpus of Irish liturgical material available for scholarly study, and tools such as my identified text list and fragment database will assist specialists in extracting further information from this complex artefact. In addition to the 'floating' majuscule writing fragments, there remains a collection of disjointed capitals, both Insular and geometric in style, often with blocks of colour still attached, that require identification and relocation (Fig. 8.2). These decorated letters were intended to highlight certain psalms, such as those that began the 'three fifties'. This task is complicated, as the strokes of the letters themselves are often deformed and out of position. I hope to continue work in this area, with the goal of building a more complete picture of the writing and layout of the psalter.

The observations of Françoise Henry, the famous scholar of early Irish art, were vindicated in 2006 when the FMP was discovered. In her examination of three Irish psalters in 1961, she thought it strange that no

7 Sharpe 2010, 16.

Fig. 8.3—St Anthony's Monastery, Red Sea Desert.

other psalter texts were known from the period between the *Cathach*, in the early seventh century(?), and the earliest of the psalters in her study, which dated from the tenth century. She commented that 'There cannot be the slightest doubt that many copies of the psalter have existed in Ireland in the late seventh, eighth and ninth centuries'.[8]

The FMP undoubtedly makes a worthwhile and substantial addition to the corpus of Irish early medieval manuscripts. Its stature as such is unlikely to be fully realised until a concentrated scholarly appraisal has been completed. The difficulty lies in its partial survival, physical condition and faded writing, which add a substantial challenge to any detailed study. Nevertheless, as in the cases of the Dead Sea Scrolls or the Oxyrhynchus Papyri, there is much to be learned, given time, resources and ever-improving technology. The materiality of the FMP makes an even greater contribution, adding substantially to the codicological study of early medieval book-making, and more specifically to Irish book-making. It now takes its place with the tiny number of Insular manuscripts that still retain their original covers and, like the St Cuthbert Gospel and the Cadmug Gospels, also display influence from eastern Mediterranean traditions. Uniquely, the FMP also presents the materials from that tradition and, in so doing, brings additional evidence to the Hiberno-Coptic discussion. It is to be hoped that the work completed thus far will act as a catalyst for multi-disciplinary research to begin in earnest around this extraordinary survival. My continuing work includes a search for additional historical illustrations of like structures as well as extant structures; the latter may survive on the shelves of libraries or even in monastic communities such as St Anthony's in the Red Sea Desert, where I believe that bindings like that of the FMP are to be found (Fig. 8.3). Closer to home, the study and conservation of the associated pouch is already contributing data that will better inform us about the provenance of the Faddan More Psalter and the role it played in the monastic Ireland of the eighth century.

8 Henry 1961, 24.

FADDAN MORE PSALTER

Appendices

APPENDIX 1

Vellum drying trials

Sample no.	Drying mechanism
1	Air-dry control
2	Freeze-dried
3, 4, 5, 6	Vacuum table
7, 8, 9, 10	Under weight
11, 12, 13, 14	In vacuum machine

Sample no.	**Drying solvent**
1	Air-dry control
2	No solvent exchange
3	No solvent exchange
4	Through denatured alcohol
5	Through acetone
6	Through acetone/H_2O 80:20
7	No solvent exchange
8	Through denatured alcohol
9	Through acetone
10	Through acetone/H_2O 80:20
11	No solvent exchange
12	Through denatured alcohol
13	Through acetone
14	Through acetone/H_2O 80:20

DRYING TEST RESULTS

1. Air-dry control

Placed on blotting-paper uncovered from saturated. Ambient 21°C, 57% RH.
Result: Dry in six hours, judged by touch; very distorted and less flexible; very translucent in places, leaving a 'blotchy' appearance; approx. 5% shrinkage.
Flexibility Disc C, 0.30mm. Colour value 3020-Y10 (hair side).

2. Freeze-dried (over five days)

Result: No distortion; approx. 3.5% shrinkage; opacity maintained; sample has 'pulped up' with a noticeable increase in thickness; loss of natural pigmentation on hair side, becoming almost white; surface feels 'spongy'.
Flexibility Disc B, 0.20mm. Colour value 1510-Y20 (hair side).

3, 4, 5, 6. Vacuum table

Through various (see below). Sample laid on two thicknesses of Bondina®, area masked with Mylar® film; vacuum set at 28 inches of H_2O (about 6.9kPa), with ambient values of 20°C and 57% RH; in order to slow regional drying and avoid 'cupping' of the sample, two thicknesses of Bondina® were placed over the affected areas; as drying of the sample neared completion, pressure was reduced to 13 inches of H_2O.

3. From wet state: dry in 90 minutes, judged by touch; vacuum struggled to hold sample in position; approx. 5% shrinkage; somewhat distorted; loss of flexibility and sample now translucent in areas.
Flexibility Disc C, 0.30mm. Colour value 3020-Y10 (hair side).

4. Through denatured alcohol: some slight distortion; approx. 3% shrinkage; opacity maintained; slightly blotchy appearance; considerable change in colour (lighter).
Flexibility Disc B, 0.20mm. Colour value 1510-Y20 (hair side).

5. Through acetone: some slight distortion; approx. 3% shrinkage; opacity maintained; slightly blotchy appearance; considerable change in colour (lighter).
Flexibility Disc B, 0.20mm. Colour value 1510-Y20 (hair side).

6. Through acetone/H_2O 80:20: very slight distortion; approx. 2% shrinkage; has become more transparent with loss of flexibility.
Flexibility Disc C, 0.30mm. Colour value 3020-Y10 (hair side).

7. Under weight

Sample between blotting-paper and 100% cotton heavy blotting-paper. Glass weights placed on top, 1.2kg. Blotting-paper changed after two hours, then left overnight. No distortion; approx. 3.5% shrinkage; flexibility maintained but increase in translucency.
Flexibility Disc B, 0.20mm. Colour value 3020-Y10 (hair side).

8, 9, 10. Under weight

No blotting-paper change for No. 9; weight increased for all to 2.1kg; all dry after three hours, No. 9 much sooner; ambient values of 20°C and 57% RH.

8. Through denatured alcohol: dried well; no distortion; approx. 3% shrinkage; slight increase in translucency; some colour change (lighter) to hair side.
Flexibility Disc B, 0.20mm. Colour value 2020-Y10 (hair side).

9. Through acetone: no distortion; approx. 3% shrinkage; some areas becoming more translucent, others having dramatic colour change, appearing very white.
Flexibility Disc B, 0.20mm. Colour value 2020-Y10 (hair side).

10. Through acetone/H_2O 80:20: no distortion; approx. 1.5% shrinkage;

opacity maintained.
Flexibility Disc B, 0.20mm. Colour value 2020-Y10 (hair side).

11, 12, 13, 14. Vacuum machine
Vacuum timed at 35 seconds after vacuum is reached; sample in Archipress® vacuum bag and between Bondina® and heavy 100% cotton blotting-paper sheets. For test purposes there was no change of blotting-paper and sample remained sealed for three days.

11. From wet state: no distortion; approx. 1.5% shrinkage; sample has become very translucent across most of its surface; flexibility unchanged.
Flexibility Disc B, 0.20mm. Colour value 3020-Y10 (hair side).

12. Through denatured alcohol: no distortion; approx. 3.5% shrinkage; opacity maintained; slight loss in flexibility and slight colour change (lighter).
Flexibility Disc B, 0.20mm. Colour value 2020-Y10 (hair side).

13. Through acetone: no distortion; approx. 3.5% shrinkage; opacity maintained, as was flexibility; dramatic change to colour value on hair side (lighter).
Flexibility Disc B, 0.20mm. Colour value 1010-Y10 (hair side).

14. Through acetone/H_2O 80:20: no distortion; no shrinkage; opacity maintained; flexibility maintained, as was colour value.
Flexibility Disc B, 0.20mm. Colour value 2020-Y10 (hair side).

VACUUM MACHINE—DENATURED ALCOHOL AGAINST DENATURED ALCOHOL/H_2O 98:2

Because of the successful results achieved using the vacuum machine through acetone/H_2O 80:20 in relation to the end results but concern as to activity (bubbling from the sample, leaving a skin on the surface of the solution), it was decided to conduct a trial of the denatured alcohol with a low percentage of additional water, as it is understood that even laboratory-grade alcohol has some water content (0.5% for IMS 100). As a comparison, a parallel trial using only denatured alcohol was also carried out.

Conditions
New parchment was soaked in tap water for three weeks. One sample was placed in a denatured alcohol bath and the other in a denatured alcohol/H_2O 98:2 bath. Both baths were covered and left for 48 hours. Both samples were removed and placed inside an Archipress® vacuum bag between layers of Bondina® and double layers of 100% thick cotton blotting-paper. Both bags were placed in the vacuum machine and a vacuum was pulled for 30 seconds. The vacuum bags were opened after five days.

Results
Both samples maintained opacity and showed no distortion from the wet state to the dry. Shrinkage was calculated as before on all four sides and a mean established. The alcohol-only sample showed a shrinkage of 1.5%, while the alcohol/H_2O 98:2 displayed no discernable shrinkage, with all dimensions identical to their wet values.

The results prompted a repeat of this test using nineteenth-century vellum soaked and kept at saturated values between wet sheets of blotting-paper for five weeks. As before, the samples were then placed in the two different solutions and left overnight. The same conditions for the vacuum machine were employed and the sealed samples left for 24 hours before opening. The blotting-paper was changed and the samples placed under vacuum again and left for a further seventeen hours.

RESULTS

Alcohol: sample maintained opacity; no distortion; good flexibility.
Flexibility Disc B, 0.20mm. Colour value 2020-Y10 (hair side).
Alcohol/H_2O 98:2: sample maintained opacity; no distortion; good flexibility.
Flexibility Disc B, 0.20mm. Colour value 2020-Y10 (hair side).

Sample 1, alcohol	Thickness wet: 0.41–0.55mm	Average: 0.48mm
Sample 1, alcohol	Thickness dry: 0.19–0.28mm	Average: 0.23mm
Sample 1, alcohol/H_2O	Thickness wet: 0.53–0.59mm	Average: 0.56mm
Sample 1, alcohol/H_2O	Thickness dry: 0.25–0.32mm	Average: 0.28mm

In both samples there was an average reduction of 50% in thickness from wet to dry.

Test sample dimensions

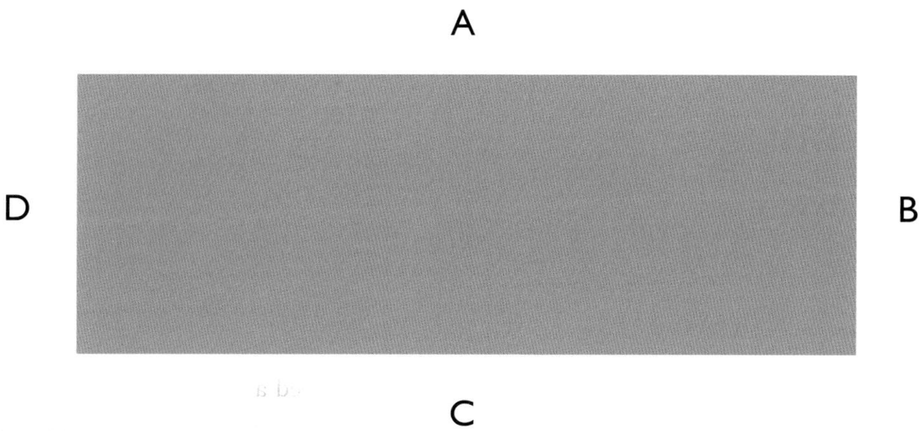

SAMPLE	WET/DRY	A	B	C	D	MEAN
Alcohol	Wet	110mm	42mm	91mm	46mm	
Alcohol	Dry	108mm	42mm	90mm	46mm	0.7%
Alcohol/H_2O	Wet	88mm	46mm	106mm	42.5mm	
Alcohol/H_2O	Dry	86mm	46mm	104.5mm	42.5mm	0.9%

APPENDIX 2

Faddan More Psalter databases

SAMPLE PAGE FROM MAIN DATABASE

FADDAN MORE PSALTER CONSERVATION FILE

Tag No. P-A85 **Date** 08/12/2008 **Session No.** 22 **Level** 1

Left/Right Left — Position of fragment prior to removal L/R based on facing the open Ms.

Quire 1st **folio** 04 - 09 — Quire and folio numbers are based on the last examination of the fragment and are updated as new information becomes available.

Grid Reference

N/A

Comments

A good percentage of this bifolium has survived with some interesting features. There are unusual capitals on both folios, with colour. There is also some interlinear work, both single letter and a complete word (4v), these appear to be corrections for omitted text, or "eye skip". The hand and the ink appear different to the text. There is also a small area on 4v where vertical ruling can be seen and what appears to be double lines and associated pricking, further investigation is needed here. With added fragments from f1-12 f4 has become almost complete, with only f29-32 more intact

Insert Photo

Folio / Psalm

4r 8.6-10 9.2-10
4v 9.13-28
9r 19.5-23 20.10-12
9v 20.14 21.10

Fragment Added

From P-A69 Ps20.10-12 <te>mpor<e>.....de terra....<homi>num....<cogi>taveru<nt>
From P-A77 f1-12 f4r Ps9.5-6 *(et causam mea<m>.....<sae>culi)* and f4vPs9.21-24 *(Domine legislatorem <su>per eos..... cogitant quoniam)* Other fragments from f1-12 have added to f4, with text on recto and verso identified

SAMPLE PAGE FROM LEATHER DRYING TRIALS

Faddan More Psalter Leather Drying Trials

No. 56 Thickness based on average of several readings

Batch Grades

Thickness wet 1.6 mm **Species** Calf **Batch** 4 **Incised** Yes

Test: Solvent Dry through I.M.S and blottings

Observations; Pre Close grained piece.

Observations; Post Good result.

Thickness dry 1.2 mm

Flex Disc C

Thickness loss -.4 mm **Shrinkage** 12 %

APPENDIX 3

Folio and psalm number

FOLIO/BIFOLIO	VERSO	RECTO
Q1_1v+12r	1v—Ps.1:3	
Q1_2v+11r	2v—Ps.4:8–10	
Q1_3v+10r	3v—Ps.7:7	10r—Ps.21:23
Q1_4v+9r	4v—Ps.9:13–28	9r—Ps.19:5–10, Ps.20:2–3, Ps.20:10–12
Q1_5r		5r—Ps.9:29–39, Ps.10:1–5
Q1_5v	5v—Ps.10:6–8, Ps.11:2–9, Ps.12:1	
Q1_6v+7r	6v—Ps.15:1–10, Ps.16:1–3	
Q1_7v+6r	7v—Ps.17:8–26	6r—Ps.13:1–6, Ps.14:2–3
Q1_8r		8r—Ps.17:28–41
Q1_8v	8v—Ps.17:50, Ps.18:2–8	
Q1_9v+4r	9v—Ps.20:14, Ps.21:2–10	4r—Ps.8:6–10, Ps.9:2–10
Q1_10v+3r		3r—Ps.6:2
Q1_11v+2r		2r—Ps.2:12–13
Q1_12v+1r		1r—Ps.1:1
Q2_13v+25r	13v—Ps.31:4–10	25r—Ps.60:2–9, Ps.61:2–4
Q2_14v+24r	14v—Ps.33:18–21, Ps.34:1–4	24r—Ps.56:5–6, Ps.57:2–9
Q2_15r		15r—Ps.34:15–21
Q2_15v	15v—Ps.35:8–13, Ps.36:1–3	
Q2_16v+23r	16v—Ps.37:2-10	23r—Ps.54:10-20
Q2_17v+22r	17v—Ps.39:7–13, Ps.40:2–4	22r—Ps.50:19–20, Ps.51:3
Q2_18v+21r		21r—Ps.48:18–20
Q2_19v+20r		
Q2_20v+19r		
Q2_21v+18r	21v—Ps.49:20	
Q2_22v+17r	22v—Ps.52:3–6	17r—Ps.38:4–9
Q2_23v+16r	23v—Ps.55:7–11	16r—Ps.36:18–27

Folio and psalm number

FOLIO/BIFOLIO	VERSO	RECTO
Q2_24v+14r	24v—Ps.58:9–13	14r—Ps.32:11–22
Q2_25v+13r	25v—Ps.62:3–9	13r—Ps.30:13–24
Q3_26v+35r	26v—Ps.64:10	35r—Ps.83:4–9
Q3_27v+34r	27v—Ps.68:2	34r—Ps.80:4–8
Q3_28v+33r	28v—Ps.70:11–13	33r—Ps.77:69–72
Q3_29v+32r	29v—Ps.72:13–28, Ps.73:1–6	32r—Ps.77:30–50
Q3_30v+31r	30v—Ps.74:6–11	31r—Ps.76:8–15
Q3_31v+30r	31v—Ps.77:9–12	30r—Ps.73:7–10
Q3_32v+29r	32v—Ps.77:50–69	29r—Ps.71:10–19, Ps.72:1–13
Q3_33v+28r	33v—Ps.78:13, Ps.79:2–4	28r—Ps.68:25
Q3_34v+27r	34v—Ps.82:2–6	27r—Ps.67:12–13
Q3_35v+26r	35v—Ps.84:12–14	
Q4_36v+50r	36v—Ps.87:19, Ps.88:2–6	
Q4_37r		37r—Ps.88:24–31
Q4_37v	37v—Ps.88:51–52, Ps.89:1–8	
Q4_38v+46r	38v—Ps.92:1–5, Ps.93:1	46r—Ps.108:11–12
Q4_39r		39r—Ps.93:19–23, Ps.94:1–2
Q4_39v	39v—Ps.95:10–13, Ps.96:1–4	
Q4_42v+43r	42v—Ps.103:29–33	43r—Ps.104:20–23
Q4_43v+42r	43v—Ps.105:1–4	42r—Ps.103:5–10
Q4_45v+40r	45v—Ps.107:2–4	40r—Ps.97:5–59, Ps.98:2–5
Q4_46v+38r	46v—Ps.109:1–2	38r—Ps.90:8–14
Q4_47v+49r		
Q4_48r		
Q4_48v		
Q4_49v+47r		
Q4_50v+36r		36r—Ps.85:16–17, Ps.86:1–7
Q5_51v+60r	51v—Ps.118:117–120	60r—blank
Q5_52v+59r	52v—Ps.118:160–171	59r—Ps.146:1–11, Ps.147:12–19, Ps.148:3–9
Q5_53v+58r	53v—Ps.123:5–8, Ps.124:1–3	58r—Ps.143:1–8
Q5_54v+57r	54v—Ps.129:6–8, Ps.130:1–3, Ps.131:1–2	57r—Ps.139:2–7, Ps.140:4–6
Q5_55v+56r	55v—Ps.134:13–18	56r—Ps.135:19–26, Ps.136:1–5
Q5_56v+55r	56v—Ps.138:2–11	55r—Ps.131:16–18, Ps.132:1–3, Ps.133:1
Q5_57v+54r	57v—Ps.140:7–10, Ps.141:2–5	54r—Ps.126:4–5, Ps.127:1–5
Q5_58v+53r	58v—Ps.144:5–15, Ps.145:7–10	53r—Ps.120:1–8, Ps.121:1–4
Q5_59v+52r	59v—Ps.148:13–14, Ps.149:1–9, Ps.150:2	52r—Ps.118:135–146
Q5_60v+51r	60v—blank	51r—Ps.118:95–98

APPENDIX 4

Faddan More Psalter: identified psalm text from the Vulgate

KEY:

Black text = extant FMP text
Grey text = absent FMP text

Green highlight = variant listed in Vulgate
Yellow highlight = variant **not** listed in Vulgate
~~Strike through =~~ omitted word

1r = folio number in FMP
(1) = line number in FMP (where indicated)
1[1] = Psalm number and verse

1r(1)**1**[1] beatus
vir qui non abiit in consilio impiorum et in via
peccatorum non stetit et in cathedra pestilentiae
non sedit [2] sed in lege Domini voluntas eius et in
lege eius meditabitur die ac nocte

1v(1) [3] et erit tamquam lignum quod
(2) plantatum est secus decursus aquarum quod
(3) fructum suum dabit in tempore suo et folium
(4) eius non defluet et omnia quaecumque faciet
(5) prosperabuntur [4] non sic impii non sic; sed
tamquam pulvis
(6) quem proicit ventus a facie terrae; [5] ideo non
(7) resurgent impii in iudicio neque peccatores in
(8) consilio iustorum
[6] quoniam novit Dominus viam iustorum et iter
impiorum peribit

2[1] psalmus David quare fremuerunt gentes et
populi meditati sunt inania [2] adstiterunt reges
terrae et principes convenerunt in unum adversus
Dominum et adversus christum eius diapsalma
[3] disrumpamus vincula eorum et proiciamus
a nobis iugum ipsorum [4] qui habitat in caelis
inridebit eos et Dominus subsannabit eos [5]

tunc loquetur ad eos in ira sua et in furore suo
conturbabit eos [6] ego autem constitutus sum rex
ab eo super Sion montem sanctum eius praedicans
praeceptum eius [7] Dominus dixit ad me filius
meus es tu ego hodie genui te [8] postula a me et
dabo tibi gentes hereditatem tuam et possessionem
tuam terminos terrae [9] reges eos in virga ferrea
tamquam vas figuli confringes eos [10] et nunc
reges intellegite erudimini qui iudicatis terram [11]
servite Domino in timore et exultate ei in tremore
[12] adprehendite disciplinam
2r(1) nequando irascatur Dominus et pereatis de
via iusta [13] cum exarserit in brevi ira eius beati
omnes qui confidunt in eo

3[1] psalmus David cum fugeret a facie Abessalon
filii sui [2] Domine quid multiplicati sunt qui
tribulant me multi insurgunt adversum me [3]
multi dicunt animae meae non est salus ipsi in Deo
eius; diapsalma [4] tu autem Domine susceptor
meus es gloria mea et exaltans caput meum [5]
voce mea ad Dominum clamavi et exaudivit me
de monte sancto suo diapsalma [6] ego dormivi et
soporatus sum exsurrexi quia Dominus suscipiet
me [7] non timebo milia populi circumdantis me
exsurge Domine salvum me fac Deus meus [8]
quoniam tu percussisti omnes adversantes mihi sine
causa dentes peccatorum contrivisti [9] Domini est
salus et super populum tuum benedictio tua

4[1] in finem in carminibus psalmus David [2]
cum invocarem exaudivit me Deus iustitiae meae
in tribulatione dilatasti mihi miserere mei et exaudi
orationem meam [3] filii hominum usquequo
gravi corde ut quid diligitis vanitatem et quaeritis
mendacium diapsalma [4] et scitote quoniam
mirificavit Dominus sanctum suum Dominus
exaudiet me cum clamavero ad eum [5] irascimini
et nolite peccare quae dicitis in cordibus vestris
in cubilibus vestris conpungimini diapsalma [6]
sacrificate sacrificium iustitiae et sperate in Domino
multi dicunt quis ostendet nobis bona [7] signatum
est super nos lumen vultus tui Domine dedisti
laetitiam in corde meo [8] a fructu frumenti et vini
2v(1) et oliu sui multiplicati sunt [9] in pace in id
ipsum dormiam et requiescam [10] quoniam tu
Domine singulariter in spe constituisti me

5—No text extant

3r(1) **6**[2] Domine ne in furore tuo arguas me
neque in ira tua corripias me [3] miserere mei
Domine quoniam infirmus sum sana me Domine
quoniam conturbata sunt ossa mea [4] et anima
mea turbata est valde et tu Domine usquequo [5]
convertere Domine eripe animam meam salvum me
fac propter misericordiam tuam [6] quoniam non
est in morte qui memor sit tui in inferno autem
quis confitebitur tibi [7] laboravi in gemitu meo
lavabo per singulas noctes lectum meum in lacrimis
meis stratum meum rigabo [8] turbatus est a furore
oculus meus inveteravi inter omnes inimicos meos
[9] discedite a me omnes qui operamini iniquitatem
quoniam exaudivit Dominus vocem fletus mei
[10] exaudivit Dominus deprecationem meam
Dominus orationem meam suscepit [11] erubescant
et conturbentur vehementer omnes inimici mei
convertantur et erubescant valde velociter

7[1] psalmus David quem cantavit Domino
pro verbis Chusi filii Iemini [2] Domine Deus
meus in te speravi salvum me fac ex omnibus
persequentibus me et libera me [3] nequando rapiat
ut leo animam meam dum non est qui redimat
neque qui salvum faciat [4] Domine Deus meus
si feci istud si est iniquitas in manibus meis [5] si
reddidi retribuentibus mihi mala decidam merito
ab inimicis meis inanis [6] persequatur inimicus
animam meam et conprehendat et conculcet in
terra vitam meam et gloriam meam in pulverem
deducat diapsalma [7] exsurge Domine in ira tua
exaltare in finibus inimicorum meorum et
3v(1) exsurge Domine Deus meus in praecepto
quod mandasti [8] et synagoga populorum
circumdabit te et propter hanc in altum
regredere [9] Dominus iudicat populos iudica me
Domine secundum iustitiam meam et secundum
innocentiam meam super me [10] consummetur
nequitia peccatorum et diriges iustum et scrutans
corda et renes Deus [11] iustum adiutorium meum
a Deo qui salvos facit rectos corde [12] Deus iudex
iustus et fortis et patiens numquid irascitur per
singulos dies [13] nisi conversi fueritis gladium
suum vibrabit arcum suum tetendit et paravit
illum [14] et in eo paravit vasa mortis sagittas suas

ardentibus effecit [15] ecce parturiit iniustitiam et; concepit dolorem et peperit iniquitatem [16] lacum aperuit et effodit eum et incidet in foveam quam fecit [17] convertetur dolor eius in caput eius et in verticem ipsius iniquitas eius descendet [18] confitebor Domino secundum iustitiam eius et psallam nomini Domini altissimi

8[1] in finem pro torcularibus psalmus David
[2] Domine Dominus noster quam admirabile est
nomen tuum in universa terra quoniam elevata est
magnificentia tua super caelos [3] ex ore infantium
et lactantium perfecisti laudem propter inimicos
tuos ut destruas inimicum et ultorem [4] quoniam
videbo caelos tuos; opera digitorum tuorum lunam
et stellas quae tu fundasti [5] quid est homo quod
memor es eius aut filius hominis quoniam visitas
eum [6] minuisti eum
4r(1) Paulo minus ab angelis gloria et honore coro-
(2) nasti eum [7] et constituisti eum super opera
manu-
(3) um tuarum [8] omnia subiecisti sub pedibus
eius oves
(4) et boves universas insuper et pecora campi
[9] volucres caeliet pisces maris qui perambulant
semitas maris [10] DomineDominus noster quam
admirabile ÷ nomen tuum in universa terra

9[2] confitebor tibi Domine in toto corde
meonarrabo omnia mirabilia tua [3] letabor
et exultabo in tepsallam nomini tuo Altisime
[4] in convertendo inimicum meum retrorsum
infirmabuntur et peribunt a facie tua [5] quoniam
fecisti iudicium meum et causam meam sedisti
super thronum qui iudicas iustitiam

[6] increpasti gentes et; perit impius nomen eorum
delisti in aeternum et in saeculum saeculi; [7]
inimici defecerunt frameae in finem et civitates
destruxisti periit memoria eorum cum sonitu [8] et
Dominus in aeternum permanet paravit in iudicio
thronum suum [9] et ipse iudicabit orbem terrae
in aequitate iudicabit populos in iustitia [10] et
factus est Dominus refugium pauperi adiutor in
oportunitatibus in tribulatione

[11] et sperent in te qui noverunt nomen tuum
quoniam non dereliquisti quaerentes te Domine
[12] psallite Domino qui habitat in Sion adnuntiate
inter gentes studia eius [13] quoniam requirens
sanguinem eorum recordatus est 4v non est oblitus
clamorem pauperum [14] misserere mei Domine
vide humilitatem meam de inimicis meis [15] qui
exaltas me de portis mortisut adnuntiem omnes
laudes tuas in portis filiae Sion

[16] exultabo in salutari tuoinfixae sunt gentes
in interitu quem feceruntin laqueo isto quem
absconderunt conprehensus est pes eorum [17]
cogn *(n omitted and added above the line)* oscetur Dominus iudicia
faciensin operibus manum suarum conprehensus
est peccator [18] convertantur peccatores in
infernumomnes gentes quae obliviscuntur Deum
[19] quoniam non in finem oblivio eritpauperis
patientia pauperum non peribit in finem [20]
exsurge Domine non confortetur homo iudicentur
gentes in conspectu tuo

[21] constitue Domine legislatorem super eossciant
gentes *(omitted and added above the line)* *quoniam homines*
sunt diapsalma [22] ut quid Domine recessisti
longe dispicis in oportunitatibus in tribulation
[23] dum superbit impius incenditur pauper
conprehenduntur in consilis quibus cogitant [24]
quoniam laudatur peccator in desideriis animae
suae et iniquus benedicitur [25] exacerbavit
Dominum peccator secundum multitudinem irae
suae non quaeret

[26] non est Deus in conspectu eius inquinatae
sunt viae illius in omni tempore auferuntur iudicia
tua a facie eius omnium inimicorum suorum
dominabitur [27] dixit enim in corde suo non
movebor a generatione in generationem sine
malo [28] cuius maledictione os plenum est et
amaritudine et dolo sub lingua eius labor et dolor
[29] sedet in insidiis cum divitibus in occultis ut
interficiat

5r(1) innocentem [30] oculi eius in pauperem
respiciunt insi-
(2) diaturin abscondito quasi leo in spelunca sua
insidiatur
(3) ut rapiat pauperem repere pauperem

(4) dum aostrahit eum [31] in laqueo suo
humiliabit eum
(5) inclinabit se et cadet dum dominatus fuerit pau-
(6) perum∴ [32] Dixit enim in corde suo oblitus
÷ Deus
(7) avertit faciam ~~suam~~ ne videant in finem [33]
exsurge Domine Deus ex-
(8) altetur manus tuane oblivscaris pauperum
(9) [34] propter quod inritabit impius deum Dixit
enim in cor-
(10) de suo non requirequiret [35] vides qum tu
laborem et d-
(11) olorem considerasut tradas eos in manus tuas
(12) tibi direlictus est pauper orfano tu eras adiutor
[36] contere
(13) brachium peccatoris et maligni quaeretur pec-
(14) catum illius et non invenietur [37] Dominus
regnabit in
(15) aeternum et in saeculum saeculi; peribitis gentes
de terra illius [38] desiderium pauperum exaudivit
Dominus praeparationem cordis eorum audivit auris
tua [39] iudicare pupillo et humili ut non adponat
ultra magnificare se homo super terram

10[2] in Domino confido quomodo dicitis animae meae transmigra in montes sicut passer [3] quoniam ecce peccatores intenderunt arcum paraverunt sagittas suas in faretra ut sagittent in obscuro rectos corde [4] quoniam quae perfecisti destruxerunt iustus autem; quid fecit [5] Dominus in templo sancto suo Dominus in caelo sedis eius oculi eius in pauperem; respiciunt palpebrae eius interrogant filios hominum

[6] Dominus interrogat 5v iustum et impium qui autem diligit iniquitatem odit animam suam [7] pluet super pecatores laqueos ignis et sulphur et spiritus procellarum pars calicis eorum [8] quoniam iustus Dominus et iustitiam dilexit aequitatem vidit vultus eius∴

11[2] salvum ~~me~~ fac Domine quoniam defecit sanctus quoniam demonutae sunt veritates a filis hominum [3] vane locuti sunt unusquisque ad proximum suum labia dolosa in corde et corde locuti sunt [4] disperdat Dominus universa labia dolosa linguam magniloquam [5] qui dixerunt linguam nostram magnificabimus labia nostra a nobis sunt quis noster dominus est

[6] propter miseriam inopum et gemitum pauperum nunc exsurgam dicit Dominus ponam in salutari fiducialiter agam in eo [7] eloquia Domini eloquia casta argentum igne examinatum probatum terrae purgatum septuplum [8] tu Domine servabis nos et custodies nos a generatione hac et in aeternum [9] in circuitu impii ambulant secundum altitudinem tuam multiplicasti filios hominum

12 usquequo Domine oblivisceris me in finem usquequo avertis faciem tuam a me [2] quamdiu ponam consilia in anima mea dolorem in corde meo per diem [3] usquequo exaltabitur inimicus meus super me [4] respice exaudi me Domine Deus meus inlumina oculos meos ne umquam obdormiam in mortem [5] nequando dicat inimicus meus praevalui adversus eum qui tribulant me exultabunt si motus fuero

[6] ego autem in misericordia tua speravi exultabit cor meum in salutari tuo cantabo Domino qui bona tribuit mihi et psallam nomini Domini altissimi

13[1] 6r dixit insipiens in corde suo non est Deus corrupti sunt et abominabiles facti sunt in studis suis non est qui faciat bonum non est usque ad unum [2] Dominus de caelo prospexit super filios hominumut videat si est intellegens aut; requirens Deum [3] omnes declinaverunt simul inutiles facti sunt non est qui faciat bonum non est usque ad unum sepuclhrum patens est gutur eorum linguis suis dolose agebantvenenum aspidum sub labis eorum quorum os maledictione et amaritudine plenum est veloces pedes eorum ad efundendum sanguinem contritio et inflicitas ~~in~~ vis eorum et viam pacis non cognoverunt non est timor Dei ante oculos eorum; [4] nonne cognoscent omnes qui operantur iniquitatem qui devorant plebem meam sicut escam panis [5] Dominum non invocaverunt illic tripidaverunt timore ubi non erat timor;

[6] quoniam Deus in generatione iusta consilium inopis confudistis quoniam Dominus spes eius est

[7] quis dabit ex Sion salutare Israhel cum averterit Dominus captivitatem plebis suae exultabit Iacob et laetabitur Israhel

14[1] psalmus David Domine quis habitabit in tabernaculo tuo aut quis requiescet in monte sancto tuo [2] qui ingreditur sine macula et operatur iustitiam [3] qui loquitur veritatem in corde suo qui non egit dolum in lingua sua nec fecit proximo suo malum et obprobrium non accepit adversus proximos suos [4] ad nihilum deductus est in conspectu eius malignus timentes autem Dominum glorificat qui iurat proximo suo et non decipit [5] qui pecuniam suam non dedit ad usuram et munera super innocentes non accepit qui facit haec non movebitur in aeternum

15[1] 6v conserva me Domine quoniam in te speravi [2] dixi Domino Dominus meus es tu quoniam bonorum meorum non egis [3] sanctis qui sunt in terra eius mirificavit mihi omnes voluntates meas in eis [4] multiplicatae sunt infirmitatis eorum postea adcaeleraverunt non congregabo conventicula eorum de sanguinibus nec memor ero nomem llorum per labia mea [5] Dominus pars hereditatis meae et calicis mei tu es qui restitues hereditatem meam mihi

[6] funes ceciderunt mihi in praeclaris etenim hereditas mea praeclara ÷ mihi [7] benedicam Domino qui tribuit mihi intellectuminsuper et usque ad noctem increpaverunt me renis mei [8] providebam Dominum in conspectu meo semper quoniam a dextris est mihi ne commovear [9] propter hoc laetatum ÷ cor meum et exultavit lingua mea insuper et caro mea requiescet in spe [10] quoniam non derelinques animam meam in inferno non dabis sanctum tuum videre corruptionem notas mihi fecisti vias vitae adimplebis me laetitia cum vultu tuo delectatio in dextera tua usque in finem

16[1] exaudi Domine iustitiam meam intende deprecationem meam auribus percipe orationem meam non in labiis dolosis [2] de vultu tuo iudicium meum prodeat oculi tui videant aequitates [3] probasti cor meum visitasti nocte igne me examenasti et non ÷ inventa in me iniquitas [4] ut non loquatur os meum opera hominum propter verba labiorum tuorum ego custodivi vias duras [5] perfice gressus meos in semitis tuis ut non moveantur vestigia mea

[6] 7r ego clamavi quoniam exaudisti me Deus inclina aurem tuam mihi et exaudi verba mea [7] mirifica misericordias tuas qui ssalvos facis sperantes in te [8] a risistentibus dexterae tuae custodi me ut pupillam oculi sub umbra alarum tuarum proteges me [9] a faciae impiorum qui me adflixerunt inimici mei animam meam circumdederunt super me; [10] adipem suum conclusserunt os eorum locutum ÷ superbia

[11] proicientes me nunc circumdederunt me oculos suos statuerunt declinare in terra~~m~~ [12] susceperunt me sicut leo paratus ad praedam et sicut catulus leonis habitans in abditis [13] exsurge Domine praeveni eum et subplanta eum eripe animam ~~meam~~ abimpioframeam tuam [14] ab inimicis manus tuae Domine a paucis de terra divide eos in vita eorum de absconditis tuis adimpletus est venter eorum saturati sunt filiis et dimiserunt reliquias suas parvulis suis [15] ego autem in iustitia apparebo conspectui tuo satiabor cum apparuerit gloria tua

17[1] in finem puero Domini David quae locutus est Domino verba cantici huius in die qua eripuit eum Dominus de manu omnium inimicorum eius et de manu Saul et dixit [2] dilegam te Domine fortitudo mea [3] Dominus firmamentum meum et refugium meum et liberator meus Deus meus adiutor meus et sperabo in eum protector meus et cornu salutis meae et susceptor meus [4] laudans invocabo Dominum et ab inimicis meis salvus ero [5] circumdederunt me dolores mortis et torrentes iniquitatis conturbaverunt me

[6] dolores inferni circumdederunt me praeoccupaverunt me laquei mortis [7] cum tribularer invocavi Dominum et ad Deum meum clamavi et exaudivit de templo sancto; suo vocem meam et clamor meus in conspectu eius introibit in aures eius [8] et commota est et contremuit

terra et fundamenta 7v montium conturbata sunt~~et commota~~*(eye skip)* sunt quoniam iratus est eis [9] ascendit fumus in ira eius et ignis a facie eius exarsit carbones succensi sunt ab eo [10] inclinabit caelos et descendit et caligo sub pedibus eius

[11] et ascendit super cherubin et volavit volavit super pinnas ventorum [12] et possuit tenebras latibulum suum in circuitu eius tabernaculum eius tenebrosa aqua in nubibus aeris [13] prae fulgore in conspectu eius nubes ~~eius;~~ transierunt grando et carbones ignis [14] et intonuit de caelo Dominus et Altissimus dedit vocem suam grando et carbones ignis; [15] et misit sagittas et dissipavit eos et fulgora multiplicavit et conturbavit eos

[16] et aparuerunt fontes aquarum et revelata sunt fundamenta orbis terrarum ab increpatione tua Domine ab inspiratione spiritus irae tuae [17] misit de summo et accepit me adsumpsit me de aquis multis [18] eripiet me de inimicis meis fortissimis et ab his qui oderunt me quoniam confortati sunt super me [19] praevenerunt me in die adflictionis meae et factus est Dominus protector meus [20] et eduxit me in latitudinem salvum me faciet quoniam voluit me

[21] et; retribuit mihi Dominus secundum iustitiam meam et; secundum puritatem manuum mearum retribuet mihi [22] quia custodivi vias Domini nec impie gessi a Deo meo [23] quoniam omnia iudicia eius in conspectu meo sunt et iustitias eius non reppuli a me [24] et ero inmaculatus cum eo et observabo ab iniquitate mea [25] et retribuet mihi Dominus secundum iustitiam meam et secundum puritatem manuum mearum in conspectu oculorum eius

[26] cum sancto sanctus eris et cum viro innocente innocens eris [27] et cum electo electus eris et cum perverso perverteris [28] quoniam tu populum humilem salvum facies et oculos superborum 8r humiliabis [29] quoniam tu inluminas lucernam meam Domine Deus meus inluminas tenebras meas [30] quoniam in te eripiar a temptatione et in Deo meo transgrediar murum

[31] Deus meus inpolluta via eius eloquia Domini igne examinata protector est omnium sperantiumin eum [32] quoniam quis deus praeter Dominum et quis deus praeter Deum nostrum [33] Deus qui praecinixit me virtute et posuit inmaculatam viam meam [34] qui perfecit pedes meos tamquam cervorum et super excelsa statuens me [35] qui doces manus meas et proelium et posuisti arcum aereum brachia mea

[36] et dedisti mihi protectionem salutis tuae et dextera tua suscepit me et disciplina tua correxit me in finem et disciplina tua ipsa me docebit [37] dilatasti gressus meos subtus me et non sunt infirmata vestigia mea [38] persequar inimicos meos et conprehendam illos et non convertar donec deficiant [39] confringam illos nec poterunt stare cadent subtus pedes meos [40] et praecinxisti me virtute ad bellum subplantasti insurgentes in me subtus me

[41] et inimicos meos dedisti mihi dorsum et odientes me disperdisti [42] clamaverunt nec erat qui salvos faceret ad Dominum nec exaudivit eos [43] et comminuam illos ut pulverem ante faciem venti ut lutum platearum delebo eos [44] eripe me de contradictionibus populi constitues me in caput gentium [45] populus quem non cognovi servivit mihi in auditu auris oboedivit mihi

[46] filii alieni mentiti sunt mihi filii alieni inveterati sunt et claudicaverunt a semitis suis [47] vivit Dominus et benedictus Deus meus et exaltetur Deus salutis meae [48] Deus qui dat vindictas mihi et subdidit populos sub me liberator meus de gentibus iracundis [49] et ab insurgentibus in me exaltabis me a viro iniquo eripies me [50] propterea confitebor tibi in nationibus 8v Domine et psalmum dicam nomini tuo

[51] magnificans salutes regis ipsius et faciens misericordiam xpo suo David et semini eius usque in saeculum

18[2] caeli inarrant gloriam Dei et opera manuum eius adnuntiat firmamentum [3] dies diei eructat verbumet nox necti indicat scientiam [4] non sunt

loquellae neque sermones quorum non audientur
voces eorum [5] in omnem terram exivit sonus
eorum et in fines orbis terrae verba eorum

[6] in sole possuit tabernaculum suum et ipse
tamquam sponsus proce suo
exultavit ut gigans ad currendam viam suum; [7]
a summo caeli egressio eius et occursus eius usque
ad summum eius nec est qui se abscondat a calore
eius [8] lex Domini inmaculata convertens animas
testimonium Domini fidele sapientiam praestans
parvulis [9] iustitiae Domini rectae laetificantes
corda praeceptum Domini lucidum inluminans
oculos [10] timor Domini sanctus permanens in
saeculum saeculi iudicia Domini vera iustificata in
semet ipsa

[11] desiderabilia super aurum et lapidem
pretiosum multum et dulciora super mel et favum
[12] etenim servus tuus custodit ea in custodiendis
illis retributio multa [13] delicta quis intellegit
ab occultis meis munda me [14] et ab alienis
parce servo tuo si mei non fuerint dominati tunc
inmaculatus ero et emundabor a delicto maximo
[15] et erunt ut conplaceant eloquia oris mei et
meditatio cordis mei in conspectu tuo semper
Domine adiutor meus et redemptor meus

19[2] exaudiat te Dominus in die tribulationis
protegat te nomen Dei Iacob [3] mittat tibi
auxilium de sancto et de Sion tueatur te [4] memor
sit omnis sacrificii tui et holocaustum tuum pingue
fiat diapsalma [5] tribuat tibi 9r secundum cor
tuum et omne consilium tuum confirmet

[6] laetabimur in salutari tuo et in nomine Dei
nostri magnificabimur [7] inpleat Dominus omnes
petitiones tuas nunc cognovi quoniam salvum fecit
Dominus christum suum exaudiet illum de caelo
sancto suo in potentatibus salus dexterae eius [8]
hi in curribus et hi in equis nos autem in nomine
Domini Dei nostri magnificabimur [9] ipsi obligati
sunt et ceciderunt nos vero ressurreximus et erecti
sumus [10] Domine salvum fac regemet exaudi nos
in die qua invocaverimus te

20[2] Domine in virtute tua laetabitur rex et super
salutare tuum exultabit vehementer [3] desiderium
animae eius tribuisti ei et voluntate labiorum
eius non fraudasti eum diapsalma [4] quoniam
praevenisti eum in benedictionibus dulcedinis
posuisti in capite eius coronam de lapide pretioso
[5] vitam petiit a te et tribuisti ei longitudinem
dierum in saeculum et in saeculum saeculi

[6] magna gloria eius in salutari tuo gloriam et
magnum decorem inpones super eum [7] quoniam
dabis eum benedictionem in saeculum saeculi
laetificabis eum in gaudio cum vultu tuo [8]
quoniam rex sperat in Domino et in misericordia
Altissimi non commovebitur [9] inveniatur manus
tua omnibus inimicis tuis dextera tua inveniat
omnes; qui te oderunt [10] pones eos ut clibanum
ignis in tempore vultus tui Dominus in ira sua
conturbabit eos et devorabit eos ignis

[11] fructum eorum de terra perdes et semen
eorum a filiis hominum [12] quoniam
declinaverunt in te mala cogitaverunt consilia quae
non potuerunt stabilire; [13] quoniam pones eos
dorsum in reliquis tuis praeparabis vultum eorum
[14] exaltare Domine in virtute tua 9v cantauimus
et psallemus virtutes tuas

21[1] in finem pro adsumptione matutina psalmus
David [2] Deus Deus meus respice in me quare me
dereliquisti longe a salute mea verba delictorum
meorum [3] Deus meus clamabo per diem et non
exaudies et nocte et non ad insipientiam mihi [4]
tu autem in sancto habitas Laus Israhel [5] in te
speraverunt patres nostri speraverunt et liberasti
eos

[6] ad te clamaverunt et salvi facti sunt in te
speraverunt et non sunt confusi [7] ego autem
sum vermis et non homo obprobrium hominum
et abiectio plebis [8] omnes videntes me deriserunt
me locuti sunt labiis moverunt caput [9] speravit in
Domino eripiat eum salvum faciat eum quoniam
vult eum [10] quoniam tu es qui extraxisti me de
ventre spes mea ab uberibus matris meae

[11] in te proiectus sum ex utero de ventre
matris meae Deus meus es tu [12] ne discesseris

a me quoniam tribulatio proxima est quoniam non est qui adiuvet [13] circumdederunt me vituli multi tauri pingues obsederunt me [14] aperuerunt super me os suum sicut leo rapiens et rugiens [15] sicut aqua effusus sum et dispersa sunt universa ossa mea factum est cor meum tamquam cera liquescens in medio ventris mei

[16] aruit tamquam testa virtus mea et lingua mea adhesit faucibus meis et in limum mortis deduxisti me [17] quoniam circumdederunt me canes multi concilium malignantium obsedit me foderunt manus meas et pedes meos [18] dinumeraverunt omnia ossa mea ipsi vero consideraverunt et inspexerunt me [19] diviserunt sibi vestimenta mea et super vestem meam miserunt sortem [20] tu autem Domine ne elongaveris auxilium tuum ad defensionem meam conspice

[21] erue a framea animam meam et de manu canis unicam meam [22] salva me ex ore leonis et a cornibus unicornium humilitatem meam [23] narrabo nomen tuum 10r fratribus meis in media ecclesia laudabo te [24] qui timetis Dominum laudate eum universum semen Iacob magnificate eum [25] timeat eum omne semen Israhel quoniam non sprevit neque dispexit deprecationem pauperis nec avertit faciem suam a me et cum clamarem ad eum exaudivit me;

[26] apud te laus mea in ecclesia magna vota mea reddam in conspectu timentium eum [27] edent pauperes et saturabuntur et laudabunt Dominum qui requirunt eum vivent corda eorum in saeculum saeculi [28] reminiscentur et convertentur ad Dominum universi fines terrae et adorabunt in conspectu eius universae familiae gentium [29] quoniam Dei est regnum et ipse; dominabitur gentium [30] manducaverunt et adoraverunt omnes pingues terrae in conspectu eius cadent omnes qui descendunt in terram

[31] et anima mea illi vivet et semen meum serviet ipsi [32] adnuntiabitur Domino generatio ventura et adnuntiabunt iustitiam eius populo qui nascetur quem fecit Dominus;

22—No text extant

23—No text extant

24—No text extant

25—No text extant

26—No text extant

27—No text extant

28—No text extant

29—No text extant

30[1] in finem psalmus David [2] in te Domine speravi non confundar in aeternum in iustitia tua libera me [3] inclina ad me aurem tuam adcelera ut eruas me esto mihi in Deum protectorem et in domum refugii ut salvum me facias [4] quoniam fortitudo mea et refugium meum es tu et propter nomen tuum deduces me et enutries me [5] educes me de laqueo hoc quem absconderunt mihi quoniam tu es protector meus

[6] in manus tuas commendabo spiritum meum redemisti me Domine Deus veritatis [7] odisti observantes vanitates supervacue ego autem in Domino speravi [8] exultabo et laetabor in misericordia tua quoniam respexisti humilitatem meam salvasti de necessitatibus animam meam [9] nec conclusisti me in manibus inimici statuisti in loco spatioso pedes meos [10] miserere mei Domine quoniam tribulor conturbatus est in ira oculus meus anima mea et venter meus

[11] quoniam defecit in dolore vita mea et anni mei in gemitibus infirmata est in paupertate virtus mea et ossa mea conturbata sunt [12] super omnes inimicos meos factus sum obprobrium et vicinis meis valde et timor notis meis qui videbant me foras fugerunt a me [13] 13r oblivioni datus sum tamquam mortuus a corde factus sum tamquam vas perditum [14] quoniam audivi vituperationem multorum commorantium in circuitu in eo dum convenirent simul adversus me accipere animam

meam consiliati sunt [15] ego autem in te speravi Domine dixi Deus meus es tu

[16] in manibus tuis sortes meae eripe me de manu inimicorum meorum et a persequentibus me [17] inlustra faciem tuam super servum tuum salvum me fac in misericordia tua [18] Domine ne confundarr quoniam invocavi te erubescant impii et deducantur in infernum [19] muta fiant labia dolosa quae loquuntur adversus iustum iniquitatem in superbia et in abusione [20] quam magna multitudo dulcedinis tuae Domine; quam abscondisti timentibus te perfecisti eis qui sperant in te in conspectu filiorum hominum

[21] abscondes eos in abdito faciei tuae a conturbatione hominum proteges eos in tabernaculo a contradictione linguarum [22] benedictus Dominus quoniam mirificavit misericordiam suam mihi in civitate munita [23] ego autem dixi in excessu mentis meae proiectus sum a facie oculorum tuorum ideo exaudisti vocem orationis meae dum clamarem ad te [24] diligite Dominum omnes sancti eius quoniam; veritates requirit Dominus et retribuit abundanter facientibus superbiam [25] viriliter agite et confortetur cor vestrum omnes qui speratis in Domino

31[1] huic David intellectus beati quorum remissae sunt iniquitates et quorum tecta sunt peccata [2] beatus vir cui non inputabit Dominus peccatum nec est in spiritu eius dolus [3] quoniam tacui inveteraverunt ossa mea dum clamarem tota die [4] quoniam die ac nocte gravata est super me manus tua conversus sum in 13v aerumna mea dum configitur mihi; spina [5] delectum meum cognitum tibi; feci et iniustitiam meam non abscondi dixi confitebor adversus me iniustitiam meam Domino et tu remisisti impietatem peccati mei diapsalma

[6] pro hac orabit ad te omnis sanctus in tempore oportuno verumtamen in diluvio aquarum multarum ad eum non adproximabunt [7] tu es refugium meum a tribulatione quae circumdedit me exultatio mea erue me a circumdantibus me diapsalma [8] intellectum tibi dabo et instruam te in via hac qua gradieris firmabo super te oculos meos [9] nolite fieri sicut equus et mulus quibus non est intellectus in camo et freno maxillas eorum constringe qui non adproximant ad te [10] multa flagella peccatoris sperantem autem in Domino misericordia circumdabit

[11] laetamini in Domino et exultate iusti et gloriamini omnes recti corde

32[1] psalmus David exultate iusti in Domino rectos decet laudatio [2] confitemini Domino in cithara in psalterio decem cordarum psallite illi [3] cantate ei canticum novum bene psallite in vociferatione [4] quia rectum est verbum Domini et omnia opera eius in fide [5] diligit misericordiam et iudicium misericordia Domini plena est terra

[6] verbo Domini caeli firmati sunt et spiritu oris eius omnis virtus eorum [7] congregans sicut in utre aquas maris ponens in thesauris abyssos [8] timeat Dominum omnis terra ab eo autem commoveantur omnes inhabitantes orbem [9] quoniam ipse dixit et facta sunt ipse mandavit et creata sunt [10] Dominus dissipat consilia gentium reprobat autem cogitationes populorum et reprobat consilia principum;

[11] consilium autem Domini in aeternum manet cogitationes cordis eius in 14r generatione in generationem [12] beata gens cuius est Dominus Deus eius populus quem elegit in hereditatem sibi [13] de caelo respexit Dominus vidit omnes filios hominum [14] de praeparato habitaculo suo respexit super omnes qui habitant terram [15] qui finxit singillatim corda eorum qui intellegit omnia opera illorum

[16] non salvatur rex per multam virtutem et gigans non salvabitur in multitudine virtutis suae [17] fallax aequs ad salutem in abundantia autem virtutis suae non salvabitur [18] ecce oculi Domini super metuentes eum qui sperant super misericordia eius [19] ut eruat a morte animas eorum et alat eos in fame [20] anima nostra sustinet Dominum quoniam adiutor et protector noster est

Identified psalm text from the Vulgate

[21] quia in eo laetabitur cor nostrum et in nomine sancto eius speravimus [22] fiat misericordia tua Domine super nos quemadmodum speravimus in te

33[1] David cum inmutavit vultum suum coram Abimelech et dimisit eum et abiit [2] benedicam Dominum in omni tempore semper laus eius in ore meo [3] in Domino laudabitur anima mea audiant mansueti et laetentur [4] magnificate Dominum mecum et exaltemus nomen eius in id ipsum [5] exquisivi Dominum et exaudivit me et ex omnibus tribulationibus meis eripuit me

[6] accedite ad eum et inluminamini et facies vestrae non confundentur [7] iste pauper clamavit et Dominus exaudivit eum; et de omnibus tribulationibus eius salvavit eum [8] vallabit angelus Domini in circuitu timentium eum et eripiet eos [9] gustate et videte quoniam suavis est Dominus beatus vir qui sperat in eo [10] timete Dominum omnes; sancti eius quoniam non est inopia timentibus eum

[11] divites eguerunt et esurierunt inquirentes autem Dominum non minuentur omni bono diapsalma [12] venite filii audite me timorem Domini docebo vos [13] quis est homo qui vult vitam cupit videre dies bonos [14] prohibe linguam tuam a malo et labia tua ne loquantur dolum [15] deverte a malo et fac bonum inquire pacem et persequere eam

[16] oculi Domini super iustos et aures eius in precem eorum [17] facies Domini superfacientes mala ut perdat de terra memoriam eorum [18] clamaverunt iusti et 14v Dominus exaudivit eos et ex omnibus tribulationibus eorum liberavit eos [19] iuxta est Dominus his qui tribulato sunt corde et humiles spiritu salvabit [20] multae tribulationes iustorum et de omnibus his liberavit eos

[21] Dominus custodit omnia ossa eorum unum ex his non conteretur [22] mors peccatorum pessima ÷ et qui oderunt iustum delinquent [23] redimet Dominus animas servorum suorum et non derelinquet omnes qui sperant in eum

34[1] huic David iudica Domine nocentes me expugna inpugnantes me [2] adprehende arma et scutum et exsurge in adiutorium mihi [3] effunde frameam et conclude adversus eos qui persequuntur me dic animae meae salus tua ego sum [4] confundantur et

revereantur quaerentes animam meam avertantur retrorsum et confundantur cogitantes mihi mala [5] fiant tamquam pulvis ante faciem venti et angelus Domini coartans eos

[6] fiat via illorum tenebrae et lubricum et angelus Domini persequens eos [7] quoniam gratis absconderunt mihi interitum laquei sui supervacue exprobraverunt animam meam [8] veniat illi laqueus quem ignorat et captio quam abscondit conprehendat eum et in laqueo cadat in ipso [9] anima autem mea exultabit in Domino delectabitur super salutari suo [10] omnia ossa mea dicent Domine quis similis tui eripiens inopem de manu fortiorum eius egenum et pauperem a diripientibus eum

[11] surgentes testes iniqui quae ignorabam interrogabant me [12] retribuebant mihi mala pro bonis sterilitatem animae meae [13] ego autem cum mihi molesti essent induebar cilicio humiliabam in ieiunio animam meam et oratio mea in sinum meum convertetur [14] quasi proximum quasi fratrem nostrum sic conplacebam quasi lugens et contristatus sic humiliabar [15] et adversum me laetati sunt et convenerunt congregata sunt super me 15r flagella et ignoravi

[16] dissipati sunt nec conpuncti temptaverunt me subsannaverunt me subsannatione frenduerunt super me dentibus suis [17] Domine quando respicies restitue animam meam a malignitate eorum a leonibus unicam meam [18] confitebor tibi in eclesia magna in populo gravi laudabo te [19] non supergaudeant mihi qui adversantur mihi inique qui oderunt me gratis et annuunt oculis [20] quoniam mihi quidem pacifice loquebantur et in iracundia terrae loquentes; dolos cogitabant

[21] et dilataverunt super me os suum dixerunt

euge euge viderunt oculi nostri [22] vidisti Domine ne sileas Domine ne discedas a me [23] exsurge et intende iudicio meo Deus meus et Dominus meus in causam meam [24] iudica me secundum iustitiam tuam Domine Deus meus et non supergaudeant mihi [25] non dicant in cordibus suis euge euge animae nostrae nec dicant devoravimus eum

[26] erubescant et revereantur simul qui gratulantur malis meis induantur confusione et reverentia qui magna loquuntur super me [27] exultent et laetentur qui volunt iustitiam meam et dicant semper magnificetur Dominus qui volunt pacem servi eius [28] et lingua mea meditabitur iustitiam tuam tota die laudem tuam

35[1] in finem servo Domini David [2] dixit iniustus ut delinquat in semet ipso non est timor Dei ante oculos eius [3] quoniam dolose egit in conspectu eius ut inveniatur iniquitas eius ad odium [4] verba oris eius iniquitas et dolus noluit intellegere ut bene ageret [5] iniquitatem meditatus est in cubili suo adstetit omni viae non bonae malitiam autem non odivit

[6] Domine in caelo misericordia tua et veritas tua usque ad nubes [7] iustitia tua sicut montes Dei iudicia tua abyssus multa homines et iumenta salvabis Domine **[8]** quemadmodum 15v multiplica**sti misericordia**m tuam Deus filii autem hominum in tegmine **alarum tuar**um **sper**abunt **[9]** inebriabuntur ab ubertate **domus tuae et** torren**te** voluntatis tuae potabis eos **[10] quoniam apud te fons vitae** in lumine tuo videbimus lumen

[11] praetende misericordiam tuam scientibus te et iu**stitiam tuam his qui recto sunt corde [12]** non veniat mihi pes superbiae et manus peccatoris non moveat me **[13]** ibi ceciderunt qui o**perant**ur ini**quitatem** expulsi sunt nec potuerunt stare

36[1] ipsi David noli aemulari in malignantibus n**e**qu**e** **zelaver**is facientes iniquitatem **[2]** Quoniam **tam**quam faen**um vel**ociter arescent et quemadm**odum holera** herb**arum** cito decident **[3]** spera in Domino et fa**c bonitat**em et inhabita terram et pasceris in divitiis eius [4] delectare in Domino et dabit tibi petitiones cordis tui [5] revela Domino viam tuam et spera in eum et ipse faciet

[6] et educet quasi lumen iustitiam tuam et iudicium tuum tamquam meridiem [7] subditus esto Domino et ora eum noli aemulari in eo qui prosperatur in via sua in homine faciente iniustitias [8] desine ab ira et derelinque furorem noli aemulari ut maligneris [9] quoniam qui malignantur exterminabuntur sustinentes autem Dominum ipsi hereditabunt terram [10] et adhuc pusillum et non erit peccator et quaeres locum eius et non invenies

[11] mansueti autem hereditabunt terram et delectabuntur in multitudine pacis [12] observabit peccator iustum et stridebit super eum dentibus suis [13] Dominus autem inridebit eum quia prospicit quoniam veniet dies eius [14] gladium evaginaverunt peccatores intenderunt arcum suum ut decipiant pauperem et inopem ut trucident rectos corde [15] gladius eorum intret in corda ipsorum et arcus ipsorum confringatur

[16] melius est modicum iusto super divitias peccatorum multas [17] quoniam brachia peccatorum conterentur confirmat autem iustos Dominus **[18]** novit Dominus dies inmaculatorum et hereditas eorum in 16r aete**rnu**m erit **[19]** non con**fun**dentur in tempore malo et in diebus **famis saturabun**tur **[20]** quia peccatores peribunt inimici ver**o** **Domini mox ho**norificati fuerint et exaltati **defecientes quemad**modum fumus defecerunt

[21] mutu**ab**itur **pecca**tor **et non solvet** iustus autem miseretur et tribuet **[22] quia benedicentes ei hered**itabunt terram maledicentes autem ei di**speribunt [23] apud Dominum** gressus hominis dirigentur et viam eius **vo**let **[24]** cum ceciderit non conlidetur quia **Dominus su**bponit manum suam **[25]** iunior fui et senui et non vidi iustum de**r**eli**ctumnec** semen eius quaerens panes

[26] tota die miseretu**rr** **et** co**m**modat et semen

Identified psalm text from the Vulgate

illius in benedictione erit [27] declina a malo et fac bonum et inhabita in saeculum saeculi [28] quia Dominus amat iudicium et non derelinquet sanctos suos in aeternum conservabuntur iniusti punientur et semen impiorum peribit [29] iusti autem hereditabunt terram et inhabitabunt in saeculum saeculi; super eam [30] os iusti meditabitur sapientiam et lingua eius loquetur iudicium

[31] lex Dei eius in corde ipsius et non subplantabuntur gressus eius [32] considerat peccator iustum et quaerit mortificare eum [33] Dominus autem non derelinquet eum in manus eius nec damnabit eum cum iudicabitur illi [34] expecta Dominum et custodi viam eius et exaltabit te ut hereditate capias terram cum perierint peccatores videbis [35] vidi impium superexaltatum et elevatum sicut cedros Libani

[36] et transivi et ecce non erat et quaesivi eum et non est inventus locus eius [37] custodi innocentiam et vide aequitatem quoniam sunt reliquiae homini pacifico [38] iniusti autem disperibunt simul reliquiae impiorum peribunt [39] salus autem iustorum a Domino et protector eorum in tempore tribulationis [40] et adiuvabit eos Dominus et liberabit eos et eruet eos a peccatoribus et salvabit eos quia speraverunt in eo

37[2] 16v Domine ne in furore tuo arguas me neque in ira tua corripias me [3] quoniam sagitae tuae infixae sunt mihi et confirmasti super me manum tuam [4] non ÷ sanitas carni meae a facie irae tuae non est pax ossibus meis a facie peccatorum meorum [5] quoniam iniquitatus meae supergresae sunt caput meum sicut onus grave gravatae sunt super me

[6] putruerunt et corruptae sunt cicatrices meaea facie insipientiae meae [7] miser factus sum et curvatus sum usque in finem tota die contristatus ingrediebar [8] quoniam lumbi mei impleti sunt inlusionibus et non est sanitas in carne mea [9] adflictus sum et humiliatus sum nimis rugiebam a gemitu cordis mei [10] Domine ante te omne desiderium meum et gemitus meus a te non est absconditus

[11] cor meum conturbatum est dereliquit me virtus mea et lumen oculorum meorum et ipsum non est mecum [12] amici mei et proximi mei adversus me adpropinquaverunt et steterunt et qui iuxta me erant de longe steterunt [13] et vim faciebant qui quaerebant animam meam et qui inquirebant mala mihi locuti sunt vanitates et dolos tota die meditabantur [14] ego autem tamquam surdus non audiebam et sicut mutus non aperiens os suum [15] et factus sum sicut homo non audiens et non habens in ore suo redargutiones

[16] quoniam in te Domine speravi tu exaudies Domine Deus meus [17] quia dixi nequando supergaudeant mihi inimici mei et dum commoventur pedes mei super me magna locuti sunt [18] quoniam ego in flagella paratus et dolor meus in conspectu meo semper [19] quoniam iniquitatem meam adnuntiabo et; cogitabo pro peccato meo [20] inimici autem mei vivent et firmati sunt super me et multiplicati sunt qui oderunt me inique

[21] qui retribuunt mala pro bonis detrahebant mihi quoniam sequebar bonitatem [22] non derelinquas me Domine Deus meus ne discesseris a me [23] intende in adiutorium meum Domine salutis meae

38[2] dixi custodiam vias meas ut non delinquam in lingua mea posui ori meo custodiam cum consisteret peccator adversum me [3] obmutui et humiliatus sum et silui a bonis et dolor meus renovatus est

17r(1) [4] concaluit cor meum intra me et in
(2) meditatione*(eye skip)* mea exardescet ignis [5] locutus sum in lingua mea notum fac mihi Domine finem meum et
(3) numerum dierum meorum quis est ut sciam quid
(4) desit mihi[6] ecce mensurabiles posuisti dies meos
(5) et substantia mea tamquam nihilum ante te
(6) verumtamen universa vanitas omnis homo vivens
(7) diapsalma [7] verumtamen in imagine pertransit homo

(8) sed et frustra conturbatur thesaurizat et ignorat
cui congregabit ea
(9) [8] et nunc quae est expectatio mea nonne
Dominus et substantia
(10) mea apud te est [9] ab omnibus iniquitatibus
meis erue me

obprobrium insipienti dedisti me [10] obmutui et;
non aperui os meum quoniam tu fecisti

[11] amove a me plagas tuas [12] a fortitudine
manus tuae ego defeci in increpationibus propter
iniquitatem corripuisti hominem et tabescere
fecisti sicut araneam animam eius verumtamen
vane conturbatur; omnis homo diapsalma [13]
exaudi orationem meam Domine et deprecationem
meam auribus percipe lacrimas meas ne sileas
quoniam advena sum apud te et peregrinus sicut
omnes patres mei [14] remitte mihi ut refrigerer
priusquam abeam et amplius non ero

39[1] in finem David psalmus [2] expectans
expectavi Dominum et intendit mihi [3] et
exaudivit preces meas et eduxit me de lacu miseriae
et de luto fecis et statuit super petram pedes meos
et direxit gressus meos [4] et inmisit in os meum
canticum novum carmen Deo nostro videbunt
multi et timebunt et sperabunt in Domino [5]
beatus vir cuius est nomen Domini spes ipsius et
non respexit in vanitates et insanias falsas

[6] multa fecisti tu Domine Deus meus mirabilia
tua et cogitationibus tuis non est qui similis sit
tibi adnuntiavi et locutus sum multiplicati sunt
supernumerum
17v(1) [7] sacrificium et oblationem noluisti aures
autem
(2) perfecisti mihi holocaustums et pro peccato non
postulasti [8]
(3) tunc dixi ecce venio in capite libri scriptum est
de me [9] ut
(4) facerem voluntatem tuam Deus meus volui et
legem tuam
(5) in medio cordis mei [10] adnuntiavi iustitiam in
ecclesia
(6) magna ecce labia mea non prohibebo Domine
tu scisti [11] iustitiam

(7) tuam non abscondi in corde meoveritatem
tuam et salutare
(8) tuum dixi non abscondi missericordiam tuam et
veritatem
(9) tuam a concilio multo [12] tu autem Domine ne
longe facias
(10) miserationes tuas a me misericordia tua et
veritas tua semper
(11) susceperunt me [13] quoniam circumdederunt
me mala quorum

non est numerus conprehenderunt me iniquitates
meae et non potui ut viderem multiplicatae
sunt super capillos capitis mei et cor meum
dereliquit me [14] conplaceat tibi Domine ut
eruas me Domine ad adiuvandum me respice [15]
confundantur et revereantur simul qui quaerunt
animam meam ut auferant eam convertantur
retrorsum et revereantur qui volunt mihi mala

[16] ferant confestim confusionem suam qui dicunt
mihi euge euge [17] exultent et laetentur super te
omnes quaerentes te et dicant semper magnificetur
Dominus qui diligunt salutare tuum [18] ego
autem mendicus sum et pauper Dominus sollicitus
est mei adiutor meus et protector meus tu es Deus
meus ne tardaveris

40(1a) [2] beatus qui intellegit super egenum et
pauperem in die mala
(2a) liberavit eum Dominus [3] Dominus conservet
eum et vivificet
(3a) eum et beatum faciat eum in terra et non
tradat eum
(4a) in animam inimicorum eius [4] Dominus
opem ferat illi
(5a) super lectum doloris eius universum stratum
eius versasti in infirmitate eius

[5] ego dixi Domine miserere mei sana animam
meam quoniam peccavi tibi

[6] inimici mei dixerunt mala mihi quando
morietur et peribit nomen eius [7] et si
ingrediebatur ut videret vane loquebatur cor
eius congregavit iniquitatem sibi egrediebatur
foras et loquebatur [8] in id ipsum adversum

me susurrabant omnes inimici mei adversus
me cogitabant mala mihi [9] verbum iniquum
constituerunt adversus me numquid qui dormit
non adiciet ut resurgat [10] etenim homo pacis
meae in quo speravi qui edebat panes meos
magnificavit super me subplantationem

[11] tu autem Domine miserere mei et resuscita
me et retribuam eis [12] in hoc cognovi quoniam
voluisti me quoniam non gaudebit inimicus meus
super me [13] me autem propter innocentiam
suscepisti et confirmasti me in conspectu tuo in
aeternum [14] benedictus Dominus Deus Israhel a
saeculo et in saeculum fiat fiat

41—No text extant

42—No text extant

43—No text extant

44—No text extant

45—No text extant

46—No text extant

47—No text extant

48[1] in finem filiis Core psalmus [2] audite haec
omnes gentes auribus percipite omnes qui habitatis
orbem [3] quique terriginae et filii hominum
in unum dives et pauper [4] os meum loquetur
sapientiam et meditatio cordis mei prudentiam [5]
inclinabo in parabolam aurem meam aperiam in
psalterio propositionem meam

[6] cur timebo in die malo iniquitas calcanei mei
circumdabit me [7] qui confidunt in virtute sua et
in multitudine divitiarum suarum gloriantur [8]
frater non redimit redimet homo non dabit Deo
placationem suam [9] et pretium redemptionis
animae suae et laboravit in aeternum [10] et vivet
adhuc; in finem

[11] non videbit interitum cum viderit sapientes
morientes simul insipiens et stultus peribunt et
relinquent alienis divitias suas [12] et; sepulchra
eorum domus illorum in aeternum tabernacula
eorum in progeniem et progeniem vocaverunt
nomina sua in terris suis [13] et homo cum
in honore esset non intellexit conparatus est
iumentis insipientibus et similis factus est illis
[14] haec via illorum scandalum ipsis et postea
in ore suo conplacebunt diapsalma [15] sicut
oves in inferno positi sunt mors depascet eos
et dominabuntur eorum iusti in matutino et
auxilium eorum veterescet in inferno a gloria
eorum

[16] verumtamen Deus redimet animam meam
de manu inferi cum acceperit me diapsalma
[17] ne timueris cum dives factus fuerit homo et
cum multiplicata fuerit gloria domus eius [18]
quoniam cum interierit non sumet omnia neque
descendet cum eo 21r pone; gloria eius [19] quia
anima eius in vita ipsius benedicetur confitebitur
tibi cum benefeceris ei [20] introibit usque in
progenies patrum suorum usque in aeternum non
videbit lumen

[21] homo in honore cum esset non intellexit
conparatus est iumentis insipientibus; et similis
factus est illis

49[1] psalmus Asaph Deus deorum Dominus
locutus est et vocavit terram a solis ortu usque
ad occasum [2] ex Sion species decoris eius [3]
Deus manifeste veniet Deus noster et non silebit
ignis in conspectu eius exardescet et in circuitu
eius tempestas valida [4] advocabit caelum
desursum et terram discernere populum suum
[5] congregate illi sanctos eius qui ordinant
testamentum eius super sacrificia

[6] et adnuntiabunt caeli iustitiam eius quoniam
Deus iudex est diapsalma [7] audi populus meus
et loquar tibi Israhel et testificabor tibi Deus Deus
tuus ego sum [8] non in sacrificiis tuis arguam
te holocausta autem tua in conspectu meo sunt
semper [9] non accipiam de domo tua vitulos
neque de gregibus tuis hircos [10] quoniam meae
sunt omnes ferae silvarum iumenta in montibus et
boves

[11] cognovi omnia volatilia caeli et pulchritudo
agri mecum est [12] si esuriero non dicam tibi
meus est enim orbis terrae et plenitudo eius
[13] numquid manducabo carnes taurorum aut
sanguinem hircorum potabo [14] immola Deo
sacrificium laudis et redde Altissimo vota tua [15]
et invoca me in die tribulationis et eruam te et
honorificabis me diapsalma

[16] peccatori autem dixit Deus quare tu enarras
iustitias meas et adsumis testamentum meum per
os tuum [17] tu vero odisti disciplinam et proiecisti
sermones meos retrorsum [18] si videbas furem
currebas cum eo et cum adulteris portionem tuam
ponebas [19] os tuum abundavit malitia et lingua
tua concinnabat dolos [20] sedens adversus fratrem
tuum loquebaris et adversus filium matris 21v tuae
ponebas scandalum

[21] haec fecisti et tacui existimasti inique quod
ero tui similis arguam te et statuam contra faciem
tuam [22] intellegite nunc haec qui obliviscimini
Deum nequando rapiat et non sit qui eripiat [23]
sacrificium laudis honorificabit me et illic iter quod
ostendam illi salutare Dei

50[1] in finem psalmus David [2] cum venit
ad eum Nathan propheta quando intravit ad
Bethsabee [3] miserere mei Deus secundum
magnam; misericordiam tuam et; secundum
multitudinem miserationum tuarum dele
iniquitatem meam [4] amplius lava me ab
iniquitate mea et a peccato meo munda me [5]
quoniam iniquitatem meam ego cognosco et
peccatum meum contra me est semper

[6] tibi soli peccavi et malum coram te feci ut
iustificeris in sermonibus tuis et vincas cum
iudicaris [7] ecce enim in iniquitatibus conceptus
sum et in peccatis concepit me mater mea [8]
ecce enim veritatem dilexisti incerta et occulta
sapientiae tuae manifestasti mihi [9] asparges me
hysopo et mundabor lavabis me et super nivem
dealbabor [10] auditui meo dabis gaudium et
laetitiam exultabunt ossa humiliata

[11] averte faciem tuam a peccatis meis et omnes
iniquitates meas dele [12] cor mundum crea in
me Deus et spiritum rectum innova in visceribus
meis [13] ne proicias me a facie tua et spiritum
sanctum tuum ne auferas a me [14] redde mihi
laetitiam salutaris tui et spiritu principali confirma
me [15] docebo iniquos vias tuas et impii ad te
convertentur

[16] libera me de sanguinibus Deus Deus salutis
meae exultabit lingua mea iustitiam tuam [17]
Domine labia mea aperies et os meum adnuntiabit
laudem tuam [18] quoniam si voluisses sacrificium
dedissem utique holocaustis non delectaberis
[19] sacrificium Deo spiritus contribulatus cor
contritum et

22r(1) humiliatum Deus non spernet [20] benigne
fac Domine
(2) in bona voluntates tua Sion et aedificentur
(3) muri Hierusalem [21] tunc acceptabis
(4) sacrificium iustitiae obblationes et holocausta
(5) tunc inponent super altare tuum vitulos

51(6) [3] QUID*(decorated lettering here)*gloriatur in malitia
qui potens est iniquitate [4] tota die iniustitiam
cogitavit lingua tua sicut novacula acuta fecisti
dolum [5] dilexisti malitiam super benignitatem
iniquitatem magis quam loqui aequitatem
diapsalma

[6] dilexisti omnia verba praecipitationis linguam
dolosam [7] propterea Deus destruet te in finem
evellet te et emigrabit te de tabernaculo et radicem
tuam de terra viventium diapsalma [8] videbunt
iusti et timebunt et super eum ridebunt et dicent [9]
ecce homo qui non posuit Deum adiutorem suum
sed speravit in multitudine divitiarum suarum et
praevaluit in vanitate sua [10] ego autem sicut
oliva fructifera in domo Dei speravi in misericordia
Dei in aeternum et in saeculum saeculi

[11] confitebor tibi in saeculum quia fecisti et
expectabo nomen tuum quoniam bonum in
conspectu sanctorum tuorum

52[1] in finem pro Melech intellegentiae
David dixit insipiens in corde suo non est Deus

[2] corrupti sunt et abominabiles facti sunt in
iniquitatibus non est qui faciat bonum [3] Deus de
caelo prospexit in filios hominum ut videat si

22v (1) est intellegens aut;requirens Deum [4] omnes
(2) declinaverunt simul inutiles facti sunt non est qui
faciat bonum
(3) non est usque ad unum [5] nonne scient omnes;
qui operantur iniquitatem
(4) qui devorant plebem meam ut cibum panis [6]
Deum non
(5) invocaverunt illic trrepidabunt timore ubi non
fuit timor
(6) quoniam Deus dissipavit ossa eorum qui
hominibus placent confusi
(7) sunt quoniam Deus sprevit eos [7] quis dabit ex
Sion salutare
(8) Israhel dum convertit Deus captivitatem plebis
suae
(9) exultabit Iacob et laetabitur Israhel

53 [3] Deus in nomine
(10) tuo salvum me facet in virtute tua iudica me
[4] Deus
(11) exaudi orationem meam auribus percipe
verba oris mei
(12) [5] quoniam alieni insurrexerunt adversum
me et fortes
(13) quaesierunt animam meam et non
proposuerunt Deum ante
(14) conspectum suum diapsalma [6] ecce enim
Deus adiuvat me Dominus susceptor animae
meae [7] avertet mala inimicis meis in veritate
tua disperde illos [8] voluntarie sacrificabo tibi
confitebor nomini tuo Domine quoniam bonum
[9] quoniam ex omni tribulatione eripuisti me et
super inimicos meos despexit oculus meus

54[1] in finem in carminibus intellectus
David [2] exaudi Deus orationem meam et ne
despexeris deprecationem meam [3] intende mihi
et exaudi me contristatus sum in exercitatione
mea et conturbatus sum [4] a voce inimici et a
tribulatione peccatoris quoniam declinaverunt in
me iniquitatem et in ira molesti erant mihi [5] cor
meum conturbatum est in me et formido mortis
cecidit super me

[6] timor et tremor venit super me et contexit
me tenebra [7] et dixi quis dabit mihi pinnas
sicut columbae et volabo et requiescam [8]
ecce elongavi fugiens et mansi in solitudine
diapsalma [9] expectabam eum qui salvum me
fecit a pusillanimitate spiritus et a tempestate [10]
praecipita Domine divide linguas eorum quoniam
vidi iniquitatem et contradictionem in 23r civitate

[11] die et nocte circumdabit eam super muros eius
et iniquitas et labor in medio eius [12] et iniustitia
et non defecit de plateis eius usura et dolus [13]
quoniam si inimicus maledixisset mihi sustinuissem
utique et si is qui oderat me super me magna
locutus fuisset abscondissem me forsitan ab eo [14]
tu vero homo unianimis dux meus et notus meus
[15] qui simul mecum dulces capiebas cibos in
domo Dei ambulavimus cum consensu

[16] veniat mors super illos et descendant in
infernum viventes quoniam nequitiae in habitaculis
eorum in medio eorum [17] ego autem; ad Deum
clamavi et Dominus salvabit me [18] vespere et
mane et meridie narrabo et adnuntiabo et exaudiet
vocem meam [19] redimet in pace animam
meam ab his qui adpropinquant mihi quoniam
inter multos erant mecum [20] exaudiet Deus et
humilhiabit illos qui est ante saecula diapsalma
non enim est illis commutatio et non timuerunt
Deum

[21] extendit manum suam in retribuendo
contaminaverunt testamentum eius [22] divisi
sunt ab ira vultus eius et adpropinquavit cor
illius molliti sunt sermones eius super oleum et
ipsi sunt iacula [23] iacta super Dominum curam
tuam et ipse te enutriet non dabit in aeternum
fluctuationem iusto [24] tu vero Deus deduces
eos in puteum interitus viri sanguinum et doli non
dimidiabunt dies suos ego autem sperabo in te
Domine

55[1] in finem pro populo qui a sanctis longe
factus est David in tituli inscriptione cum tenuerunt
eum Allophili in Geth [2] miserere mei Deus
quoniam conculcavit me homo tota die inpugnans
tribulavit me [3] conculcaverunt me inimici mei

tota die quoniam multi bellantes adversum me [4]
ab altitudine diei timebo ego vero in te sperabo [5]
in Deo laudabo sermones meos in Deo speravi non
timebo quid faciat mihi caro

[6] tota die verba mea execrabantur adversum me
omnia consilia eorum in malum [7] inhabitabunt et
abscondent ipsi calcaneum meum observabunt 23v
sicut sustinuerunt animam meam [8] pro nihilo
salvos facies illos in ira populos confringes Deus
[9] vitam meam adnuntiavi tibi posuisti lacrimas
meas in conspectu tuo sicut et in promissione
tua [10] tunc convertentur inimici mei retrorsum
in quacumque die invocavero te ecce cognovi
quoniam Deus meus es

[11] in Deo laudabo verbumin Domino laudabo
sermonem in Deo speravi non timebo quid faciat
mihi homo [12] in me sunt Deus vota tua; quae;
reddam laudationes tibi [13] quoniam eripuisti
animam meam de morte et pedes meos de lapsu ut
placeam coram Deo in lumine viventium

56[1] in finem ne disperdas David in tituli
inscriptione cum fugeret a facie Saul in spelunca
[2] miserere mei Deus miserere mei quoniam
in te confidit anima mea et in umbra alarum
tuarum sperabo donec transeat iniquitas [3]
clamabo ad Deum altissimum Deum qui benefecit
mihi [4] misit de caelo et liberavit me dedit in
obprobrium conculcantes me diapsalma misit
Deus misericordiam suam et veritatem suam [5] et
eripuit animam meam de medio catulorum leonum
dormivi conturbatus filii hominum dentes eorum
arma et sagittae et lingua eorum gladius 24r acutus

[6] exaltare super caelos Deus et in omnem
terramgloria tua [7] laqueum paraverunt pedibus
meis et incurvaverunt animam meam foderunt
ante faciem meam foveam et inciderunt in
eam diapsalma [8] paratum cor meum Deus
paratum cor meum cantabo et psalmum dicam
[9] exsurge gloria mea exsurge psalterium et
cithara exsurgam diluculo [10] confitebor tibi in
populis Domine psalmum dicam tibi in gentibus
[11] quoniam magnificata est usque ad caelos
misericordia tua et usque ad nubes veritas tua

[12] exaltare super caelos Deus et super omnem
terram Gloria*(eye skip here)* tua

57[2] si vere utique iustitiam loquimini recta
iudicate filii hominum [3] etenim in corde
iniquitates operamini in terra iniustitiam manus
vestrae concinnant [4] alienati sunt peccatores a
vulva erraverunt ab utero locuti sunt falsa [5] furor
illis secundum similitudinem serperntis sicut aspidis
surdae et obturantis aures suas

[6] quae non exaudiet vocem incantantium et
venefici incantantes sapienter [7] Deus conteret
dentes eorum in ore ipsorum molas leonum
confringet Dominus [8] ad nihilum devenient
tamquam aqua decurrens intendit arcum suum
donec infirmentur [9] sicut cera quae fluit
auferentur supercecidit ignis et non viderunt
solem [10] priusquam intellegerent spinae vestrae
ramnum sicut viventes sicut in ira absorbet vos

[11] laetabitur iustus cum viderit vindictam manus
suas lavabit in sanguine peccatoris [12] et dicet
homo si utique est fructus iusto utique est Deus
iudicans eos in terra

58[1] in finem ne disperdas David in tituli
inscriptione quando misit Saul et custodivit
domum eius ut interficeret eum [2] eripe me de
inimicis meis Deus et ab insurgentibus in me libera
me [3] eripe me de operantibus iniquitatem et de
viris sanguinum salva me [4] quia ecce ceperunt
animam meam inruerunt in me fortes [5] neque
iniquitas mea neque peccatum meum Domine sine
iniquitate cucurri et direxi

[6] exsurge in occursum meum et vide et tu
Domine Deus virtutum Deus Israhel intende ad
visitandas omnes gentes non miserearis omnibus
qui operantur iniquitatem diapsalma [7]
convertentur ad vesperam et famem patientur ut
canes et circuibunt civitatem [8] ecce loquentur
in ore suo et gladius in labiis eorum quoniam
quis audivit [9] et tu 24v Domine deridebis
eos ad nihilum deduces omnes gentes [10]
fortitudinem meam ad te custodiam quia Deus
susceptor meus

[11] Deus meus voluntas eius praeveniet me∴
[12] Deus ostendet mihi super inimicos meos ne
occidas eosnequando obliviscantur populi mei
disperge illos in virtute tua et depone eos protector
meus Domine [13] dilectumoris eorum sermonem
labiorum ipsorum et conprehendantur in superbia
sua et de execratione et mendacio adnuntiabuntur
[14] in consummatione in ira consummationis et
non erunt et scient quia Deus dominatur Iacob
finium terrae diapsalma [15] convertentur ad
vesperam et famem patientur ut canes et circuibunt
civitatem

[16] ipsi dispergentur ad manducandum si vero
non fuerint saturati et murmurabunt [17] ego
autem cantabo fortitudinem tuam et exultabo
mane misericordiam tuam quia factus es susceptor
meus et refugium meum in die tribulationis meae
[18] adiutor meus tibi psallam quia Deus susceptor
meus es Deus meus misericordia mea

59—No text extant

60[2] 25r *(larger letter e here)* exaudi Deus deprecationem
meam intende orationi meae [3] a finibus terrae
d te clamavi dum anxiaretur cor meum in petra
exaltasti me deduxisti me [4] quia factus es spes
mea turris fortitudinis a facie inimici [5] inhabitabo
in tabernaculo tuo in saecula protegar in velamento
alarum tuarum diapsalma

[6] quoniam tu Deus ~~meus~~ exaudisti orationem
meam dedisti hereditatem timentibus nomen tuum
[7] dies super dies regis adicies annos eius usque
in deim generationis et generationis [8] permanet
in aeternum in conspectu Dei misericordiam et
veritatem quis requiret eius [9] sic psalmum dicam
nomini tuo in saeculum saeculi ut reddam vota
mea de die in diem

61[2] *(decorated lettering here)* nonne Deo subiecta erit
anima mea ab ipso enim salutare meum [3] nam et
ipse Deus meus et salutaris meus susceptor meus
non movebor amplius [4] quousque inruitis in
hominem interficitis universi vos tamquam parieti
inclinato et maceriae depulsae [5] verumtamen
pretium meum cogitaverunt repellere cucurri in siti
ore suo benedicebant et corde suo maledicebant
diapsalma

[6] verumtamen Deo subiecta esto anima mea
quoniam ab ipso patientia mea [7] quia ipse Deus
meus et salvator meus adiutor meus non emigrabo
[8] in Deo salutare meum et gloria mea Deus
auxilii mei et spes mea in Deo est [9] sperate in
eo omnis congregatio populi effundite coram illo
corda vestra Deus adiutor noster in aeternum [10]
verumtamen vani filii hominum mendaces filii
hominum in stateris ut decipiant ipsi de vanitate in
id ipsum

[11] nolite sperare in iniquitate et rapinas nolite
concupiscere divitiae si affluant nolite cor adponere
[12] semel locutus est Deus duo haec audivi quia
potestas Dei [13] et tibi Domine misericordia quia
tu reddes unicuique iuxta opera sua

62[1] psalmus David cum esset in deserto Iudaeae
[2] Deus Deus meus ad te de luce vigilo sitivit in
te anima mea quam multipliciter tibi caro mea
[3] in terra deserta et 25v invia et inaquosa sic in
sancto apparui tibi ut viderem virtutem tuam et
gloriam tuam [4] quoniam melior est misericordia
tua super vitas labia mea laudabunt te [5] sic
benedicam te in vita mea in nomine tuo levabo
manus meas

[6] sicut adipe et pinguidine repleatur anima mea et
labia exultationis laudabit os meum [7] si memor
fui tui super stratum meum in matutinis meditabar
in te [8] quia fuisti adiutor meus et in velamento
alarum tuarum exultabo [9] adhesit anima mea
post te me suscepit dextera tua [10] ipsi vero in
vanum quaesierunt animam meam introibunt in
inferiora terrae

[11] tradentur in manus gladii partes vulpium
erunt [12] rex vero laetabitur in Deo laudabitur
omnis qui iurat in eo quia obstructum est os
loquentium iniqua

63—No text extant

64—No text extant

65[1] in finem canticum psalmi resurrectionis iubilate Deo omnis terra [2] psalmum dicite nomini eius date gloriam laudi eius [3] dicite Deo quam terribilia sunt opera tua Domine in multitudine virtutis tuae mentientur tibi inimici tui [4] omnis terra adorent te et psallant tibi psalmum dicant nomini tuo diapsalma [5] venite et videte opera Dei terribilis in consiliis super filios hominum

[6] qui convertit mare in aridam in flumine pertransibunt pede ibi laetabimur in ipso [7] qui dominatur in virtute sua in aeternum oculi eius super gentes respiciunt qui exasperant non exaltentur in semet ipsis diapsalma [8] benedicite gentes Deum nostrum et auditam facite vocem laudis eius [9] qui posuit animam meam ad vitam et non dedit in commotionem pedes meos [10] quoniam probasti nos Deus igne nos examinasti sicut examinatur argentum

[11] induxisti nos in laqueum posuisti tribulationes in dorso nostro [12] inposuisti homines super capita nostra transivimus per ignem et aquam et eduxisti nos in refrigerium [13] introibo in domum tuam in holocaustis reddam tibi vota mea [14] quae distinxerunt labia mea et locutum est os meum in tribulatione mea [15] holocausta medullata offeram tibi cum incensu arietum offeram tibi boves cum hircis diapsalma

[16] venite audite et narrabo omnes qui 26v timetis Deum quando fecit animae meae [17] ad ipsum ore meo clamavi et exaltavi sub lingua mea [18] iniquitatem si aspexi in corde meo non exaudiat Dominus [19] propterea exaudivit Deus adtendit voci deprecationis meae [20] benedictus Deus qui non amovit orationem meam et misericordiam suam a me

66—No text extant

67[1] in finem David psalmus cantici [2] exsurgat Deus et dissipentur inimici eius et fugiant qui oderunt eum a facie eius [3] sicut deficit fumus deficiant sicut fluit cera a facie ignis sic pereant peccatores a facie Dei [4] et iusti epulentur exultent in conspectu Dei delectentur in laetitia [5] cantate Deo psalmum dicite nomini eius iter facite ei qui ascendit super occasum Dominus nomen illi et exultate in conspectu eius turbabuntur a facie eius

[6] patris orfanorum et iudicis viduarum Deus in loco sancto suo [7] Deus inhabitare facit unius moris in domo qui educit vinctos in fortitudine similiter eos qui exasperant qui habitant in sepulchris [8] Deus cum egredereris in conspectu populi tui cum pertransieris in deserto diapsalma [9] terra mota est etenim caeli distillaverunt a facie Dei Sinai a facie Dei Israhel [10] pluviam voluntariam segregabis Deus hereditati tuae et infirmata est tu vero perfecisti eam

[11] animalia tua habitant in ea parasti in dulcedine tua pauperi Deus [12] Dominus dabit verbum evangelizantibus 27r virtute multa [13] rex virtutum dilecti dilecti; et speciei domus dividere spolia [14] si dormiatis inter medios cleros pinnae columbae deargentatae et posteriora dorsi eius in pallore auri [15] dum discernit Caelestis reges super eam nive dealbabuntur in Selmon

[16] mons Dei mons pinguis mons coagulatus mons pinguis [17] ut quid suspicamini montes coagulatos mons in quo beneplacitum est Deo habitare in eo etenim Dominus habitabit in finem [18] currus Dei decem milibus multiplex milia laetantium Dominus in eis in Sina in sancto [19] ascendisti in altum cepisti captivitatem accepisti dona in hominibus etenim non credentes inhabitare Dominum Deus [20] benedictus Dominus die cotidie prosperum iter faciet nobis Deus salutarium nostrorum diapsalma

[21] Deus noster Deus salvos faciendi et Domini Domini exitus mortis [22] verumtamen Deus confringet capita inimicorum suorum verticem capilli perambulantium in delictis suis [23] dixit Dominus ex Basan convertam convertam in profundis maris [24] ut intinguatur pes tuus in sanguine lingua canum tuorum ex inimicis ab ipso [25] viderunt ingressus tui Deus ingressus Dei mei regis mei qui est in sancto

[26] praevenerunt principes coniuncti psallentibus in medio iuvencularum tympanistriarum [27] in ecclesiis benedicite Deum Dominum de fontibus Israhel [28] ibi Beniamin adulescentulus in mentis excessu principes Iuda duces eorum principes Zabulon principes Nepthali [29] manda Deus virtutem tuam confirma Deus hoc quod operatus es nobis [30] a templo tuo in Hierusalem tibi adferent reges munera

[31] increpa feras harundinis congregatio taurorum in vaccis populorum ut excludant eos qui probati sunt argento dissipa gentes quae bella volunt [32] venient legati ex Aegypto Aethiopia praeveniet manus eius Deo [33] regna terrae cantate Deo psallite Domino diapsalma psallite Deo; [34] qui ascendit super caelum caeli ad orientem ecce dabit voci suae vocem virtutis [35] date gloriam Deo super Israhel magnificentia eius et virtus eius in nubibus

[36] mirabilis Deus in sanctis suis Deus Israhel ipse dabit virtutem et fortitudinem plebi suae benedictus Deus

68[1] in finem pro his qui commutabuntur David [2] 27v *(enlarged S)*salvum me fac Deus quoniam intraverunt aquae usque ad animam meam [3] infixus sum in limum profundi et non est substantia veni in altitudines maris et tempestas demersit me [4] laboravi clamans raucae factae sunt fauces meae defecerunt oculi mei dum spero in Deum meum [5] multiplicati sunt super capillos capitis mei qui oderunt me gratis confortati sunt qui persecuti sunt me inimici mei iniuste quae non rapui tunc exsolvebam

[6] Deus tu scis insipientiam meam et delicta mea a te non sunt absconditа [7] non erubescant in me qui expectant te Domine Domine virtutum non confundantur super me qui quaerunt te Deus Israhel [8] quoniam propter te sustinui obprobrium operuit confusio faciem meam [9] extraneus factus sum fratribus meis et peregrinus filiis matris meae [10] quoniam zelus domus tuae comedit me et obprobria exprobrantium tibi ceciderunt super me

[11] et operui in ieiunio animam meam et factum est in obprobrium mihi [12] et posui vestimentum meum cilicium et factus sum illis in parabolam [13] adversum me exercebantur qui sedebant in porta et in me psallebant qui bibebant vinum [14] ego vero orationem meam ad te Domine tempus beneplaciti Deus in multitudine misericordiae tuae exaudi me in veritate salutis tuae [15] eripe me de luto ut non infigar liberer ab his qui oderunt me et de profundis aquarum

[16] non me demergat tempestas aquae neque absorbeat me profundum neque urgeat super me puteus os suum [17] exaudi me Domine quoniam benigna est misericordia tua secundum multitudinem miserationum tuarum respice me [18] et ne avertas faciem tuam a puero tuo quoniam tribulor velociter exaudi me [19] intende animae meae et libera eam propter inimicos meos eripe me [20] tu scis inproperium meum et confusionem et reverentiam meam

[21] in conspectu tuo sunt omnes qui tribulant me inproperium expectavit cor meum et miseriam et sustinui qui simul contristaretur et non fuit et qui consolaretur et non inveni [22] et dederunt in escam meam fel et in siti mea potaverunt me aceto [23] fiat mensa eorum coram ipsis in laqueum et in retributiones et in scandalum [24] obscurentur oculi eorum ne videant et dorsum eorum semper incurva [25] 28r effunde super eos iram tuam et furor irae tuae conprehendat eos

[26] fiat habitatio eorum deserta et in tabernaculis eorum non sit qui inhabitet [27] quoniam quem tu percussisti persecuti sunt et super dolorem vulnerum meorum addiderunt [28] adpone iniquitatem super iniquitatem eorum et non intrent in iustitia tua [29] deleantur de libro viventium et cum iustis non scribantur [30] ego sum pauper et dolens salus tua Deus suscepit me

[31] laudabo nomen Dei cum cantico magnificabo eum in laude [32] et placebit Deo super vitulum novellum cornua producentem et ungulas [33] videant pauperes et laetentur quaerite Deum et vivet anima vestra [34] quoniam exaudivit

pauperes Dominus et vinctos suos non despexit [35] laudent illum caeli et terra mare et omnia reptilia in eis

[36] quoniam Deus salvam faciet Sion et aedificabuntur civitates Iudaeae et inhabitabunt ibi et hereditate adquirent eam [37] et semen servorum eius possidebunt eam et qui diligunt nomen eius habitabunt in ea

69—No text extant

70[1] David psalmus filiorum Ionadab et priorum captivorum in te Domine speravi non confundar in aeternum [2] in iustitia tua libera me et eripe me inclina ad me aurem tuam et salva me [3] esto mihi in Deum protectorem et in locum munitum ut salvum me facias quoniam firmamentum meum et refugium meum es tu [4] Deus meus eripe me de manu peccatoris de manu contra legem agentis et iniqui [5] quoniam tu es patientia mea Domine Domine spes mea a iuventute mea

[6] in te confirmatus sum ex utero de ventre matris meae tu es protector meus in te cantatio mea semper [7] tamquam prodigium factus sum multis et tu adiutor fortis [8] repleatur os meum laude ut cantem gloriam tuam tota die magnitudinem tuam [9] non proicias me in tempore senectutis cum deficiet virtus mea ne derelinquas me [10] quia dixerunt inimici mei mihi et qui custodiebant animam meam consilium fecerunt in unum

[11] dicentes Deus dereliquit eum persequimini et conprehendite eum quia non est qui 28v eripiat [12] Deus ne elongeris a me Deus meus in adiutorium meum respice [13] confundantur et deficiant detrahentes animae meae operieantur confusione et pudore qui quaerunt mala mihi [14] ego autem semper sperabo et adiciam super omnem laudem tuam [15] os meum adnuntiabit iustitiam tuam tota die salutem tuam quoniam non cognovi litteraturam

[16] introibo in potentiam Domini Domine memorabor iustitiae tuae solius [17] Deus docuisti me ex iuventute mea et usque nunc pronuntiabo mirabilia tua [18] et usque in senectam et senium Deus ne derelinquas me donec adnuntiem brachium tuum generationi omni quae ventura est potentiam tuam [19] et iustitiam tuam Deus usque in altissima quae fecisti magnalia Deus quis similis tibi [20] quantas ostendisti mihi tribulationes multas et malas et conversus vivificasti me et de abyssis terrae iterum reduxisti me

[21] multiplicasti magnificentiam tuam et conversus consolatus es me [22] nam et ego confitebor tibi in vasis psalmi veritatem tuam Deus psallam tibi in cithara Sanctus Israhel [23] exultabunt labia mea cum cantavero tibi et anima mea quam redemisti [24] sed et lingua mea tota die meditabitur iustitiam tuam cum confusi et reveriti fuerint qui quaerunt mala mihi

71[1] in Salomonem [2] Deus iudicium tuum regi da et iustitiam tuam filio regis iudicare populum tuum in iustitia et pauperes tuos in iudicio [3] suscipiant montes pacem populo et colles iustitiam [4] iudicabit pauperes populi et salvos faciet filios pauperum et humiliabit calumniatorem [5] et permanebit cum sole et ante lunam generationes generationum

[6] descendet sicut pluvia in vellus et sicut stillicidia stillantia super terram [7] orietur in diebus eius iustitia et abundantia pacis donec auferatur luna [8] et dominabitur a mari usque ad mare et a flumine usque ad terminos orbis terrarum [9] coram illo procident Aethiopes et inimici eius terram lingent [10] reges Tharsis et insulae munera offerent

29r(1) reges Arabum et Saba dona aducent [11] et adorabunt
(2) eum omnes reges omnes gentes servient ei [12] quia
(3) liberabit pauperum a potente et pauperum cui non
(4) erat adiutor [13] paret pauperi et inopi et animas pau-
(5) perum salvas faciet [14] exs ussuris et

iniquitate redimet
(6) animas eorum et honorabile nomen eorum
(7) coram illo [15] et vivet et dabitur ei de auro Arabia et adora-
(8) bunt de ipso semper tota die benedicant ei [16] erit fir-
(9) mamentum in terra in summis montium superextolletur
(10) super Libanum fructus eius et florebunt de civitate sicut
(11) fenum terrae [17] sit nomen eius benedictum in saecula ante solem permanet nomen eius
et benedicentur in *(eye skip here—*benedictum *to* benedicentur*)*
ipso~~omne~~stribus
(12) terrae omnes gentes magificabunt eum [18] benedictus
(13) Dominus Deus Deus Israhel qui facit mirabilia solus [19] et bedictum
(14) nomen maiestatis eius in aeternum et replebitur
(15) maiestate eius omnis terra fiat fiat

72(16) [1] quam bonus Israhel Deus ~~his~~ quirecto sunt
(17) corde [2] mei autem paene moti sunt ~~pedes~~ paene effussi sunt
(18) gressus mei [3] quia zelavi super iniquipacem pec-
(19) catorum videns [4] quia non est respectus morti
(20) eorum et firmamentum inplaga eorum [5] in lab-
(21) orehominum non sunt et cum hominibus non flagillabuntur [6] ideo
(22) tenuit eos superbia operti sunt iniquitate etimpie-
(23) tatesua [7] prodiet quasi ex adipe iniquitas eorum tra-
(24) nsierunt in affectum cordis [8] cogitaverunt et locuti sunt
(25) in nequitia iniquitatem in excelso locuti sunt [9] possuerunt
(26) in caelum os suum et lingua eorum transivit in
(27) terra [10] ideo convertetur populus meus hic et dies
(28) pleni invenienturin eis [11] et dixerunt
quomodo scit Deus et si
(29) est scientia in Excelso [12] ecce ipsi peccatores et habun-
(30) dantes in saeculo obtinuerunt divitias [13] et dixi sine
(31) ergo cusa iustificavi cor meum et lavi inter

29v(1) innogentes manus meas [14] et fui flagellatus tota die
(2) et castigatio mea in matutino [15] si dicebam narrabo sic
(3) ecce in nationem filiorum tuorum reprobavi [16] et existima-
(4) bam cognoscere hoc labor est ante me [17] donec intrem
(5) in sanctuarium Dei intellegem in novissimis eorum [18] verum-
(6) tamen propter dolos possuisti eis deiecisti eos dum adli-
(7) berent [19] quomodo facti sunt in desolatione subito defe-
(8) cerunt perierunt propter iniquitatem suam [20] velut som-
(9) nium surgentium Domine in *(possible eye skip?)*
inquitatem tua imaginem ipsorum
(10) ad nihilum rediges [21] quia inflammatum est cor meum et renn-
(11) es mei commotati sunt [22] et ego ad nihilum redactus sum et nesci-
(12) vi [23] ut iumentum factus sum apud te et ego semper tecum
(13) [24] tenuisti dñ manum dexteram meam et in voluntate
(14) tua deduxisti me et cum gloriam suscepisti me [25] quidenim
(15)mihi est in caelo et a te quid volui super terram [26] defecit caro
(16) mea et cor meum Deus cordis mei et pars mea Deus mie
(17) aeternum [27] quia ecce qui elongant se a te peribunt
(18) perdidisti omnem qui fornicatur abs te [28] mihi autem
(19) adherere Deo bonum est ponere in Domino Deo spem meam
(20) ut adnuntiem omnes predicationes tuas in
(21) portis filiae Sion ∴

73(22) [1] ut quid Deus repulisti in finem iratus est
(23) furor tuus super oves pascuae tuae [2] me-
(24) mor esto congregationis tuae quam posse-
(25) disti ab initia redemisti virgam hereditatis tuae
(26) mons Sion in quo habitasti in eo [3] leva manus tuas in
(27) superbias eorum in finem quanta malignatus est
(28) inimicus in sancto [4] et gloriati sunt qui oderunt te in medio
(29) sollemnitatis tuae posuerunt signa sua ~~signa~~ [5] et non
(30) cognoverunt sicut in exitu super summumquasi
(31) in silva lignorum securibus [6] exciderunt ianuas
(32) eius in id ipsumin securi et ascia deiecerunt eam; [7] incenderunt

30r igni sanctuarium tuum in terra polluerunt tabernaculum nominis tui [8] dixerunt in corde suo cognatio eorum simul quiescere faciamus omnes dies festos Dei a terra [9] signa nostra non vidimus iam non est propheta et nos non cognoscet amplius [10] usquequo Deus inproperabit inimicus inritat adversarius nomen tuum in finem

[11] ut quid avertis manum tuam et dexteram tuam de medio sinu tuo in finem [12] Deus autem rex noster ante saeculum operatus est salutes in medio terrae [13] tu confirmasti in virtute tua mare contribulasti capita draconum in aquis [14] tu confregisti capita draconis dedisti eum escam populis Aethiopum [15] tu disrupisti fontem et torrentes tu siccasti fluvios Aetham;

[16] tuus est dies et tua est nox tu fabricatus es auroram et solem [17] tu fecisti omnes terminos terrae aestatem et ver tu plasmasti ea [18] memor esto huius inimicus inproperavit Dominum et populus insipiens incitavit nomen tuum [19] ne tradas bestiis animam confitentem tibi animas pauperum tuorum ne obliviscaris in finem [20] respice in testamentum tuum quia repleti sunt qui obscurati sunt terrae domibus iniquitatum

[21] ne avertatur humilis factus confusus pauper et inops laudabunt nomen tuum [22] exsurge Deus iudica causam tuam memor esto inproperiorum tuorum eorum qui ab insipiente sunt tota die [23] ne obliviscaris voces inimicorum tuorum superbia eorum qui te oderunt ascendit semper

74[1] in finem ne corrumpas psalmus Asaph cantici [2] confitebimur tibi Deus confitebimur et invocabimus nomen tuum narrabimus mirabilia tua [3] cum accepero tempus ego iustitias iudicabo [4] liquefacta est terra et omnes qui habitant in ea ego confirmavi columnas eius diapsalma [5] dixi iniquis nolite inique facere et delinquentibus nolite exaltare cornu

[6] nolite extollere in altum cornu vestrum nolite loqui adversus Deum 30v iniquitatem [7] quia neque ab oriente neque ab occidente neque a desertis montibus [8] quoniam Deus iudexest hunc humiliat et hunc exaltat [9] quia calix in manu Domini veni meri plenus mixto et inclinavit ex hoc in hoc verum fex eius non est exinanita bibent omnes peccatores terrae [10] ego autem adnuntiabo in saeculuo cantabo Deo Iacob

[11] et omnia cornua peccatorum confringam et exaltabuntur cornua iusti

75—No text extant

76[1] in finem pro Idithun psalmus Asaph [2] voce mea ad Dominum clamavi voce mea ad Deum et intendit me [3] in die tribulationis meae Deum exquisivi manibus meis nocte contra eum et non sum deceptus rennuit consolari anima mea [4] memor fui Dei et delectatus sum exercitatus sum et defecit spiritus meus diapsalma [5] anticipaverunt vigilias oculi mei turbatus sum et non sum locutus

[6] cogitavi dies antiquos et annos aeternos in mente habui [7] et meditatus sum nocte cum corde meo exercitabar et scobebam spiritum meum [8] numquid in aeternum proiciet Deus et non adponet 31r ut conplacitior sit adhuc [9] aut in finem misericordiam suam abscidet a generatione in generationem [10] aut obliviscetur misereri

Deus aut continebit in ira sua missericordias suas diapsalma

[11] et dixi nunc coepi haec mutatio dexterae Excelsi [12] memor fui operum Domini quia memor ero ab initio mirabilium tuorum [13] et meditabor in omnibus operibus tuis et in adinventionibus tuis exercebor [14] Deus in sancto via tua quis deus magnus sicut Deus noster [15] tu es Deus qui facis mirabilia notam fecisti in populis virtutem tuam

[16] redemisti in brachio tuo populum tuum filios Iacob et Ioseph diapsalma [17] viderunt te aquae Deus viderunt te aquae et timuerunt et turbatae sunt abyssi [18] multitudo sonitus aquarum vocem dederunt nubes etenim sagittae tuae transeunt [19] vox tonitrui tui in rota inluxerunt coruscationes tuae orbi terrae commota est et contremuit terra [20] in mari via tua et semitae tuae in aquis multis et vestigia tua non cognoscentur

[21] deduxisti sicut oves populum tuum in manu Mosi et Aaron

77[1] intellectus Asaph adtendite populus meus legem meam inclinate aurem vestram in verba oris mei [2] aperiam in parabola os meum eloquar propositiones ab initio [3] quanta audivimus et cognovimus ea et patres nostri narraverunt nobis [4] non sunt occultata a filiis eorum in generationem alteram narrantes laudes Domini et virtutes eius et mirabilia eius quae fecit [5] et suscitavit testimonium in Iacob et legem posuit in Israhel quanta mandavit patribus nostris nota facere ea filiis suis

[6] ut cognoscat generatio altera filii qui nascentur et exsurgent et narrabunt filiis suis [7] ut ponant in Deo spem suam et non obliviscantur opera Dei et mandata eius exquirant [8] ne fiant sicut patres eorum generatio prava et exasperans generatio quae non direxit cor suum et non est creditus cum Deo spiritus eius [9] filii 31v Effrem intendentes et mittentes arcus conversi sunt in die belli [10] non custodierunt testamentum Dei et in lege eius noluerunt ambulare

[11] et obliti sunt benefactorum eius et mirabilium eius quae ostendit eis [12] coram patribus eorum quae fecit mirabilia in terra Aegypti in campo Taneos [13] interrupit mare et perduxit eos statuit aquas quasi utrem [14] et deduxit eos in nube diei et tota nocte in inluminatione ignis [15] interrupit petram in heremo et adaquavit eos velut in abysso multa

[16] et eduxit aquam de petra et deduxit tamquam flumina aquas [17] et adposuerunt adhuc peccare ei in ira excitaverunt Excelsum in inaquoso [18] et temptaverunt Deum in cordibus suis ut peterent escas animabus suis [19] et male locuti sunt de Deo dixerunt numquid poterit Deus parare mensam in deserto [20] quoniam percussit petram et fluxerunt aquae et torrentes inundaverunt numquid et panem potest dare aut parare mensam populo suo

[21] ideo audivit Dominus et distulit et ignis accensus est in Iacob et ira ascendit in Israhel [22] quia non crediderunt in Deo nec speraverunt in salutare eius [23] et mandavit nubibus desuper et ianuas caeli aperuit [24] et pluit illis manna ad manducandum et panem caeli dedit eis [25] panem angelorum manducavit homo cibaria misit eis in abundantiam

[26] transtulit austrum de caelo et induxit in virtute sua africum [27] et pluit super eos sicut pulverem carnes et sicut harenam maris volatilia pinnata [28] et ceciderunt in medio castrorum eorum circa tabernacula eorum [29] et manducaverunt et saturati sunt nimis et desiderium eorum adtulit eis [30]

32r(1) non sunt fraudati a desiderio suo adhuc escae eorum
(2) erat in ore ipsorum [31] et ira Dei ascendit in eos et occi-
(3) dit pingues eorum et electos Issrahel inedivit [32] in om-
(4) nibus his peccaverunt adhuc et non crediderunt ~~erunt~~ mirabbilibus eius [33]
(5) et defecerunt in vanitates ~~dies~~ eorum et anni ~~eorum~~ cum festinatei-

(6) one [34] cum occideret eos quaerebant eum et revertebantur
(7) et deluculo veniebant ad Deum [35] et rememorati sunt quia Deus
(8) adiutor est eorum et Deus excelsus redemptor eorum est [36]
(9) et dilexerunt eum in ore suo ~~et lingua sua~~ mentiti sunt ei [37]
(10) cor autem ipsorum non erat rectum eorum eo nec fid-
(11) eles habiti sunt in testamento eius [38] ipse ~~autem~~ est misericors et p-
(12) ropitius fiet peccatis eorum et non disperdit eos et abundabit ut avertat iram suam et non accendet (eye skip here?) omnem iram suam [39] et
(13) recordatus est quia caro sunt spiritus vadens et non rediens [40]
(14) quotiens exacerbaverunt eum in deserto in ira
(15) concitaverunt eum in inaquoso [41] et conversi sunt et temp-
(16) taverunt Deum et Sanctum Israhel exacerbaverunt [42]
(17) non sunt recordati manus eius die qua redemit eos de manu
(18) tribulantis [43] sicut posuit in Aeegypto signa sua et
(19) prodigia sua in campo Taneos [44] et convertit in sanguine flumina eorum et imbres
(20) eorum ne biberent [45] misit in eos cynomiam
(21) et comedit eos et ranam et disperdit eos

(22) [46] et dedit erugini fructus eorum et labores eorum
(23) lucustae [47] et occiditin grandine iumenta eorum et moros eorum
(24) in pruina [48] et tradidit grandini iumenta eorum
(25) et possessionem eorum igni iumenta eorum [49] misit in eos iram indigna-
(26) tionis suae indignationem et iram et tribulation-
(27) nem inmissionem per singulas males [50] viam
(28) fecit semitae irae suae non pepercit a morte
(29) animarum eorum etiumenta eorum in morte

32v(1) conclussit [51] et percussit omne primitivum in ~~terra~~ Aegypto
(2) praemitinm laborum eorum in tabernaculis
(3) Cham [52] et abstullit sicut oves populum suum et per-
(4) duxit eos tamquam gregem in deserto [53] etdeduxit
(5) eos in spe et non timuerunt et inimicos eorum ope-
(6) ruit mare [54] et induxit eos in montem sanctifica-
(7) tionis suae montem quem adquisivit dextera
(8) eius et eiecit a facie eorum gentes et sorte div-
(9) isit eis tamquam in funiculo ~~dis~~tributionis [55] et ha-
(10) bitare fecit in tabernaculis eorum tribus Isra-
(11) hel [56] et temptaverunt et ex-
(12) acerbaverunt Deum excelsum et testimonia eiusnon custodierunt [57] et avertterunt
(13) se et non servaverunt pactum quemadmodum patres
(14) eorum conversi sunt in arcum pravum [58] ~~et~~ in ira concita-
(15) verunt eum in collibus suis ~~et~~ in scluptilibus suis ad
(16) aemulationem eum provocaverunt [59] audivit Deus et spre-
(17) vit et ad nihilum redegit valde Israhel [60] et repullit
(18) tabernaculum Selo tabernaculum suum ubi
(19) habitavit in hominibus [61] et tradidit in captivitatem virtutem
(20) eorum et pulchritudinem eorum in ma-
(21) nus inimici [62] et conclusit in gladio populum suum
(22) et heriditatem suam sprevit [63] iuvenes eorum come-
(23) dit ignis et virgines eorum non sunt lamentatae [64] sa-
(24) cerdotes eorum in gladio ciciderunt et viduae eorum
(25) non plorabuntur [65] et excitatus est tamquam dor-
(26) miens Dominus tamquam potans crapulatus a v-
(27) ino [66] et percussit inimicos suos in posteriora obpprobrium
(28) sempiternum dedit illis [67] et repullit tabernaculum

(29) Iosephet tribum Effrem non ellegit [68] ~~et elegit~~ tribum Iuda montem
(30) Sion quem dilexit [69] et aedificavit sicut
(31) unicornium sanctificium

33r suum in terra quam fundavit in saecula [70] et elegit David servum suum et sustullit eum de gregibus ovium de post fetantes accepit eum

[71] pascere Iacob servum suum et Israhel hereditatem suam [72] et pavit eos in innocentia cordis sui et in intellectibus manuum suarum deduxit eos

78[1] psalmus Asaph Deus venerunt gentes in hereditatem tuam polluerunt templum sanctum tuum posuerunt Hierusalem in pomorum custodiam [2] posuerunt morticina servorum tuorum escas volatilibus caeli carnes sanctorum tuorum bestiis terrae [3] effuderunt sanguinem ipsorum tamquam aquam in circuitu Hierusalem et non erat qui sepeliret [4] facti sumus obprobrium vicinis nostris subsannatio et inlusio his qui circum nos sunt [5] usquequo Domine irasceris in finem accendetur velut ignis zelus tuus

[6] effunde iram tuam in gentes quae te non noverunt et in regna quae nomen tuum non invocaverunt [7] quia comederunt Iacob et locum eius desolaverunt [8] ne memineris iniquitatum nostrarum antiquarum cito anticipent nos misericordiae tuae quia pauperes facti sumus nimis [9] adiuva nos Deus salutaris noster propter gloriam nominis tui Domine libera nos et propitius esto peccatis nostris propter nomen tuum [10] ne forte dicant in gentibus ubi est Deus eorum et innotescat in nationibus coram oculis nostris ultio sanguinis servorum tuorum qui effusus est

[11] introeat in conspectu tuo gemitus conpeditorum secundum magnitudinem brachii tui posside filios mortificatorum [12] et redde vicinis nostris septuplum in sinu eorum inproperium ipsorum quod exprobraverunt tibi Domine [13] nos autem populus tuus et oves pascuae tuae confitebimur tibi in 33v saeculum in generationem et generationem adnuntiabimus laudem tuam

79[2] qui regis Israhel intende qui deducis tamquam oves Ioseph qui sedes super cherubin manifestare [3] coram Effraim et Beniamin et Manasse excita potentiam tuam et veni ut salvos facias nos [4] Deus converte nos et ostende faciem tuam et salvi erimus [5] Domine Deus virtutum quousque irasceris super orationem servi tui

[6] cibabis nos pane lacrimarum et potum dabis nobis in lacrimis in mensura [7] posuisti nos in contradictionem vicinis nostris et inimici nostri subsannaverunt nos [8] Deus virtutum converte nos et ostende faciem tuam et salvi erimus [9] vineam de Aegypto transtulisti eiecisti gentes et plantasti eam [10] dux itineris fuisti in conspectu eius et plantasti radices eius et implevit terram

[11] operuit montes umbra eius et arbusta eius cedros Dei [12] extendit palmites suos usque ad mare et usque ad Flumen propagines eius [13] ut quid destruxisti maceriam eius et vindemiant eam omnes qui praetergrediuntur viam [14] exterminavit eam aper de silva et singularis ferus depastus est eam [15] Deus virtutum convertere respice de caelo et vide et visita vineam istam

[16] et perfice eam quam plantavit dextera tua et super filium quem confirmasti tibi [17] incensa igni et suffossa ab increpatione vultus tui peribunt [18] fiat manus tua super virum dexterae tuae et super filium hominis quem confirmasti tibi [19] et non discedimus a te vivificabis nos et nomen tuum invocabimus [20] Domine Deus virtutum converte nos et ostende faciem tuam et salvi erimus

80[1] in finem pro torcularibus Asaph [2] exultate Deo adiutori nostro iubilate Deo Iacob [3] sumite psalmum et date tympanum psalterium iucundum cum cithara [4] bucinate in neomenia tuba in insigni die sollemnitatis 34r nostrae [5] quia praeceptum Israhel est et iudicium Dei Iacob

[6] testimonium in Iosephp osuit illud cum exiret de terra Aegypti linguam quam non noverat audivit [7] devertit ab oneribus dorsum eius manus eius in cofino servierunt [8] in tribulatione invocasti me et liberavi te exaudivi te in abscondito

tempestatis probavi te apud aquam Contradictionis diapsalma [9] audi populus meus et contestabor te Israhel si audias me [10] non erit in te deus recens nec adorabis deum alienum

[11] ego enim sum Dominus Deus tuus qui eduxi te de terra Aegypti dilata os tuum et implebo illud [12] et non audivit populus meus vocem meam et Israhel non intendit mihi [13] et dimisi illos secundum desideria cordis eorum ibunt in adinventionibus suis [14] si populus meus audisset me Israhel si in viis meis ambulasset [15] pro nihilo forsitan inimicos eorum humiliassem et super tribulantes eos misissem manum meam

[16] inimici Domini mentiti sunt ei et erit tempus eorum in saeculo [17] et cibavit illos ex adipe frumenti et de petra melle saturavit illos

81—No text extant

82[2] 34v Deus quis similis erit tibi ne taceas neque conpescaris Deus [3] quoniam ecce inimici tui sonaverunt et qui oderunt te extullerunt caput [4] super populum tuum malignaverunt consilium et cogitaverunt adversus sanctos tuos [5] dixerunt venite et disperdamus eos de gente et non memoretur nomen Israhel ultra

[6] quoniam cogitaverunt unianimiter simul adversum te testamentum disposuerunt [7] tabernacula Idumeorum et Ismahelitae Moab et Aggareni [8] Gebal et Ammon et Amalech alienigenae cum habitantibus Tyrum [9] etenim Assur venit cum illis facti sunt in adiutorium filiis Loth diapsalma [10] fac illis sicut Madiam et Sisarae sicut Iabin in torrente Cison

[11] disperierunt in Endor facti sunt ut stercus terrae [12] pone principes eorum sicut Oreb et Zeb et Zebee et Salmana omnes principes eorum [13] qui dixerunt hereditate possideamus sanctuarium Dei [14] Deus meus pone illos ut rotam sicut stipulam ante faciem venti [15] sicut ignis qui conburit silvam sicut flamma conburens montes

[16] ita persequeris illos in tempestate tua et in ira tua turbabis eos [17] imple facies illorum ignominia et quaerent nomen tuum Domine [18] erubescant et conturbentur in saeculum saeculi et confundantur et pereant [19] et cognoscant quia nomen tibi Dominus tu solus Altissimus in omni terra

83[1] in finem pro torcularibus filiis Core psalmus [2] quam dilecta tabernacula tua Domine virtutum [3] concupiscit et defecit anima mea in atria Domini cor meum et caro mea exultavit in Deum vivum [4] etenim passer invenit sibi; domum et turtur nidum sibi ubi ponat pullos suos altaria tua Domine virtutum 35r rex meus et Deus meus [5] beati qui habitant in domo tua in saecula saeculorum laudabunt te diapsalma

[6] beatus cui vir est auxilium abs te ascensiones in corde suo disposuit [7] in valle lacrimarum in loco quem posuit [8] etenim benedictiones dabit legis dator ibunt de virtute in virtutem videbitur Deus deorum in Sion [9] Domine Deus virtutum exaudi orationem meam auribus percipe Deus Iacob diapsalma [10] protector noster aspice Deus et respice in faciem christi tui

[11] quia melior est dies una in atriis tuis super milia elegi abiectus esse in domo Dei mei magis quam habitare in tabernaculis peccatorum [12] quia misericordiam et veritatem diligit; Deus gratiam et gloriam dabit Dominus [13] non privabit bonis eos qui ambulant in innocentia Domine virtutum beatus vir qui sperat in te

84[1] in finem filiis Core psalmus [2] benedixisti Domine terram tuam avertisti captivitatem Iacob [3] remisisti iniquitates plebis tuae operuisti omnia peccata eorum diapsalma [4] mitigasti omnem iram tuam avertisti ab ira indignationis tuae [5] converte nos Deus salutum nostrarum et averte iram tuam a nobis

[6] numquid in aeternum irasceris nobis aut extendes iram tuam a generatione in generationem [7] Deus tu conversus vivificabis nos et plebs tua laetabitur in te [8] ostende nobis Domine misericordiam tuam et salutare tuum da nobis

[9] audiam quid loquatur in me; Dominus Deus quoniam loquetur pacem in plebem suam et super sanctos suos et in eos qui convertuntur ad cor [10] verumtamen prope timentes eum salutare ipsius ut inhabitet gloria in terra nostra

[11] misericordia et veritas obviaverunt sibi; iustitia et pax osculatae sunt [12] veritas de terra orta 35v et iustitia de caelo prospexit [13] etenim Dominus dabit benignitatem et terra nostra dabit fructum suum [14] iustitia ante eum ambulabit et ponet in via gressus suos

85[1] oratio ipsi David inclina Domine aurem tuam et; exaudi me quoniam inops et pauper sum ego [2] custodi animam meam quoniam sanctus sum salvum fac servum tuum Deus meus sperantem in te [3] miserere mei Domine quoniam ad te clamabo tota die [4] laetifica animam servi tui quoniam ad te Domine animam meam levavi [5] quoniam tu Domine suavis et mitis et multae misericordiae omnibus invocantibus te

[6] auribus percipe Domine orationem meam et intende voci orationis meae [7] in die tribulationis meae clamavi ad te quia exaudisti me [8] non est similis tui in diis Domine et non est secundum opera tua [9] omnes gentes quascumque fecisti venient et adorabunt coram te Domine et glorificabunt nomen tuum [10] quoniam magnus es tu et faciens mirabilia tu es Deus solus

[11] deduc me Domine in via tua et ingrediar in veritate tua laetetur cor meum ut timeat nomen tuum [12] confitebor tibi Domine Deus meus in toto corde meo et glorificabo nomen tuum in aeternum [13] quia misericordia tua magna est super me et eruisti animam meam ex inferno inferiori [14] Deus iniqui insurrexerunt super me et synagoga potentium quaesierunt animam meam et non proposuerunt te in conspectu suo [15] et tu Domine Deus miserator et misericors patiens et multae misericordiae et verax

[16] respice in me et miserere mei da imperium tuum puero tuo et 36r salvum fac filium ancillae tuae [17] fac mecum signum in bono et videant qui oderunt me et confundantur quoniam tu Domine adiuvasti me et consolatus es me: *(continuation of text from line below)* omnia tabernacula

86[1] fundamenta eius in montibus sanctis [2] delegit Dominus portas Sion super omnia tabernacula Iacob [3] gloriosa dicta sunt de decivtas Dei diapsalma [4] memor ero Raab et Babylonis scientibus te ~~ecce alienigenae et Tyrus et populus~~ Aethiopum hii fuerunt illic [5] numquid Sion dicet homo et homo natus est in ea et ipse fundavit eam Altissimus

[6] Dominus narrabit in scriptura populorum et principum horum qui fuerunt in ea diapsalma [7] sicut laetantium omnium habitatio in te

87[1] canticum psalmi filiis Core in finem pro Maeleth ad respondendum intellectus Eman Ezraitae [2] Domine Deus salutis meae die clamavi et nocte coram te [3] intret in conspectu tuo oratio mea inclina aurem tuam ad precem meam [4] quia repleta est malis anima mea et vita mea in inferno adpropinquavit [5] aestimatus sum cum descendentibus in lacum factus sum sicut homo sine adiutorio

[6] inter mortuos liber sicut vulnerati dormientes in sepulchris quorum non es memor amplius et ipsi de manu tua repulsi sunt [7] posuerunt me in lacu inferiori in tenebrosis et in umbra mortis [8] super me confirmatus est furor tuus et omnes fluctus tuos induxisti super me diapsalma [9] longe fecisti notos meos a me posuerunt me abominationem sibi traditus sum et non egrediebar [10] oculi mei languerunt prae inopia clamavi ad te Domine tota die expandi ad te manus meas

[11] numquid mortuis facies mirabilia aut medici suscitabunt et confitebuntur tibi diapsalma [12] numquid narrabit aliquis in sepulchro misericordiam tuam et veritatem tuam in perditione [13] numquid cognoscentur in tenebris mirabilia tua et iustitia tua in terra oblivionis [14] et ego ad te Domine clamavi et mane oratio mea praeveniet te [15] ut quid Domine repellis orationem meam avertis faciem tuam a me

[16] pauper sum ego et in laboribus a iuventute mea exaltatus autem humiliatus sum et conturbatus [17] in me transierunt irae tuae et terrores tui conturbaverunt me [18] circuierunt me sicut aqua tota die circumdederunt me simul [19] 36v elongasti a me amicum et proximum et notos meos a miseria

88[2] misericordias Domini in aeternum cantabo in generationem et generationem adnuntiabo veritatem tuam in ore meo.·. [3] quoniam dixisti in aeternum misericordia aedificabitur in caelis praeparabitur veritas tua in eis; [4] disposui testamentum electis meis iuravi David servo meo [5] usque in aeternum praeparabo semen tuum et aedificabo in generationem et generationem sedem tuam diapsalma

[6] confitebuntur caeli mirabilia tua Domine etenim veritatem tuam in ecclesia sanctorum [7] quoniam quis in nubibus aequabitur Domino similis erit Domino in filiis Dei [8] Deus qui glorificatur in consilio sanctorum magnus et horrendus super omnes qui in circuitu eius sunt [9] Domine Deus virtutum quis similis tibi potens es Domine et veritas tua in circuitu tuo [10] tu dominaris potestatis maris motum autem fluctuum eius tu mitigas

[11] tu humiliasti sicut vulneratum superbum in brachio virtutis tuae dispersisti inimicos tuos [12] tui sunt caeli et tua est terra orbem terrae et plenitudinem eius tu fundasti [13] aquilonem et mare tu creasti Thabor et Hermon in nomine tuo exultabunt [14] tuum brachium cum potentia firmetur manus tua et exaltetur dextera tua [15] iustitia et iudicium praeparatio sedis tuae misericordia et veritas praecedent faciem tuam

[16] beatus populus qui scit iubilationem Domine in lumine vultus tui ambulabunt [17] et in nomine tuo exultabunt tota die et in iustitia tua exaltabuntur [18] quoniam gloria virtutis eorum tu es et in beneplacito tuo exaltabitur cornu nostrum [19] quia Domini est adsumptio nostra; et Sancti Israhel regis nostri [20] tunc locutus es in visione sanctis tuis et dixisti posui adiutorium in potentem exaltavi electum de plebe mea

[21] inveni David servum meum in oleo sancto meo linui eum [22] manus enim mea auxiliabitur ei et brachium meum confirmabit eum [23] nihil proficiet inimicus in eo et filius iniquitatis non adponet nocere eum [24] et concidam a facie 37r ipsius inimicos eius et odientes eum in fugam convertam [25] et veritas mea et missericordia mea cum ipso et in nomine meo exaltabitur cornu eius

[26] et ponam in mari manum eius et in fluminibus dexteram eius [27] ipse invocabit me pater meus es tu Deus meus et susceptor salutis meae [28] et ego primogenitum ponam illum excelsum prae regibus terrae [29] in aeternum servabo illi misericordiam meam et testamentum meum fidele ipsi [30] et ponam in saeculum saeculi semen eius et thronum eius sicut dies caeli

[31] si dereliquerint filii eius legem meam et in iudicis meis non ambulaverint [32] si iustitias meas profanaverint et mandata mea non custodierint [33] visitabo in virga iniquitates eorum et in verberibus peccata eorum [34] misericordiam autem meam non dispergam ab eo neque nocebo in veritate mea [35] neque profanabo testamentum meum et quae procedunt de labiis meis non faciam irrita

[36] semel iuravi in sancto meo si David mentiar [37] semen eius in aeternum manebit [38] et thronus eius sicut sol in conspectu meo et sicut luna perfecta in aeternum et testis in caelo fidelis diapsalma [39] tu vero reppulisti et despexisti distulisti christum tuum [40] evertisti testamentum servi tui profanasti in terram sanctuarium eius

[41] destruxisti omnes sepes eius posuisti firmamenta eius formidinem [42] diripuerunt eum omnes transeuntes viam factus est obprobrium vicinis suis [43] exaltasti dexteram deprimentium eum laetificasti omnes inimicos eius [44] avertisti adiutorium gladii eius et non es auxiliatus ei in bello [45] destruxisti eum a mundatione sedem eius in terram conlisisti

[46] minorasti dies temporis eius perfudisti eum confusione diapsalma [47] usquequo Domine avertis in finem exardescet sicut ignis ira tua [48] memorare quae mea substantia numquid enim vane constituisti omnes filios hominum [49] quis est homo qui vivet et non videbit mortem eruet animam suam de manu inferi diapsalma [50] ubi sunt misericordiae tuae antiquae Domine sicut iurasti David in veritate tua

[51] memor esto Domine obprobrii servorum tuorum quod continui in sinu meo multarum 37v gentium [52] quod exprobraverunt inimici tui Domine quod commuta tionem exprobraverunt *(these two words switched position)* christi tui [53] benedictus Dominus in aeternum fiat fiat

89[1] Domine refugium tu factus es nobis in generatione et generatione [2] prius quam montes fierent et formaretur terra et orbis a saeculo usque in saeculum tu es Deus [3] ne avertas hominem in humilitatem et dixisti convertimini filii hominum [4] quoniam mille anni ante oculos tuos tamquam ~~dies~~ hesterna quae praeteriit et custodia in nocte [5] quae pro nihilo habentur eorum anni conerunt

[6] mane sicut herba transeat mane floreat et transeat vespere decidat induret et arescat [7] quia defecimus in ira tua et in furore tuo turbati sumus [8] posuisti iniquitates nostras in conspectu tuo saeculum nostrum in inluminatione vultus tui [9] quoniam omnes dies nostri defecerunt in ira tua defecimus anni nostri sicut aranea meditabantur [10] dies annorum nostrorum in ipsis septuaginta anni si autem in potentatibus octoginta anni et amplius eorum labor et dolor quoniam supervenit mansuetudo et corripiemur

[11] quis novit potestatem irae tuae et prae timore tuo iram tuam [12] dinumerare dexteram tuam sic notam fac et conpeditos corde in sapientia [13] convertere Domine usquequo et deprecabilis esto super servos tuos [14] repleti sumus mane misericordia tua et exultavimus et delectati sumus in omnibus diebus nostris [15] laetati sumus pro diebus quibus nos humiliasti annis quibus vidimus mala

[16] et respice in servos tuos et in opera tua et dirige filios eorum [17] et sit splendor Domini Dei nostri super nos et opera manuum nostrarum dirige super nos et opus manuum nostrarum dirige;

90[1] laus cantici David qui habitat in adiutorio Altissimi in protectione Dei caeli commorabitur [2] dicet Domino susceptor meus es tu et refugium meum Deus meus sperabo in eum [3] quoniam ipse liberabit me de laqueo venantium et a verbo aspero [4] in scapulis suis obumbrabit te et sub pinnis eius sperabis [5] scuto circumdabit te veritas eius non timebis a timore nocturno

[6] a sagitta volante in die a negotio perambulante in tenebris ab incursu et daemonio meridiano [7] cadent a latere tuo mille et decem milia a dextris tuis ad te autem non adpropinquabit [8] verumtamen oculis tuis 38r consederabis et retributionem peccatorum videbis [9] quoniam tu Domine spes mea Altissimum posuisti refugium tuum [10] non accedent ad te malaet flagellum non adpropinquabit tabernaculo tuo

[11] quoniam angelis suis mandabit de te ut custodiant te in omnibus viis tuis [12] in manibus portabunt te ne forte offendas ad lapidem pedem tuum [13] super aspidem et basilliscum ambulabis et; conculcabis leonem et draconem [14] quoniam in me speravit et liberabo eum protegam eum quoniam cognovit nomen meum [15] clamabit ad me et exaudiam eum cum ipso sum in tribulatione eripiam eum et clarificabo eum

[16] longitudine dierum replebo eum et ostendam illi salutare meum

91—No text extant

92[1] laus cantici David in die ante sabbatum quando inhabitata est terra 38v Dominus regnabit decore indutus est indutus est Dominus fortitudine et praecignxit se etenim firmavit orbem terrae qui non commovebitur [2] parata sedis tua ex tunc a saeculo tu es [3] elevaverunt flumina Domine elevaverunt flumina vocem suam elevabunt flumina fluctus suos; [4] a vocibus aquarum multarum mirabiles elationes maris mirabilis in altis Dominus [5] testimonia tua credibilia facta sunt nimis domum tuam decet sanctitudo Domine in longitudine dierum

: ~ : ~ : ~ : ~ : ~ : ~ : ~ : ~ : ~ : ~ : ~

93[1] psalmus David quarta sabbati Deus ultionum Dominus Deus ultionum libere egit [2] exaltare qui iudicas terram redde retributionem superbis [3] usquequo peccatores Domine usquequo peccatores gloriabuntur [4] effabuntur et loquentur iniquitatem loquentur omnes qui operantur iniustitiam [5] populum tuum Domine humiliaverunt et hereditatem tuam vexaverunt

[6] viduam et advenam interfecerunt et pupillos occiderunt [7] et dixerunt non videbit Dominus nec intelleget Deus Iacob [8] intellegite qui insipientes estis in populo et stulti aliquando sapite [9] qui plantavit aurem non audiet aut qui finxit oculum non considerat [10] qui corripit gentes non arguet qui docet hominem scientiam

[11] Dominus scit cogitationes hominum quoniam vanae sunt [12] beatus homo quem tu erudieris Domine et de lege tua docueris eum [13] ut mitiges ei a diebus malis donec fodiatur peccatori fovea [14] quia non repellet Dominus plebem suam et hereditatem suam non derelinquet [15] quoadusque iustitia convertatur in iudicium et qui iuxta illam omnes qui recto sunt corde diapsalma

[16] quis consurget mihi adversus malignantes aut quis stabit mecum adversus operantes iniquitatem [17] nisi quia Dominus adiuvit me paulo minus habitavit in inferno anima mea [18] si dicebam motus est pes meus misericordia tua Domine adiuvabat me [19] secundum multitudinem dolorum meorum in corde meo consolationes tuae laetificaverunt 39r animam meam [20] numquid aderit tibi sedis iniquitatis qui fingis dolorem in praecepto

[21] captabunt in animam iusti et sanguinem innocentem condemnabunt [22] et factus est Dominus mihi in refugium et Deus meus in adiutorem spei meae [23] et reddet illis iniquitatem ipsorum et in malitia eorum disperdet eos disperdet illos Dominus Deus noster

94[1] laus cantici David venite exultemus Domino iubilemus Deo salutari nostro [2] praeoccupemus faciem eius in confessione et in psalmis iubilemus ei [3] quoniam Deus magnus Dominus et rex magnus super omnes deos [4] quia in manu eius fines terrae et altitudines montium ipsius sunt [5] quoniam ipsius est mare et ipse fecit illud et siccam manus eius formaverunt

[6] venite adoremus et procidamus et ploremus ante Dominum qui fecit nos [7] quia ipse est Deus noster et nos populus pascuae eius et oves manus eius [8] hodie si vocem eius audieritis nolite obdurare corda vestra [9] sicut in inritatione secundum diem temptationis in deserto ubi temptaverunt me patres vestri probaverunt me; et viderunt opera mea [10] quadraginta annis offensus fui generationi illi et dixi semper errant corde

[11] et isti non cognoverunt vias meas ut iuravi in ira mea si intrabunt in requiem meam

95[1] quando domus aedificabatur post captivitatem canticum huic David cantate Domino canticum novum cantate Domino omnis terra [2] cantate Domino benedicite nomini eius adnuntiate diem de die salutare eius [3] adnuntiate inter gentes gloriam eius in omnibus populis mirabilia eius [4] quoniam magnus Dominus et laudabilis valde terribilis est super omnes deos [5] quoniam omnes dii gentium daemonia at vero Dominus caelos fecit

[6] confessio et pulchritudo in conspectu eius sanctimonia et magnificentia in sanctificatione eius [7] adferte Domino patriae gentium adferte Domino gloriam et honorem [8] adferte Domino gloriam nomini eius tollite hostias et introite in atria eius [9] adorate Dominum in atrio sancto eius commoveatur a facie eius universa terra [10] dicite in gentibus quia Dominus

39v(1) regnabit etenim correxit orbem qui terrae non
(2) movebitur iudicabit populos in aequitate [11] laetentur caeli et exultet
(3) terra commoveatur mare et plenitudo eius [12] gaudebunt
(4) campi et omnia quae in eis sunt tunc exultabunt omnia ligna
(5) silvarum [13] a facie Domini quia venit quoniam venit
(6) iudicare ~~terram~~ iudicabit orbem terrae *remi...* *(different word here?)* in aequitate et populos in
(7) veritate sua:-multae [2] nubes* *(this is text from 96:1–2, see line 8)*

96[1] Dominus regnavit
(8) exultet terra laetentur insulae *et caligo in
(9) circuitu eius iustitia et iudicium correctio sedis eius
(10) [3] ignis ante ipsum praecedet et inflammabit in circuitu inimicos eius
(11) [4] adluxerunt fulgora eius orbi terrae vidit et commota est terra [5] montes sicut cera fluxerunt a facie Domini; a facie Domini omnis terrae

[6] adnuntiaverunt caeli iustitiam eius et viderunt omnes populi gloriam eius [7] confundantur omnes qui adorant sculptilia qui gloriantur in simulacris suis adorate eum omnes angeli eius [8] audivit et laetata est Sion et exultaverunt filiae Iudaeae propter iudicia tua Domine [9] quoniam tu Dominus Altissimus super omnem terram nimis superexaltatus es super omnes deos [10] qui diligitis Dominum odite malum custodit animas sanctorum suorum de manu peccatoris liberabit eos

[11] lux orta est iusto et rectis corde laetitia [12] laetamini iusti in Domino et confitemini memoriae sanctificationis eius

97[1] psalmus David cantate Domino canticum novum quoniam mirabilia fecit salvavit sibi dextera eius et brachium sanctum eius [2] notum fecit Dominus salutare suum in conspectu gentium revelavit iustitiam suam [3] recordatus est misericordiae suae et veritatem suam domui Israhel viderunt omnes termini terrae salutare Dei nostri [4] iubilate Domino omnis terra cantate et exultate et psallite [5] psallite Domino in cithara in cithara et 40r*('abec' penned on the top of this folio)* voce psalmi

[6] in tubis ductilibus et voce tubae corneae iubilate in conspectu regis Domini [7] moveatur mare et plenitudo eius orbis terrarum et qui habitant in eo [8] flummina plaudent manu simul montes exultabunt [9] in conspectu Domini quoniam venit iudicare terram iudicabit orbem terrarum in iustitia et populos in aequitate∴

98[1] psalmus David Dominus regnavit irascanter populi qui sedet super cherubin moveatur terra [2] Dominus in Sion magnus et excelsus est super omnes populos [3] confiteantur nomini tuo magno quoniam terribile et sanctum est [4] et honor regis iudicium diligit tu parasti directiones iudicium et iustitiam in Iacob tu fecisti [5] exaltate Dominum Deum nostrum et adorate scabillum pedum eius quoniam sanctum est

[6] Moses et Aaron in sacerdotibus eius et Samuhel inter eos qui invocant nomen eius invocabant Dominum et ipse exaudiebat illos [7] in columna nubis loquebatur ad eos custodiebant testimonia eius et praeceptum quod dedit illis [8] Domine Deus noster tu exaudiebas illos Deus tu propitius fuisti eis et ulciscens in omnes adinventiones eorum [9] exaltate Dominum Deum nostrum et adorate in monte sancto eius quoniam sanctus Dominus Deus noster

99—No text extant

100[1] David psalmus misericordiam et iudicium cantabo tibi Domine psallam [2] et intellegam in via inmaculata quando venies ad me perambulabam in innocentia cordis mei in medio domus meae [3] non proponebam ante oculos meos rem iniustam facientes praevaricationes odivi non adhesit 40v mihi [4] cor pravum declinante a me maligno non cognoscebam [5] detrahentem secreto proximo suo hunc persequebarsuperbo oculo et insatiabili corde cum hoc non edebam

[6] oculi mei ad fideles terrae ut sederent mecum ambulans in via inmaculata hic mihi ministrabat [7] non habita in medio domus meae qui facit superbiam qui loquitur iniqua non direxit in conspectu oculorum meorum [8] in matutino interficiebam omnes pecatores terrae ut disperderem de civitate Domini omnes operantes iniquitatem

101 [1] oratio pauperis cum anxius fuerit et coram Domino effuderit precem suam [2] Domine exaudi orationem meam et clamor meus ad te veniat [3] non avertas faciem tuam a me in quacumque die tribulor inclina ad me aurem tuam in quacumque die invocavero te velociter exaudi me [4] quia defecerunt sicut fumus dies mei et ossa mea sicut gremium aruerunt [5] percussum est ut faenum et aruit cor meum quia oblitus sum comedere panem meum

[6] a voce gemitus mei adhesit os meum carni meae [7] similis factus sum pelicano solitudinis factus sum sicut nycticorax in domicilio [8] vigilavi et factus sum sicut passer solitarius in tecto [9] tota die exprobrabant mihi inimici mei et qui laudabant me adversus me iurabant [10] quia cinerem tamquam panem manducavi et poculum meum cum fletu miscebam

[11] a facie irae et indignationis tuae quia elevans adlisisti me [12] dies mei sicut umbra declinaverunt et ego sicut faenum arui [13] tu autem Domine in aeternum permanes 41r et memoriale tuum in generationem et generationem [14] tu exsurgens missereberis Sion quia tempus miserendi eius quia venit tempus [15] quoniam placuerunt servis tuis lapides eius et terrae eius miserebuntur

[16] et timebunt gentes nomen Domini et omnes reges terrae gloriam tuam∴ [17] quia aedificauit Dominus Sion et videvit in gloria sua [18] respexit in orationem humilium et non sprevit precem eorum [19] screbantur haec in generationem alteram et populus qui creabitur laudrait Dominum [20] quia prospexit de excelso sancto suo Dominus de caelo in terram aspexit

[21] ut audiret gemitum conpetitorum ut solvat filios interemptorum [22] ut adnuntiet in Sion nomen Domini et laudem suam in Hierusalem [23] in conveniendo populos in unum et reges ut serviant Domino [24] respondit ei in via virtutis suae paucitatem dierum meorum nuntia mihi [25] ne revoces me in dimidio dierum meorum in generationem et generationem anni tui

[26] initio tu Domine terram fundasti et opera manuum tuarum sunt caeli [27] ipsi peribunt tu autem permanes et omnes sicut vestimentum veterescent et sicut opertorium mutabis eos et mutabuntur [28] tu autem idem ipse es et anni tui non deficient [29] filii servorum tuorum habitabunt et semen eorum in saeculum dirigetur

102 [1] ipsi David benedic anima mea Domino et omnia quae intra me sunt nomini sancto eius [2] benedic anima mea Domino et noli oblivisci omnes retributiones eius [3] qui propitiatur omnibus iniquitatibus tuis qui sanat omnes infirmitates tuas [4] qui redimit de interitu vitam tuam qui coronat te in misericordia et miserationibus [5] qui replet in bonis desiderium tuum renovabitur ut aquilae iuventus tua

[6] faciens misericordias Dominus et iudicium omnibus 41v iniuriam patientibus [7] notas fecit vias suas Mosi filiis Israhel voluntates suas∴ [8] misserator et misericors Dominus longanimis et multum missericors [9] non in perpetuum ~~irascetur neque in aeternum~~ *(eye skip 'um')* comminabitur [10] non secundum peccata nostra fecit nobiss nec secundum iniustitias nostras retribuit nobis

[11] quoniam secundum altitudinem caeli a terra corroboravit misericordiam suam super timentes se∴ [12] quantum distat ortus ab occidente longe fecit a nobis iniquitates nostras [13] quomodo miseretur pater filiorum misertus est Dominus timentibus se [14] quoniam ipse cognovit figmentum nostrum recordatus est quoniam pulvis sumus [15] homo sicut faenum dies eius tamquam flos agri sic efflorebit

Identified psalm text from the Vulgate

[16] quoniam spiritus pertransivit in illo et non
subsistet et non cognoscet amplius locum suum
[17] misericordia autem Domini ab aeterno
et usque in aeternum super timentes eum et
iustitia illius in filios filiorum [18] his qui servant
testamentum eius et memores sunt mandatorum
ipsius ad faciendum ea [19] Dominus in caelo
paravit sedem suam et regnum ipsius omnibus
dominabitur [20] benedicite Domino angeli
eius potentes virtute facientes verbum illius ad
audiendam vocem sermonum eius

[21] benedicite Domino omnes virtutes eius
ministri eius qui facitis voluntatem eius [22]
benedicite Domino omnia opera eius in omni loco
dominationis ipsius benedic anima mea Domino

103[1] ipsi David benedic anima mea Domino
Domine Deus meus magnificatus es vehementer
confessionem et decorem induisti [2] amictus
lumine sicut vestimento extendens caelum sicut
pellem [3] qui tegis in aquis superiora eius qui
ponis nubem ascensum tuum qui ambulas super
pinnas ventorum [4] qui facis angelos tuos spiritus
et ministros tuos ignem urentem **[5]** qui fundasti
terram super stabilitatem suam non inclinabitur in
saeculum 42r **saeculi**

[6] abyssus sicut vestimentum amictus eius
super **montes stab**unt **aquae [7] ab in**crepatione
tua fugi**ent a voce ton**itrui tui formidabunt **[8]**
ascendunt **montes et d**escendunt campi in locum
quem fun**dasti eis [9]** terminum posuisti quem non
transgredientur **neque conve**rtentur operire terram
[10] qui emittis **fontes** in convallibus inter medium
montium pertransibunt aquae

[11] potabunt omnes bestiae agri expectabunt
onagri in siti sua [12] super ea volucres caeli
habitabunt de medio petrarum dabunt vocem
[13] rigans montes de superioribus suis de fructu
operum tuorum satiabitur terra [14] producens
faenum iumentis et herbam servituti hominum ut
educas panem de terra [15] et vinum laetificat cor
hominis ut exhilaret faciem in oleo et panis cor
hominis confirmat

[16] saturabuntur ligna campi et cedri Libani
quas plantavit [17] illic passeres nidificabunt
erodii domus dux est eorum [18] montes excelsi
cervis petra refugium erinaciis [19] fecit lunam in
tempora sol cognovit occasum suum [20] posuisti
tenebras et facta est nox in ipsa pertransibunt
omnes bestiae silvae

[21] catuli leonum rugientes ut rapiant et quaerant
a Deo escam sibi [22] ortus est sol et congregati
sunt et in cubilibus suis conlocabuntur [23]
exibit homo ad opus suum et ad operationem
suam usque ad vesperum [24] quam magnificata
sunt opera tua Domine omnia in sapientia fecisti
impleta est terra possessione tua [25] hoc mare
magnum et spatiosum manibus; illic reptilia
quorum non est numerus animalia pusilla cum
magnis

[26] illic naves pertransibunt draco iste quem
formasti ad inludendum ei [27] omnia a te
expectant ut des illis escam in tempore [28] dante
te illis colligent aperiente te manum tuam omnia
implebuntur bonitate **[29]** avertente autem te
faciem 42v turb**abuntur ~~au~~feres spiritum eorum**
et deficient et in pulverem suum reverten**tur** [30]
emittes spiritum tuum et creabuntur et renovabis
faciem terrae

[31] sit gloria Domini in saeculum laetabitur
Dominus in operibus suis **[32]** qui respicit terram
et facit eam **tremere** qui tangit montes et fumigant
[33] cantabo **Domino in** vita mea psallam Deo meo
quamdiu sum [34] iucundum sit ei eloquium meum
ego vero delectabor in Domino [35] deficiant
peccatores a terra et iniqui ita ut non sint benedic
anima mea Domino

104[1] alleluia confitemini Domino et invocate
nomen eius adnuntiate inter gentes opera eius [2]
cantate ei et psallite ei narrate omnia mirabilia
eius [3] laudamini in nomine sancto eius laetetur
cor quaerentium Dominum [4] quaerite Dominum
et confirmamini quaerite faciem eius semper [5]
mementote mirabilium eius quae fecit prodigia eius
et iudicia oris eius

[6] semen Abraham servi eius filii Iacob electi eius [7] ipse Dominus Deus noster in universa terra iudicia eius [8] memor fuit in saeculum testamenti sui verbi quod mandavit in mille generationes [9] quod disposuit ad Abraham et iuramenti sui ad Isaac [10] et statuit illud Iacob in praeceptum et Israhel in testamentum aeternum

[11] dicens tibi dabo terram Chanaan funiculum hereditatis vestrae [12] cum essent numero breves paucissimos et incolas eius [13] et pertransierunt de gente in gentem et de regno ad populum alterum [14] non reliquit hominem nocere eis et corripuit pro eis reges [15] nolite tangere christos meos et in prophetis meis nolite malignari

[16] et vocavit famem super terram omne firmamentum panis contrivit [17] misit ante eos virum in servum venundatus est Ioseph [18] humiliaverunt in conpedibus pedes eius ferrum pertransiit anima eius [19] donec veniret verbum eius eloquium Domini inflammavit eum [20] misit rex et solvit eum princeps 43r populorum et dimisit eum

[21] constituit eum dominum domus suae et principem omnis possessionis suae [22] ut erudiret principes eius sicut semet ipsum et senes eius prudentiam doceret [23] et intravit Israhel in Aegyptumet Iacob accola fuit in terra Cham [24] et auxit populum eius vehementer et firmavit eum super inimicos eius [25] convertit cor eorum ut odirent populum eius ut dolum facerent in servos eius

[26] misit Mosen servum suum Aaron quem elegit ipsum [27] posuit in eis verba signorum suorum et prodigiorum in terra Cham [28] misit tenebras et obscuravit et non exacerbavit sermones suos [29] convertit aquas eorum in sanguinem et occidit pisces eorum [30] dedit terra eorum ranas in penetrabilibus regum ipsorum

[31] dixit et venit cynomia et scinifes in omnibus finibus eorum [32] posuit pluvias eorum grandinem ignem conburentem in terra ipsorum [33] et percussit vineas eorum et ficulneas eorum et contrivit lignum finium eorum [34] dixit et venit lucusta et bruchus cuius non erat numerus [35] et comedit omne faenum in terra eorum et comedit omnem fructum terrae eorum

[36] et percussit omne primogenitum in terra eorum primitias omnis laboris eorum [37] et eduxit eos in argento et auro et non erat in tribubus eorum infirmus [38] laetata est Aegyptus in profectione eorum quia incubuit timor eorum super eos [39] expandit nubem in protectionem eorum et ignem ut luceret eis per noctem [40] petierunt et venit coturnix et panem caeli saturavit eos

[41] disrupit petram et fluxerunt aquae abierunt in sicco flumina [42] quoniam memor fuit verbi sancti sui quod habuit ad Abraham puerum suum [43] et eduxit populum suum in exultatione et; electos suos in laetitia [44] et dedit illis regiones gentium et labores populorum possederunt [45] ut custodiant iustificationes eius et legem eius requirant

105[1] alleluia 43v confitemini Domino quoniam bonus quoniam in saeculum misericordia eius [2] quis loquetur potentias Domini auditas faciet omnes laudes eius [3] beati qui custodiunt iudicium et faciunt iustitiam in omni tempore [4] memento nostri Domine in beneplacito populi tui visita nos in salutari tuo [5] ad videndum in bonitate electorum tuorum ad laetandum in laetitia gentis tuae et lauderis cum hereditate tua

[6] peccavimus cum patribus nostris iniuste egimus iniquitatem fecimus [7] patres nostri in Aegypto non intellexerunt mirabilia tua non fuerunt memores multitudinis misericordiae tuae et inritaverunt ascendentes in mare mare; Rubrum [8] et salvavit eos propter nomen suum ut notam faceret potentiam suam [9] et increpuit mare Rubrum et exsiccatum est et deduxit eos in abyssis sicut in deserto [10] et salvavit eos de manu odientium et redemit eos de manu inimici

[11] et operuit aqua tribulantes eos unus ex eis non remansit [12] et crediderunt in verbis eius et

laudaverunt laudem eius [13] cito fecerunt obliti
sunt operum eius non sustinuerunt consilium eius
[14] et concupierunt concupiscentiam in deserto
et temptaverunt Deum in inaquoso [15] et dedit
eis petitionem ipsorum et misit saturitatem in
anima eorum

[16] et inritaverunt Mosen in castris Aaron
sanctum Domini [17] aperta est terra et degluttivit
Dathan et operuit super congregationem Abiron
[18] et exarsit ignis in synagoga eorum flamma
conbusit peccatores [19] et fecerunt vitulum
in Choreb et adoraverunt sculptile [20] et
mutaverunt gloriam suam in similitudine vituli
comedentis faenum

[21] obliti sunt Deum 44r ~~qui~~ salvavit eos qui
fecit magnalia in Aegypto [22] mirabilia in terra
Cham terribilia in mari Rubro [23] et dixit ut
disperderet eos si non Moses electus eius stetisset
in confractione in conspectu eius ut averteret iram
eius ne disperderet eos [24] et pro nihilo habuerunt
terram desiderabilem non crediderunt verbo eius
[25] et murmurabant in tabernaculis suis non
exaudierunt vocem Domini

[26] et elevavit manum suam super eos ut
prosterneret eos in deserto [27] et ut deiceret
semen eorum in nationibus et dispergeret eos
in regionibus [28] et initiati sunt Beelphegor
et comederunt sacrificia mortuorum [29] et
inritaverunt eum in adinventionibus suis et
multiplicata est in eis ruina [30] et stetit Finees et
placavit et cessavit quassatio

[31] et reputatum est ei in iustitiam in generatione
et generationem usque in sempiternum [32] et
inritaverunt ad aquam Contradictionis et vexatus
est Moses propter eos [33] quia exacerbaverunt
spiritum eius et distinxit in labiis suis [34] non
disperdiderunt gentes quas dixit Dominus illis
[35] et commixti sunt inter gentes et didicerunt
opera eorum

[36] et servierunt sculptilibus eorum et factum
est illis in scandalum [37] et immolaverunt filios
suos et filias suas daemoniis [38] et effuderunt
sanguinem innocentem sanguinem filiorum
suorum et filiarum suarum; quas sacrificaverunt
sculptilibus Chanaan et interfecta est terra in
sanguinibus [39] et contaminata est in operibus
eorum et fornicati sunt in adinventionibus suis
[40] et iratus est furore Dominus in populo suo et
abominatus est hereditatem suam

[41] et tradidit eos in manus 44v gentium et
dominati sunt eorum qui oderant eos [42] et
tribulaverunt eos inimici eorum et humiliati sunt
sub manibus eorum [43] saepe liberavit eos ∴ ipse
~~autem~~ exacerbaverunt eum in consilio suo et
humiliati sunt in iniquitatibus suis [44] et vidit
cum tribularentur et audiret orationem eorum
[45] et memor fuit testamenti sui et paenituit eum
secundum multitudinem misericordiae suae

[46] et dedit eos in misericordias in conspectu
omnium qui ceperant eos [47] salvos fac nos
Domine Deus noster et congrega nos de nationibus
ut confiteamur nomini tuo sancto et gloriemur in
laude tua [48] benedictus Dominus Deus Israhel
a saeculo et usque in saeculum et dicet omnis
populus fiat fiat

106[1] alleluia confitemini Domino quoniam
bonus quoniam in saeculum misericordia eius [2]
dicant qui redempti sunt a Domino quos redemit
de manu inimici de regionibus congregavit eos [3]
a solis ortu et occasu et ab aquilone et mari [4]
erraverunt in solitudine in inaquoso viam civitatis
habitaculi non invenerunt [5] esurientes et sitientes
anima eorum in ipsis defecit

[6] et clamaverunt ad Dominum cum tribularentur
et de necessitatibus eorum eripuit eos [7] et
deduxit eos in viam rectam ut irent in civitatem
habitationis [8] confiteantur Domino misericordiae
eius et mirabilia eius filiis hominum [9] quia
satiavit animam inanem et animam esurientem
satiavit bonis [10] sedentes in tenebris et umbra
mortis vinctos in mendicitate et ferro

[11] quia exacerbaverunt eloquia Dei et consilium
Altissimi inritaverunt [12] et humiliatum est in
laboribus cor eorum infirmati sunt nec fuit qui

adiuvaret [13] et clamaverunt ad Dominum cum
tribularentur et de necessitatibus eorum liberavit
eos [14] et eduxit eos de tenebris et umbra mortis
et vincula eorum disrupit [15] confiteantur
Domino misericordiae eius et mirabilia eius filiis
hominum

[16] quia contrivit portas aereas et vectes ferreos
confregit [17] suscepit eos de via iniquitatis
eorum propter iniustitias enim suas humiliati
sunt [18] omnem escam abominata est anima
eorum et adpropinquaverunt usque ad 45r portas
mortis∴ [19] et clamaverunt ad Dominum cum
tribularentur et de necessitatibus eorum liberavit
eos [20] misit verbum suum et sanavit eos et eripuit
eos de interitionibus eorum

[21] confiteantur Domino misericordiae eius et
mirabilia eius filiis hominum [22] et sacrificent
sacrificium laudis et adnuntient opera eius in
exultatione [23] qui descendunt mare in navibus
facientes operationem in aquis multis [24] ipsi
viderunt opera Domini et mirabilia eius in
profundo [25] dixit et stetit spiritus procellae et
exaltati sunt fluctus eius

[26] ascendunt usque ad caelos et descendunt
usque ad abyssos anima eorum in malis tabescebat
[27] turbati sunt et moti sunt sicut ebrius et omnis
sapientia eorum devorata est [28] et clamaverunt
ad Dominum cum tribularentur et de necessitatibus
eorum eduxit eos [29] et statuit procellam eius; in
auram et siluerunt fluctus eius [30] et laetati sunt
quia siluerunt et deduxit eos in portum voluntatis
eorum

[31] confiteantur Domino misericordiae eius et
mirabilia eius filiis hominum [32] exaltent eum in
ecclesia plebis et in cathedra seniorum laudent eum
[33] posuit flumina in desertum et exitus aquarum
in sitim [34] terram fructiferam in salsuginem a
malitia inhabitantium in ea [35] posuit desertum
in stagna aquarum et terram sine aqua in exitus
aquarum

[36] et conlocavit illic esurientes et constituerunt
civitatem habitationis [37] et seminaverunt agros et
plantaverunt vineas et fecerunt fructum nativitatis
[38] et benedixit eis et multiplicati sunt nimis et
iumenta eorum non minoravit [39] et pauci facti
sunt et vexati sunt a tribulatione malorum et
dolore [40] effusa est contemptio super principes et
errare fecit eos in invio et non in via

[41] et adiuvit pauperem de inopia et posuit sicut
oves familias [42] videbunt recti et laetabuntur
et omnis iniquitas oppilabit os suum [43]
quis sapiens et custodiet haec et intellegent
misericordias Domini

107[1] canticum psalmi David [2] 45v paratum
cor meum Deus paratum cor meum cantabo et
psallam in gloria mea [3] exsurge psalterium et
cithara exsurgam dilucelo [4] confitebor tibi in
populis Domine et psallam tibi in nationibus [5]
quia magna super caelos misericordia tua et usque
ad nubes veritas tua

[6] exaltare super caelos Deus et super omnem
terram gloria tua [7] ut liberentur dilecti tui salvum
fac dextera tua et exaudi me [8] Deus locutus
est in sancto suo exaltabor et dividam Sicima et
convallem tabernaculorum dimetiar [9] meus est
Galaad et meus est Manasse et Effraim susceptio
capitis mei Iuda rex meus [10] Moab lebes spei
meae in Idumeam extendam calciamentum meum
mihi alienigenae amici facti sunt

[11] quis deducet me in civitatem munitam
quis deducet me usque in Idumeam [12] nonne
tu Deus qui reppulisti nos et non exibis Deus
in virtutibus nostris [13] da nobis auxilium de
tribulatione quia vana salus hominis [14] in Deo
faciemus virtutem et ipse ad nihilum deducet
inimicos nostros

108[1] in finem David psalmus [2] Deus laudem
meam ne tacueris quia os peccatoris et os dolosi
super me apertum est [3] locuti sunt adversum
me lingua dolosa et sermonibus odii circuierunt
me et expugnaverunt me gratis [4] pro eo ut me
diligerent detrahebant mihi ego autem orabam
[5] et posuerunt adversus me mala pro bonis et
odium pro dilectione mea

[6] constitue super eum peccatorem et diabulus stet a dextris eius [7] cum iudicatur exeat condemnatus et oratio eius fiat in peccatum [8] fiant dies eius pauci et episcopatum eius accipiat alter [9] fiant filii eius orfani et uxor eius vidua [10] nutantes transferantur filii eius et mendicent eiciantur de habitationibus suis

[11] scrutetur fenerator omnem 46r substantiam eius et diripiant alieni labores eius [12] non sit illi adiutor nec sit qui misereatur pupillis eius [13] fiant nati eius in interitum in generatione una deleatur nomen eius [14] in memoriam redeat iniquitas patrum eius in conspectu Domini et peccatum matris eius non deleatur [15] fiant contra Dominum semper et dispereat de terra memoria eorum

[16] pro eo quod non est recordatus facere misericordiam [17] et persecutus est hominem inopem et mendicum et conpunctum corde mortificare [18] et dilexit maledictionem et veniet ei et noluit benedictionem et elongabitur ab eo et induit maledictionem sicut vestimentum et intravit sicut aqua in interiora eius et sicut oleum in ossibus eius [19] fiat ei sicut vestimentum quo operitur et sicut zona qua semper praecingitur [20] hoc opus eorum qui detrahunt mihi apud Dominum et qui loquuntur mala adversus animam meam

[21] et tu Domine Domine fac mecum propter nomen tuum quia suavis misericordia tua libera me [22] quia egenus et pauper ego sum et cor meum turbatum est intra me [23] sicut umbra cum declinat ablatus sum excussus sum sicut lucustae [24] genua mea infirmata sunt a ieiunio et caro mea inmutata est propter oleum [25] et ego factus sum obprobrium illis viderunt me moverunt capita sua

[26] adiuva me Domine Deus meus salvum fac me secundum misericordiam tuam [27] et sciant quia manus tua haec tu Domine fecisti eam [28] maledicent illi et tu benedices qui insurgunt in me confundantur servus autem tuus laetabitur [29] induantur qui detrahunt mihi pudore et operiantur sicut deploide confusione sua [30] confitebor Domino nimis in ore meo et in medio multorum laudabo eum

[31] quia adstetit a dextris pauperis ut salvam faceret a persequentibus animam meam

109[1] David psalmus dixit Dominus 46v Domino ~~meo~~ sede a dextris meis donec ponam inimicos tuos scabillum pedum tuorum [2] virgam virtutis tuae emittet Dominus ex Sion dominare in medio inimicorum tuorum [3] tecum principium in die virtutis tuae in splendoribus sanctorum ex utero ante luciferum genui te [4] iuravit Dominus et non paenitebit eum tu es sacerdos in aeternum secundum ordinem Melchisedech [5] Dominus a dextris tuis confregit in die irae suae reges

[6] iudicabit in nationibus implebit cadavera conquassabit capita in terra multorum [7] de torrente in via bibet propterea exaltabit caput

110—No text extant

111—No text extant

112—No text extant

113—No text extant

114—No text extant

115—No text extant

116—No text extant

117—No text extant

118[1] alleluia aleph beati inmaculati in via qui ambulant in lege Domini [2] beati qui scrutantur testimonia eius in toto corde exquirent eum [3] non enim qui operantur iniquitatem in viis eius ambulaverunt [4] tu mandasti mandata tua custodire nimis [5] utinam dirigantur viae meae ad custodiendas iustificationes tuas

[6] tunc non confundar cum perspexero in omnibus mandatis tuis [7] confitebor tibi in

directione cordis in eo quod didici iudicia iustitiae tuae [8] iustificationes tuas custodiam non me derelinquas usquequaque [9] beth in quo corriget adulescentior viam suam in custodiendo sermones tuos [10] in toto corde meo exquisivi te non repellas me a mandatis tuis

[11] in corde meo abscondi eloquia tua ut non peccem tibi [12] benedictus es Domine doce me iustificationes tuas [13] in labiis meis pronuntiavi omnia iudicia oris tui [14] in via testimoniorum tuorum delectatus sum sicut in omnibus divitiis [15] in mandatis tuis exercebor et considerabo vias tuas

[16] in iustificationibus tuis meditabor non obliviscar sermones tuos [17] gimel retribue servo tuo vivifica me et custodiam sermones tuos [18] revela oculos meos et considerabo mirabilia de lege tua [19] incola ego sum in terra non abscondas a me mandata tua [20] concupivit anima mea desiderare iustificationes tuas in omni tempore

[21] increpasti superbos maledicti qui declinant a mandatis tuis [22] aufer a me obprobrium et contemptum quia testimonia tua exquisivi [23] etenim sederunt principes et adversum me loquebantur servus autem tuus exercebatur in iustificationibus tuis [24] nam et testimonia tua meditatio mea et consilium meum iustificationes tuae [25] deleth adhesit pavimento anima mea vivifica me secundum verbum tuum

[26] vias meas enuntiavi et exaudisti me doce me iustificationes tuas [27] viam iustificationum tuarum instrue me et exercebor in mirabilibus tuis [28] dormitavit anima mea prae taedio confirma me in verbis tuis [29] viam iniquitatis amove a me et lege tua miserere mei [30] viam veritatis elegi iudicia tua non sum oblitus

[31] adhesi testimoniis tuis Domine noli me confundere [32] viam mandatorum tuorum cucurri cum dilatasti cor meum [33] he legem pone mihi Domine viam iustificationum tuarum et exquiram eam semper [34] da mihi intellectum et scrutabor legem tuam et custodiam illam in toto corde meo

[35] deduc me in semita mandatorum tuorum quia ipsam volui

[36] inclina cor meum in testimonia tua et non in avaritiam [37] averte oculos meos ne videant vanitatem in via tua vivifica me [38] statue servo tuo eloquium tuum in timore tuo [39] amputa obprobrium meum quod suspicatus sum quia iudicia tua iucunda [40] ecce concupivi mandata tua in aequitate tua vivifica me

[41] vav et veniat super me misericordia tua Domine salutare tuum secundum eloquium tuum [42] et respondebo exprobrantibus mihi verbum quia speravi in sermonibus tuis [43] et ne auferas de ore meo verbum veritatis usquequaque quia in iudiciis tuis supersperavi [44] et custodiam legem tuam semper in saeculum et in saeculum saeculi [45] et ambulabam in latitudine quia mandata tua exquisivi

[46] et loquebar in testimoniis tuis in conspectu regum et non confundebar [47] et meditabar in mandatis tuis quae dilexi [48] et levavi manus meas ad mandata quae dilexi et exercebar in iustificationibus tuis [49] zai memor esto verbi tui servo tuo in quo mihi spem dedisti [50] haec me consolata est in humilitate mea quia eloquium tuum vivificavit me

[51] superbi inique agebant usquequaque a lege autem tua non declinavi [52] memor fui iudiciorum tuorum a saeculo Domine et consolatus sum [53] defectio tenuit me prae peccatoribus derelinquentibus legem tuam [54] cantabiles mihi erant iustificationes tuae in loco peregrinationis meae [55] memor fui in nocte nominis tui Domine et custodivi legem tuam

[56] haec facta est mihi quia iustificationes tuas exquisivi [57] heth portio mea Dominus dixi custodire legem tuam [58] deprecatus sum faciem tuam in toto corde meo miserere mei secundum eloquium tuum [59] cogitavi vias meas et avertisti pedes meos in testimonia tua [60] paratus sum et non sum turbatus ut custodiam mandata tua

Identified psalm text from the Vulgate

[61] funes peccatorum circumplexi sunt me et legem tuam non sum oblitus [62] media nocte surgebam ad confitendum tibi super iudicia iustificationis tuae [63] particeps ego sum omnium timentium te et custodientium mandata tua [64] misericordia Domini plena est terra iustificationes tuas doce me [65] teth bonitatem fecisti cum servo tuo Domine secundum verbum tuum

[66] bonitatem et disciplinam et scientiam doce me quia mandatis tuis credidi [67] priusquam humiliarer ego deliqui propterea eloquium tuum custodivi [68] bonus es tu et in bonitate tua doce me iustificationes tuas [69] multiplicata est super me iniquitas superborum ego autem in toto corde scrutabor mandata tua [70] coagulatum est sicut lac cor eorum ego vero legem tuam meditatus sum

[71] bonum mihi quia humiliasti me ut discam iustificationes tuas [72] bonum mihi lex oris tui super milia auri et argenti [73] ioth manus tuae fecerunt me et plasmaverunt me da mihi intellectum et discam mandata tua [74] qui timent te videbunt me et laetabuntur quia in verba tua supersperavi [75] cognovi Domine quia aequitas iudicia tua et veritate humiliasti me

[76] fiat misericordia tua ut consoletur me secundum eloquium tuum servo tuo [77] veniant mihi miserationes tuae et vivam quia lex tua meditatio mea est [78] confundantur superbi quia iniuste iniquitatem fecerunt in me ego autem exercebor in mandatis tuis [79] convertantur mihi timentes te et qui noverunt testimonia tua [80] fiat cor meum inmaculatum in iustificationibus tuis ut non confundar

[81] caf defecit in salutare tuum anima mea in verbum tuum supersperavi [82] defecerunt oculi mei in eloquium tuum dicentes quando consolaberis me [83] quia factus sum sicut uter in pruina iustificationes tuas non sum oblitus [84] quot sunt dies servo tuo quando facies de persequentibus me iudicium [85] narraverunt mihi iniqui fabulationes sed non ut lex tua

[86] omnia mandata tua veritas inique persecuti sunt me adiuva me [87] paulo minus consummaverunt me in terra ego autem non dereliqui mandata tua [88] secundum misericordiam tuam vivifica me et custodiam testimonia oris tui [89] lamed in aeternum Domine verbum tuum permanet in caelo [90] in generationem et generationem veritas tua fundasti terram et permanet

[91] ordinatione tua perseverat dies quoniam omnia serviunt tibi [92] nisi quod lex tua meditatio mea est tunc forte perissem in humilitate mea [93] in aeternum non obliviscar iustificationes tuas quia in ipsis vivificasti me [94] tuus sum ego salvum me fac quoniam iustificationes tuas exquisivi [95] me expectaverunt peccatores ut perderent me testimonia tua 51r intellexi

[96] omni consummationi vidi finem latum mandatum tuum nimis [97] mem quomodo dilexi legem tuam tota die meditatio mea est [98] super inimicos meos prudentem me fecisti mandato tuo quia in aeternum mihi est [99] super omnes docentes me intellexi quia testimonia tua meditatio mea est [100] super senes intellexi quia mandata tua quaesivi

[101] ab omni via mala prohibui pedes meos ut custodiam verba tua [102] a iudiciis tuis non declinavi quia tu legem posuisti mihi [103] quam dulcia faucibus meis eloquia tua super mel ori meo [104] a mandatis tuis intellexi propterea odivi omnem viam iniquitatis [105] nun lucerna pedibus meis verbum tuum et lumen semitis meis

[106] iuravi et statui custodire iudicia iustitiae tuae [107] humiliatus sum usquequaque Domine vivifica me secundum verbum tuum [108] voluntaria oris mei beneplacita fac Domine et iudicia tua doce me [109] anima mea in manibus meis semper et legem tuam non sum oblitus [110] posuerunt peccatores laqueum mihi et de mandatis tuis non erravi

[111] hereditate adquisivi testimonia tua in aeternum quia exultatio cordis mei sunt [112]

inclinavi cor meum ad faciendas iustificationes tuas in aeternum propter retributionem [113] samech iniquos odio habui et legem tuam dilexi [114] adiutor meus et susceptor meus es tu in verbum tuum supersperavi [115] declinate a me maligni et scrutabor mandata Dei mei

[116] suscipe me secundum eloquium tuum et vivam et non confundas me ab expectatione mea [117] adiuva me et salvus ero et 51v meditabor in iustificationibus tuis semper [118] sprevisti omnes discedentes a iustitiis tuis quia iniusta cogitatio eorum [119] praevaricantes reputavi omnes peccatores terrae ideo dilexi testimonia tua [120] confige timore tuo carnes meas a iudiciis enim; tuis timui

[121] ain feci iudicium et iustitiam non tradas me calumniantibus me [122] suscipe servum tuum in bonum non calumnientur me superbi [123] oculi mei defecerunt in salutare tuum et in eloquium iustitiae tuae [124] fac cum servo tuo secundum misericordiam tuam et iustificationes tuas doce me [125] servus tuus sum ego da mihi intellectum et sciam testimonia tua

[126] tempus faciendi Domino dissipaverunt legem tuam [127] ideo dilexi mandata tua super aurum et topazion [128] propterea ad omnia mandata tua dirigebar omnem viam iniquam odio habui [129] fe mirabilia testimonia tua ideo scrutata est ea anima mea [130] declaratio sermonum tuorum inluminat et intellectum dat parvulis

[131] os meum aperui et adtraxi spiritum quia mandata tua desiderabam [132] aspice in me et miserere mei secundum iudicium diligentium nomen tuum [133] gressus meos dirige secundum eloquium tuum et non dominetur mei omnis iniustitia [134] redime me a calumniis hominum et custodiam mandata tua [135] faciem tuam inlumina super 52r servum tuum et doce me iustificationes tuas

[136] exitus aquarum deduxerunt oculi mei quia non custodierunt legemtuam∴ iustiam test...*(inserted from net line)* [137] SADE IUstus Domine et rectum iudicium tuum [138] mandasti iustitiam testimonia tua et veritatem tuam nimis [139] tabescere me fecit zelus meus quia obliti sunt verba tua inimici mei [140] ignitum eloquium tuum vehimenter et servus tuus dilexit illud

[141] adulescentulus sum ego et contemptus iustificationes tuas non sum oblitus [142] iustitia tua iustitia in aeternum et lex tua veritas [143] tribulatio et angustia invenerunt me mandata tua meditatio mea [144] aequitas testimonia tua in aeternum intellectum da mihi et vivam [145] cof clamavi in toto corde exaudi me Domine iustificationes tuas requiram

[146] clamavi te salvum me fac et custodiam mandata tua [147] praeveni in maturitate et clamavi in verba tua supersperavi [148] praevenerunt oculi mei ad diluculum ut meditarer eloquia tua [149] vocem meam audi secundum misericordiam tuam Domine secundum iudicium tuum vivifica me [150] adpropinquaverunt persequentes me iniquitate a lege autem tua longe facti sunt

[151] prope es tu Domine et omnes viae tuae veritas [152] initio cognovi de testimoniis tuis quia in aeternum fundasti ea [153] res vide humilitatem meam et eripe me quia legem tuam non sum oblitus [154] iudica iudicium meum et redime me propter eloquium tuum vivifica me [155] longe a peccatoribus salus quia iustificationes tuas non exquisierunt

[156] misericordiae tuae multae Domine secundum iudicia tua vivifica me [157] multi qui persequuntur me et tribulant me a testimoniis tuis non declinavi [158] vidi praevaricantes et tabescebam quia eloquia tua non custodierunt [159] vide quoniam mandata tua dilexi Domine in misericordia tua vivifica me [160] principium verborum tuorum veritas et in 52v aeternum omnia iudicia iustitiae tuae

[161] sen principes persecuti sunt me gratis et a verbis tuis formidavit cor meum [162] laetabor ego super eloquia tua sicut qui invenit spolia

multa [163] iniquitatem odio habui et abominatus sum legem autem tuam dilexi [164] septies in die laudem dixi tibi super iudicia iustitiae tuae [165] pax multa diligentibus legem tuam et non est illis scandalum

[166] expectabam salutare tuum Domine et mandata tua dilexi [167] custodivit anima mea testimonia tua et dilexi ea vehementer [168] servavi mandata tua et testimonia tua quia omnes viae meae in conspectu tuo [169] thau adpropinquet deprecatio mea in conspectu tuo Domine iuxta eloquium tuum da mihi intellectum [170] intret postulatio mea in conspectu tuo secundum eloquium tuum eripe me

[171] eructabunt labia mea hymnum cum docueris me iustificationes tuas [172] pronuntiabit lingua mea eloquium tuum quia omnia mandata tua aequitas [173] fiat manus tua ut salvet me quoniam mandata tua elegi [174] concupivi salutare tuum Domine et lex tua meditatio mea [175] vivet anima mea et laudabit te et iudicia tua adiuvabunt me

[176] erravi sicut ovis quae periit quaere servum tuum quia mandata tua non sum oblitus

119—No text extant

120[1] canticum graduum levavi oculos meos in montes unde veniet auxilium 53r mihi [2] auxilium meum a Domino qui fecit caelum et terram [3] non det in commotionem pedem tuum neque dormitet qui custodit te [4] eccenon dormitabit neque dormiet qui custodit Israhel [5] Dominus custodit te Dominus ptectio tua super manum dexteram tuam

[6] per diem sol non uret te ~~neque~~*(different word here?)*luna per noctum [7] Dominus custodit te ab omni malo custodiat animam tuam Dominus [8] Dominus custodiat introitum tuum et exitum tuumex hoc nunc et usque in saeculum

121[1] laetatus sum in his quae dicta sunt mihi in domum Domini ibimus [2] stantes erant pedes nostri in atriis tuis Hierusalem [3] Hierusalem quae aedificatur ut civitas cuius participatio eius in id ipsum [4] illic enim ascenderunt tribus tribus Domini testimonium Israhel ad confitendum nomini Domini [5] quia illic sederunt sedes in iudicium sedes super domum David

[6] rogate quae ad pacem sunt Hierusalem et abundantia diligentibus te [7] fiat pax in virtute tua et abundantia in turribus tuis [8] propter fratres meos et proximos meos loquebar pacem de te [9] propter domum Domini Dei nostri quaesivi bona tibi

122—No text extant

123[1] canticum graduum huic David nisi quia Dominus erat in nobis dicat nunc Israhel [2] nisi quia Dominus erat in nobis cum exsurgerent in nos homines [3] forte vivos degluttissent nos cum irasceretur furor eorum in nos [4] forsitan aqua absorbuisset nos [5] torrentem pertransivit anima nostra forsitan 53v pertranssiset anima nostra aquam intolerabilem

[6] benedictus Dominus qui non dedit nos in captione dentibus eorum [7] anima nostra sicut passer erepta est de laqueo venantium laqueus contritus est et nos liberati sumus [8] adiutorium nostrum in nomine Domini qui fecit caelum et terram

124[1] qui confidunt in Domino sicut mons Sion non commovebitur in aeternum qui habitat [2] in Hierusalem montes in circuitu eius et Dominus in circuitu populi sui ex hoc nunc et usque in saeculum [3] quia non relinquet Dominus virgam peccatorum super sortem iustorum ut non extendant iusti ad iniquitatem manus suas [4] benefac Domine bonis et rectis corde [5] declinantes autem in obligationes adducet Dominus cum operantibus iniquitatem pax super Israhel

125—No text extant

126[1] canticum graduum Salomonis nisi Dominus aedificaverit domum in vanum

laboraverunt qui aedificant eam nisi Dominus
custodierit civitatem frustra vigilavit qui custodit
[2] vanum est vobis ante lucem surgere surgere
postquam sederitis qui manducatis panem doloris
cum dederit dilectis suis somnum [3] ecce hereditas
Domini filii mercis fructus ventris [4] 54r sicut
sagitae in manu potentis ita filii excussorum [5]
beatus vir qui impleuit desiderium suum ex ipsis
non confundentur cum loquentur inimiciss suis in
porta

127[1] beati omnes qui timent Dominum qui
ambulant in viis eius [2] ~~labors~~ manuum tuarum
qui manducabis beatus es et bene tibi erit [3] uxor
tuae sicut vitis abundans in lateribus domus tuae
fili tui sicut novella olivarum in circuitu mensae
tuae [4] ecce sic benedicetur homo qui timet
Dominum [5] benedicat te Dominus ex Sion et
videas bona Hierusalem omnibus diebus vitae tuae

[6] et videas filios filiorum tuorum pax super
Israhel

128—No text extant

129[1] canticum graduum de profundis clamavi
ad te Domine [2] Domine exaudi vocem meam
fiant aures tuae intendentes in vocem deprecationis
meae [3] si iniquitates observabis Domine Domine
quis sustinebit [4] quia apud te propitiatio est
propter legem tuam sustinui te Domine sustinuit
anima mea in verbum eius [5] speravit anima mea
in Domino

[6] a custodia 54v matudina usque ad noctem
speret Israhel in Domino [7] quia apud Dominum
missericordia et copiosa apud eum redemptio [8]
et ipse redemet Israhel ex omnibus iniquitatibus
eius :~

130[1] oculi mei neque ambulavi in magnis
exaltatum cormeum in Domino non est neque
elati sunt neque in mirabilibus super me [2] si non
humiliter sentiebam sed exaltavi animam meam
sicut ablactatum super matrem suam ita retributio
in anima mea [3] speret Israhel in Domino ex hoc
nunc et usque in saeculum:~

131[1] canticum graduum memento Domine
David et omnis mansuetudinis eius [2] sicut iuravit
Domino votum vovit Deo Iacob [3] si introiero
in tabernaculum domus meae si ascendero in
lectum strati mei [4] si dedero somnum oculis meis
et palpebris meis dormitationem [5] et requiem
temporibus meis donec inveniam locum Domino
tabernaculum Deo Iacob

[6] ecce audivimus eam in Efrata invenimus eam
in campis silvae [7] introibimus in tabernacula
eius adorabimus in loco ubi steterunt pedes eius
[8] surge Domine in requiem tuam tu et arca
sanctificationis tuae [9] sacerdotes tui induentur
iustitia et sancti tui exultabunt [10] propter David
servum tuum non avertas faciem christi tui

[11] iuravit Dominus David veritatem et non
frustrabit eum de fructu ventris tui ponam
super sedem tuam [12] si custodierint filii tui
testamentum meum et testimonia mea haec quae
docebo eos et filii eorum usque in saeculum
sedebunt super sedem tuam [13] quoniam elegit
Dominus Sion elegit eam in habitationem sibi [14]
haec requies mea in saeculum saeculi hic habitabo
quoniam elegi eam [15] viduam eius benedicens
benedicam pauperes eius saturabo panibus

[16] sacerdotes eius 55r induam salutari et sancti
eius exultatione exultabunt [17] illic producam
cornu David paravi lucernam christo meo [18]
inimicos eius induam confusione super ipsum
autem efflorebit sanctificatio mea: ~

132[1] ecce quam bonum et quam iucundum
habitare fratres in unum [2] sicut unguentum in
capite quod descendit in barbam barbam Aaron
quod descendit in ora vestimenti eius [3] sicut ros
Hermon qui descendit in montes Sion quoniam illic
mandavit Dominus benedictionem et vitam usque
in saeculum

133[1] ecce nunc benedicite Dominum omnes servi
Domini qui statis in domo Domini in atriis domus
Dei nostri; [2] in noctibus extollite manus vestras
in sancta et benedicite Domino [3] benedicat te
Dominus ex Sion qui fecit caelum et terram

134[1] alleluia laudate nomen Domini laudate servi Dominum [2] qui statis in domo Domini in atriis domus Dei nostri [3] laudate Dominum quia bonus Dominus psallite nomini eius quoniam suave [4] quoniam Iacob elegit sibi Dominus Israhel in possessionem sibi [5] quia ego cognovi quod magnus est Dominus et Deus noster prae omnibus diis

[6] omnia quae voluit Dominus fecit in caelo et in terra in mare et in omnibus abyssis [7] educens nubes ab extremo terrae fulgora in pluviam fecit qui producit ventos de thesauris suis [8] qui percussit primogenita Aegypti ab homine usque ad pecus [9] emisit signa et prodigia in medio tui Aegypte in Pharaonem et in omnes servos eius [10] qui percussit gentes multas et occidit reges fortes

[11] Seon regem Amorreorum et Og regem Basan et omnia regna Chanaan [12] et dedit terram eorum hereditatem hereditatem Israhel populo suo [13] 55v Domine nomen tuum in aeternum Domine memoriale tuum in generationem et generationem [14] quia iudicabit Dominus populum suum et in servis suis deprecabitur [15] simulacra gentium argentum et aurum opera manuum hominum

[16] os habent et non loquentur oculos habent et non videbunt [17] aures habent et non audient neque enim est spiritus in ore eorum [18] similes illis fiant qui faciunt ea et omnes qui confidunt in eis [19] domus Israhel benedicite Domino domus Aaron benedicite Domino [20] domus Levi benedicite Domino qui timetis Dominum benedicite Domino

[21] benedictus Dominus ex Sion qui habitat in Hierusalem

135[1] alleluia confitemini Domino quoniam bonus quoniam in aeternum misericordia eius [2] confitemini Deo deorum quoniam in aeternum misericordia eius [3] confitemini Domino dominorum quoniam in aeternum misericordia eius [4] qui facit mirabilia magna solus quoniam in aeternum misericordia eius [5] qui fecit caelos in intellectu quoniam in aeternum misericordia eius

[6] qui firmavit terram super aquas quoniam in aeternum misericordia eius [7] qui fecit luminaria magna quoniam in aeternum misericordia eius [8] solem in potestatem diei quoniam in aeternum misericordia eius [9] lunam et stellas in potestatem noctis quoniam in aeternum misericordia eius [10] qui percussit Aegyptum cum primogenitis eorum quoniam in aeternum misericordia eius

[11] qui eduxit Israhel de medio eorum quoniam in aeternum misericordia eius [12] in manu potenti et brachio excelso quoniam in aeternum misericordia eius [13] qui divisit Rubrum mare in divisiones quoniam in aeternum misericordia eius [14] et duxit Israhel per medium eius quoniam in aeternum misericordia eius [15] et excussit Pharaonem et virtutem eius in mari Rubro quoniam in aeternum misericordia eius

[16] qui transduxit populum suum in deserto quoniam in aeternum misericordia eius [17] qui percussit reges magnos quoniam in aeternum misericordia eius [18] et occidit reges fortes quoniam in aeternum misericordia eius [19] Seon 56r regem Amorreorum quoniam ~~in aeternum misericordia eius~~ [20] et Og regem Basan quoniam in aeternum misericordia eius

[21] et dedit terram eorum hereditatem∴ quoniam ~~in aeternum misericordia eius~~ [22] hereditatem Israhel servo suo quoniam in aeternum misericordia eius [23] quoniam quia in umilitate nostra memor fuit nostri quoniam in aeternum misericordia eius [24] et redemit nos ab inimicis nostris quoniam in aeternum misericordia eius [25] qui dat escam omni carni∴ quoniam ~~in aeternum misericordia eius~~

[26] confitemini Deo caeli quoniam in aeternum misericordia eius confitemini Domino dominorum∴ quoniam bonus *(eye skip; see 135:1)* in aeternum misericordia eius

136[1] super flumina Babylonis illic sedimus et flevimus cum recordaremur Sion [2] in salicimus in medio eius suspendimus organa nostra [3] quia illic interrogaverunt nos qui captivos duxerunt nos verba cantionum et qui abduxerunt nos hymnum cantate nobis de canticis Sion [4] quomodo cantabimus canticum Domini in terra aliena [5] si oblitus fuero tui Hierusalem oblivioni detur dextera mea

[6] adhereat lingua mea faucibus meis si non meminero tui si non praeposuero Hierusalem in principio laetitiae meae [7] memor esto Domine filiorum Edom diem Hierusalem qui dicunt exinanite exinanite usque ad fundamentum in ea [8] filia Babylonis misera beatus qui retribuet tibi retributionem tuam quam retribuisti nobis [9] beatus qui tenebit et adlidet parvulos tuos ad petram

137—No text extant

138[1] in finem David psalmus [2] Domine probasti 56v me et cognovisti me tu cognovisti sessionem meam et surrectionem meam [3] intellexisti cogitationes meas de longe semitam meam et funiculum meum investigasti [4] et omnes vias meas praevidisti quia non est sermo ~~in~~ lingua mea [5] ecce Domine tu cognovisti omnia novissima et antiqua tu formasti me et posuisti super me manum ~~tuam~~

[6] mirabilis facta est scientia tua ex me confortata est non potero ad eam [7] quo ibo ab spiritu tuo et quo a facie tua fugiam [8] si ascendero in caelum tu illic es si descendero ad infernum ades [9] si sumpsero pinnas meas diluculo et habitavero in extremis maris [10] etenim illuc manus tua deducet me et tenebit me dextera tua

[11] et dixi forsitan tenebrae conculcabunt me et nox inluminatio in deliciis meis [12] quia tenebrae non obscurabuntur a te et nox sicut dies inluminabitur sicut tenebrae eius ita et lumen eius [13] quia tu possedisti renes meos suscepisti me de utero matris meae [14] confitebor tibi quia terribiliter magnificatus es mirabilia opera tua et anima mea cognoscit nimis [15] non est occultatum os meum a te quod fecisti in occulto et substantia mea in inferioribus terrae

[16] inperfectum meum viderunt oculi tui et in libro tuo omnes scribentur die formabuntur et nemo in eis [17] mihi autem nimis honorificati sunt amici tui Deus nimis confirmati sunt principatus eorum [18] dinumerabo eos et super harenam multiplicabuntur exsurrexi et adhuc sum tecum [19] si occideris Deus peccatores et viri sanguinum declinate a me [20] quia dices in cogitatione accipient in vanitate civitates tuas

[21] nonne qui oderunt te Domine oderam et super inimicos tuos tabescebam [22] perfecto odio oderam illos inimici facti sunt mihi [23] proba me Deus et scito cor meum interroga me et cognosce semitas meas [24] et vide si via iniquitatis in me est et deduc me in via aeterna

139[1] in finem psalmus David [2] 57r eripe me Domine ab homine malo a viro iniquo eripe me [3] qui cogitaverunt iniquitates in corde tota die cogitaverunt(eye skip) proelia [4] acuerunt linguam suam sicut serpentis:~venenum aspidum sub labiis eorum [5] ~~diapsalma~~ custodi me Domine de menu peccatoris ab hominibus iniquis eripe me qui cogitaverunt subplantare gressus meos

[6] absconderunt superbi laqueum mihi et funes extenderunt ~~in~~ laqueum iuxta iter scandalum posuerunt mihi diapsalma [7] dixi Domino Deus meus es tu exaudi Domine vocem deprecationis meae [8] Domine Domine virtus salutis meae obumbrasti super caput meum in die belli [9] non tradas Domine desiderio meo peccatori cogitaverunt contra me ne derelinquas me ne forte exaltentur diapsalma [10] caput circuitus eorum labor labiorum ipsorum operiet eos

[11] cadent super eos carbones in igne deicies eos in miseriis non subsistent [12] vir linguosus non dirigetur in terra virum iniustum mala capient in interitu [13] cognovi quia faciet Dominus iudicium inopis et vindictam pauperum [14] verumtamen iusti confitebuntur nomini tuo habitabunt recti cum vultu tuo

Identified psalm text from the Vulgate

140[1] psalmus David Domine clamavi ad te exaudi me intende voci meae cum clamavero ad te [2] dirigatur oratio mea sicut incensum in conspectu tuo elevatio manuum mearum sacrificium vespertinum [3] pone Domine custodiam ori meo et ostium circumstantiae labiis meis [4] non declines cor meum in verba malitiae ad excusandas excusationes in peccatis cum hominibus operantibus iniquitatem et non communicabo cum electis eorum [5] corripiet me iustus in misericordia et increpabit me oleum autem; peccatoris non inpinguet caput meum quoniam adhuc et oratio mea in beneplacitis eorum

[6] absorti sunt iuncti petrae iudices eorum audient verba mea quoniam potuerunt [7] 57v sicut crassitudo ~~terrae~~ erupta est super terram dissipata sunt ossa nostra secus infernum [8] quia ad te Domine Domine oculi mei in te speravi non auferas animam meam [9] custodi me a laqueo quem statuerunt mihiet ab scandalis operantium iniquitatem [10] cadent in retiaculo eius peccatores singularit sum ego donec transeam

141[2] voce mea ad Dominum clamavi vote mea ad Dominum deprecatus sum [3] effundo in conspectu eius deprecationem meam tribulationem meam ante ipsum pronuntio [4] in deficiendo ex me spiritum meum et tu cognovisti semitas meas in via hac qua ambulabam absconderunt laqueum mihi [5] considerabam ad dexteram et videbam et non erat qui cognosceret me periit fuga a me et non est qui requirit animam meam

[6] clamavi ad te Domine dixi tu es spes mea portio mea in terra viventium [7] intende ad deprecationem meam quia humiliatus sum nimis libera me a persequentibus me quia confortati sunt super me [8] educ de custodia animam meam ad confitendum nomini tuo me expectant iusti donec retribuas mihi

142[1] psalmus David quando filius eum persequebatur Domine exaudi orationem meam auribus percipe obsecrationem meam in veritate tua exaudi me in tua iustitia [2] et non intres in iudicio cum servo tuo quia non iustificabitur in conspectu tuo omnis vivens [3] quia persecutus est inimicus animam meam humiliavit in terra vitam meam conlocavit me in obscuris sicut mortuos saeculi [4] et anxiatus est super me spiritus meus in me turbatum est cor meum [5] memor fui dierum antiquorum meditatus sum in omnibus operibus tuis in factis manuum tuarum meditabar

[6] expandi manus meas ad te anima mea sicut terra sine aqua tibi diapsalma [7] velociter exaudi me Domine defecit spiritus meus non avertas faciem tuam a me et similis ero descendentibus in lacum [8] auditam mihi fac mane misericordiam tuam quia in te speravi notam fac mihi viam in qua ambulem quia ad te levavi animam meam [9] eripe me de inimicis meis Domine ad te confugi [10] doce me facere voluntatem tuam quia Deus meus es tu spiritus tuus bonus deducet me in terra recta

[11] propter nomen tuum Domine vivificabis me in aequitate tua educes de tribulatione animam meam [12] et in misericordia tua disperdes inimicos meos et perdes omnes qui tribulant animam meam quoniam ego servus tuus sum

143[1] David adversus Goliad 58r benedictus Dominus Deus meus qui docet manus meas ad proelium degetos meos ad pellum [2] misericordia mea et refugium meum susceptor meus et liberator meus protector meus et in eo speravi qui subdis populum meum sub me [3] Domine quid est homo quia innotuisti ei aut filis hominis quia reputas eum [4] homo vanitati similis factus est dies eius sicut umbra praetereunt [5] Domine inclina caelos tuos et descende tange montes et fumigabunt

[6] fulgora coruscationem et dissipabis eos emitte sagittas tuas et conturbabis eos [7] emitte manum tuam de alto eripe me et libera me de aquis multis de manu filiorum alienorum [8] quorum os locutum est vanitatem et dextera eorum dextera iniquitatis [9] Deus canticum novum cantabo tibi in psalterio decacordo psallam tibi [10] qui das salutem regibus qui redimit David servum suum de gladio maligno

[11] eripe me et eripe me de manu filiorum
alienigenarum quorum os locutum est vanitatem
et dextera eorum dextera iniquitatis [12] quorum
filii sicut novella plantationis in iuventute sua filiae
eorum conpositae circumornatae ut similitudo
templi [13] promptuaria eorum plena eructantia
ex hoc in illud oves eorum fetosae abundantes in
egressibus suis [14] boves eorum crassi non est
ruina maceriae neque transitus neque clamor in
plateis eorum [15] beatum dixerunt populum cui
haec sunt beatus populus cuius Dominus Deus eius

144[1] laudatio David exaltabo te Deus meus
rex et benedicam nomini tuo in saeculum et in
saeculum saeculi [2] per singulos dies benedicam
tibi et laudabo nomen tuum in saeculum et
in saeculum saeculi [3] magnus Dominus et
laudabilis nimis et magnitudinis eius non est
finis [4] generatio et generatio laudabit opera
tua et potentiam tuam pronuntiabunt [5] 58v
magnificentiam gloriae sanctitatis tuae loquentur et
mirabilia tua narrabunt

[6] et virtutem terribilium tuorum dicent et
magnitudinem tuam narrabunt [7] memoriam
abundantiae suavitatis tuae eructabunt et iustitia
tua exultabunt [8] miserator et misericors Dominus
patiens et multum misericors [9] suavis Dominus
universis et miserationes eius super omnia opera
eius [10] confiteantur tibi Domine omnia opera tua
et sancti tui confiteantur tibi

[11] gloriam regni tui dicent et potentiam tuam
loquentur [12] ut notam faciant filiis hominum
potentiam tuam et gloriam magnificentiae regni tui
[13] regnum tuum regnum omnium saeculorum
et dominatio tua in omni generatione et ~~progenie~~
generatione *(eye skip)* fidelis Dominus in omnibus
verbis suis et sanctus in omnibus operibus suis
[14] adlevat Dominus omnes qui corruunt et
erigit omnes elisos [15] oculi omnium in te spirant
Domine et tu das escam illorum in tempore
oportuno

[16] aperis tu manum tuam et imples omne animal
benedictione [17] iustus Dominus in omnibus viis
suis et sanctus in omnibus operibus suis [18] prope
est Dominus omnibus invocantibus eum omnibus
invocantibus eum in veritate [19] voluntatem
timentium se faciet et deprecationem eorum
exaudiet et salvos faciet eos [20] custodit Dominus
omnes diligentes se et omnes peccatores disperdet

[21] laudationem Domini loquetur os meum
et benedicat omnis caro nomini sancto eius in
saeculum et in saeculum saeculi

145[1] alleluia Aggei et Zacchariae [2] lauda
anima mea Dominum laudabo Dominum in
vita mea psallam Deo meo quamdiu fuero nolite
confidere in principibus [3] in filiis hominum
quibus non est salus [4] exibit spiritus eius et
revertetur in terram suam in illa die peribunt
omnes cogitationes eorum [5] beatus cuius Deus
Iacob adiutor eius spes eius in Domino Deo ipsius

[6] qui fecit caelum et terram mare et omnia
quae in eis [7] qui custodit veritatem in saeculum
facit iudicium iniuriam patientibus dat escam
esurientibus Dominus solvit conpeditos [8]
Dominus inluminat caecos Dominus erigit adlisos
Dominus diligit iustos [9] Dominus custodit
advenas pupillum et viduam suscipiet et viam
peccatorum disperdet [10] regnabit Dominus
in saecula Deus tuus Sion in generationem et
generationem

146[1] 59r Laudate Dominum quoniam bonum
psalmus Deo nostro sit iucunda decoraque;
laudatio [2] aedificans Hierusalem Dominus
dispersiones Israhel congregabit [3] qui sanat
contritos corde et alligat contritiones illorum [4]
qui numerat multitudinem stellarum et omnibus
eis nomina vocans [5] magnus Dominus noster
et magna virtus eius et sapientiae eius non est
numerus

[6] suscipiens mansuetos Dominus humilians
autem peccatores usque ad terram [7] praecinite
Domino in confessione psallite Deo nostro in
cithara [8] qui operate caelum nubibus et parat
terrae pluviam qui producit in montibus faenum

et herbam servituti hominum [9] et dat iumentis escam ipsorum et pullis corvorum invocantibus eum [10] non in fortitudine equi voluntatem habebit nec in tibiis viri beneplacitum erit ei

[11] beneplacitum est Domino super timentes eum et in eis qui sperant super missericordia eius

147[12] alleluia lauda Hierusalem Dominum lauda Deum tuum Sion [13] quoniam confortavit seras portarum tuarum benedixit filis tuis in te [14] qui posuit fines tuos pacem et adipe frumenti satiat te [15] qui emittit eloquium suum terrae velociter currit sermo eius

[16] qui dat nivem sicut lanam nebulam sicut cinerem spargit [17] mittit cristallum suum sicut buccellas ante faciem frigoris eius quis sustinebit [18] emittet verbum suum et liquefaciet ea flabit spiritus eius et fluent aquae [19] qui adnuntiat verbum suum Iacob iustitias et iudicia sua Israhel [20] non fecit taliter omni nationi et iudicia sua non manefestavit eis

148[1] alleluia laudate Dominum de caelis laudate eum in excelsis [2] laudate eum omnes angeli eius laudate eum omnes virtutes eius [3] laudate eum sol et luna laudate eum omnes stellae et lumen [4] laudate eum caeli caelorum et aqua quae super caelum est [5] laudent nomen Domini quia ipse dixit et facta sunt ipse mandavit et creata sunt

[6] statuit ea in saeculum et in saeculum saeculi praeceptum posuit et non praeteribit [7] laudate Dominum de terra dracones et omnes abyssi [8] ignis grando nix glacies spiritus procellarum quae faciunt verbum eius [9] montes et omnes colles ligna fructifera et omnes cedri [10] bestiae et universa pecora serpentes et volucres pinnatae

[11] reges terrae et omnes populi principes et omnes iudices terrae [12] iuvenes et virgines senes cum iunioribus laudent nomen Domini [13] quia
59v exaltatum est nomen eius solius [14] confessio eius super caelum et terram et exaltabit cornu populi sui hymnus omnibus sanctis eius filis Israhel populo adpropinquanti sibi

149[1] alleluia cantate Domino canticum novum laud eius in ecclesia sanctorum [2] laetetur Israhel in eo qui fecit eum et filii Sion exultent in rege suo [3] laudent nomen eius in choro in tympano et psalterio psallant ei [4] quia beneplacitum est Domino in populo suo et exaltabit mansuetos in salute [5] exultabunt sancti in gloria laetabuntur in cubilibus suis

[6] exaltationes Dei in gutture eorum et gladii ancipites in manibus eorum [7] ad faciendam vindictam in nationibus increpationes in populis [8] ad alligandos reges eorum in conpedibus et nobiles eorum in manicis ferreis [9] ut faciant in eis iudicium conscriptum gloria haec est omnibus sanctis eius

150[1] alleluia laudate Dominum in sanctis eius laudate eum in firmamento virtutis eius [2] laudate eum in virtutibus eius laudate eum secundum multitudinem magnitudinis eius [3] laudate eum in sono tubae laudate eum in psalterio et cithara [4] laudate eum in tympano et choro laudate eum in cordis et organo [5] laudate eum in cymbalis bene sonantibus laudate eum in cymbalis iubilationis

APPENDIX 5

Extant psalm beginnings in the Faddan More Psalter

1r	1.1	[B]eatus vir
3r	6.2	D[omine ne in furore]
4r	9.2	Confiteor tibi Domine.
5r	10.2	IN [Domino]
5v	11.2	Salvum me fac Domine
5v	12.1	Usqueq[uo Domine]
6r	13.1	Dixit insipiens
6v	15.1	Conserva me Domine quoniam …
6v	16.1	Ex[audi]
8v	18.2	Caeli inarrant glor[iam]
8v	19.2	Exau[diat].
9r	20.2	Domine in virtut[e]
9v	21.2	Deus Deus [m]eus respice in me
16v	37.2	D[omine ne in furore]
16v	38.2	Dixi cus[todiam]
17v	40.2	B[eatus qui]
22r	51.3	Quid g[loriatur]
25r	60.2	Exaudi Deus
25r	61.2	Nonne Deo subiect[a]
27v	68.2	S[al]vum me [fac Deus]
29r	72.1	Quam bonus Israhel Deus
29v	73.1	Ut qui[d] Deus
33v	80.2	Ex[ultate Deo adiutori]
34v	82.2	Deus quis [similis] erit.
58r	143.1	Benedictus Dominus Deus meus.
59r	146.1	Laudate Dominum quoniam

APPENDIX 6

Abbreviations in the Faddan More text

terrae is a suspension, the syllable *ter* to a with a stroke (macron) above.

cum is a suspension to *c* with a stroke above.

david contracts to *dd* with a stroke through the ascenders.

deprecationem contracts the syllable *pre* to a *p* with a stroke above.

Abbreviations in the Faddan More text

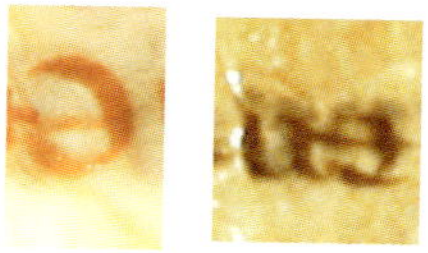

eius uses two symbols, an upside-down *e* or back-to-front *e*.

est employs the symbol ÷

sunt is a contraction to *st* with a stroke over the two letters.

hominis is a suspension of the final letter to a double-curved stroke (tilde) over the *i*.

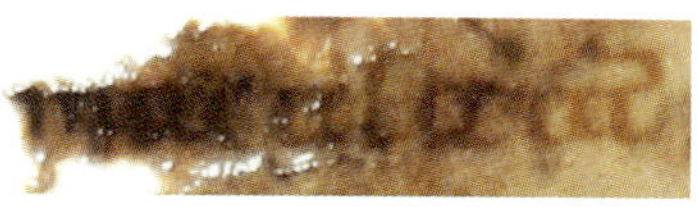

inmaculatam abbreviates the final letter with a curved stroke over the *a*.

non is a suspension to *n* with an upward curve over the letter.

per is a suspension to *p* with a curved stroke from the top of the bow. Bischoff sees this as an Irish invention based on the knowledge of the Latin *notae tironiane*.[1]

quia is a suspension to *q* with a stroke through the descender.

1 Bischoff 1990, 86.

quoniam is a contraction to *qm* with a short curved line over the *m*.

sanctis is a suspension to *scis* with a stroke over the *i*.

sancto is a suspension to *sco* with a stroke over the *o*.

spiritu is a suspension to *spir* with a stroke over the *i*.

sunt ... et ego ad—contractions and ligatures combined on all four words; *sunt* is ligatured to *st* with a curved stroke off the arch of the *s; et ego* is ligatured.

Insular punctuation makes an appearance in the form of ∴ (known as a trigon). It was used to indicate a point of emphasis or the end of a section. This, according to Paul Saenger, is 'The most enduring of insular emblematic punctuation'[2]. Another punctuation form appears repeated in a row between Psalms 92 and 93. The colon to the left of an upward curve : ~ (positura) is an indication of the end of a section. There are a number of extant areas in the text of the FMP between two psalms, none of which displays this feature.

2 Saenger 1997, 73.

APPENDIX 7

Radiocarbon dating results from the ^{14}CHRONO Centre, Queen's University, Belfast

Highlighting the calendar dates @ 95% probability from the data below (i.e. calculated to 2 sigma).

Sample 1	AD 784–991	Papyrus, cover lining
Sample 2	AD 677–883	Vellum text block
Sample 3	AD 718–941	Pigskin bag
Sample 4	AD 779–977	Animal pelt, covering material
Sample 5	AD 712–889	Plant matter, leaf inside cover

UBA no.	Sample ID	^{14}C age	±	AMS δ^{13}C	F14C	±
UBA-15215	#1 Papyrus	1124	28	-23.8	0.8695	0.0031
UBA-15218	#2 Vellum	1241	43	-29.8	0.8568	0.0046
UBA-15220	#3 Bag-collagen	1194	30	-27.6	0.8619	0.0032
UBA-15222	#4 Animal pelt	1148	33	-27.0	0.8668	0.0035
UBA-15223	#5 Plant- Leaf	1212	26	-26.8		

SAMPLE 1:
UBA-15215
Radiocarbon age BP 1124 ± 28
Calibration data set: intcal09.14c # Reimer *et al.* 2009
% area enclosed cal. AD age ranges relative area under probability distribution
68.3 (1 sigma) cal. AD 892–903 0.173
914–969 0.827
95.4 (2 sigma) cal. AD 784–786 0.002
826–841 0.015
863–991 0.983

SAMPLE 2:
UBA-15218
Radiocarbon age BP 1241 ± 43
Calibration data set: intcal09.14c # Reimer *et al.* 2009
% area enclosed cal. AD age ranges relative area under probability distribution
68.3 (1 sigma) cal. AD 689–753 0.532
760–783 0.179
788–815 0.193
843–859 0.095
95.4 (2 sigma) cal. AD 677–883 1.000

SAMPLE 3:
UBA-15220
Radiocarbon age BP 1194 ± 30
Calibration data set: intcal09.14c # Reimer *et al.* 2009
% area enclosed cal. AD age ranges relative area under probability distribution
68.3 (1 sigma) cal. AD 780–792 0.141
805–878 0.859
95.4 (2 sigma) cal. AD 718–743 0.041
769–896 0.933
923–941 0.026

SAMPLE 4:
UBA-15222
Radiocarbon age BP 1148 ± 33
Calibration data set: intcal09.14c # Reimer *et al.* 2009
% area enclosed cal. AD age ranges relative area under probability distribution
68.3 (1 sigma) cal. AD 784–786 0.013
827–839 0.079
864–903 0.370
914–969 0.539
95.4 (2 sigma) cal. AD 779–793 0.045
802–977 0.955

SAMPLE 5:
UBA-15223
Radiocarbon age BP 1212 ± 26
Calibration data set: intcal09.14c # Reimer *et al.* 2009
% area enclosed cal. AD age ranges relative area under probability distribution
68.3 (1 sigma) cal. AD 775–830 0.640
837–868 0.360
95.4 (2 sigma) cal. AD 712–745 0.100
767–889 0.900

FADDAN MORE PSALTER

Bibliography

Abbott, T.K. and Gwynn, E.J. 1921 *Catalogue of the Irish manuscripts in the Library at Trinity College, Dublin.* Hodges, Figgis and Co., Dublin.

Agati, M.L. 2017 *The manuscript book: a compendium of codicology.* L'Erma di Bretschneider, Rome.

Aldhouse-Green, M. 2015 *Bog bodies uncovered.* Thames and Hudson, London.

Alexander, J. 1978a *Insular manuscripts, 6th to the 9th century.* Harvey Miller, London.

Alexander, J. 1978b *The decorated letter.* Thames and Hudson, London.

Anderson, A.O. and Anderson, M.O. (eds) 1961 *Adomnán's Life of Columba.* Oxford University Press, Edinburgh.

Avrin, L. 1991 *Scribes, script and books.* British Library, London.

Backhouse, J. 1981 *The Lindisfarne Gospels.* Phaidon/British Library, Oxford.

Baldwin, J. and Gillis, J. 2006 Conservation of a thirteenth-century Biblia Sacra Latine. *Care and Conservation of Manuscripts* **9**, 59–69.

Baring-Gould, S. 1882 *The lives of the saints*, Vol. 1. John Hodges, London.

Baum, P.F. (trans.) 1963 *Anglo-Saxon riddles of the Exeter Book.* Duke University Press, North Carolina.

Bell, R. 1937 *The Qur'ān.* T. and T. Clark, Edinburgh.

Betham, W. 1827 *Irish antiquarian researches, Vol. 2.* William Curry Jun. and Co., Dublin.

Bhreathnach, E. 2014 *Ireland in the medieval world, AD 400–800.* Four Courts Press, Dublin.

Biddle, M. 1990 *Object and economy in medieval Winchester.* Clarendon Press, Oxford.

Bieler, L. and Binchy, D.A. 1963 *The Irish penitentials.* Dublin Institute for Advanced Studies, Dublin.

Bischoff, B. 1990 *Latin palaeography* (trans. D. Ó Cróinín and D. Ganz). Cambridge University Press, Cambridge.

Bitel, L. 1993 *Isle of the Saints: monastic settlement and Christian community in early Ireland.* Cork University Press, Cork.

Bolger, T., Moloney, C. and Troy, C. 2012 Archaeological excavations at Lorrha, Co. Tipperary. *Journal of Irish Archaeology* **21**, 113–37.

Bologna, G. 1978 *Il libro attraverso gli esemplari della Biblioteca Trivulziana.* Comune Di Milano, Milan.

Bostock, J. and Riley, H.T. (trans.) 1855 *The Natural History of Pliny*, Vol. 3. H.G. Bohn, London.

Boudalis, G. 2018 *The codex and crafts in Late Antiquity.* Brad Graduate Center, New York.

Brown, J. 1972 Northumbria and the Book of Kells. *Anglo-Saxon England* **1**, 219–46.

Brown, J. 1993 *A palaeographer's view.* Harvey Miller, London.

Brown, M.P. 1994 *Understanding illuminated manuscripts: a guide to technical terms.* J. Paul Getty Museum/British Library Board, London.

Brown, M.P. 1996 Pigments and their uses in manuscripts. *Bibliologia Elementa ad Librorum Studia Pertinentia* **14**, 136–45.

Brown, M.P. 2003 *The Lindisfarne Gospels: society, spirituality and the scribe.* British Library, London.

Brown, M.P. 2006a *How Christianity came to Britain and Ireland.* Lion Hudson, Oxford.

Brown, M.P. 2006b Spreading the word. In M.P. Brown (ed.), *In the beginning: bibles before the year 1000*, 45–76. Smithsonian Institution Press, Washington.

Brown, M.P. 2007 *A guide to western historical scripts from Antiquity to 1600.* British Library, London.

Brown, M.P. 2011 Southumbrian book culture: the interface between Insular and Anglo-Saxon. In C. Hourihane (ed.), *Insular and Anglo-Saxon art and thought in the early medieval period*, 31–42. Princeton University Press, Princeton, NJ.

Brown, M.P. 2012 Writing in the Insular world. In R. Gameson (ed.), *The Cambridge History of the Book in Britain, Vol. I: c. 400–1100*, 121–66. Cambridge University Press, Cambridge.

Brown, M.P. 2016 *Art of the islands: Celtic, Pictish, Anglo-Saxon and Viking visual culture c. 450–1050.* Bodleian Library, Oxford.

Brown, T.J. 1974 The distribution and significance of membrane prepared in the Insular manner. In *La paléographie hébraïque médiévale: Paris, 11–13 septembre 1972*, 127–35. Colloques Internationaux du Centre National de la Récherche Scientifique no. 547. Paris.

Brownrigg, L. (ed.) 1995 *Making the medieval book: techniques and production.* Red Gull Press, London.

Buckley, J.J. 1915 Some early ornamented leatherwork. *Journal of the Royal Society of Antiquaries of Ireland* **5** (4), 300–9.

Budny, M. 2001 Deciphering the art of interlace. In C. Hourihane (ed.), *From Ireland coming: Irish art from the early Christian to the late Gothic period and its European context*, 183–211. Princeton University Press, Princeton, NJ.

Byrne, F.J. 2001 *Irish kings and high-kings* (2nd edn). Four Courts Press, Dublin.

Byrne, F.J. 2005a The Viking Age. In D. Ó Cróinín (ed.), *A New History of Ireland, Vol. I. Prehistoric and early Ireland*, 609–31. Oxford University Press, Oxford.

Byrne, F.J. 2005b Church and politics, *c.* 750–*c.* 1100. In D. Ó Cróinín (ed.), *A New History of Ireland, Vol. I. Prehistoric and early Ireland*, 656–79. Oxford University Press, Oxford.

Cains, A. 1990 The vellum. In P. Fox (ed.), *The Book of Kells: MS 58, Trinity College Library Dublin: commentary*, 177–81. Faksimile Verlag, Luzern.

Cains, A. 1992 The vellum of the Book of Kells. *The Paper Conservator: Journal of the Institute of Paper Conservation* **16**, 50–61.

Cameron, E. 1998 Pre-Conquest leather on English bookbindings, arms and armour, AD 400–1100. In E. Cameron (ed.), *Leather and fur: aspects of early medieval trade and technology*, 45–56. Archetype Press, London.

Cameron, E. 2000 *Sheaths and scabbards in England AD 400–1100.* British Archaeological Reports, British Series 301. Archaeopress, Oxford.

Cameron, E. 2007 *Scabbards*

and sheaths from Viking and medieval Dublin. National Museum of Ireland, Dublin.

Cameron, E., Spriggs, J. and Wills, B. 2006 The conservation of archaeological leather. In M. Kite and R. Thomson (eds), *Conservation of leather and related materials* (1st edn), 244–61. Butterworth-Heinemann, Oxford.

Campbell, J. (ed.) 1991 *The Anglo-Saxons*. Penguin Books, London.

Carey, J. 2009 Compilations of lore and legend: Leabhar na hUidhre and the books of Uí Mhaine. In B. Cunningham and S. Fitzpatrick (eds), *Treasures of the Royal Irish Academy Library*, 17–32. Royal Irish Academy, Dublin.

Cartwright, C. 2010 Report on the identification of the organic cover lining of the Faddan More Psalter and other associated organic remains. Unpublished report for the National Museum of Ireland.

Carver, M. 2008 *Portmahomack, monastery of the Picts*. Edinburgh University Press, Edinburgh.

Chadwick, N.K. 1997 *The druids*. University of Wales Press, Cardiff.

Charles-Edwards, G. 2001 The East Cross inscription from Toureen Peacaun: some concrete evidence. *Journal of the Royal Society of Antiquaries of Ireland* **132**, 114–26.

Charles-Edwards, G. 2002 The Springmount Bog tablets: their implications for Insular epigraphy and palaeography. *Studia Celtica* **36**, 27–45.

Charles-Edwards, G. 2006 The origin and development of Insular geometric letters. Unpublished Ph.D thesis, University of Wales, Bangor.

Charles-Edwards, G. 2007 Insular display capitals and their origins. In R. Moss (ed.), *Making and meaning in Insular art*, 228–41. Four Courts Press, Dublin.

Charles-Edwards, T. 2000 *Early Christian Ireland*. Cambridge University Press, Cambridge.

Claffey, J. 2003 A very puzzling Irish missal. *Journal of the Galway Archaeological and Historical Society* **55**, 1–12.

Clarke, M. 2008 Book satchels in early mediaeval British Isles. *Gazette du Livre Medieval* **52–3**, 16–24 (https://www.persee.fr/doc/galim_0753-5015_2008_num_52_1_1773).

Clarkson, C. 1997 Some representations of the book and book-making, from the earliest codex forms to Jost Amman. In J.L. Sharpe III and K. Van Kampen (eds), *The Bible as book: the manuscript tradition*, 197–203. British Library, London.

Cleaver, L. 2015 Illustrating the Psalter. In L. Cleaver and H. Conrad O'Briain, *Latin psalter manuscripts in Trinity College Dublin and the Chester Beatty Library*, 23–38. Four Courts Press, Dublin.

Clements, R. and Graham, T. 2007 *An introduction to manuscript studies*. Cornell University Press, New York.

Comber, M. 2001 Trade and communication networks in early historic Ireland. *Journal of Irish Archaeology* **10**, 73–92.

Cramp, R. 1986 Northumbria and Ireland. In P.E. Szarmach and V.D. Oggins (eds), *Sources of Anglo-Saxon culture*, 185–201. Studies in Medieval Culture 20. Medieval Institute Publications, Kalamazoo.

Cunningham, G. 1987 *The Anglo-Norman advance into the south-west midlands of Ireland 1185–1221*. Parkmore Press, Roscrea.

Cunningham, G. 2012 The holy island of Loch Cré: Monaincha, the thirty-first wonder of the world. In S. Ryan and B. Leahy (eds), *Treasures of Irish Christianity: people and places, images and texts*, 53–6. Veritas, Dublin.

Curzon, R. 1955 *Visits to monasteries in the Levant*. Arthur Barker, London.

Davenport, C. 1902 Bagford's notes on bookbindings. *The Library: Transactions of the Bibliographical Society* **7**, **123–30**.

Davies, P.R., Brooke, G.J. and Callaway, P.R. 2002 *The complete world of the Dead Sea Scrolls*. Thames and Hudson, London.

de Bhaldraithe, E. 2009 *The high crosses of Moone and Castledermot: a journey back to the early church.* Rainsford Publishing, Kildare.

de Hamel, C. 1994 *A history of illuminated manuscripts.* BCA, London.

de Hamel, C. 2009 *Scribes and illuminators.* British Museum Press, London.

de Paor, L. 1977 The Christian triumph: the Golden Age. In P. Cone (ed.), *Treasures of early Irish art, 1500 BC to 1500 AD*, 93–104. Metropolitan Museum of Art, New York.

de Paor, M. 1977 The Viking impact. In P. Cone (ed.), *Treasures of early Irish art, 1500 BC to 1500 AD*, 144–52. Metropolitan Museum of Art, New York.

de Paor, M. and de Paor, L. 1964 *Early Christian Ireland.* Thames and Hudson, London.

Diebold, W.J. 2000 *Word and image: an introduction to early medieval art.* Westview Press, Colorado.

Diringer, D. 1982 *The book before printing.* Dover Publications, New York.

Doan, J.E. 1982 Mediterranean influences on Insular manuscript illumination. In J.T. Koch and J. Rittmueller (eds), *Proceedings of the Harvard Celtic Colloquium, Vol. 2*, 31–8. Harvard University Press, Cambridge, Massachusetts.

Dodwell, C.R. 1993 *The pictorial arts of the West.* Yale University Press, New Haven.

Doherty, C. 1980 Exchange and trade in medieval Ireland. *Journal of the Royal Society of Antiquaries of Ireland* **110**, 67–89.

Dora, C. 2018 The Irish Gospels of St Gall and its family. In C. Dora and F. Schnoor (eds), *The cradle of European culture: early medieval Irish book art*, **74–85**. Verlag am Klosterhof, St Gallen/Schwabe Verlag, Basel.

Dora, C. and Schnoor, F. (eds) 2018 *The cradle of European culture: early medieval Irish book art.* Verlag am Klosterhof, St Gallen/Schwabe Verlag, Basel.

Doyle, I. 2009 Mediterranean and Frankish pottery imports in early medieval Ireland. *Journal of Irish Archaeology* **18**, 17–62.

Drogin, M. 1980 *Medieval calligraphy: its history and technique.* Annalheld, Osmun and Co., New Jersey.

Duft, J. and Meyer, P. 1954 *The Irish miniatures in the Abbey Library of St Gall.* Urs Graf-Verlag, Olten, Berne and Lausanne.

Dumville, D.N. 2004 *Abbreviations used in Insular script before AD 850.* Department of Anglo-Saxon and Celtic, University of Cambridge.

Edwards, N. 1999 *The archaeology of early medieval Ireland.* Routledge, London.

Elliott, J.K. (ed.) 2004 *The collected biblical writings of T.C. Skeat.* Brill, Leiden.

Endres, W. 2017 Canon table II in the Book of Kells. In R. Moss, F. O'Mahony and J. Maxwell (eds), *An Insular odyssey: manuscript culture in Early Christian Ireland and beyond*, 213–30. Four Courts Press, Dublin.

Ettinghausen, R. 1954 Near Eastern book covers and their influence on European bindings. In *Ars Orientalis: the arts of Islam and the East*, 113–31. Freer Gallery of Art, Washington.

Ettinghausen, R. 1965 Foundation-moulded leather—a rare Egyptian technique also used in Britain. In *Studies in Islamic art and architecture in honour of Professor K.A.C. Creswell*, 63–71. The American University in Cairo Press, Cairo.

Farr, C.A. 2017 Reused, rescued and recycled: the art historical and palaeographic contexts of the Irish fragments, St Gallen Codex 1395. In R. Moss, F. O'Mahony and J. Maxwell (eds), *An Insular odyssey: manuscript culture in Early Christian Ireland and beyond*, 175–93. Four Courts Press, Dublin.

Feehan, J. 1987 Foreword: The medieval landscape. In G. Cunningham, *The Anglo-Norman advance into the south-west midlands of Ireland, 1185–1221*, xiii–xxviii. Parkmore Press, Roscrea.

Fitzpatrick, E. 1998 The early church in Offaly. In W. Nolan and T.P. O'Neill (eds), *Offaly history and society*, 93–129. Geography Publications, Dublin.

Fitzpatrick, E. and O'Brien, C. 1988 *The medieval churches of County Offaly*. Government of Ireland, Dublin.

Follett, W. 2012 *Céli Dé in Ireland: monastic writing and identity in the early Middle Ages*. Cambridge University Press, Cambridge.

Gabra, G. 2002 *Coptic monasteries: Egypt's monastic art and architecture*. American University in Cairo Press, Cairo.

Gamble, H.Y. 1997 *Books and readers in the early church: a history of early Christian texts*. Yale University Press, New Haven.

Gameson, R. 1994 The Royal 1.B.vii Gospels and English book production in the seventh and eighth centuries. In R. Gameson (ed.), *The early medieval bible: its production, decoration and use*, 24–52. Cambridge University Press, Cambridge.

Gameson, R. 2017 *Codex Amiatinus: making and meaning*. Parish Church Council of St Paul's, Newcastle.

Ganiaris, H., Keen, S. and Starling, K. 1982 A comparison of some treatments for excavated leather. *The Conservator* **6**, 12–23.

Gaskell-Brown, C. and Harper, A.E.T. 1984 Excavations on Cathedral Hill, Armagh, 1968. *Ulster Journal of Archaeology* (3rd ser.) **47**, 109–61.

Gathercole, S. 2012 *The earliest manuscript title of Matthew's Gospel*. Novum Testamentum 54. Brill, Leiden.

Gillis, J. 2012 The methodology used for dewatering the vellum from the Faddan More Psalter. *Journal of the Institute of Conservation* **35** (2), 137–51.

Gillis, J. and Meehan, B. 2017 Examining the Book of Dimma, the scribe Dianchride and the Gospel of John. In R. Moss, F. O'Mahony and J. Maxwell (eds), *An Insular odyssey: manuscript culture in Early Christian Ireland and beyond*, 86–113. Four Courts Press, Dublin.

Gleeson, J. 2014 Materials and methods: fine metalwork. In R. Moss (ed.), *Art and architecture of Ireland, Vol. 1. Medieval,* c. *400–*c. *1600*, 112–13. Royal Irish Academy, Dublin.

Goldman, N. 2001 Roman footwear. In J.L. Sebesta and L. Bonfante (eds), *The world of Roman costume*, 101–17. University of Wisconsin Press, Wisconsin.

Graham, H. 1925 Irish monks and the transmission of learning. *Catholic Historical Review* **11** (3), 431–42.

Gray, N. 1986 *A history of lettering: creative experiment and letter identity*. Phaidon, Oxford.

Gulácsi, Z. 2005 *Medieval Manichaean book art*. Brill, Leiden.

Gullick, M. 2012 Bookbindings. In R. Gameson (ed.), *The Cambridge History of the Book in Britain, Vol. I:* c. *400–1100*, 294–310. Cambridge University Press, Cambridge.

Gumbert, J.P. 2009 Time and places for initials. *Quaerendo* **39**, 304–27.

Haines, B. 2006 Collagen: 'the leather making protein'. In M. Kite and R. Thomson (eds), *Conservation of leather and related materials* (1st edn), 4–10. Butterworth-Heinemann, Oxford.

Hamlin, A. and Hughes, K. 2004 *The modern traveller to the early Irish church* (2nd edn). Four Courts Press, Dublin.

Haran, M. 1991 Technological heritage in the preparation of skins for biblical text in medieval oriental Jewry. In P. Rück (ed.), *Pergament: Geschichte, Struktur, Restaurierung, Herstellung*, 35–43. Thorbecke, Sigmaringen.

Harbison, P. 1992 *Guide to the national and historic monuments of Ireland*. Gill and Macmillan, Dublin.

Harbison, P. 1999 *The Golden Age of Irish art: the medieval achievement, 600–1200*. Thames and Hudson, London.

Harmon, J.A. 1984 *Codicology of the Court School of Charlemagne. Gospel book production, illumination, and emphasized script*. Peter Lang, Frankfurt.

Harthan, J.P. 1961 *Bookbindings [in the Victoria and Albert Museum]*. HMSO, London.

Haughton, J.P. 2005 The physical environment. In D. Ó Cróinín (ed.), *A New History of Ireland, Vol. I. Prehistoric and early Ireland*, 32–48. Oxford University Press, Oxford.

Hawthorne, J.G. and Stanley-Smith, C. (trans.) 1963 *On Divers Arts. The treatise of Theophilus*. University of Chicago Press, Chicago.

Hemphill, S. 1911 The Gospels of MacRegol of Birr: a study in Celtic illumination. *Proceedings of the Royal Irish Academy* **29**, 1–10.

Henderson, G. 1987 *From Durrow to Kells: the Insular gospel-books 650–800*. Thames and Hudson, London.

Henderson, G. and Henderson, I. 2004 *The art of the Picts*. Thames and Hudson, London.

Henry, F. 1961 Remarks on the decoration of three Irish psalters. *Proceedings of the Royal Irish Academy* **61**C, 23–40.

Henry, F. 1964 *Irish high crosses*. Three Candles, Dublin.

Henry, F. 1965 *Irish art in the Early Christian period to AD 800*. Cornell University Press, New York.

Herman, M. 2017 Built upon tradition: setting the stage for the evolution of Insular art. In C. Newman, M. Mannion and F. Gavin (eds), *Islands in a global context. Proceedings of the Seventh International Conference on Insular Art*, 111–22. Four Courts Press, Dublin.

Herren, M.W. 1974 *The Hisperica Famina: I. The A-text*. Pontifical Institute of Mediaeval Studies, Toronto.

Higgins, J.G. 1987 *The Early Christian cross slabs, pillar stones and related monuments of County Galway, Ireland*. British Archaeological Reports, International Series 375. Archaeopress, Oxford.

Higgitt, J. 1982 The Pictish Latin inscription at Tarbat in Ross-Shire. *Proceedings of the Society of Antiquaries of Scotland* **112**, 300–21.

Higgitt, J. 1994 The display script of the Book of Kells and the tradition of Insular decorative capitals. In F. O'Mahony (ed.), *The Book of Kells. Proceedings of a conference at Trinity College Dublin*, 209–33. Scholar Press, Aldershot.

Hillgarth, J.N. 1963 Visigothic Spain and Early Christian Ireland. *Proceedings of the Royal Irish Academy* **62**C, 167–94.

Hobson, G.D. 1929 *English binding before 1500*. Cambridge University Press, Cambridge.

Hogan, M. 2007 *The gospel book of MacRegol of Birr*. Offaly County Council, Offaly.

Horn, W. and Born, E. 1986 The medieval monastery as a setting for the production of manuscripts. *Journal of the Walters Art Gallery* **44**, 16–47.

Hughes, K. 2008 The church in Irish society. In D. Ó Cróinín (ed.), *A New History of Ireland, Vol. I. Prehistoric and early Ireland* (2nd edn), 301–30. Clarendon Press, Oxford.

Johnson, R. 2014 Viking art. In R. Moss (ed.), *Art and architecture of Ireland, Vol. 1. Medieval,* c. *400–*c. *1600*, 43–6. Royal Irish Academy, Dublin.

Johnston, E. 1906 *Writing and illumination and lettering*. John Hogg, London.

Jones, L.W. 1944 Where are the Prickings? *Transactions and Proceedings of the American Philological Association* **75**, 71–86.

Jones, L.W. 1946 Pricking manuscripts: the instruments and their significance. *Speculum* **21** (4), 389–403.

Joyce, P. 1997 [1903] *A social history of ancient Ireland*, Vol. 1. Celtic Bookshop, Limerick.

Kelly, A. 2010 The discovery of Phocaean Red Slip Ware (PRSW) Form 3 and Bii ware (LR1 amphorae) on sites in Ireland—an analysis within a broader framework. *Proceedings of the Royal Irish Academy* **110C**, 35–88.

Kelly, E.P. 2006 The manuscript discovered. *Archaeology Ireland* **20** (3) (supplement).

Kenney, J.F. 1929 *The sources for the early history of Ireland: ecclesiastical. An introduction and guide.* Columbia University Press, New York.

Krause, M. (ed.) 1975 *Essays on the Nag Hammadi texts in honour of Pahor Labib.* Brill, Leiden.

Laing, L. 2010 *European influence on Celtic art.* Four Courts Press, Dublin.

Langwe, M. 2013 *Limp bindings from the Vatican Library.* Langwe, Mora.

Larsen, R., Vestergaard Poulsen Sommer, D. and Vest, M. 2002 The hydrothermal stability (shrinkage activity) of parchment measured by the micro hot table method (MHT). In R. Larsen (ed.), *Microanalysis of parchment*, 55–62. Archetype Publications, London.

Larsen, R., Vestergaard Poulsen Sommer, D. and Fazlic, N. 2007 *Analyses of samples from the Irish psalter: analytical report.* School of Conservation, Royal Danish Academy of Fine Arts, Copenhagen.

Lawlor, H.C. 1925 *The monastery of Saint Mochaoi of Nendrum.* Belfast Natural History and Philosophical Society, Belfast.

Leach, B. 2005 Mounting papyri at the British Museum. In J. Rayner, J.M. Kosek and B. Christensen (eds), *Art on paper: mounting and housing*, 193–8. Archetype Publications, London.

Leask, H. 1920 Monaincha, Co. Tipperary. Historical notes. *Journal of the Royal Society of Antiquaries of Ireland* (6th ser.) **10** (1), 19–35.

Lowe, E.A. 1935 *Codices Latini Antiquiores, Part II: Great Britain and Ireland.* Oxford University Press, Oxford.

Lowe, E.A. 1959 *Codices Latini Antiquiores, Part IX.* Clarendon Press, Oxford.

Lowe, E.A. 1966 *Codices Latini antiquiores.* Clarendon Press, Oxford.

Lucas, A.T. 1956 Footwear in Ireland. *Journal of the County Louth Archaeological Society* **13** (4), 309–94.

Lucas, A.T. 1967 The plundering and burning of churches in Ireland, 7th to 16th century. In E. Rynne (ed.), *North Munster studies: essays in commemoration of Monsignor Michael Moloney*, 172–229. Thomond Archaeological Society, Limerick.

Lucas, A.T. 1986 The social role of relics and reliquaries in ancient Ireland. *Journal of the Royal Society of Antiquaries of Ireland* **116**, 5–37.

Lucas, A.T. 1989 *Cattle in ancient Ireland.* Boethius Press, Kilkenny.

Macalister, R.A. 1996 *Corpus inscriptionum insularum Celticarum.* Four Courts Press, Dublin.

McCormick, F. 2014 Agriculture, settlement and society in early medieval Ireland. *Quaternary International* **346**, 119–30.

McGrath, F. 1979 *Education in ancient and medieval Ireland.* Studies Special Publications, Dublin.

MacGregor, A. 1985 *Bone, antler, ivory and horn: the technology of skeletal materials since the Roman period.* Croom Helm, London.

McGurk, P. 1994 The oldest manuscripts of the Latin Bible. In R. Gameson (ed.), *The early medieval bible: its production, decoration and use*, 1–23. Cambridge University Press, Cambridge.

McGurk, P. 2009 The oldest manuscripts of the Latin Bible. In R. Gameson (ed.), *The early medieval bible: its production, decoration and use*, 1–23. Cambridge University Press, Cambridge.

McKitterick, R. 1996 The historic context: Carolingian wealth, faith and culture. In K. van der Horst, W. Noel and W.C.M. Wüstefeld (eds), *The Utrecht Psalter in medieval art: picturing the Psalms of David*, 1–21. Harvey Miller, London.

McNamara, M. 1973 Psalter text and psalter study in the early Irish church (AD 600–1200). *Proceedings of the Royal Irish Academy* 73C, 201–98.

Madan, F. and Craster, H.H.E. 1922 *A summary catalogue of the Western manuscripts in the Bodleian Library at Oxford: Pt 1*. Clarendon Press, Oxford.

Manning, C. 1995 *Early Irish monasteries*. Town House and Country House, Dublin.

Meehan, B. 1994 *The Book of Kells: an illustrated introduction to the manuscript in Trinity College, Dublin*. Thames and Hudson, London.

Meehan, B. 2000 *The Book of Durrow*. Town House and Country House, Dublin.

Meehan, B. 2005 Book satchels in medieval Scotland and Ireland. In A. Crone and E. Campbell (eds), *A crannog of the first millennium AD: excavations by Jack Scott at Loch Glashan, Argyll*, 85–90. Society of Antiquaries of Scotland, Edinburgh.

Meehan, B. 2012 *The Book of Kells*. Thames and Hudson, London.

Meehan, B. 2014 Hagiographies, Book of Armagh. In R. Moss (ed.), *Art and architecture of Ireland, Vol. 1. Medieval, c. 400–c. 1600*, 276. Royal Irish Academy, Dublin.

Meehan, B. 2015 Irish pocket gospel books. In C. Breay and B. Meehan (eds), *The St Cuthbert Gospel: studies on the Insular manuscript of the Gospel of John*, 83–102. British Library, London.

Meehan, B. 2018 Interactions with Ireland. In C. Breay and J. Story (eds), *Anglo-Saxon kingdoms: art, word, war*, 39–46. British Library, London.

Meyer, E. 2007 Roman tabulae, Egyptian Christians and the adoption of the codex. *Chiron* 37, 295–347.

Meyer, K. 1912a Neu aufgefundene altirische Glossen. *Zeitschrift für celtische Philologie* 8, 173–7.

Meyer, K. 1912b Sanas Cormaic. An Old-Irish glossary compiled by Cormac úa Cuilennáin, king-bishop of Cashel in the tenth century. In O.J. Bergin, R.I. Best, K. Meyer and J.G. O'Keeffe (eds), *Anecdota from Irish manuscripts*, Vol. 4, 1–128. Hodges Figgis, Dublin.

Meyer, M.W. 2005 *The gnostic discoveries: the impact of the Nag Hammadi library*. Harper Collins, New York.

Mez, A. 1937 *The renaissance of Islam* (trans. S. Khuda Bukhsh and D.S. Margoliouth). Jubilee Printing and Publishing, Patna.

Miller, J. 2010 *Books will speak plain: a handbook for identifying and describing historical bindings*. Legacy Press, Ann Arbor.

Mitchell, F. and Ryan, M. 2003 *Reading the Irish landscape*. Town House and Country House, Dublin.

Morris, I. 1965 The significance of dot-patterns in Carolingian manuscripts. Unpublished MA thesis, University of British Columbia.

Morton, H.V. 1930 *In search of Ireland*. Methuen, London.

Moss, R. 2014a Movements, motifs and meanings. In R. Moss (ed.), *Art and architecture of Ireland, Vol. 1. Medieval, c. 400–c. 1600*, 39–80. Royal Irish Academy, Dublin.

Moss, R. 2014b Materials and methods, fine metalwork. In R. Moss (ed.), *Art and architecture of Ireland, Vol. 1. Medieval, c. 400–c. 1600*, 107–10. Royal Irish Academy, Dublin.

Moss, R. 2014c Art of worship and devotion: gospel books. In R. Moss (ed.), *Art and architecture of Ireland, Vol. 1. Medieval, c. 400–c. 1600*, 225–43. Royal Irish Academy, Dublin.

Moss, R. 2014d The Book of Leinster. In R. Moss (ed.),

Art and architecture of Ireland, Vol. 1. Medieval, c. 400–c. 1600, 421–3. Royal Irish Academy, Dublin.

Moss, R. 2018 *The Book of Durrow*. Thames and Hudson, London.

Mullarkey, P. 2000 Irish book shrines: a reassessment. Unpublished Ph.D thesis, Trinity College Dublin.

Mullarkey, P. 2014 Book-shrines. In R. Moss (ed.), *Art and architecture of Ireland, Vol. 1. Medieval, c. 400–c. 1600*, 297–303. Royal Irish Academy, Dublin.

Murray, G. 2015 Insular crosiers from Viking-age Scandinavia. *Acta Archaeologica* **86** (2), 95–121.

Mynors, R.A.B. (ed.) 1937 *Cassiodori Senatoris Institutiones*. Clarendon Press, Oxford.

Mytum, H. 1992 *The origins of Early Christian Ireland*. Routledge, London.

Needham, P. 1979 *Twelve centuries of bookbinding: 400–1600*. Pierpont Morgan Library, New York.

Nees, L. 1978 A fifth century book cover and the origin of the Four Evangelist symbols page in the Book of Durrow. *Gesta* **17** (1), 3–8.

Nees, L. 2002 *Early medieval art*. Oxford University Press, Oxford.

Netzer, N. 2011 The narrative on Insular gospel books. In C. Hourihane (ed.), *Insular and Anglo-Saxon art and thought in the early medieval period*, 3–13. Princeton University, Princeton, NJ.

Ní Mheara, R. 2001 *Early Irish saints in Europe: their sites and their stories*. Cumann Seanchais Ard Mhacha, Armagh.

Nordenfalk, C. 1988 *Early medieval book illumination*. Rizzoli, New York.

O'Brien, C. 2006 *Stories from a sacred landscape: Croghan Hill to Clonmacnoise*. Mercier Press, Dublin.

Ó Carragáin, T. 2010 *Churches in early medieval Ireland*. Yale University Press, New Haven.

O'Carroll, E. 2001 *The archaeology of Lemanaghan: the story of an Irish bog*. Wordwell, Dublin.

Ó Corráin, D. 1980 *Ireland before the Normans*. Gill and Macmillan, Dublin.

Ó Corráin, D. 2011–12 What happened to Ireland's medieval manuscripts? *Peritia* **22–3**, 191–223.

Ó Cróinín, D. 1995 *Early medieval Ireland 400–1200*. Longman, London.

Ó Cróinín, D. 2005 Ireland, 400–800. In D. Ó Cróinín (ed.), *A New History of Ireland, Vol. I. Prehistoric and early Ireland*, 182–233. Oxford University Press, Oxford.

Ó Cróinín, D. 2009 The Cathach and Domnach Airgid. In B. Cunningham and S. Fitzpatrick (eds), *Treasures of the Royal Irish Academy Library*, 1–10. Royal Irish Academy, Dublin.

Ó Cróinín, D. 2018 Ireland and St Gall. In C. Dora and F. Schnoor (eds), *The cradle of European culture: early medieval Irish book art*, 8–25. Schwabe Verlagsgruppe AG, Basel.

O'Dwyer, P. 1981 *Célí Dé: spiritual reform in Ireland 750–900*. Editions Tailliura, Dublin.

Ó Floinn, R. 1982 The shrine of the Book of Dimma. *Éile: Journal of the Roscrea Heritage Society* **1**, 25–39.

Ó hÉaildhe, P. 1967 The crosses and slabs at St Berrihert's Kyle in the Glen of Aherlow. In E. Rynne (ed.), *North Munster studies: essays in commemoration of Monsignor Michael Moloney*, 102–26. Thomond Archaeological Society, Limerick.

O'Loughlin, T. 2001 Monasteries and manuscripts: the transmission of learning in early medieval Ireland. In H. Morgan (ed.), *Information, media and power through the ages*, 46–64. Historical Studies 22. University College Dublin Press, Dublin.

Ó Maídín, U. 1996 *The Celtic monk: rules and writings of early Irish monks*. Cistercian Publications, Kalamazoo.

O'Meadhra, U. 1979 *Early*

Christian, Viking and Romanesque art motif-pieces from Ireland. Almqvist and Wiksell International, Stockholm.

O'Neill, T. 2014 *The Irish hand: scribes and their manuscripts from the earliest times.* Cork University Press, Cork.

O'Neill, T. 2017 Initial wanderings: continuity and development of the smaller initials in Irish manuscripts, *c.* 500–*c.* 1500. In R. Moss, F. O'Mahony and J. Maxwell (eds), *An Insular odyssey: manuscript culture in Early Christian Ireland and beyond*, 283–301. Four Courts Press, Dublin.

Ó Riain, P. 1991 The shrine of the Stowe Missal, redated. *Proceedings of the Royal Irish Academy* **91**C, 285–95.

Ó Riain, P. 2009 The Stowe Missal. In B. Cunningham and S. Fitzpatrick (eds), *Treasures of the Royal Irish Academy Library*, 11–16. Royal Irish Academy, Dublin.

Ó Riain, P. 2011 *A dictionary of Irish saints.* Four Courts Press, Dublin.

Ó Riain, P. 2014 *Four Tipperary saints.* Four Courts Press, Dublin.

Ó Súilleabháin, M. 1997 *The illustrated guide to Seir Kieran, County Offaly.* Seir Kieran Project, Clareen.

Ó Súilleabháin, M., Downey, L. and Downey, D. 2018 *Antiquities of rural Ireland.* Wordwell, Dublin.

O'Sullivan, A. 2007 Exploring past people's interactions with wetland environments in Ireland. *Proceedings of the Royal Irish Academy* **107**C, 147–203.

O'Sullivan, A. and Boland, D. 1998 Clonmacnoise: early medieval bridge. In I. Bennett (ed.), *Excavations 1997: summary accounts of archaeological excavations in Ireland*, 75–6. Wordwell, Dublin.

O'Sullivan, M. and Downey, L. 2015 Early historic routeways. *Archaeology Ireland* **29** (3), 14–17.

O'Sullivan, W. 1985 Insular calligraphy: current state and problems. *Peritia* **4**, 346–59.

O'Sullivan, W. 2005 Manuscripts and palaeography. In D. Ó Cróinín (ed.), *A New History of Ireland, Vol. I. Prehistoric and early Ireland*, 511–47. Oxford University Press, Oxford.

Okasha, E. and Forsyth, K. 2001 *Early Christian inscriptions of Munster: a corpus of the inscribed stones.* Cork University Press, Cork.

Pächt, O. 1986 *Book illumination in the Middle Ages: an introduction.* Oxford University Press, Oxford.

Parkes, M.B. 1991 Insular scribes and the grammar of legibility. In M.B. Parkes, *Scribes, scripts and readers: studies in the communication, presentation and dissemination of medieval texts*, 1–18. Hambledon Press, London.

Parkinson, R. and Quirke, S. 1995 *Papyrus.* British Museum Press, London.

Peacock, E.E. 1992 Drying archaeological textiles. In L. Bender Jørgensen and E. Munksgaard (eds), *Archaeological textiles in northern Europe*, 195–207. Tidens Tand 5. Konservatorskolen, Det Kongelige danske kunstakademi, Copenhagen.

Pedersen, H. 1909–13 *Vergleichende Grammatik der keltischen Sprachen* (2 vols). Vandenhoeck & Ruprecht, Göttingen.

Pickwoad, N. 2015 The binding. In C. Breay and B. Meehan (eds), *The St Cuthbert Gospel: studies on the Insular manuscript of the Gospel of John*, 41–63. British Library, London.

Plummer, C. (ed.) 1910 *Vitae sanctorum Hiberniae* (2 vols). Oxford University Press, Oxford.

Plunkett, G., Watson, J. and Coulter, S. 2009 Palaeoenvironmental research relating to the Faddan More manuscript: final report. Unpublished report for the School of Geography, Archaeology and Palaeoecology, Queen's University Belfast.

Powell, E. 2007 *The high crosses of Ireland.* Liffey

Press, Dublin.

Pulliam, H. 2011 Looking to Byzantium: light, color and cloth in Insular art. In C. Hourihane (ed.), *Insular and Anglo-Saxon art and thought in the early medieval period*, 59–78. Princeton University, Princeton, NJ.

Raaijmakers, J. 2012 *The making of the monastic community of Fulda, c. 744–c. 900*. Cambridge University Press, Cambridge.

Raftery, B. 1965 'Ex Oriente …'. *Journal of the Royal Society of Antiquaries of Ireland* **95** (1–2), 193–204.

Raftery, B. 2005 Iron-age Ireland. In D. Ó Cróinín (ed.), *A New History of Ireland, Vol. I. Prehistoric and early Ireland*, 134–79. Oxford University Press, Oxford.

Rand, E.K. 1929 *A survey of the manuscripts of Tours*. Mediaeval Academy of America, Cambridge, Mass.

Reed, R. 1972 *Ancient skins, parchments and leathers*. Seminar Press, London.

Reed, R. 1975 *The nature and making of parchment*. Elmete Press, Leeds.

Reeves, W. and Keller, F. 1860 Early Irish calligraphy. *Ulster Journal of Archaeology* (1st ser.) **8**, 291–308.

Richardson, H. 1984 Number and symbol in Early Christian art. *Journal of the Royal Society of Antiquaries of Ireland* **114**, 28–47.

Richardson, H. 1996 Lozenges and logos. *Archaeology Ireland* **10** (2), 24–5.

Richter, M. 2008 *Bobbio in the early Middle Ages*. Four Courts Press, Dublin.

Rippin, A. 2013 *The Islamic world*. Routledge, London.

Robb, D.M. 1973 *The art of the illuminated manuscript*. A.S. Barnes and Co., New Jersey.

Roberts, C.H. and Skeat, T.C. 2004 *The birth of the codex*. Oxford University Press, Oxford.

Roberts, J. 2005 *Guide to scripts used in English writings up to 1500*. British Library, London.

Romilly Allen, J. 1903 *The Early Christian monuments of Scotland*. Society of Antiquaries of Scotland, Edinburgh.

Roosen-Runge, H. and Warner, A.E.A. 1960 Pigments and medium of the Lindisfarne Gospels, and comparisons with some related manuscripts. In T.D. Kendrick (ed.), *Evangeliorum Quattuor Codex Lindisfarnensis*, Vol. 2, 261–95. Urs Graf, Basel.

Ryan, J. 1972 *Irish monasticism: origins and early development*. Irish University Press, Dublin.

Ryan, J. 1993 *Irish monasticism*. Four Courts Press, Dublin.

Ryan, M. 1983 Metalwork and style in the Early Christian period, 7th–10th centuries AD. In M. Ryan (ed.), *Treasures of Ireland: Irish art 3000 BC–1500 AD*, 34–47. Royal Irish Academy, Dublin.

Ryan, M. 1988 Fine metalworking and early Irish monasteries: the archaeological evidence. In J. Bradley (ed.), *Settlement and society in medieval Ireland*, 33–48. Boethius Press, Kilkenny.

Ryan, M. 1989 Church metalwork in the eighth and ninth centuries. In S. Youngs (ed.), *'The work of angels': masterpieces of Celtic metalwork, 6th–9th centuries AD*, 125–49. British Museum, London.

Ryan, M. 2002 *Studies in medieval Irish metalwork*. Pindar Press, London.

Ryder, M.L. 1960 Parchment—its history, manufacture and composition. *Journal of the Society of Archivists* **2** (9), 391–9.

Ryder, M.L. 1983 *Sheep and man*. Duckworth, London.

Rynne, E. 1987 The date of the Ardagh Chalice. In M. Ryan (ed.), *Ireland and Insular art, AD 500–1200*, 85–9. Royal Irish Academy, Dublin.

Saenger, P. 1997 *Space between words: the origins of silent reading*. Stanford University Press, Stanford, CA.

Sanders, K. 2009 *Bodies in the bog and the archaeological imagination*. University of Chicago Press, Chicago.

Savage, E.A. 1970 *Old English libraries: the making, collection and use of books during the Middle Ages*. Barnes and Noble, New York.

Schutz, H. 2004 *The Carolingians in central Europe, their history, arts, and architecture: a cultural history of central Europe, 750–900*. Brill, Leiden.

Scott, B.G. 1981 Varia II. *Ériu* **32**, 153–7.

Sharpe, J. 1996 Wooden books and the history of the codex: Isocrates and the Farm Account, evidence from the Egyptian desert. In J.L. Sharpe III (ed.), *Roger Powell: The Compleat Binder*, 107–29. Bibliologia: Elementa ad librorum studia pertinentia 14. Brepols, Turnhout.

Sharpe, R. 1985 Latin and Irish words for 'book-satchel'. *Peritia* **4**, 152–6.

Sharpe, R. (trans.) 1995 *Adomnán of Iona: Life of St Columba*. Penguin, London.

Sharpe, R. 2010 Books from Ireland, fifth to ninth centuries. *Peritia* **21**, 1–55.

Sheehan, J. 2014 Caherlehillan: art and architecture. In R. Moss (ed.), *Art and architecture of Ireland, Vol. 1. Medieval,* c. *400–*c. *1600*, 132–3. Royal Irish Academy, Dublin.

Sikora, M. and Kelly, E. 2009 Preliminary report, Faddan More, Co. Tipperary, 06E0786; 06R0141. Unpublished report for the National Museum of Ireland.

Singer, B.W. 2008 Investigation of a black paint/ink sample from the Faddan More Psalter for the National Museum of Ireland. Unpublished report, Northumbria University.

Skeat, T.C. 1969 Book production: papyri and manuscripts. In P.R. Ackroyd, C.F. Evans, S.L. Greenslade and G.W.H. Lampe (eds), *The Cambridge History of the Bible*, Vol. 3, 54–79. Cambridge University Press, London.

Sly, D. 1996 *Philo's Alexandria*. Routledge, London.

Stevenson, J. 1989 The beginning of literacy in Ireland. *Proceedings of the Royal Irish Academy* **89C**, 127–65.

Stevenson, J. 1997 The monastic Rules of Columbanus. In M. Lapidge (ed.), *Columbanus: studies on the Latin writings*, 203–15. Boydell and Brewer, Woodbridge.

Stevick, R. 2000 The coherent geometry of two Irish high crosses. *Peritia* **14**, 297–322.

Stokes, G.T. 1899 *Ireland and the Celtic Church*. Hodder and Stoughton, London.

Stokes, M. 1932 *Early Christian art in Ireland.* Stationery Office, Dublin.

Stokes, W. (ed. and trans.) 1887 *The Tripartite Life of Patrick, with other documents relating to that saint*. Eyre and Spottiswoode, London.

Stokes, W. (ed.) 1905 *Félire Óengusso Céli Dé: The Martyrology of Oengus the Culdee*. Henry Bradshaw Society, London.

Stopford Green, A. 1925 *History of the Irish state to 1014*. Macmillan, London.

Stout, M. 1998 Early Christian settlement, society and economy in Offaly. In W. Nolan and T.P. O'Neill (eds), *Offaly history and society*, 29–92. Geography Publications, Dublin.

Stout, M. 2017 *Early medieval Ireland, 431–1169*. Wordwell, Dublin.

Szirmai, J.A. 1999 *The archaeology of medieval bookbinding*. Ashgate Publishing Ltd, Aldershot.

Telepneff, Fr G. 2008 *The Egyptian desert in the Irish bogs*. Center for Traditionalist Orthodox Studies, Etna, CA.

Thomas, C. 1971 *Britain and Ireland in Early Christian times, AD 400–800*. Thames and Hudson, London.

Thompson, D.V. (trans.) 1954 *The craftsman's handbook*. Dover Publications, New York.

Thompson, D.V. 1956 *The materials of medieval painting*. George Allen and Unwin, London.

Thomson, R. 2006a The nature and properties of leather. In M. Kite and R. Thomson (eds),

Conservation of leather and related materials, 1–3. Elsevier Butterworth-Heinemann, Oxford.

Thomson, R. 2006b The manufacture of leather. In M. Kite and R. Thomson (eds), *Conservation of leather and related materials*, 66–81. Elsevier Butterworth-Heinemann, Oxford.

Todd, J.H. (trans.) 1867 *The war of the Gaedhil with the Gaill, or, The invasions of Ireland by the Danes and other Norsemen*. Longmans, London.

Toswell, M.J. 2016 Psalters. In R. Gameson (ed.), *The Cambridge History of the Book in Britain, Vol. I: c. 400–1100*, 468–81. Cambridge University Press, Cambridge.

Van Regemorter, B. 1957 La reliure souple des manuscrits carolongiens de Fulda. *Scriptorium: International Review of Manuscript Studies* **11**, 249–57.

Van Regemorter, B. 1978–9 The bound codex from its origin to the early Middle Ages. *Guild of Book Workers Journal* **17**, 1–24.

Van Regemorter, B. 1992 *Binding structures in the Middle Ages* (trans. J. Greenfield). Bibliotheca Wittockiana, Brussels.

Van Stone, M. 1994 Ornamental techniques in Kells and its kin. In F. O'Mahony (ed.), *The Book of Kells. Proceedings of a conference at Trinity College Dublin, 6–9 September, 1992*, 234–42. Scholar Press, Aldershot.

Veldmeijer, A.J. 2012 *Sandals, shoes and other leatherwork from the Coptic monastery of Deir el-Bachit: analysis and catalogue*. Sidestone Press, Leiden.

Vezin, J. 1982 Une reliure carolingienne de cuir souple. *Revue Française d'Histoire du Livre* **36**, 235–41.

Wächter, O. 1962 The restoration of the 'Vienna Dioscorides'. *Studies in Conservation* **7** (1), 22–6.

Wallace, P.F. and Ó Floinn, R. (eds) 2002 *Treasures of the National Museum of Ireland: Irish antiquities*. Gill and Macmillan, Dublin.

Walsh, J. and Bradley, T. 2003 *A history of the Irish Church 400–700 AD*. Columba Press, Dublin.

Walton Rogers, P. 2008 Interim report for archive: Investigation of organic materials from Faddan More, Co. Tipperary, Ireland. Unpublished report for the National Museum of Ireland.

Warren, F.E. 1987 *The liturgy and ritual of the Celtic Church* (2nd edn by J. Stevenson). Boydell Press, Woodbridge.

Waterer, J.W. 1950 *Leather and craftsmanship*. Faber and Faber, London.

Waterer, J.W. 1968 Irish book satchel or budgets. *Medieval Archaeology* **12**, 70–82.

Waterer, J.W. 1972 *A guide to the conservation and restoration of objects made wholly or in part of leather*. G. Bell and Sons, London.

Webster, L. and Backhouse, J. (eds) 1991 *The making of England: Anglo-Saxon art and culture AD 600–900*. British Museum, London.

Weston Joyce, P. 1997 *A social history of Ireland*, Vol. 1. The Celtic Bookshop, Limerick.

Whitley, K.P. 2000 *The gilded page*. British Library, London.

Wild, J.P. 1966 Papyrus in pre-Roman Britain. *Antiquity* **40** (158), 139–42.

Wilde, W.R. 1848 Description of an ancient shrine called the 'Mias Tighernain'. *Transactions of the Royal Irish Academy* **21** (2), 16–19.

Wilde, W.R. 1857–61 Ancient and modern races of oxen in Ireland. *Proceedings of the Royal Irish Academy* **7**, 64–75.

Willingham, E.M. 2003 Celtic ornament, Irish gospel book decoration, and the illustrated prose *Lancelot* of Yale 229. *Proceedings of the Harvard Celtic Colloquium* **23**, 299–326.

Wilson, D. 1961 An Anglo-Saxon bookbinding at Fulda (Codex Bonifatianus I). *Antiquaries Journal* **41** (3–4), 199–217.

Wood, I. 2013 Entrusting Western Europe to the Church. *Transactions of the Royal Historical Society* **23**,

37–73.

Woods, C. 2006 The conservation of parchment. In M. Kite and R. Thomson (eds), *Conservation of leather and related materials*, 200–24. Elsevier Butterworth-Heinemann, Oxford.

Woods, D. 2016 Adomnán, Arculf and the mosque on the Temple Mount. *Ériu* **66**, 179–90.

Woolf, A. 2018 The Scandinavian intervention. In B. Smith (ed.), *The Cambridge History of Ireland, Vol. 1: 600–1550*, 107–30. Cambridge University Press, Cambridge.

Youngs, S. (ed.) 1989 *'The work of angels': masterpieces of Celtic metalwork, 6th–9th centuries AD*. British Museum, London.

Zarnecki, G. 1972 *The monastic achievement*. Thames and Hudson, London.